PRAYING THE PSALMS

Finding Your Voice in Israel's Prayer Book

Claude F. Mariottini

z

PRAYING THE PSALMS

Finding Your Voice in Israel's Prayer Book

Library of Congress Control Number: 2026907983

ISBN: 979-8-9938752-3-1

Published by Ancient Path Press

Printed in the United States of America

CONTENTS

Book Two: Psalms 42–72

Book Three: Psalms 73–89

Book Four: Psalms 90–106

PREFACE

The book you hold in your hands was not written so much as lived. Its pages grew out of more than half a century of ministry — from early-morning journal entries in a California parsonage to seminary lecture halls to the quiet of retirement, where the Psalms have remained my most faithful companions. If this book has any virtue, it is that it does not merely describe the Psalms from a safe scholarly distance. It comes from within the experience of praying them.

My journey with the Psalms began in earnest during my years as a pastor in San Jose, California, long before I entered the academy. Each morning, I would open the Psalter to a single verse, and from that verse, I would write a prayer in my journal, not a polished theological reflection, but an honest conversation with God, shaped by whatever joy or burden that day before had brought. I did not know then that this daily discipline would sustain me through the next five decades of ministry. I know it now.

When I joined the faculty of Southwest Baptist University in Bolivar, Missouri, in 1983 as Professor of Old Testament, the Psalms followed me into the classroom. Every other year, I taught a course on Wisdom Literature, and throughout each semester, I continued the habit I had developed as a pastor: selecting a verse from a Psalm and composing a prayer or meditation around it. Over the course of thirty-three years of teaching, both at Southwest Baptist and Northern Seminary, those entries accumulated into a considerable body of reflection. This book is their fruit.

The title of this book, *Praying the Psalms: Finding Your Voice in Israel's Prayer Book*, derives from a paper I delivered at the Symposium on Theological Interpretation of Scripture, held at North Park Theological Seminary in Chicago on September, 26–28, 2002. The paper, titled "Praying the Psalms: A Response to John C. Endres," explored the Psalter not simply as sacred literature to be studied but as a living instrument of prayer to be inhabited. That conviction has never left me, and it animates every page of this book.

Because this is a book of devotion and prayer rather than a work of technical scholarship, I have made certain deliberate choices about its form. The reader will find no footnotes. I have read widely in the scholarly literature on the Psalms throughout my academic career, and the ideas of many gifted interpreters have shaped my thinking. I acknowledge that debt at the end of this volume in a brief bibliography of the works that have most profoundly influenced my spiritual and intellectual formation. But to burden these meditations with apparatus would be to change their character entirely: to turn an invitation to prayer into an exercise in academic documentation. That is not my purpose here.

Similarly, I have largely set aside the Hebrew vocabulary of the Old Testament. This is not because the Hebrew text is unimportant; to the contrary, it is the irreplaceable foundation of everything written here. But because this book is intended for the broadest possible audience, I have chosen to discuss the meanings of Hebrew words and verbal forms without requiring readers to navigate the language itself.

In select instances, I have retained a transliterated Hebrew term because its theological weight cannot be captured by translation alone. The most important of these is the word *hesed*. No English equivalent does it justice. "Love" is too vague; "kindness" too mild; "loyalty" too cold. *Hesed* names the covenant commitment of a God who binds himself to his people not by compulsion but by choice, and who keeps that commitment through every season of human failure and divine faithfulness. It is steadfast love as a promise kept, mercy as a policy of the heart. Where this word appears in the Psalms, I have retained it in transliteration and paused to let the reader feel its weight.

A word is also necessary regarding the divine name. The God of Israel revealed himself to Moses by a personal name: the four consonants of the Hebrew Tetragrammaton, YHWH, most likely pronounced

Yahweh. In the academic study of the Old Testament, the use of this name has become standard practice, and with good reason: "the LORD" risks obscuring the intimacy and specificity of the relationship between Israel and its God. Throughout my scholarly writing, I employ "Yahweh" without hesitation.

In this devotional volume, however, I have chosen a different path. When citing biblical texts, I follow the well-established convention of rendering the Tetragrammaton as "LORD" in small caps, indicating to the informed reader that the divine name stands in the Hebrew text. Beyond that convention, I refer to God simply as "the Lord." I do so out of pastoral sensitivity. The Psalms have always been more than a scholar's text; they are the prayer book of the church, sung and spoken by believers who may never have encountered the name Yahweh in their devotional practice. I do not wish to place a stumbling block before readers whose encounter with God in the Psalms is being renewed or begun. The name matters enormously; the relationship it names matters more.

The question of authorship requires a frank but gentle word. The Book of Psalms attributes seventy-three psalms to David through superscriptions bearing the Hebrew phrase commonly rendered "of David." The Septuagint, the ancient Greek translation of the Hebrew scriptures, extends Davidic attribution to additional psalms, bringing the total to approximately eighty-four. Twelve psalms are assigned to Asaph, eleven to the Sons of Korah, two to Solomon, and one each to Moses, Heman, and Ethan. Forty-nine psalms carry no authorial notice at all; scholars have long called these the "orphan psalms."

Modern scholarship has rightly noted that the Hebrew preposition underlying "of David" can bear multiple meanings: it may indicate authorship, dedication, or association with the Davidic tradition. The critical question of which psalms David himself composed, and which were composed in his name or spirit by later generations, is one that cannot be resolved with certainty on current evidence. I am not unaware of these discussions; they have occupied Old Testament scholarship for the better part of two centuries.

For the purposes of this devotional work, I have chosen to employ the traditional attributions not as historical claims requiring defense but as interpretive contexts that enrich the reading of the psalms. Thirteen of the Davidic psalms carry historical superscriptions that explicitly connect them to identifiable moments in David's narrative as preserved in 1–2 Samuel: his flight from Saul, his sin with Bathsheba, his exile from Jerusalem during Absalom's revolt. Whether these notes are original to the psalms or later editorial additions, they represent an ancient and theologically rich tradition of reading the Psalter as the personal prayer of a man who encountered God in the full range of human experience. To read Psalm 51 in light of David's confession of adultery and murder is to hear the cry for mercy with a specificity that abstract theology cannot provide. That is the spirit in which I invoke the traditional attributions throughout this book.

One of the persistent marvels of the Psalter is its refusal to become dated. These poems and prayers were composed in a world of ancient Near Eastern kingship, temple worship, tribal memory, and agrarian crisis. They speak of enemies who lurk like lions, of harvests that fail and rivers that clap their hands, of a God who rides upon the storm and bends down to hear the cry of the poor. The cultural distance between the psalmists and the twenty-first century reader is immense.

And yet the Psalms endure, not despite their particularity but because of it. The psalmist who cries out from the pit of despair, who rages at the prosperity of the wicked, who trembles at the silence of God in the hour of greatest need, this psalmist speaks for every generation that has known darkness and waited for light. The woman who weeps by the waters of Babylon and cannot bring herself to sing is every person in exile, literal or spiritual. The shepherd-king who walks through the valley of the shadow of death is every believer who has faced mortality and reached for a hand beyond their own. The Psalms survive because human need does not change, and neither does the God who meets it.

I have organized this book to lead the reader through the Psalter in an accessible way without being superficial. Each reflection begins with a biblical text, moves through the historical and literary context that illuminates it, and arrives at an application for the life of prayer. Where the Hebrew opens a window onto a meaning that English cannot quite reach, I have paused to let the reader look through it. Where the ancient world of the psalmist illuminates a human experience that is still very much our own, I have tried to name that connection with care.

My hope is not that readers will finish this book knowing more about the Psalms, though I trust that will happen. My deeper hope is that they will finish it praying more honestly, more persistently, and more hopefully than they did when they began — that the voice of the psalmist will have become, in some measure, their own voice before God.

The Psalms have carried me for more than fifty years. They have been my language in seasons of joy that outran my own words, and my shelter in seasons of grief that silenced me entirely. I offer this book as a doorway into that spiritual wilderness, trusting that the God who spoke to the psalmist continues to inhabit those same quiet places.

Claude F. Mariottini
Professor Emeritus of Old Testament
Northern Baptist Seminary

THE TWO WAYS

Blessed is the one who does not walk in step with the wicked or stand in the way that sinners take or sit in the company of mockers, but whose delight is in the law of the Lord, and who meditates on his law day and night (Psalm 1:1–2).

The book of Psalms opens not with a lament or a petition, but with a profound declaration of blessing. Psalm 1 serves as a gateway into the entire psalter, establishing the fundamental spiritual principle that distinguishes the righteous from the wicked. This opening psalm presents two contrasting individuals whose lives exemplify diametrically opposed responses to God and his word. In meditating upon these figures, we discover essential truths about the nature of genuine blessing and the peril of spiritual compromise.

The psalmist introduces us first to the one "who does not walk in step with the wicked." Notice the specificity of this negative formulation. Blessing is described not primarily in terms of what this person does, but in terms of what they deliberately avoid. The Hebrew word for "blessed" is perhaps better translated as "how happy" or "how fortunate," suggesting a condition of flourishing that extends far beyond momentary happiness. This is a comprehensive well-being rooted in a right relationship with God.

The psalmist uses three verbs in descending degrees of involvement: "walk," "stand," and "sit." This progression reveals the insidious nature of spiritual compromise. It begins with a casual walk alongside the wicked, a seemingly innocent association. If unchecked, this develops into standing in the way of sinners, suggesting a deliberate pause and contemplation of their counsel. Finally, one sits in the company of mockers, implying a settled, comfortable position of identification with those who ridicule faith and righteousness. The blessed individual refuses this entire trajectory.

Yet Psalm 1 does not leave us with mere negatives. The truly blessed person's delight is in the law of the Lord—the *Torah*, God's instruction and revelation. This is not a grudging obedience born of obligation, but genuine delight, deep satisfaction found in God's Word. The Hebrew word for "delight" conveys a sense of desire and pleasure. The psalmist is describing someone who loves God's instruction the way one loves what brings joy and life.

This delight issues in meditation, not casual reading, but the kind of deep, contemplative dwelling upon Scripture that continues day and night. This is the constant return of the mind to God's Word, the persistent turning of thoughts toward divine truth. Such meditation becomes the foundation of a flourishing life, like a tree planted by streams of water (verse 3), bearing fruit in its season with leaves that do not wither.

In stark contrast stands the wicked, the sinner, and the mocker. The psalmist describes not their activity but their ultimate fate: they are like chaff that the wind blows away. Where the righteous are rooted and stable, bearing fruit, the wicked are rootless and insubstantial. Their judgment is certain because they "will not stand in the place of judgment, nor sinners in the assembly of the righteous." This is not merely social exclusion; it is cosmic separation, a reality that will be fully revealed when God judges all humanity.

The fundamental difference between these two individuals lies in their relationship to God's Word and God's way. The blessed one deliberately cultivates separation from evil and passionate engagement with Scripture. The wicked, by contrast, abandon God's instruction and follow their own desires, mocking those who walk in righteousness. Their apparent freedom is, in fact, slavery to destructive impulses; their confidence in human wisdom becomes their undoing.

We who read this psalm must honestly assess which trajectory characterizes our own lives. Are we cultivating genuine delight in God's Word, meditating upon it day and night? Or are we slowly drifting into compromise, beginning with innocent associations and settling into the comfortable company of those who mock faith and truth? The blessing promised in Psalm 1 is not a magic formula but a natural consequence: those who root their lives in God's Word flourish, while those who abandon his instruction inevitably wither.

PRAYER

Gracious God, we come to you this day recognizing our tendency toward compromise and our weakness against the world's subtle allurements. Grant us the courage to walk apart from wickedness, the wisdom to discern the voices of mockers, and the holy dissatisfaction with anything less than your truth. Cultivate within us a genuine delight in your word. Help us to meditate upon your revelation, not out of duty but out of deepening love. Plant us by streams of living water, that we might flourish and bear fruit in season. And when we are tempted to drift, redirect our hearts and minds toward you. In Jesus's name, Amen.

CELEBRATING WITH TREMBLING

Serve the Lord with fear and celebrate his rule with trembling (Psalm 2:11).

The paradox at the heart of Psalm 2:11 confronts us with a tension that defines authentic faith: we are called both to fear and to celebrate, to tremble and to serve. These seemingly contradictory postures reveal something profound about the nature of God and our relationship with him.

At first glance, this verse might strike us as odd. We live in an age that prefers a comfortable God, one who affirms our choices and stays safely within the boundaries we have drawn. The idea of fearing God feels antiquated, even oppressive to modern ears. Yet the psalmist insists that genuine worship begins with fear, not the cringing terror of an abused child, but the awe-filled recognition of who God actually is.

This fear is the trembling we feel when standing at the edge of the Grand Canyon, when holding a newborn child, when witnessing something so magnificent that our smallness suddenly becomes startlingly clear. It is the catch in our breath when we realize we are in the presence of someone infinitely greater than ourselves. The fear of the Lord is wisdom's beginning because it shatters our illusions of self-sufficiency and puts us in right relationship with reality.

But notice that the verse does not end with fear. We are to "celebrate his rule with trembling." Here is where the paradox deepens and becomes beautiful. Our God is not a distant tyrant to be dreaded but a King whose reign is cause for joy. His rule means justice for the oppressed, hope for the broken, and life for those walking in death's shadow. To celebrate his rule is to rejoice that the universe is not random, that history has a direction, that love and truth will ultimately triumph.

Yet even our celebration must be marked by trembling. This is where cheap grace and casual Christianity fall short. We cannot approach the throne of heaven with a flippant familiarity that forgets who sits there. Even as we rejoice in the intimate access we have through Christ, we must remember that we are drawing near to consuming fire, to holy love that will not compromise with evil, to a God who is both infinitely tender and infinitely terrible.

Consider how this plays out in our daily walk. To serve the Lord with fear means bringing our best, our whole selves, to the work he has given us. It means we do not phone it in, do not treat our faith as a casual hobby to be picked up when convenient. Whether we are changing diapers, preparing presentations, or praying in secret, we are serving the King of kings. That reality should infuse even mundane moments with weight and purpose.

At the same time, celebrating his rule with trembling keeps our joy from becoming presumptuous. We do not celebrate because we have figured out God or because we are confident in our own righteousness. We celebrate because he is good, because his mercies are new every morning, because he has shown us grace upon grace. Our trembling reminds us that this grace is amazing precisely because it is undeserved.

This balance protects us from two dangerous extremes. On one side lies a religion of fear alone, cold, joyless duty that sees God only as taskmaster and judge. On the other side lies a religion of celebration alone, superficial happiness that has never grappled with the cost of grace or the seriousness of holiness. The psalmist calls us to hold both together, and in that tension, we find true worship.

Think of Peter on the Mount of Transfiguration, simultaneously wanting to build shelters to stay forever and falling on his face in terror. Think of Isaiah in the temple, crying "Woe is me!" even as the seraph touches his lips with purifying fire. Think of John on Patmos, falling at the feet of the risen Christ as though dead, only to hear, "Fear not." This is the faith we are called to: eyes wide open to both God's holiness and his love, hearts gripped by both reverence and rejoicing. In a world that wants either a buddy or a tyrant, Christianity offers us a Father who is also king, a savior who is also judge, a friend who is also Lord. As we go about our days, may we carry this dual awareness. Let every act of service be marked by the reverence due our Creator. Let every moment of celebration be grounded in the humble recognition of who he is and who we are. In this holy tension, we discover what it means to truly worship.

PRAYER

Almighty God, teach us to fear you rightly, not with cowering dread, but with awe-filled wonder at your majesty and holiness. Help us to celebrate your reign with trembling hearts, never forgetting the grace that allows us to approach your throne. May our service be marked by reverence, and may our joy be anchored in humble gratitude. Through Christ our Lord, Amen.

RESTING IN DIVINE SUSTENANCE

I lie down and sleep; I wake again, because the LORD *sustains me* (Psalm 3:5).

"I lie down and sleep; I wake again, because the LORD sustains me." These deceptively simple words of the psalmist contain profound theological truth about trust, divine providence, and the nature of faithful rest. As we examine this verse from Psalm 3, we discover an invitation to surrender our anxieties and to embrace the sustaining grace of God, which operates even in our vulnerability and sleep.

The context of Psalm 3 provides a crucial interpretive framework. The superscription attributes this psalm to David, "when he fled from his son Absalom." We encounter David at a moment of existential crisis, betrayed by his own son, fleeing Jerusalem, surrounded by enemies who declare, "there is no deliverance for him in God." The opening verses capture David's anguish: "LORD, how many are my foes! How many rise up against me!" Yet by verse 5, we discover a remarkable transformation. David has moved from anxiety to rest, from desperation to sleep. This is not the sleep of escape or denial, but the sleep of trust.

The Hebrew verb translated "lie down" carries significance beyond mere physical resting. In biblical usage, it signifies vulnerability, trust, and the relinquishment of active control. When David says, "I lie down," he positions himself in profound dependence. He is not preparing for battle or taking a defensive posture; rather, he is making himself vulnerable before God. This posture of lying down embodies the surrender that authentic faith requires.

The "sleep" deepens this surrender. Sleep represents the ultimate cessation of human vigilance and effort. In sleep, we abandon our attempts to control circumstances. We cannot protect ourselves. We cannot strategize or defend. We simply rest. That David can sleep amid crisis, pursued by Absalom's forces, betrayed by those he loved, testifies to a faith that transcends rational circumstances. His sleep is not thoughtlessness but trustfulness.

The crucial phrase "I wake again" signals restoration and continuity. David does not merely survive the night; he awakens renewed. In Hebrew, the verb suggests habitual action. This is not a single instance of divinely sustained sleep but a pattern of life. Night after night, amid genuine threat, David experiences the cycle of rest and restoration. This cyclical pattern reflects the deeper theological claim: God sustains not through a single dramatic intervention but through continuous, faithful provision.

The most theologically dense word appears at the end of the verse. The Hebrew verb translated "sustains me" literally means "keeps me" or "preserves me." The Hebrew verb denotes careful watch, protection, and the maintenance of integrity. God does not simply allow David to rest; God *watches over* him in his sleep. The Lord is the vigilant guardian while David sleeps. This inversion, the human rests while God remains wakeful, encapsulates the economy of grace. Our weakness becomes the venue for God's strength.

The theological implications deserve careful consideration. First, this verse affirms that rest itself is an act of faith. In our contemporary culture of productivity and anxiety, rest often feels irresponsible. Yet the psalmist presents sleep as an expression of trust. When we lie down despite unresolved problems, we declare that we are not ultimately responsible for our own protection. We depend upon God.

Second, Psalm 3:5 teaches that God's sustenance operates in our apparent helplessness. David does not rest because the threat has disappeared. He sleeps while Absalom pursues him, while enemies surround him. Yet he awakens, sustained by the Lord. Our circumstances need not be resolved for us to experience God's care. Divine providence often operates not by removing difficulties but by enabling us to rest within them.

Third, this verse establishes a rhythm of grace. The cycle of lying down and waking represents life itself, daily death and resurrection, nightly vulnerability and morning restoration. Each awakening testifies to God's faithfulness. Each new day becomes evidence of sustained mercy.

For contemporary readers, Psalm 3:5 challenges our addiction to control. We lie awake, minds racing, attempting to solve tomorrow's problems. We fear sleep because it represents our powerlessness. Yet the psalmist invites us into a countercultural practice: to embrace rest as spiritual discipline, to sleep as an expression of faith, to awake with gratitude for God's faithful sustenance.

As you face your own crises, perhaps not as dramatic as David's, but genuinely threatening, consider this ancient word. Will you lie down? Will you trust that God watches while you sleep? Will you wake up tomorrow and acknowledge that the Lord has sustained you?

PRAYER

Eternal God, in the darkness of night and the uncertainty of our days, teach us to rest. Quiet our anxious minds; still our restless thoughts. Grant us the faith of David, who could sleep while pursued, trusting in your faithful watch. As we close our eyes tonight, remind us that you neither slumber nor sleep, that your care extends over every moment of our vulnerability. Awaken us tomorrow with grateful hearts, aware anew that we live only by your sustaining grace. Through Jesus Christ, our true rest and our eternal keeper, we pray. Amen.

WHEN DISTRESS DRIVES US TO PRAYER

Answer me when I call to you, my righteous God. Give me relief from my distress; have mercy on me and hear my prayer (Psalm 4:1).

There is something profoundly honest about the opening words of Psalm 4. David does not ease into his prayer with polite formalities or careful theological preambles. He comes to God with urgency, with need, with the raw honesty of someone who knows what it means to be in distress. "Answer me when I call to you, my righteous God."

This is not the prayer of someone enjoying a peaceful afternoon of meditation. This is the cry of a soul under pressure, and it teaches us something essential about the nature of authentic prayer: it begins with acknowledging our need.

Notice how David addresses God as "my righteous God." Amid his distress, he anchors himself in who God is. The circumstances may be chaotic, the pressure may be mounting, but God's character remains unchanging. His righteousness stands firm. This is where faith finds its footing when everything else shifts beneath us. We may not understand our circumstances, but we can trust the character of the One to whom we cry.

David then makes a simple request: "Give me relief from my distress." There is no shame in asking God for relief. Sometimes we spiritualize suffering to the point where we feel guilty for wanting it to end, as if the holiest response to hardship is stoic endurance. But the psalmist shows us a different way. Bring your distress to God. Name it. Ask for relief. God is not offended by our desire for deliverance; he invites it.

What strikes me most about this verse is the progression David models for us. He calls out to God, acknowledges God's righteousness, asks for relief, and then appeals to God's mercy. "Have mercy on me and hear my prayer." Mercy is what we need when we have no claim, no leverage, no bargaining chip to offer. David does not approach God on the basis of his own merit but on God's character. This is the posture of authentic faith, not presuming upon God's favor because we deserve it, but appealing to his nature because he is merciful.

The phrase "hear my prayer" reminds us that prayer is fundamentally relational. David is not reciting a formula or performing a ritual; he is seeking an audience with a God who listens. In our distress, we can sometimes feel as though our prayers bounce off the ceiling, that God is distant or uninterested. But Scripture consistently affirms that God hears the cries of his people. The question is not whether he hears, but whether we truly believe he does.

Living in a culture that prizes self-sufficiency and solutions, we often treat prayer as a last resort rather than a first response. We exhaust our own resources, consult our own wisdom, and only when we have reached the end of ourselves do we finally cry out to God. But David shows us that distress is meant to drive us immediately to prayer, not merely to it eventually.

Consider what happens when we delay. We carry burdens we were never meant to carry. We make decisions without divine wisdom. We allow anxiety to take root when we could be experiencing the peace that comes from casting our cares upon him. The relief David seeks is not found in the absence of problems but in the presence of God.

This verse also confronts our tendency to compartmentalize our spirituality. We sometimes think certain concerns are too small for God's attention or too messy for proper prayer. But David brings everything to God: his fears, his frustrations, his desperate need for intervention. There is no circumstance too trivial and no distress too complicated to bring them before our righteous God.

As we reflect on Psalm 4:1, we are invited to examine our own prayer lives. When distress comes, do we turn to God immediately or as a last resort? Do we come with honesty or with carefully curated requests? Do we anchor ourselves in God's character or allow our circumstances to define our faith?

David's prayer reminds us that God welcomes us in our distress, hears us in our desperation, and responds according to his mercy and righteousness. Whatever pressure you are facing today, whatever distress is weighing on your heart, you have a God who invites you to call upon him, and he will answer.

PRAYER

Righteous God, I come to you today with my burdens and my distress. Hear my prayer, have mercy on me, and grant me the relief that only you can provide. Help me to trust not in my own strength but in your unfailing grace. Teach me to turn to you first, to pray honestly, and to rest in your faithfulness. In Jesus' name, Amen.

MORNING PETITION AND DIVINE AUDIENCE

*In the morning, LORD, you hear my voice; in the morning I lay
my requests before you and wait expectantly* (Psalm 5:3).

The psalmist opens the fifth psalm with a declaration that strikes at the
heart of spiritual practice: the morning is the season when the heavens
open to receive our prayers, when God leans close to listen. "In the
morning, LORD, you hear my voice; in the morning I lay my requests
before you and wait expectantly." This simple yet profound statement
encapsulates a theology of prayer that transforms our understanding
of petition, timing, and the nature of our relationship with God.

The Hebrew word translated "hear" carries far more weight than mere
auditory reception. To hear in the biblical sense is to listen with intent,
pay attention, acknowledge, and respond. The psalmist is not merely
hoping that sound waves carrying his words will reach the divine ears;
rather, he affirms that God actively listens and that his voice finds an
audience in the throne room of heaven. The repetition of "in the
morning" is no accident. The morning represents a new beginning, a
renewal of mercies, and a fresh opportunity to approach the throne of
grace. Throughout Scripture, the morning is the time for significant
encounters with God, when Abraham rises early to worship, when
Moses receives the Torah, and when the women encounter the risen
Christ. There is something about the dawn that quickens the human
spirit toward the divine.

The phrase "I lay my requests before you" employs a Hebrew word
which means "to arrange or set in order." The psalmist does not
haphazardly cast his concerns heavenward; rather, he carefully
arranges them, presenting them with intention and deliberation. This

is prayer as a disciplined practice, not merely as spontaneous emotion. The Jewish morning prayer tradition that would develop in later centuries reflects this understanding: prayers are structured, ordered, and thoughtful. There is reverence in the very act of arranging our petitions, acknowledging that we come before God with care and respect, not as though God were some cosmic vending machine to be approached carelessly.

Yet perhaps most striking is the final phrase: "and wait expectantly." The Hebrew word behind this translation means to wait, to hope, and to look forward with confidence. This is not passive resignation but active expectation. The psalmist has presented his requests and now waits, not with anxiety, not with doubt, but with expectancy. This is the paradox of biblical prayer: we both act and rest, both speak and listen. We lay our requests before God and then position ourselves to receive his response. In our modern world of instant communication and immediate gratification, such waiting feels countercultural. Yet the psalmist knew something we desperately need to relearn: that the waiting itself is part of the prayer, that expectant waiting is a form of faith.

The theological implications are transformative. First, this verse assures us that God is accessible. We do not approach an indifferent deity; we address one who actively hears. Second, it teaches us about the proper ordering of our days. The psalmist prioritizes morning prayer, the first offering of the day, before the pressures and distractions mount. When we give God the first and best hours of our consciousness, we establish the proper hierarchy of allegiances. Third, it models prayer as a relationship rather than a transaction. We are not placing orders; we are speaking to a God who knows us and loves us, and we wait for his response, knowing that he attends to us.

For those of us who struggle with prayer, who wonder if anyone is listening, who doubt that our small voices matter in this vast universe, Psalm 5:3 offers radical reassurance. Your voice matters. Your requests are heard. Not sometime, not eventually, but in the morning. Not by a distant, preoccupied deity, but by a God who has turned his full attention toward you. The God who spoke creation into existence pauses to listen to your petition. This is the miracle of prayer: not that we are powerful enough to change God's mind, but that we are loved enough that God wants to hear what is on ours.

Let this morning be your season of petition and expectation.

PRAYER

O Lord, as dawn breaks upon this day, I come before your throne with an expectant heart. Receive these requests that I lay before you: my hopes, my needs, my deepest longings. Grant me the faith to wait upon you with confidence, knowing that you hear me and that your mercies are new with each sunrise. Still my anxious heart and quiet my restless thoughts, that I might perceive your voice speaking to my own. In Jesus' name, I wait expectantly upon you. Amen.

THE LORD HAS HEARD MY CRY

The LORD has heard my cry for mercy; the LORD accepts my prayer (Psalm 6:9).

There is a moment that comes to every person of faith when the heavens seem silent and our prayers feel as if they are bouncing off an impenetrable ceiling. We cry out in anguish, pour our hearts out before God, and wonder whether anyone is listening at all. Into this profound human experience speaks Psalm 6:9, a declaration of absolute confidence that our prayers do not disappear into a void but reach the ears of the God who cares for us.

The structure of Psalm 6 mirrors the journey we often take from despair to hope. In verses 2 through 7, the psalmist vividly depicts distress: terror, trembling, weariness of spirit, and anguish of soul. The prayers offered are laments, the desperate petitions that arise only when we have exhausted our own resources and must cast ourselves on divine mercy. Yet verse 9 arrives as a sudden, resolute affirmation. The crisis is not yet resolved in material circumstances, but something has shifted in the psalmist's spiritual perception. The Lord has heard. The prayer has been accepted.

The Hebrew verb "to hear" carries profound theological weight throughout Scripture. When God hears, it is never a matter of mere auditory reception, as if God were simply a cosmic listening device. Rather, the Hebrew concept of hearing encompasses understanding, responding, and acting. When the Scriptures declare that God has heard a cry, they announce that the Almighty has received it with full comprehension and genuine concern. The psalmist uses the expression "has heard," suggesting an action already completed and now standing as an accomplished fact. This is not tentative hope but genuine confidence rooted in the character of God.

The phrase "cry for mercy" in Hebrew is "the voice of my supplications." The expression derives from a root that suggests earnest pleading, the passionate petition that arises from genuine need. This is not the polite request of one who has confidence in their own resources. Rather, it is the desperate appeal of one who recognizes utter dependence on divine grace. The psalmist has brought before God not reasoned arguments or claims of personal merit, but raw human vulnerability. And this cry, this authentic expression of need, has reached the ears of the God who delights in mercy.

The second line reinforces and deepens the first: "The LORD accepts my prayer." The verb here emphasizes reception and approval. God does not merely hear our prayers in the sense of tolerating them; the Lord receives them with favor. This is a remarkable claim for anyone who has ever struggled with doubt about whether their prayers matter, whether they are worthy of divine attention, or whether God truly cares about their particular circumstances. The psalm assures us that our prayers are accepted, received with approval by the one whose opinion alone truly matters.

Yet we must note something vital: the psalmist declares that the Lord has heard and accepted while still sitting amid distress. Verse 10 continues the lament: "All my enemies will be ashamed and greatly troubled; they will turn back in sudden disgrace." The prayer of confidence does not depend on the immediate resolution of the crisis. Rather, it rests on something more fundamental: the conviction that the Lord hears and cares, that petition reaches the divine ear and finds reception there.

This is the essential comfort Psalm 6:9 offers us. Our prayers matter. God listens. The Almighty receives our petitions with favor. We need not wait for circumstances to change before we trust this reality. We need not wonder whether God is paying attention or whether our prayers are too small, too insignificant, or too personal to catch God's notice. The God revealed throughout Scripture is one who bends his ear to listen, who receives our cries for mercy, and who accepts the prayers of those who come before him in honest need and genuine faith.

When you find yourself in the dark places of life, when confusion reigns, when fears assault you, when you are uncertain whether anyone is listening, remember Psalm 6:9. Your cry has reached the Lord. Your prayer has been accepted. The God of all creation has heard you, and in that hearing lies your deepest assurance and your truest hope.

PRAYER

Merciful Father, I thank you for not turning away from my cries for mercy. I am grateful that my prayers reach your ears and are accepted by you. In those times when my faith wavers and I wonder whether you are listening, help me to remember this truth: that you hear me, that you care about my concerns, and that my petitions matter to you. Strengthen my confidence in your character and your responsiveness. Grant me the courage to bring my whole self before you, my fears, my doubts, my desperate needs, knowing that you receive me with favor. May I rest not upon changing circumstances but upon the unchanging reality that you hear my cry for mercy. In the name of Jesus Christ, who taught us to pray with confidence and who intercedes for us before your throne, I pray. Amen.

THE SHIELD OF THE UPRIGHT

My shield is God Most High, who saves the upright in heart (Psalm 7:10).

There is something profoundly comforting about the image of a shield. In the ancient world, a shield was not merely a piece of military equipment; it was the difference between life and death. A warrior without his shield was vulnerable, exposed to every arrow and spear. When David writes, "My shield is God Most High, who saves the upright in heart," he is drawing on this visceral understanding of protection, declaring a truth that transcends the battlefield and speaks to the deepest needs of the human soul.

Notice first what David does not say. He does not claim that God is the shield of the perfect, the flawless, or those who have their spiritual lives completely together. Instead, God shields "the upright in heart." This is a crucial distinction. The upright in heart are not those who never stumble or fail, but those whose fundamental orientation is toward God. Their hearts, despite their imperfections, are aligned with righteousness. They desire what is good, they hunger for what is true, and when they fall, they turn back toward the light.

This matters because many of us disqualify ourselves from God's protection based on our failures. We look at our inconsistencies, our repeated struggles, our persistent weaknesses, and assume we have forfeited our right to claim God as our shield. But David, who wrote this psalm while fleeing from enemies and dealing with false accusations, understood something essential: God's protection is not earned through flawless performance but received through sincere devotion. The upright in heart are not those who never fall; they are those who refuse to stay down.

The title David uses here is significant: "God Most High." In Hebrew, this is "El Elyon," a name that emphasizes God's supremacy over all other powers. When we face threats, whether they are physical dangers, emotional assaults, spiritual attacks, or the accusations of others, we need more than a temporary shelter. We need a shield that stands higher than every arrow aimed at us. We need protection that no enemy can circumvent. This is what God Most High provides. He does not just stand between us and danger; he towers over it.

Consider what a shield does. It does not eliminate the battle. David's enemies were still real; their accusations still stung; the danger was still present. A shield does not make you immune to conflict; it protects you in the midst of it. God does not always remove our difficulties, but he positions himself between us and the full force of what would destroy us. The arrows still fly, but they strike his shield before they reach our hearts.

There is also something deeply personal in David's declaration: "My shield is God Most High." Not "a shield" or "our shield," but "my shield." This is the language of intimate relationship, of personal trust forged through experience. David had tested this truth in the wilderness, in the palace, in caves, and on battlefields. He knew from lived experience that God was faithful. Our faith, too, must move from abstract theology to personal testimony. We must each discover for ourselves that God is not just the shield of the righteous in general, but my shield, my protector, my defender in the specific circumstances of my life.

The verse also reminds us that God "saves" the upright in heart. Salvation here is not just a past-tense event or a future hope; it is a present, ongoing reality. God saves us from the schemes of the wicked, from the weight of false accusations, from the despair that threatens to overwhelm us, and from the spiritual forces that would separate us from his love. This saving work is continuous, daily, moment by moment.

What does this mean for us today? It means we can face our challenges, whatever they are, with confidence, not in our own strength or cleverness, but in the God who shields us. It means that when accusations come, whether from others or from our own conscience, we can stand firm knowing that God himself defends those whose hearts are turned toward him. It means that uprightness of heart, not perfection of performance, is what God looks for and protects.

So examine your heart today. Is it oriented toward God, even imperfectly? Then you can claim this promise as your own: "My shield is God Most High."

PRAYER

God Most High, you are my shield and my defender. When arrows fly and enemies surround me, you stand between me and all that would destroy me. Keep my heart upright before you, not through my own strength but through your sustaining grace. Let me trust not in my perfection but in your protection, and find my refuge in you alone. Amen.

THE MAJESTY ABOVE

When I consider your heavens, the work of your fingers, the moon and the stars, which you have set in place, what is mankind that you are mindful of them, human beings that you care for them? (Psalm 8:3–4).

There are moments in life when the sheer scale of creation stops us in our tracks. Perhaps it is standing beneath a canopy of stars far from city lights, or watching the moon rise over a darkened ocean, or seeing the first photographs from the James Webb Space Telescope revealing galaxies billions of light-years away. In these moments, we feel simultaneously small and significant, humbled and honored. This is precisely the paradox David captures in Psalm 8.

When David writes "your heavens, the work of your fingers," he invites us into an intimate portrait of divine creativity. He does not speak of God's mighty arms or powerful hands, but of his fingers, the language of an artisan, a craftsman who shapes with precision and care. The universe is not the product of careless explosion or impersonal force, but of deliberate, personal attention. Every star hung in its place, every orbital path calculated, every physical law calibrated with intention. The fingerprints of God are everywhere in creation.

Yet David's contemplation of cosmic grandeur leads him not to despair but to wonder. "What is mankind that you are mindful of them?" This question emerges not from insecurity but from astonishment. The God who speaks galaxies into existence and names every star turns his attention toward us. The word "mindful" here carries the sense of active remembering, of keeping someone continually in one's thoughts. It is not that God occasionally checks in on humanity; rather, we occupy his constant awareness.

This divine mindfulness reveals a profound aspect of God's nature. He is not diminished by vastness nor distracted by complexity. The same God who governs the movements of celestial bodies concerns himself with the movements of your heart. The God who set the stars in their courses has set his affection on you. There is no cosmic distance that separates God's majesty from his mercy, no unbridgeable gap between his transcendence and his tenderness.

In our modern age, we know far more about the heavens than David ever could. We understand that the moon is a quarter-million miles away, that the sun is a star burning at 27 million degrees Fahrenheit, that our galaxy contains hundreds of billions of stars, and that there are more galaxies in the observable universe than grains of sand on all Earth's beaches. This knowledge could make David's question even more acute: in a universe of such incomprehensible scale, what are we but cosmic dust?

But the biblical answer remains unchanged. We are the ones God cares for. Not angels. Not distant civilizations that may or may not exist. Us. Human beings made in his image, crowned with glory and honor, given dominion over creation, and invited into a relationship with the Creator himself. The incarnation makes this truth even more stunning: the God who hung the stars took on human flesh, walked dusty roads, and died on a wooden cross for us.

This should transform how we view ourselves and others. If the God of galaxies is mindful of humanity, who are we to dismiss our own significance or the worth of any person? Every individual you encounter today carries eternal weight, bears the divine image, and has captured God's attention. The homeless man on the corner, the difficult coworker, the stranger in line behind you, each one matters infinitely to the God of infinite space.

Yet this truth should also cultivate humility. We are not the center of the universe, even if we are central to God's heart. Our smallness in cosmic terms should check our pride and our pretensions. We live on a pale blue dot in a vast universe, here for a brief moment in cosmic time. But in that brief moment, we have the staggering privilege of knowing and being known by the God who made it all.

David's question, then, is not one of existential dread but of grateful amazement. It is the question of a child who cannot fathom why a king would stoop to notice him, the wonder of the beloved who knows the love is undeserved yet utterly real. We consider the heavens and find ourselves considered by the One in heaven. We gaze upward at glory and discover Glory gazing back at us in love.

PRAYER

Heavenly Father, when I consider your vast creation, the endless stars, the turning galaxies, the precision of every natural law, I am amazed that you would turn your attention toward me. Thank you for your mindfulness, for caring about the details of my life even as you uphold the universe. Help me to live today with both humility and confidence: humble before your majesty, confident in your love. May I see others as you see them, precious, worthy of notice, beloved. In Jesus' name, Amen.

FINDING SHELTER IN THE STORM

The LORD *is a refuge for the oppressed, a stronghold in times of trouble* (Psalm 9:9).

There is something profoundly human about seeking shelter. When the storm clouds gather, and the first drops of rain begin to fall, we instinctively look for cover. We run toward doorways, duck under awnings, or hurry home where we know we will be safe and dry. This ancient impulse, this need for refuge, runs deeper than our desire to stay dry. It touches something essential about what it means to be vulnerable, finite, and in need of protection.

The psalmist understood this when he wrote, "The LORD is a refuge for the oppressed, a stronghold in times of trouble." These are not merely pretty words meant to comfort us in abstract ways. They speak to the concrete reality of human suffering and God's response to it. The Hebrew word translated as "refuge" carries the imagery of a high place, a fortified position where enemies cannot reach. It is a place of elevation and safety, where the vulnerable can find protection from those who would harm them.

Notice who this refuge is for: the oppressed. Not the strong. Not those who have everything together. Not those who have managed to build their own fortresses through wealth, power, or self-sufficiency. The oppressed are those who are crushed down, those who bear weight they cannot carry alone, those who face forces beyond their control. This is God's particular concern, not those who need no help, but those who are desperate for it.

Throughout the Psalms, we encounter this theme again and again. God presents himself as the defender of the defenseless, the father of the fatherless, and the hope of the hopeless. This is not because God loves the weak more than the strong, but because the weak recognize their need. They have no illusions about their self-sufficiency. They understand, in ways the comfortable often do not, that they need a refuge beyond themselves.

What troubles are you facing today? Perhaps it is a relationship that is broken beyond your ability to fix. Maybe it is a financial crisis that keeps you awake at night, or a health diagnosis that has shaken your sense of security. It could be the weight of injustice, the pain of betrayal, or simply the accumulated stress of living in a world that often feels hostile and overwhelming. The psalmist does not minimize these troubles. He acknowledges them as real, as times when we genuinely need a stronghold.

A stronghold is more than a temporary shelter. It is a fortified place designed to withstand prolonged assault. Ancient strongholds were not just for weathering brief storms; they were built for sieges, for times when the enemy camps at your gates and will not leave. This is the nature of many of our troubles. They do not pass quickly. They settle in. They exhaust us. And it is precisely for these extended battles that God offers himself as our stronghold.

But here is what we must understand: taking refuge in God requires humility. It means admitting we cannot save ourselves. It means running to him rather than toward the hundred other things we typically try first: our own strength, our carefully constructed plans, our attempts to control outcomes, or our tendency to numb ourselves through distraction and denial. Taking refuge means dropping the pretense of self-sufficiency and saying to God, "I need you. I cannot do this alone."

In our culture, this kind of dependence can feel like weakness. We are told to be strong, to be resilient, to pull ourselves up by our bootstraps. But the biblical vision is different. It suggests that true strength is found not in denying our vulnerability but in knowing where to take it. The strongest people are not those who never need help; they are those who know where to find it.

When you run to God as your refuge, you are not running to an idea or a philosophy. You are running to a God who sees you, knows you, and cares about your specific pain. You are running to the God who has demonstrated his love not through empty promises but through the costly sacrifice of his own Son. This is a refuge you can trust because it has been tested and proven.

So today, whatever oppression weighs on you, whatever trouble surrounds you, know this: there is a place of safety. There is a stronghold that will not crumble. The Lord himself invites you to take shelter in him, not just for a moment, but for as long as you need. And that is more than just good news; it is the difference between despair and hope.

PRAYER

Lord, you are my refuge and my stronghold. When troubles surround me, and I feel oppressed by circumstances beyond my control, help me to run to you rather than relying on my own failing strength. Teach me the humility to admit my need and the faith to trust in your protection. In Jesus' name, Amen.

THE GOD WHO HEARS

*You, LORD, hear the desire of the afflicted; you encourage them,
and you listen to their cry* (Psalm 10:17).

"You, LORD, hear the desire of the afflicted; you encourage them, and you listen to their cry." These words arrive at the culmination of a psalm that begins in bewilderment and ends in assurance. To understand this verse properly, we must recognize it as the psalmist's resolution to the anguish expressed in the preceding lines. Psalm 10 opens with the anguished question, "Why, LORD, do you stand far off? Why do you hide yourself in times of trouble?" (Psalm 10:1). The psalmist then catalogs the wickedness of the proud and the suffering of the vulnerable. Yet by verse 17, a dramatic shift occurs. The psalmist moves from questioning God's absence to affirming God's attentiveness. This transformation speaks profoundly to the human condition and to the nature of our relationship with God.

The Hebrew term translated as "desire" carries the sense of intention, purpose, or determination. When the psalmist speaks of God hearing the desire of the afflicted, the text suggests that God does not merely hear our words; he perceives our deepest longings and intentions. This moves beyond mere acoustic reception. God understands what the suffering person truly seeks: not merely relief from pain, but restoration, dignity, and vindication. The afflicted one may struggle to articulate their needs adequately, yet God penetrates to the core of their being. This realization should comfort us profoundly. Our halting prayers, our inarticulate cries in the night, our desperate whispers, all are perfectly understood by the God who created us.

The second phrase intensifies this assurance: "you encourage them." The Hebrew verb literally means "to establish" or "to prepare." God does not merely listen passively; he actively strengthens and fortifies the hearts of those who suffer. This encouragement is not a dismissive platitude or hollow sentiment. Rather, it reflects a concrete divine engagement with human suffering. When we face affliction, God provides both the hearing ear and the steadying hand. The psalmist recognizes that divine attention itself becomes a source of strength. To know that one is heard by the transcendent Creator transforms the nature of suffering itself. It no longer seems meaningless or abandoned; it becomes a space where God's presence is made known.

The final clause, "you listen to their cry," brings the thought full circle. The repetition of auditory imagery, hearing, and listening emphasizes God's receptivity. The Hebrew word translated "cry" refers to a cry of distress or anguish, often an involuntary expression of pain. These are not carefully constructed theological arguments or eloquent supplications. They are the raw, sometimes inarticulate expressions of human suffering. That God listens to such cries tells us that divine attention is not reserved for the eloquent or the theologically sophisticated. The widow's silent tears, the orphan's confused sobs, the refugee's desperate prayers in broken language, all receive the attention of the God who created them.

This verse emerges from a specific historical and theological context that remains relevant to contemporary believers. Ancient Israel experienced oppression, injustice, and the apparent triumph of the wicked. The psalmist writes from a position of vulnerability. Yet rather than counseling resignation or passive acceptance, the psalm affirms that God's character includes an active concern for the vulnerable. This reflects the broader Old Testament emphasis on God as a defender of the defenseless, a recurring theme in the Prophets and the Torah. The God of Israel is not remote or indifferent; he is committed to the welfare of those who cannot defend themselves.

For modern readers, this verse speaks across the centuries to our experiences of pain, injustice, and abandonment. In moments when suffering feels overwhelming and God feels distant, Psalm 10:17 offers an alternative perspective. It invites us to trust that our Creator hears not merely our words but our deepest needs. It assures us that God actively strengthens us in our affliction. Most importantly, it reminds us that divine listening is not merely passive reception but an engagement that transforms the one who cries out. The psalmist's journey from "Why do you hide?" (Psalm 10:1) to "You listen to their cry" (Psalm 10:17) models our own spiritual journey.

Doubt, anger, and questioning are not obstacles to faith; they are often the pathway to deeper trust. When we voice our anguish before God rather than suppressing it, we discover that he is already present in our suffering, already attending to our deepest needs, already preparing encouragement for our weary hearts.

PRAYER

Gracious God, I come before you today, sometimes with words and sometimes only with the inarticulate longings of my heart. Thank you for the assurance that you hear not merely my words but my deepest desires. Strengthen me in the midst of my affliction, that I might know your presence even in darkness. Grant me the faith to cry out to you, trusting that you listen with full attention and deep compassion. Draw me, I pray, from doubt toward trust, from abandonment toward assurance, from despair toward the confidence that you are indeed attending to every cry of my soul. Amen.

PSALM 11

THE FACE OF DIVINE JUSTICE

For the LORD *is righteous, he loves justice; the upright will see his face* (Psalm 11:7).

The psalmist concludes this brief psalm with a declaration that cuts through the despair and fear expressed in earlier verses. After describing the wicked archers taking aim at the righteous, having questioned why one should "flee like a bird to the mountains," the poet arrives at a profound theological affirmation grounded not in circumstance but in the very character of God. This final verse offers us the essential counterbalance to our anxiety, a reminder that divine justice and righteousness are not abstract theological concepts but are intimately connected to the presence and favor of God himself.

The Hebrew word translated as "righteous" encompasses both moral rectitude and relational reliability. When the psalmist declares "The LORD is righteous," the affirmation transcends mere ethical correctness. It asserts that God is faithful to his covenant commitments, that he can be trusted to uphold justice not capriciously but according to the deepest principles of his nature. This righteousness is not distant or impersonal; rather, it is the foundation upon which the entire universe rests. In the midst of social chaos and personal threat, the apparent context of Psalm 11, this declaration anchors us to an immovable reality: God is dependable in his moral character.

More striking still is the phrase "he loves justice." The word "he loves" conveys an affectionate commitment, not merely a cold adherence to legal principle. God does not merely enforce justice as a judge who finds the work tedious; he delights in it. Justice is not something God must reluctantly perform as an obligation, but something his heart embraces. This profoundly transforms our understanding of divine justice. When we suffer injustice, when the wicked prosper, and the righteous languish, as the earlier verses describe, we can trust that God shares our distress. His love for justice means that the present disorder grieves him as well. He is not indifferent to the cries of the oppressed, nor is he resigned to moral chaos. His very nature propels him toward the establishment of what is right and true.

The consequence of divine righteousness and God's love for justice is encapsulated in one of Scripture's most luminous promises: "the upright will see his face." To see God's face was understood in ancient Israel as the highest blessing imaginable, the pinnacle of intimate communion with the divine. In the temple liturgy, the faithful would pray to "gaze on the beauty of the LORD" (Psalm 27:4). Yet this seeing was never merely mystical or eschatological. The psalmist promises it to those who walk in uprightness, suggesting that ethical living and spiritual vision are inseparably linked.

The term "upright" describes not perfection but integrity: a life oriented toward God and aligned with his righteous purposes. This is crucial: the promise is not to the spiritually elite or mystically gifted, but to ordinary people who orient their lives toward righteousness. We need not possess exceptional piety or supernatural insight. Rather, we must commit ourselves to walking in alignment with God's moral character. And in doing so, we become those who can perceive his presence in a way that the unrighteous cannot.

In our contemporary context, bombarded with images of injustice, corruption, and moral inversion, where the crooked climb to prominence and the honest are exploited, this psalm speaks with remarkable power. It does not deny the reality of wickedness or counsel passive resignation. Rather, it invites us to see through the confusion to God's steady, unwavering character. It reminds us that righteousness is not determined by circumstance or success but by fidelity to God's nature.

Furthermore, the promise that the upright "will see his face" transforms our present suffering. Even in circumstances where injustice seems to triumph, we are promised the ultimate privilege of standing before God himself. This is not escapism but eschatological realism, the confidence that God's final word will not be spoken by those who presently wield power unjustly, but by the God whose character is eternally righteous and eternally oriented toward justice.

As we navigate our uncertain world, we are invited to do what the psalmist does: move from fear to faith by anchoring our trust in the unchanging character of our God. We choose righteousness not because it promises earthly advantage but because it aligns us with the God who loves justice, and in that alignment, we are promised the supreme blessing of knowing his presence.

PRAYER

Righteous God, in a world where injustice often flourishes and the wicked prosper, strengthen our faith in your unwavering character. Grant us courage to walk in integrity and uprightness, trusting that you love justice as we do. May we be among those who shall see your face, not through extraordinary spiritual achievement but through genuine commitment to righteousness. Help us to endure present injustice with the confidence that your final word will be spoken in perfect justice. Amen.

PSALM 12

FINDING CERTAINTY IN GOD'S WORD

And the words of the LORD are flawless, like silver purified in
a crucible, like gold refined seven times (Psalm 12:6).

In a world saturated with information, misinformation, and competing voices clamoring for our attention, Psalm 12:6 offers us an anchor: "And the words of the LORD are flawless, like silver purified in a crucible, like gold refined seven times." This verse comes to us from a psalm lamenting the prevalence of deceit and flattery among people, making its declaration about God's Word all the more striking. When human words fail us, when they mislead, manipulate, or simply fall short, God's words stand utterly reliable.

The psalmist does not merely say God's words are "good" or "helpful." He reaches for the strongest possible metaphor available in his ancient context: precious metals refined to absolute purity. In the ancient world, the refining process was meticulous and demanding. Silver and gold ores contained impurities that had to be burned away at high temperatures. The refiner would place the metal in a crucible and subject it to fire again and again, carefully skimming off the dross that rose to the surface. With each successive heating, more impurities were removed. Seven times, a number signifying completeness and perfection in Hebrew thought, suggests the ultimate degree of purity.

This imagery invites us to consider what makes God's Word fundamentally different from human speech. Our words, even at their best, contain flaws. We speak from limited knowledge, biased perspectives, and mixed motives. We communicate imperfectly what we understand imperfectly. We make promises we cannot keep and assertions we cannot verify. But God's Word has passed through the refiner's fire. There is no dross of error, no impurity of deception, no mixture of truth and falsehood.

34

The flawlessness of Scripture is not primarily about its literary beauty, though the Psalms themselves demonstrate profound poetic artistry. Rather, it is about trustworthiness. When God speaks, his words accomplish exactly what he intends. They reveal reality as it truly is. They make promises that will certainly be fulfilled. They provide guidance that will never lead us astray. In an age of "fake news" and algorithmic echo chambers, this is no small claim.

Yet we might wonder: if God's Word is so pure and perfect, why does it sometimes seem difficult to understand? Why do interpretations differ? Here we must distinguish between the perfection of the text itself and our imperfect capacity to comprehend it. A flawless diamond remains flawless whether viewed in brilliant sunlight or dim candlelight, but our ability to perceive its facets changes with the conditions. Similarly, Scripture remains perfect even when our understanding is clouded by cultural distance, personal bias, or spiritual immaturity.

This is why approaching God's Word requires humility. We come not as critics evaluating whether Scripture meets our standards, but as students sitting before a perfect teacher. We ask not whether God's Word is true, but what truth it reveals to us. The refining process the psalmist describes is not something we apply to Scripture; it is something Scripture applies to us. Just as fire purifies metal, God's Word refines our thinking, challenges our assumptions, and burns away the dross of worldly wisdom that accumulates in our hearts.

The practical implications are profound. If God's Word is truly flawless, we can stake our lives on it. When Scripture offers comfort, that comfort is reliable. When it convicts, that conviction is righteous. When it makes promises, those promises are guaranteed. When it gives commands, those commands lead to flourishing. We need not anxiously fact-check every verse or nervously wonder if God really meant what he said.

This does not mean reading Scripture is always easy or comfortable. Refined gold, after all, must pass through intense heat. God's perfect Word often confronts our imperfect hearts. It challenges our cherished sins and comfortable compromises. It calls us to trust when circumstances seem to contradict its promises. But like gold that emerges stronger and more valuable from the crucible, we emerge from genuine engagement with Scripture refined and transformed.

In the end, Psalm 12:6 invites us to a posture of confidence and surrender. Confidence that God's Word will never fail us or mislead us. Surrender to its authority over every area of our lives. In a world of unreliable voices, we have access to words refined seven times over, words worthy of our complete trust.

PRAYER

Gracious Father, thank you for the gift of your perfect Word. In a world where truth feels increasingly elusive, I praise you that your words stand flawless and pure. Help me to approach Scripture with humility, trusting its reliability even when I do not fully understand. Refine my heart through your truth, burning away the impurities of doubt, pride, and worldly thinking. May your Word be the foundation on which I build my life. In Jesus' name, Amen.

TRUST AND REJOICING

But I trust in your unfailing love; my heart rejoices in your salvation. I will sing the Lord's praise, for he has been good to me (Psalm 13:5–6).

The final verses of Psalm 13 present one of the most dramatic shifts in biblical literature. The psalm begins with anguished questions, "How long, O LORD? Will you forget me forever?" and moves through desperate pleading. Yet suddenly, without explanation or resolution of circumstances, the psalmist declares absolute trust and breaks into jubilant praise. This sudden transformation invites us to explore the nature of a faith that transcends external circumstances and finds its foundation in God's character rather than in our changing situations.

The Hebrew word translated as "trust" conveys confidence and security, often depicting someone reclining peacefully. It suggests more than intellectual assent; it represents a posture of complete reliance. The psalmist does not say, "I trust in your unfailing love *when* my circumstances improve" or "I trust *if* you answer my prayer." Rather, the trust is declared absolutely and unconditionally. This is crucial for understanding biblical faith. Trust in God's character remains independent of our present distress. The psalmist has not yet seen deliverance, yet the affirmation of trust appears before any indication that God has answered.

The phrase "unfailing love" translates the Hebrew word *hesed*, perhaps the most theologically rich word in the Old Testament. *Hesed* encompasses covenant loyalty, steadfast mercy, and enduring kindness. It is not sentimental affection but rather the faithful commitment God made to his people through the covenant. When the psalmist declares his trust in God's *hesed*, he anchors his confidence in

God's unchanging, covenantal nature. God's character does not fluctuate with circumstances. His love is not conditional upon our worthiness or dependent upon our present prosperity. This is the foundation upon which genuine trust is built.

The psalmist then declares, "My heart rejoices in your salvation." The word "heart" refers to the inner person, the seat of understanding, will, and emotion. The rejoicing is not a superficial celebration but a deep, internal gladness rooted in recognition of divine deliverance. Importantly, the psalmist uses the Hebrew term for salvation, which encompasses God's saving work. Yet, the text uses what appears to be a completed action. The psalmist rejoices not only in anticipated future salvation but also in the very fact that God is his savior and that salvation is part of God's established relationship with him through the covenant.

This movement from trust to rejoicing demonstrates a spiritual reality often overlooked in our modern therapeutic spirituality: joy is not primarily dependent on our circumstances changing, but on our reconnection with God's unchanging character. The psalmist has not received notice that his enemies will depart or his illness will be healed. Rather, he has done something internally: he has reoriented his focus from his problems to God's faithfulness, and in that reorientation, his heart finds genuine rejoicing.

The final statement completes the transformation: "I will sing the LORD's praise, for he has been good to me." The resolution moves from internal emotional reorientation to external, public action. The psalmist commits to singing praise. This commitment to praise is not contingent upon future circumstances; it is grounded in "he has been good to me." The Hebrew past tense here is significant. The psalmist reflects on God's historical goodness, his demonstrated faithfulness throughout life's journey.

This ending provides an important corrective to a common misconception about faith. Some believe that genuine faith means never experiencing doubt or distress. But Psalm 13 demonstrates that authentic faith includes honest lament; the entire first section of the psalm expresses real anguish. followed by a deliberate choice to trust. The psalm models for us that faith is not the absence of struggle but the movement through struggle toward trust in God's character.

For those of us who struggle with doubt, depression, or anxiety, this psalm offers profound encouragement. It legitimizes our pain while calling us beyond it. We need not pretend that our circumstances are not difficult. But we are invited to ask, as the psalmist does, whether we will allow our temporary circumstances to define our understanding of God or whether we will allow God's character and covenant faithfulness to redefine our circumstances.

The psalmist's declaration to "sing the LORD's praise" becomes our calling as well. Not because everything is resolved, but because God himself has proven good. That is sufficient.

PRAYER

O God of unfailing love, I confess that my trust often fluctuates with my circumstances. When life is good, I rejoice in you easily; when trouble comes, I question your faithfulness. Teach me to anchor my confidence not in changing situations but in your unchanging character. Help me to remember your historical goodness in my life and in the lives of your people. Give me courage to move from my honest laments to genuine trust, and strengthen my resolve to praise you, not because my struggles have ended, but because you yourself are worthy of all praise. In Jesus' name, Amen.

THE FOOL AND THE EMPTY HEART

The fool says in his heart, "There is no God" (Psalm 14:1).

The psalmist opens with a declaration that strikes at the very foundation of human existence: "The fool says in his heart, 'There is no God.'" These opening words of Psalm 14 present us not merely with an intellectual proposition but with a profound spiritual diagnosis of the human condition. To understand this verse fully, we must look beyond the surface denial and into the theological and linguistic depths that make this statement so enduring in Scripture.

The Hebrew word translated as "fool" here is *nābāl,* a term that carries far more weight than simple intellectual deficiency. The "fool" is not primarily someone who lacks intelligence but rather someone who lacks moral and spiritual perception. This is the fool who possesses the capacity to understand but refuses to do so, one whose folly is fundamentally a matter of the will and the heart, not the mind. The fool has sufficient evidence for God's existence, yet deliberately chooses opacity over clarity, hardness over responsiveness.

Notice that the psalmist does not say the fool *thinks* or *believes* there is no God. Instead, the fool says this "in his heart." This distinction is crucial. In Hebrew anthropology, the heart is the seat of intellect, emotion, will, and moral capacity, the control center of human existence. The fool's denial does not emerge from rigorous philosophical argumentation but from an inner posture of rebellion. It is a declaration made in the privacy of one's inner self, as though the fool imagines that by confining this heresy to his heart, he might escape the consequences of his own words. Yet Scripture knows that what dwells in the heart cannot remain hidden; it will eventually overflow into speech and action, manifesting itself in the way one lives.

The theology of this statement becomes even more striking when we recognize what assumption undergirds it. The psalmist does not feel compelled to argue for God's existence. There is no apologetic here in the technical sense. Rather, the very denial of God is presented as self-evidently foolish. The psalmist's worldview assumes a framework in which God's existence is so manifest, so woven into the fabric of creation and human experience, that to deny it is to declare oneself foolish. This reflects the perspective articulated elsewhere in Scripture, particularly in Romans 1, where Paul argues that God's invisible attributes are clearly seen in creation, leaving those who deny him without excuse.

Yet we must ask: what leads someone to make such a declaration? What circumstances produce this heart-posture of denial? The broader context of Psalm 14 provides some answers. Following this opening declaration, the psalmist observes corrupt and devious behavior: "The LORD looks down from heaven upon the children of men, to see if there are any who understand, any who seek God. All have turned aside, they have together become corrupt" (Psalm 14:2–3). The fool's denial of God is intimately connected with moral and spiritual corruption. The denial is not merely intellectual; it is practical atheism, living as though God does not exist and therefore as though moral accountability is illusory.

This insight speaks powerfully to our contemporary moment. We live in an age where explicit atheism and agnosticism have gained philosophical respectability in certain quarters. Yet the psalmist's diagnosis remains accurate: the real issue is not primarily intellectual but moral. Many who deny God do so because such denial provides convenient justification for living according to their own desires, unencumbered by divine accountability. The fool says in his heart what he wishes to be true because its truth would suit his purposes.

For those of us who confess our faith in God, this verse calls for several reflections. First, it reminds us that faith is fundamentally a matter of the heart, not mere intellectual assent but a reorientation of our innermost being toward God. Second, it warns us against subtle forms of practical atheism, those moments when we live as though God does not see, does not care, or does not hold us accountable. Third, it invites us to be grateful for the grace that has opened our hearts to perceive what the fool cannot see.

Most profoundly, this verse calls us to recognize that authentic wisdom begins not with intellectual sophistication but with a humble heart that says to God: "You are. You matter. You are Lord." In that simple acknowledgment lies the beginning of all true knowledge, all genuine understanding, and all authentic flourishing.

PRAYER

Eternal God, open the eyes of our hearts to perceive your presence in all things. Guard us from the subtle forms of foolishness that tempt us to live as though you do not see or care. Grant us the wisdom that fears you and the courage to acknowledge your lordship not merely with our lips but with the whole orientation of our lives. We confess that you are God, and we commit ourselves afresh to seeking you and following your ways. In Jesus' name we pray. Amen.

THE PATH TO GOD'S PRESENCE

LORD, who may dwell in your sacred tent? Who may live on your holy mountain? The one whose walk is blameless, who does what is righteous, who speaks the truth from their heart (Psalm 15:1–2).

When David posed his question to the Lord: "Who may dwell in your sacred tent?" he was not asking out of idle curiosity. He was voicing the deepest longing of the human heart: to live in intimate communion with God. The tabernacle, God's dwelling place among his people, represented something far greater than a physical structure. It symbolized the very presence of God, that sacred space where heaven touched earth and where humans could encounter God.

David's question echoes through the centuries to us today. We may not have a physical tent or temple, but the yearning remains the same. We long to know that we are welcomed into God's presence, that we belong in his household, that we can call his holy mountain our home. And like any earnest seeker, we want to know: What does God require of us?

The answer David receives is both straightforward and profound. God does not demand elaborate rituals or impossible feats. Instead, he calls us to a way of being, a transformation that begins in the heart and radiates outward into every aspect of our lives. The one who dwells with God is the one "whose walk is blameless."

Notice that word: "walk." Not someone whose past is perfect, but whose present journey is characterized by integrity. A walk implies movement, direction, and consistency. It is not about never stumbling; it is about the daily choice to move in the right direction, to get back up when we fall, to pursue holiness not as an achievement but as a way of life. Blamelessness here does not mean sinless perfection; it means wholeness, sincerity, a life where our inner convictions and outer actions align.

This person "does what is righteous." Righteousness in Scripture is not merely personal piety divorced from practical living. It encompasses justice, fairness, and compassion: how we treat our neighbors, how we conduct our business, and how we respond to the vulnerable. The righteous person not only avoids evil but also actively pursues good. They see a need and respond. They witness injustice and speak up. Their faith has hands and feet.

Then comes perhaps the most challenging requirement: they "speak the truth from their heart." How easy it is to speak truth with our lips while harboring deception in our hearts! We can say the right words while nursing secret resentments, hidden agendas, or quiet prejudices. But God looks deeper. He desires truth in our innermost being, a radical honesty that begins with ourselves, extends to our relationships, and ultimately rests in our relationship with him.

Speaking truth from the heart means our words carry the weight of authenticity. We do not flatter to manipulate. We do not gossip to elevate ourselves. We do not bear false witness to protect our reputation. Instead, our speech becomes an extension of a truthful heart: sometimes gentle, sometimes bold, but always anchored in integrity.

The beautiful paradox of Psalm 15 is this: while it describes the character required to dwell with God, it simultaneously reveals God's own character. The God who requires blameless walking is himself faithful and true. The God who demands righteousness is perfectly just. The God who values truthfulness cannot lie. To dwell with God is to become like God, not in power or glory, but in moral character and loving action.

For those of us walking this journey of faith, these verses serve as both a mirror and a compass. They reflect who we are, often falling short of this standard, while pointing us toward who we are becoming through God's grace. We do not achieve this character through sheer willpower; we receive it as we abide in Christ, allowing his Spirit to transform us from the inside out.

The invitation to dwell in God's presence is not reserved for the spiritually elite. It is extended to all who would honestly pursue him, who would allow their lives to be shaped by his truth, and who would daily choose the path of righteousness over the broad road of compromise. God's holy mountain has room for you. His sacred tent welcomes all who come with sincere hearts.

PRAYER

Gracious Father, you have invited us into your presence, not because we are worthy, but because you are merciful. Give us the courage to walk blamelessly before you, to pursue righteousness in all we do, and to speak truth from hearts made pure by your Spirit. When we stumble, lift us up. When we wander, call us back. Make us people who dwell continually in the light of your presence. In Jesus' name, Amen.

PSALM 16

UNSHAKEABLE IN HIS PRESENCE

I keep my eyes always on the LORD. *With him at my right hand, I will not be shaken* (Psalm 16:8).

In a world that seems determined to knock us off balance, David's declaration in Psalm 16:8 offers us an anchor for the soul. These words, penned thousands of years ago, speak directly to our contemporary struggles with anxiety, uncertainty, and the constant distractions vying for our attention. David understood something profound: where we fix our gaze determines the stability of our stance.

The first half of this verse reveals a deliberate choice. "I keep my eyes always on the LORD" is not passive chance but active discipline. The Hebrew word translated "keep" carries the sense of setting something before oneself, of placing it deliberately in one's line of sight. David is not describing an occasional glance heavenward during emergencies, but a sustained, intentional focus that becomes the orienting principle of daily life.

Consider how this works in practice. When Peter stepped out of the boat to walk on water toward Jesus, he succeeded as long as he kept his eyes fixed on the Lord. The moment he looked at the wind and waves, his circumstances, rather than Jesus, began to sink. We face the same choice countless times each day. Will we focus on the turbulent circumstances around us, or will we keep our eyes on Jesus, the one who commands the wind and the waves?

This kind of focus does not mean ignoring reality or pretending difficulties do not exist. Rather, it means interpreting our reality through the lens of God's presence and character, rather than allowing our circumstances to define our view of God. When we keep our eyes on the Lord, we remember his faithfulness in past trials, we anchor ourselves in his unchanging nature, and we view present challenges against the backdrop of his sovereign purposes.

The second half of the verse flows naturally from the first: "With him at my right hand, I will not be shaken." In ancient cultures, the right-hand position was a place of honor, strength, and protection. A warrior's most trusted ally would guard his right side, his sword arm, leaving him free to fight effectively. David pictures God in exactly this position, not distant or disengaged, but intimately present and actively protective.

Notice David's confidence: "I will not be shaken." Not "I might not be shaken" or "I hope not to be shaken," but a resolute declaration of stability. This is not presumption but the natural result of maintaining focus on God's presence. When we truly comprehend that the creator of the universe stands at our right hand, that the God who holds all things together is personally invested in our well-being, fear loses its power to destabilize us.

This does not promise the absence of storms. David himself faced betrayal, warfare, family tragedy, and years of exile. He was not shaken, not because his life was easy, but because his foundation was secure. Buildings withstand earthquakes not by avoiding seismic activity, but by being built on solid foundations with proper structural support. Similarly, we remain unshaken not by eliminating life's tremors but by anchoring ourselves to the immovable rock.

The practical application of our faith challenges us daily. In moments of anxiety, will we rehearse our worries or rehearse God's character? When facing decisions, will we be paralyzed by fear or steadied by his wisdom? When relationships fracture, health fails, or finances crumble, will we be shaken by what we have lost or stabilized by the God we cannot lose?

Keeping our eyes always on the Lord requires practice. It means starting our day by consciously acknowledging his presence. It means developing the habit of turning our thoughts toward him throughout the day, not just in crisis but in ordinary moments. It means ending our day reflecting on his faithfulness rather than ruminating on our failures or fears.

David's words in Psalm 16:8 offer us more than comforting poetry. They present a practical strategy for spiritual stability in times of instability. By deliberately and consistently focusing on the Lord and recognizing his protective presence at our right hand, we discover an unshakeable foundation that no circumstance can erode. The question is not whether storms will come, but where our eyes will be when they arrive.

PRAYER

Lord, teach me to keep my eyes always on you. In the distractions and difficulties of this day, help me to remember that you stand at my right hand. When circumstances threaten to overwhelm me, anchor my soul in your unchanging presence. Give me the discipline to return my focus to you again and again, until seeing you becomes as natural as breathing. May I walk through whatever comes today confident that with you beside me, I cannot be shaken. Amen.

TREASURED AND PROTECTED

Keep me as the apple of your eye; hide me in the shadow of your wings (Psalm 17:8).

David stands at a crossroads between desperation and faith. Pursued by enemies who seek to destroy him, the psalmist turns not to weapons or alliances but to the God who sees all things. Psalm 17 emerges as a prayer of the falsely accused, a cry for vindication rooted in the confidence that God knows the human heart better than any earthly judge. Yet within this context of conflict and anxiety, David expresses something profoundly intimate: the desire to be held by God with tender, protective care. In verse 8, the pursued fugitive articulates the deepest longings of the human soul: to be cherished, to be safe, to be truly seen by the One who matters most.

The phrase "keep me as the apple of your eye" translates a Hebrew expression that literally means "the daughter of your eye." This evocative image refers to the pupil of the eye, that small, dark aperture through which light enters and vision becomes possible. The Hebrews understood this innermost part of the eye as essential to sight itself; without it, vision fails. To be the "apple" of someone's eye is to occupy the most vital, precious position in their awareness.

The use of "apple" in English translations carries particular weight in the context of ancient Near Eastern thought. In Egyptian and Mesopotamian imagery, the eye represents wholeness, protection, and divine vigilance. It was also a symbol of tender regard and intimate protection. When the psalmist asks God to keep him as the apple of his eye, he is not merely requesting attention; he is asking to be preserved at the very center of God's consciousness, as essential to the divine vision as the pupil is to human sight.

This is an extraordinary request. David does not ask God to be merely aware of him or even to defend him. He asks to be cherished as the most precious thing in God's awareness. The language invites us into a reality often obscured by theological abstraction: God's relationship with us is intensely personal. We are not cosmic incidents or statistical abstractions in God's universe; we are treasured, beloved, held at the center of divine consciousness.

The second image shifts our perspective from the interior sanctuary of God's eye to the protective shelter of God's wings. The Hebrew expression "in the shadow of your wings" evokes multiple layers of meaning throughout the Old Testament. This metaphor appears frequently in the psalms and prophetic literature, drawing on the imagery of mother birds sheltering their young and the great protective wings of cherubim overshadowing the mercy seat in the holy of holies.

Exodus 19:4 recalls how the Lord carried Israel "on eagles' wings," emphasizing divine protection during the wilderness wandering. Ruth 3:9 uses similar language when Ruth asks Boaz to "spread his wings" over her, seeking protection and a covenant relationship. The wings of God represent not weakness or sentimentality but fierce, decisive protection, the kind a mother eagle employs against threats to her nest, the kind that covered the Ark of the Covenant itself.

The "shadow" of these wings is significant. In the ancient Near Eastern world, particularly in desert contexts familiar to Israel, shadow represents shelter from destructive heat, a place of refuge and respite. To dwell in God's shadow is to experience protection from exposure, vulnerability, and harm. It is an active, deliberate placement, not accidental proximity but intentional sheltering.

These two images, the apple of the eye and the shadow of wings, complement each other perfectly. The first emphasizes intimacy and being cherished; the second emphasizes protection and security. Together, they express the completeness of what we seek in God: to be known deeply, held preciously, and protected completely. The pursued David does not merely need rescue; he needs assurance that he matters to God, that he is seen and valued even when earthly circumstances suggest otherwise.

In our own seasons of struggle, uncertainty, and fear, this verse invites the same twofold confidence. We can come to God, not primarily with elaborate theological arguments, but with the simple, profound request: Remember me. Hold me. Let me matter to you.

PRAYER

Almighty God, I thank you that I am never invisible to your sight, never insignificant in your heart. When I feel exposed and vulnerable, when my enemies press close and my circumstances seem overwhelming, remind me that I am the apple of your eye, precious, treasured, held at the center of your awareness. Hide me in the shadow of your wings, that I might find strength in your protection and peace in your presence. Grant me the faith of David, who knew that being held by you was worth more than any earthly safety. In the name of Jesus Christ, my refuge and my strength, I pray. Amen.

PSALM 18

THE UNSHAKEABLE REFUGE

I love you, LORD, my strength. The LORD is my rock, my fortress and my deliverer; my God is my rock, in whom I take refuge, my shield and the horn of my salvation, my stronghold (Psalm 18:1–2).

There is something profoundly intimate about the opening words of Psalm 18. David does not begin with theology or doctrine. He begins with a relationship: "I love you, LORD." Before cataloging God's attributes or recounting his mighty deeds, David makes a simple, personal declaration of affection. This is not the love of obligation or duty; it is the love born from experience, from knowing God in the trenches of life.

What follows is a cascade of metaphors, each building on the last, as David strives to capture the magnitude of who God has been to him. He calls God his strength, his rock, his fortress, his deliverer, his refuge, his shield, his horn of salvation, his stronghold. It is as if one image were not enough. David reaches for metaphor after metaphor because no single word can contain the fullness of God's faithfulness.

Consider what these images meant to an ancient warrior-king. A rock was not just a stone; it was the foundation upon which everything else stood, immovable and reliable when everything around it shifted. A fortress was the difference between life and death, a place of protection when enemies surrounded. A shield meant survival in battle, the barrier between a sword and your heart. These were not poetic abstractions for David; they were visceral realities drawn from his life as a shepherd defending his flock and a soldier facing Goliath and countless other threats.

What transforms this psalm from beautiful poetry into powerful devotion is recognizing that David wrote these words from experience.

This was not theoretical faith. The superscription tells us David sang this "when the LORD delivered him from the hand of all his enemies and from the hand of Saul." He had known the terror of hiding in caves, the exhaustion of running for his life, the loneliness of being hunted by the very king he had served faithfully. Yet in all of it, God had proven himself to be exactly what David proclaims: unshakeable, protective, delivering.

The progression of David's metaphors reveals a crucial aspect of how we experience God's presence in our struggles. God is our strength, the power to keep going when we have nothing left. He is our rock, the stable ground beneath us when everything feels uncertain. He is our fortress. the safe place we run to when we are overwhelmed. He is our deliverer, actively working to rescue us from what threatens to destroy us. He is our refuge, the shelter we desperately need. He is our shield, standing between us and the arrows aimed at our hearts. He is the horn of our salvation, the symbol of power and victory. He is our stronghold, the secure place from which we cannot be dislodged.

Notice that David does not say God was these things once, in some distant past. He speaks in the present tense: "The LORD is my rock, my fortress." This is the language of an ongoing relationship, of present reality. The God who delivered David from the lion and the bear, from Goliath and from Saul, is the same God who is with him now, and will be with him tomorrow.

For us, living millennia after David, these words carry the same power because we face our own lions and giants. Our fortresses may not be made of stone, but we still need refuge from the storms of life, from anxiety that keeps us awake at night, from grief that threatens to overwhelm us, from circumstances that feel impossibly hard. We still need a rock when the ground beneath us feels like it is giving way. We still need a deliverer when we are trapped in situations we cannot escape on our own.

The beauty of Psalm 18 is that it invites us into the same relationship David enjoyed. We can speak the same words and make the same declarations because the God David knew is our God, too. He has not changed. He is still the rock, still the fortress, still the deliverer. And he is still worthy of our love.

When we face our darkest valleys, we can anchor ourselves in these truths. God is not distant or indifferent. He is near, strong, and our deliverer. We can take refuge in him. We can trust him as our shield. We can depend on him as our stronghold. And we can love him, not from fear or obligation, but from the deep gratitude of hearts that have known his faithfulness.

PRAYER

Lord, you are my rock and my fortress. When everything around me shakes, you remain steady. When I am weak, you are my strength. When I am afraid, you are my refuge. Help me to trust you more deeply, to run to you more quickly, and to love you more fully. Thank you for being my deliverer, my shield, my salvation. In every battle I face, remind me that you are my stronghold, and in you I am secure. Amen.

THE PERFECT LAW

The law of the LORD is perfect, refreshing the soul. The statutes of the Lord are trustworthy, making wise the simple (Psalm 19:7).

The psalmist's declaration in Psalm 19:7 stands as one of Scripture's most profound statements about the nature and power of God's law. In our contemporary world, where legal codes are often viewed with skepticism and regulations feel burdensome, this verse invites us to reconsider what it means to embrace the law of the Lord, not as an external constraint but as a spiritual treasure. The opening words of this verse present law not as limitation, but as a gift, and the imagery that follows reveals why believers throughout the ages have found in God's Word the deepest source of renewal and wisdom.

The psalmist declares that "the law of the LORD is perfect." The Hebrew word translated as "perfect" conveys wholeness, completeness, and integrity. This is not perfection in the sense of mechanical precision, but rather the wholeness that lacks nothing essential, a completeness that addresses the full range of human need. When we speak of God's law as perfect, we affirm that it requires nothing to be added to it and suffers no deficiency. Unlike human legislation, which must constantly be revised, amended, and updated to address unforeseen circumstances, God's law encompasses eternal principles that apply across all generations and contexts. This perfection speaks to its comprehensive nature: God's law touches every dimension of human existence: our relationships with God, with one another, and with ourselves.

The second phrase declares that God's law is "refreshing the soul." The Hebrew verb conveys both restoration and return; it speaks of bringing something back to its original state or purpose. When we find our souls parched by the demands of a self-centered existence, wearied by the relentless pursuit of hollow achievements, or depleted by sin's consequences, God's law offers restoration. It refreshes us by calling us back to our intended purpose and by reconnecting us with the God in whose image we were created. The soul that has wandered finds its way home through the guiding light of God's Word. The psalmist knows from experience what we too can discover: that the direction God's law provides is not restrictive, but liberating; not burdensome, but revitalizing.

The verse continues with equal affirmation: "The statutes of the LORD are trustworthy." The Hebrew word here translated as "statutes" refers to God's testimonies, the witnesses he has given to his own character and will. To call these trustworthy is to affirm their reliability, their faithfulness, their sure foundation. In a universe where so much deceives us, where human promises prove empty, and our own plans crumble into dust, God's statutes stand firm. We may rely upon them absolutely. They will not fail us, mislead us, or abandon us when we need them most. This trustworthiness extends beyond their intellectual correctness to their transformative power.

The verse concludes with the remarkable claim that God's statutes make "wise the simple." The Hebrew word here rendered as "simple" refers not to foolishness in the moral sense but to openness, naïveté, or lack of discernment. It describes those who lack the cunning of the world, those without street wisdom or sophisticated understanding. Yet God's law has the extraordinary power to impart genuine wisdom even to such persons. This is profoundly inclusive; the acquisition of true wisdom does not depend upon formal education, social status, or natural intellectual gifts. Rather, it flows to anyone who will receive God's Word and order their lives by it.

Here lies the gospel in this verse: the perfect law of the Lord is available not to the elite or the already-wise, but to all who hunger for truth. A child can discern wisdom in God's Word; an uneducated laborer can become wise by meditating on Scripture; a person marked by past failures can find direction and restoration through God's statutes. This is why the psalmist treasures God's law more than fine gold: because it alone offers what every human soul truly needs: restoration, trustworthiness, and the path to genuine wisdom.

As we read and study Scripture, may we approach it not as dry doctrine to be mastered, but as the living Word of the living God. May we discover in its perfect principles the refreshment our souls desperately need, and may we embrace the wisdom it offers, that our lives might reflect the image of our Creator.

PRAYER

O Lord, grant to us grateful hearts that recognize your law not as a burden, but as a blessing. Restore our weary souls through your perfect Word. Teach us to trust your statutes completely, knowing that they alone lead to true wisdom and lasting peace. Make us wise, we pray, through the knowledge of your truth. Amen.

PSALM 20

WHERE WE PLACE OUR TRUST

Some trust in chariots and some in horses, but we trust in the name of the Lord our God (Psalm 20:7).

In ancient Israel, chariots and horses represented the pinnacle of military might. They were the advanced technology of warfare, the difference between victory and defeat, the symbols of security and power. For surrounding nations, these weapons were the foundation of confidence. Egypt had chariots. Assyria had cavalry. The great empires built their strength on what they could see, count, and control.

The psalmist presents us with a stark choice that echoes across the millennia into our modern lives. Where will we place our trust?

This verse does not condemn the existence of chariots and horses. Ancient Israel had its own military resources, and God never demanded that his people be foolish or unprepared. The issue is not the possession of resources but the placement of trust. The question is whether we rely ultimately on what our hands can hold or on the name of the One who holds all things.

What are our chariots and horses today? For some, it is financial security, the size of a bank account, the stability of investments, the comfort of a steady income. For others, it is reputation and social standing, the network of connections that opens doors and creates opportunities. For many, it is education and expertise, the credentials that promise control over our futures. For still others, it is health and vitality, the physical strength that seems to guarantee independence.

None of these things is wrong in itself. Like the chariots of old, they are good gifts that can serve good purposes. The danger arises when they become the ultimate foundation of our confidence, when we believe that these things can deliver what only God can: true security, lasting peace, and hope that cannot be shaken.

The contrast in this verse is profound. While some trust in tangible resources, "we trust in the name of the LORD our God." In Hebrew thought, the "name" represents a person's full character and nature. To trust in God's name is to trust in his faithfulness, his power, his wisdom, his love. It is to anchor our hope not in the gifts but in the giver, not in the provision but in the provider.

This trust is tested most severely when our chariots fail us. When the economy collapses, savings vanish. When relationships fracture, and support systems crumble. When health fails and bodies weaken. When our carefully constructed plans fall apart. In these moments, we discover what we truly trusted all along. Those who built their lives on modern chariots find themselves in despair. But those who trust in the name of the Lord discover a foundation that cannot be moved.

The beautiful irony of this verse is that God often provides material blessings, wisdom, resources, relationships, and strength to those who trust primarily in him. But these gifts remain servants rather than masters. They are held loosely, used gratefully, but never allowed to usurp the throne that belongs to God alone.

Living this way requires daily intention. Our culture constantly pressures us toward self-reliance and material confidence. We are surrounded by voices insisting that security comes from what we can accumulate, control, and calculate. To trust instead in an invisible God, to stake our lives on his character rather than our circumstances, requires countercultural courage.

Yet this trust is not blind optimism or passive resignation. It is an active choice rooted in God's proven faithfulness throughout history and in our own lives. The God who delivered Israel, who sent his Son to redeem us, who has walked with us through past valleys, this is the God whose name we trust. His track record invites our confidence.

As you move through your day, notice where you instinctively reach for security. Notice what makes you feel safe, what causes anxiety when threatened, and what you protect most fiercely. These reveal where your functional trust lies, regardless of what you profess with your lips. Then consciously redirect that trust to the one whose name is above every name, whose power exceeds every chariot, whose faithfulness outlasts every earthly resource.

PRAYER

Lord God, forgive us for the times we have trusted in our own chariots, our money, our abilities, our plans. more than we have trusted in you. Help us to hold loosely the gifts you give while clinging tightly to you, the giver. When our resources fail, may we find you faithful. Teach us to build our lives on the solid foundation of your character. We trust in your name today and surrender our need to control. In Jesus' name, Amen.

PSALM 21

THE EXALTATION OF GOD'S STRENGTH

Be exalted in your strength, Lord; we will sing and praise your might (Psalm 21:13).

The final verse of Psalm 21 concludes a royal thanksgiving psalm with a doxological declaration that seamlessly moves from God's demonstrated power on behalf of the king to a summons to universal praise. This verse encapsulates the essential movement of the entire psalm: from recognition of God's intervention in battle to communal worship that acknowledges divine supremacy. In exploring this closing declaration, we discover a profound pattern for our own spiritual lives: the necessity of translating our theological convictions about God's power into active, sustained praise.

The imperative form "be exalted" functions not as a request that God somehow needs to achieve exaltation, but rather as an invitation to acknowledge and acclaim the exaltation that God already possesses. This grammatical form carries the sense of "lift yourself up" or "make yourself high," though God requires no elevation beyond what he eternally possesses. The psalmist issues a call to recognition rather than a petition for transformation. The strength referenced here denotes God's robust power, the force by which he accomplishes his purposes in history and in the world. It is not abstract might, but demonstrable, concrete power manifest in God's actions.

What makes this verse theologically significant is the paradigm shift in perspective. Throughout much of Psalm 21, the focus is on the king and God's blessing on his strength. The king trusts in the Lord (verse 7); the Lord's hand finds out all the king's enemies (verse 8); the Lord transforms them as a fiery furnace (verse 9). These verses celebrate God's power as it works through and for the political ruler. But in verse 13, the perspective widens beyond the individual monarch to encompass a communal "we," the people, the community of faith. The king's personal security becomes the occasion for collective praise, and the particular deliverance becomes the foundation for universal doxology.

This movement from singular to plural, from particular to universal, reflects a mature understanding of how God's work in individual lives extends into the fabric of community. We live in an age that often fragments faith into private spirituality, personal blessing, and individual spiritual experience. Yet the psalmist persistently reminds us that God's power, demonstrated in any circumstance, calls forth a communal response. When God acts on our behalf, whether through deliverance from crisis, guidance through confusion, or provision in scarcity, that divine action resonates beyond our personal experience. It becomes testimony, a witness, and the foundation for corporate praise.

The promised response in the second half of the verse, "we will sing and praise your might," employs two Hebrew verbs that deserve attention. The verb "sing" appears throughout the book of Psalms as the primary expression of joyful response to God's character and actions. To sing is to engage not merely intellectually but with our whole person: our voice, our emotion, our communal identity. Complementing this, "praise" carries the sense of playing a stringed instrument in accompaniment with the voice, suggesting orchestrated, deliberate, and skillfully executed praise. These are not casual emotional outbursts but thoughtful, intentional responses to God's might, that quality of God's strength that manifests as power in action, warrior strength, and decisive intervention.

For the contemporary believer, this verse invites us to a crucial spiritual discipline. We live in a world that often conceals God's power. Suffering surrounds us; injustice persists; the wicked frequently appear to prosper. Our circumstances may suggest that God's strength remains distant or inactive. Yet this verse calls us to an act of faith that transcends our immediate circumstances, to summon the community together and, in the face of ambiguous evidence, declare, "We will sing and praise your might." This is not a denial of difficulty; rather, it is the choice to align our corporate voice with the ultimate reality of God's sovereignty.

Psalm 21 concludes where all true theology must conclude: in doxology. The psalm does not end with an analysis of the king's military strategy or a celebration of human achievement. It ends with ascription of glory to God and commitment to corporate praise. This demonstrates that theological understanding remains incomplete until it flowers into worship. To know God's strength must necessarily issue in singing God's praise.

PRAYER

Almighty God, we acknowledge that your strength is not diminished by our doubt, nor your might dependent upon our recognition. Yet we come together as your people to declare that we have witnessed your power, that we have felt your hand of protection, that we have experienced your faithfulness. Strengthen us to sing your praises not merely when circumstances feel secure, but in every season of life. Teach us to see your mighty hand at work, even in ways hidden from our immediate vision. And grant us the grace to lift high your exaltation before a world that desperately needs to recognize that you alone are God. In Christ's name we pray, Amen.

WHEN GOD FEELS ABSENT

My God, my God, why have you forsaken me? Why are you so far from saving me, so far from my cries of anguish? (Psalm 22:1).

These words pierce through the centuries with raw, unfiltered pain. They are among the most honest words ever recorded in Scripture, and they reveal something profound about the nature of faith: a genuine relationship with God has room for our deepest questions and most desperate cries.

When we first encounter Psalm 22:1, we might feel uncomfortable. This does not sound like the triumphant faith we often expect to find in Scripture. There is no pretense here, no spiritual platitudes, no attempt to mask the agony. David, or whoever penned this lament, is experiencing what spiritual writers call "the dark night of the soul," that terrifying moment when God seems utterly absent despite our most fervent prayers.

The psalmist's repetition is significant: "My God, my God." Even in this moment of perceived abandonment, the relationship remains intact. He does not cry out to a distant deity or an abstract force. This is still "my God," personal and intimate. The pain comes precisely because the relationship matters so deeply. We can only feel forsaken by someone we trust to be present.

This psalm gives us permission for something many of us desperately need: the freedom to bring our unedited selves before God. We live in a world that often demands that we maintain appearances and project strength and certainty. Even in our churches, we may feel pressure to demonstrate unwavering faith, to always have the right answers, to never admit when we are drowning. But Psalm 22:1 demolishes these false expectations. If Scripture itself contains such raw questioning, then our honest struggles are not failures of faith; they are expressions of it.

Consider what this verse does not say. It does not say, "There is no God." It does not say, "I am done with this relationship." It does not even say, "You have forsaken me." Instead, it asks "why?" This is the cry of someone still engaged, still seeking, still believing that God is there to hear the question even when he feels impossibly far away. The question itself is an act of faith.

We also cannot read this verse without recognizing its prophetic fulfillment. Centuries after David wrote these words, Jesus cried them out from the cross: "My God, my God, why have you forsaken me?" (Matthew 27:46). In that darkest moment of human history, when the weight of the world's sin created an actual separation between Father and Son, Jesus reached for this ancient prayer. He entered fully into human suffering, experiencing the ultimate abandonment so that we would never truly be abandoned. The cry of desolation became the pathway to redemption.

This means that when we pray Psalm 22:1 today, we are not alone in our anguish. Jesus has been there. He knows what it feels like when the heavens seem brass, and our prayers seem to bounce back unanswered. He understands the particular torture of feeling forsaken by the One we love most. And because he experienced it, we can trust that God does not condemn us for feeling it.

The beauty of the Psalms is that they do not leave us in despair. While Psalm 22 begins with this cry of abandonment, it ends with triumphant praise: "For he has not despised or scorned the suffering of the afflicted one; he has not hidden his face from him but has listened to his cry for help." The psalmist discovers that God was present all along, even when he felt absent. The feelings were real, the pain was valid, but the final reality was God's faithfulness.

When you find yourself in seasons of spiritual darkness, when your prayers seem to vanish into a void, when you wonder if God has forgotten you, remember Psalm 22:1. Bring your honest questions. Voice your deepest pain. Do not perform a faith you do not feel. God is big enough to handle your doubt, strong enough to carry your anger, and loving enough to meet you in your desperation. The cry of abandonment may be where your story begins, but it is not where it ends.

PRAYER

God, sometimes you feel impossibly far away. In this moment, I bring you my honest heart, my questions, my confusion, my pain. Even when I cannot feel your presence, help me trust in your faithfulness. Thank you that Jesus entered into abandonment so I would never be truly forsaken. Be near to me now, even if I cannot sense it yet. Amen.

THE LORD IS MY SHEPHERD

The LORD is my shepherd, I lack nothing (Psalm 23:1).

The opening words of Psalm 23 strike with a simplicity that belies their profound theological weight. In these few words, the psalmist articulates a comprehensive statement of trust that has sustained believers through centuries of uncertainty, loss, and fear. Yet to understand this verse fully, we must press beyond its surface comfort into the ancient shepherd imagery that gives it shape and power.

In Israelite society, the word "shepherd" carries resonances that run deep through Israel's religious consciousness. Abraham was a shepherd; Moses encountered God while tending sheep in Midian; David himself was called from shepherding to kingship. But the shepherd metaphor extends far beyond human experience. In ancient Near Eastern texts, kings were regularly depicted as shepherds of their people, and the gods themselves were sometimes portrayed in this role. When the psalmist declares "The LORD is my shepherd," the statement encompasses protection, guidance, sustenance, and intimate personal care. This is no distant God dispensing wisdom from on high, but rather one who walks with the flock, tends each individual creature, and takes responsibility for their well-being.

What strikes many readers as curious is the conjunction of shepherd imagery with the declaration "I lack nothing." This is not naive optimism. The psalmist lived in a world of genuine danger and scarcity. Predators threatened flocks. Drought devastated pastures. Enemies pursued the vulnerable. The sheep themselves were entirely dependent upon the shepherd; they could neither find water nor navigate treacherous terrain without guidance. Yet precisely in this vulnerability lies the power of the statement. The psalmist does not claim self-sufficiency or material abundance. Rather, the claim rests upon the competence and commitment of the shepherd. Because the Lord is my shepherd, I lack nothing. My security does not derive from circumstances but from a relationship with God.

The Hebrew verb carries the sense of "to lack" or "to want for." In the context of shepherd and flock, it speaks to provision, food, water, shelter, and protection. A competent shepherd ensures that his flock lacks none of these necessities. The sheep do not worry about tomorrow's provision or construct elaborate contingency plans; they simply follow where the shepherd leads.

Yet this is precisely where modern believers often stumble. We have been trained by culture and circumstance to measure our security by material accumulation, career advancement, investment portfolios, and insurance policies. We perform calculations and forecasts; we strategize and scheme. The psalmist invites us into a radically different posture: not the abandonment of prudence, but the grounding of trust in the One whose knowledge and power infinitely exceed our own.

This opening verse of Psalm 23 must be read within the broader narrative of the psalm itself. The shepherd image will expand across subsequent verses: the psalmist will walk through dark valleys, will be anointed with oil, and will dine at a table before enemies. These concrete images suggest that lacking nothing does not mean the absence of difficulty. Valleys still come. Enemies still exist. Dangers still lurk. But the shepherd's presence transforms these experiences. The rod and staff, instruments of discipline and defense, provide both correction and protection. The anointing with oil speaks of healing and consecration. The table in the presence of enemies transforms what might have been a place of humiliation into one of honor and celebration.

For contemporary believers, this verse summons us to recalibrate our understanding of provision and security. In an age of endless anxiety, about finances, health, security, meaning, and mortality, the psalmist's declaration cuts to the heart of the matter: the question is not whether circumstances will be perfect, but whether we trust the character and commitment of our shepherd. Do we truly believe that the One who calls himself shepherd possesses both the desire and the power to ensure that we lack nothing essential for our journey?

The spiritual disciplines that follow, prayer, scripture meditation, obedience, and worship, are not means of earning God's shepherding care. Rather, they are the postures through which we align ourselves with the shepherd's guidance. We learn to follow. We learn to trust. We learn to distinguish the shepherd's voice from the many other voices that call for our allegiance and resources.

As you meditate on these opening words today, ask yourself: Do I truly believe that the Lord is my shepherd? What would change in my life if I genuinely trusted that I lack nothing that the shepherd deems essential for my journey?

PRAYER

Eternal God, shepherd of my soul, I confess that my faith often falters. I calculate and worry; I grasp and accumulate; I doubt your sufficiency. Yet in this moment, I open myself afresh to your tender care. Teach me to follow where you lead. Calm my anxious heart. Help me to release the illusion that security derives from my own efforts, and to rest instead in your faithful provision. As I journey through this day, grant me the peace that comes from knowing myself cared for, guided, and sustained by your good and capable hands. In Christ's name, I pray. Amen.

ASCENDING THE HOLY MOUNTAIN

Who may ascend the mountain of the LORD? Who may stand in his holy place? The one who has clean hands and a pure heart, who does not trust in an idol or swear by a false god (Psalm 24:3–4).

The psalmist poses a fundamental question that resonates through the centuries: What qualifies a person to approach the living God? This question assumes that access to the divine is neither automatic nor indiscriminate. The God who dwells in the heavens and rules over all creation maintains boundaries around his holy presence, and those boundaries are not arbitrary. They flow from the character of God himself: he is holy, and holiness demands a corresponding orientation in those who seek his face.

The language of ascending the mountain carries ancient resonance. In the Old Testament world, mountains served as liminal spaces where heaven and earth intersected. Mount Sinai became the place where God revealed himself to Moses and Israel. Zion, the mountain of God in Jerusalem, represented both a geographical reality and a theological symbol of God's dwelling place and the center of his redemptive purposes. When the psalmist asks, "Who may ascend the mountain of the LORD?" he invokes this rich tradition of theophanic encounter, moments when mortals stand in the presence of the divine and are transformed by that meeting.

Yet what is remarkable about Psalm 24:3–4 is that it democratizes access to this holy mountain. The answer does not restrict ascent to priests alone, though priests had particular liturgical functions in the temple. Rather, the psalmist identifies the true prerequisites: clean hands and a pure heart. These are not prerequisites available only to the spiritual elite. They are available to all who genuinely seek them.

The "clean hands and pure heart" construction employs biblical parallelism to express a unified reality viewed from different perspectives. "Clean hands" refers to external conduct, the moral actions that flow from one's life. In ancient Israel, clean hands represented innocence from wrongdoing, the conduct of one who has not violated covenantal obligations. But the psalmist does not stop at external righteousness. He presses inward to the "pure heart," the inner disposition, the motivations, the deepest commitments of one's being. Hebrew thought did not compartmentalize human existence into separate internal and external domains. Rather, the external expression and the internal disposition form an integrated whole. A person with clean hands and a pure heart is integrated, not duplicitous, not hiding corruption beneath a respectable exterior.

The second clause intensifies this requirement: "who does not trust in an idol or swear by a false god." This is remarkably direct. Access to God's holy presence is fundamentally incompatible with divided loyalty. To ascend the mountain of the Lord is to renounce all competing allegiances. An idol represents anything we trust in, rely upon, or serve in place of the true God: wealth, status, military power, or even our own competence. To "swear by a false god" indicates the language of covenant commitment, the binding oaths that establish our ultimate allegiances.

The psalmist thus presents a portrait of genuine worship: it demands integrity of life, consistency between profession and practice, and undivided loyalty to God. In our contemporary context, where compartmentalization has become almost second nature, our public personas carefully separated from our private realities, our stated values sometimes contradicted by our actual choices, this ancient word strikes with particular force.

Yet there is grace embedded in this text. The conditions are demanding, but they are not impossible. The psalmist does not announce a standard so elevated that humans cannot reach it. Rather, he calls us to the hard work of integration, to bring our external conduct into alignment with our inner convictions, to evaluate what we truly trust, and to surrender competing loyalties. This is the work of repentance and faith.

One final observation: Psalm 24 appears to have functioned in the worship life of ancient Israel, likely as a processional psalm for pilgrims entering the temple. It asks these questions not to establish barriers to worship, but to call worshippers to account before they enter God's presence. It functions as a mirror, inviting self-examination and calling us to the genuineness of heart that God desires.

In approaching our own worship today, this psalm invites us to honest self-assessment. Where do our loyalties truly rest? Are our hands clean and our hearts pure, or do we harbor hidden compromises? The ascent to God is always open to those who genuinely seek him with integrated, undivided hearts.

PRAYER

O God, you dwell in holiness that we cannot approach casually or carelessly. Yet you invite us to draw near with clean hands and pure hearts. Examine us, we pray. Reveal the places where our loyalty is divided, where we trust in idols of our own making: success, security, the approval of others. Cleanse our hands from actions that contradict your ways, and purify our hearts from the divided affections that diminish our devotion to you. Give us the courage to surrender completely to your lordship, to ascend your holy mountain with integrity and sincerity. Make us whole, O Lord, both inwardly and outwardly, so that we might stand in your holy place. In Christ's name, Amen.

LONGING FOR DIVINE DIRECTION

Show me your ways LORD, *teach me your paths. Guide me in your truth and teach me, for you are God my Savior, and my hope is in you all day long* (Psalm 25:4–5).

There is something profoundly human about feeling lost. We stand at crossroads in our careers, relationships, and faith, wondering which way to turn. We make plans only to watch them unravel. We seek certainty in an uncertain world. It is in these moments that the words of Psalm 25:4–5 become not just ancient poetry, but a lifeline: "Show me your ways, LORD, teach me your paths. Guide me in your truth and teach me, for you are God my Savior, and my hope is in you all day long."

David, the psalmist, understood what it meant to need direction. As a shepherd boy turned king, he navigated treacherous political landscapes, moral failures, and enemies on every side. Yet here we find him in a posture of remarkable humility, not demanding answers, but asking to be taught. This is the prayer of someone who has learned that God's wisdom surpasses human understanding.

Notice the progression in David's request. First, "show me your ways," a request for vision, for the ability to see as God sees. Then, "teach me your paths," a plea for instruction in walking those ways practically. This is not about receiving a one-time revelation and moving on. David asks to be taught, which implies a process, a relationship, a patient unfolding of understanding over time. The Christian life is not about getting all the answers upfront; it is about learning to walk closely with the One who is the way.

The phrase "guide me in your truth" takes us even deeper. David does not just want to know true things about God; he wants to be guided *in* truth itself. Truth here is not merely intellectual assent to correct doctrine, though that matters. It is the lived reality of God's character, the substance of who he is. When we ask God to guide us in his truth, we are asking to be immersed in his nature, to have our thoughts and actions aligned with ultimate reality rather than the shifting shadows of cultural opinion or personal preference.

What makes this request possible is what David declares next: "for you are God my Savior." This is not casual language. David anchors his entire petition in God's character and covenant faithfulness. He can ask boldly because he knows who he is asking. The God who saves is the God who cares, who intervenes, who does not abandon his people to confusion and darkness. Our confidence in asking for guidance does not rest on our worthiness but on God's identity as savior, the one who rescues, delivers, and makes a way when there seems to be no way.

The final phrase captures the constancy required of faith: "my hope is in you all day long." Not just in the morning when we are fresh and optimistic. Not only in church on Sunday, but also when surrounded by worship and community. All day long, through the mundane moments, the frustrations, the weariness of the afternoon, the uncertainties of the evening. This is hope as a sustained posture, a continuous orientation of the soul toward God regardless of circumstances.

In our fast-paced world, we often want instant direction. We pray and expect immediate clarity, a clear sign, an unmistakable voice. But David's prayer suggests a different way. He asks to be taught, which takes time. He asks to be guided, which requires ongoing attention to God's presence. He commits to hoping all day long, which means choosing trust through the hours when nothing seems to change.

This passage invites us to reconsider what it means to seek God's will. Perhaps it is less about discovering a hidden plan for our lives and more about cultivating a relationship in which we learn God's ways so thoroughly that our decisions naturally align with his heart. Perhaps divine guidance is less like consulting a map and more like walking with a trusted guide who knows the terrain intimately.

When we do not know what to do, when the path ahead is unclear, when our own wisdom fails us, we can return to this ancient prayer. We can ask the God who saves to show us his ways, teach us his paths, and guide us in his truth. And we can choose, in every moment of every day, to place our hope in him.

PRAYER

Lord, I come to you as David did, asking you to show me your ways and teach me your paths. Guide me in your truth, for you alone are my savior. When I feel lost or uncertain, remind me that my hope is secure in you. Help me to trust your timing, to remain teachable, and to walk closely with you all day long. Amen.

THE COURAGE OF EXAMINED FAITH

Test me, LORD, and try me, examine my heart and my mind;
for I have always been mindful of your unfailing love and have
lived in reliance on your faithfulness (Psalm 26:2–3).

There is something almost breathtaking about David's boldness in Psalm 26. While most of us instinctively hide our flaws and guard our hearts against scrutiny, here stands a man flinging open the doors of his inner life and inviting God to investigate every corner. "Test me, LORD, and try me, examine my heart and my mind." These are not the words of someone caught in denial or blind to his own shortcomings. Rather, they reflect a profound confidence rooted not in personal perfection, but in something far more substantial: God's unfailing love and faithfulness.

David's invitation for divine examination feels countercultural in our age of carefully curated personas. We live in a time when we craft our best social media angles, rehearse our interview answers, and present polished versions of ourselves to the world. The thought of someone, even God, truly examining our hearts and minds can feel terrifying. What might be found in those hidden places? What inconsistencies between our public declarations and private thoughts might come to light?

Yet David does not shrink from this vulnerability. The Hebrew words here suggest something more than a casual glance; they speak of refining, of testing metal in fire to reveal its true composition. David is essentially saying, "Put me in the crucible, Lord. Apply the heat. Let us see what I am really made of." This is the prayer of someone who has learned that God's scrutiny is not something to fear but to welcome, because it is always motivated by love and oriented toward our growth.

What makes such openness possible? David tells us immediately: "For I have always been mindful of your unfailing love and have lived in reliance on your faithfulness." Here lies the foundation that supports his courage. He can invite examination because he has anchored his identity not in his own righteousness but in God's unchanging character. The word "unfailing" in Hebrew carries connotations of covenant loyalty, the kind of committed love that does not waver based on performance. David has internalized this truth deeply enough that it transforms his relationship with divine scrutiny.

Notice the beautiful tension in these verses. On one hand, David invites the most thorough examination imaginable. On the other hand, he does not claim sinless perfection as his qualification. Instead, he points to his consistent orientation toward God; he has been "mindful" of God's love and has "lived in reliance" on God's faithfulness. This is the heart of authentic faith: not the absence of struggle or failure, but a persistent turning toward God, a habitual remembering of who he is, and a daily choice to lean into his faithfulness rather than our own strength.

This distinction matters profoundly for us today. Many believers live under a crushing weight, believing they must achieve moral perfection before they can approach God with confidence. But David models something different: a faith that says, "I know I am not perfect, but I also know my God. And because I know his love is unfailing, and his faithfulness is sure, I can stand before him without pretense." This kind of faith actually enables deeper transformation than fear-driven perfectionism ever could, because it removes the need for self-deception and creates space for honest growth.

Living with this kind of examined faith requires intentionality. We must regularly rehearse God's character to ourselves, reminding our hearts of his unfailing love when circumstances suggest otherwise. We must choose reliance over self-sufficiency, even when our culture celebrates independence. And we must develop the courage to look honestly at our own hearts, knowing that whatever is found there, God's love remains constant.

The invitation, then, is to join David in this daring prayer. Not because we have arrived at spiritual maturity, but precisely because we have not, and we trust that the one examining us loves us too much to leave us unchanged. In God's hands, examination is not about condemnation; it is about refinement. The searchlight of his presence reveals not to shame us, but to heal us, to show us where we still need his transforming work, and to remind us that his love never fails.

PRAYER

Lord, I confess that inviting your examination feels vulnerable and frightening. Yet I choose, like David, to open my heart and mind to your searching gaze. Test me and try me, not because I am confident in my own righteousness, but because I am confident in your unfailing love. Help me live each day mindful of your covenant faithfulness, relying not on my own strength but on yours. Transform what needs to be changed, and root me ever deeper in the truth that your love for me never wavers. Amen.

THE LIGHT THAT DISPELS ALL FEAR

*The LORD is my light and my salvation— whom shall I fear?
The LORD is the stronghold of my life— of whom shall I be
afraid?* (Psalm 27:1).

The opening line of Psalm 27 strikes with remarkable force. David
does not begin with a complaint or lament, though the psalm reveals
he faces genuine enemies and persistent uncertainty. Instead, he opens
with a declaration of confidence so fundamental and so resolute that
it frames everything that follows. This is not naive optimism. It is the
testimony of a man who has learned, through years of conflict and
exile, where true security resides.

The Hebrew word translated "light" carries profound theological
weight throughout the Old Testament. Light is not merely
illumination; it represents revelation, guidance, and the manifest
presence of the divine. When God said, "Let there be light" (Genesis
1:3), he did not simply create photons; he initiated creation itself,
separating chaos from order. To call the Lord one's light is to claim
that God stands at the center of one's existence, providing both
illumination for the path ahead and assurance in present darkness.
David's enemies may lurk in the shadows, but he walks in the radiance
of God's presence.

Equally significant is the parallelism between "light" and "salvation."
This coupling suggests they are not separate benefits but expressions
of a single reality. Salvation here encompasses rescue from immediate
danger but extends far deeper; it refers to wholeness, restoration, and
the saving activity of God that brings one into right relationship with
him. The light that saves is the light of God's face, his favorable regard
turned toward his covenant people.

Then David poses his rhetorical question: "Whom shall I fear?" The Hebrew interrogative here, "who," presupposes that the answer is "no one." This is not bravado. Rather, it is the logical consequence of making God one's light and salvation. If the infinite, all-powerful Creator has declared himself to be one's protector, what possible threat can any creature pose? Fear in such a context would represent, in essence, a rejection of God's character and ability.

The second line shifts from "light" to "fortress." The term "stronghold" evokes the mountain refuges where David fled from Saul, physical places of security. Yet the psalmist identifies the Lord himself as this stronghold. No earthly refuge compares to the security found in God. Ancient fortifications could be breached; enemies could scale walls. But God cannot be breached. His protection is not contingent upon circumstances or military strength.

The repetition of the fear-question, "of whom shall I be afraid?" emphasizes the point through Israel's characteristic parallelism. This is not mere poetic repetition; it is theological reinforcement. By asking twice, David drives home the absurdity of fear when one belongs to the God who is both light and stronghold. The structure itself becomes an argument: a statement, a question, a restatement, and another question. The form supports the content.

What makes Psalm 27:1 particularly powerful is its historical context. David wrote this during a genuine threat. The psalm later reveals enemies who falsely accuse, witnesses who lie, and the real possibility of violence ("Do not give me over to the desire of my adversaries," verse 12). This is not the confidence of one who faces no danger. This is the testimony of one who has faced danger, considerable danger, and discovered that fear is optional when one's trust is properly anchored.

This truth speaks directly into our contemporary anxiety. We live in an age of manufactured fear, where news cycles exploit our deepest vulnerabilities and social media amplifies worst-case scenarios. Many of us face genuine hardship: illness, financial uncertainty, relational fracture, and professional instability. In such seasons, the cultural message whispers that fear is not merely reasonable; it is rational.

Psalm 27:1 offers a counter-witness. It does not deny the reality of threats. Rather, it repositions them within a theological framework in which they lose their power to dominate. When the Lord becomes one's light, the darkness of circumstance no longer defines reality. When God becomes one's stronghold, no enemy's scheme can ultimately prevail.

The invitation before us is clear: to make this declaration our own. Not with eyes closed to genuine difficulty, but with eyes opened to a greater reality. To say with David, across the centuries and into our own moment of uncertainty: "The LORD is my light and my salvation—whom shall I fear?"

PRAYER

Eternal God, your light breaks through the darkness where I dwell. When anxiety threatens to overwhelm me, when enemies of circumstance and fear press close, remind me that you are my stronghold. Teach me to rest in the truth of your protection, not because danger has passed, but because you remain faithful. Grant me courage rooted not in my own strength but in your infinite power and love. Help me live this day as one illuminated by your presence and secure in your care. In the name of the one who is my light and my salvation, I pray. Amen.

PRAISE BORN FROM DELIVERANCE

Praise be to the LORD, for he has heard my cry for mercy. The LORD is my strength and my shield; my heart trusts in him, and he helps me. My heart leaps for joy, and with my song I praise him (Psalm 28:6–7).

The shift in tone at Psalm 28:6 is unmistakable. Where verses 1–5 contain urgent pleas and warnings against the wicked, verse 6 erupts in joyful praise. In Hebrew, the word translated "blessed" or "praise be" signals a dramatic theological pivot. The psalmist has moved from supplication to celebration, from anxiety to assurance. This movement teaches us something profound about the nature of faith: it is not static resignation to God's will but a dynamic response to God's action on our behalf.

The opening phrase, "Praise be to the LORD, for he has heard my cry for mercy," contains the word *shema*, which means not merely to hear audibly but to listen with intention and response. This is not passive hearing; it is engaged listening that leads to action. When the psalmist says God has "heard" his cry, he affirms that God listens with the fullness of his divine attention and care. The Hebrew word translated here as "cry" carries connotations of singing, rejoicing, and joyful sound. Yet the psalmist's cry has also become a cry of distress. God has heard both the anguish and the longing embedded within it.

The immediate basis for praise is simple but revolutionary: God responds. He does not ignore. He does not delay indefinitely. He listens and acts. This is the foundation upon which all authentic praise must rest. We do not praise God because we have successfully reasoned our way into faith or because we have mustered sufficient willpower. We praise because we have encountered his responding grace. The grammar here matters. The psalmist does not say "Praise be to the LORD because I hope he will hear" or "because he might hear." He says, "for he has heard," past tense, completed action. Something has happened. The crisis has shifted.

What has shifted becomes clear in the subsequent declarations: "The LORD is my strength and my shield." The words "strength" and "shield" draw upon the language of warfare and physical protection. In ancient Israel, a shield was not ornamental; it was essential protective equipment for the soldier facing an actual threat. The psalmist speaks not in metaphors divorced from reality but in images drawn directly from the experiences of genuine danger. His enemies were real. His vulnerability was real. His need for God's protection was not theoretical.

Yet notice how the psalmist names this protection: not as external imposition but as personal possession. "My strength and my shield." This reflects the intimate nature of the covenant relationship. God does not protect Israel as a general protects anonymous troops. God is *my* strength, available to me, personal, mine. This particularity is essential to biblical faith. The God who created all things and sustains all creation is simultaneously the God who knows me, who hears my specific cry, and who shields me individually.

The confession deepens in the next line: "my heart trusts in him." The word "trust" conveys confidence and reliance, a sense of resting securely in someone or something. The heart, the center of volition, emotion, and spiritual orientation, has repositioned itself. It no longer grips anxiously at its own resources or prospects. Instead, it trusts, it settles, it rests in the Lord. This trust is not blind or uninformed; it flows from having experienced God's responsive action. The heart trusts because it has learned through experience that God can be trusted.

And what follows? "He helps me." The Hebrew word translated "help" means to strengthen and support. God is not a distant administrator of cosmic laws but a present helper. The parallelism in the psalmist's thought is striking: the Lord is strength, the Lord is a shield, the Lord helps. Each statement reinforces the others. We are not merely protected; we are empowered. We are not merely defended; we are supported.

Then the psalmist reaches the full expression of his joy: "My heart leaps for joy, and with my song I praise him." The word "joy" suggests exultant rejoicing, the kind that cannot be contained. It moves from the interior ("my heart leaps") to the exterior ("with my song I praise him"). The entire being, emotions, voice, and spirit become an instrument of praise. The song that began as a cry of distress has been transformed into a song of triumph.

This is not false cheerfulness superimposed on genuine suffering. This is authentic joy that has passed through darkness and emerged on the other side. The psalmist has learned that God truly hears, that God truly acts, and that we can truly entrust ourselves to his care. His joy is that of one who has discovered that faith itself is validated in experience.

PRAYER

Eternal God, I praise you for your attentive ear and your responsive heart. When I cry out in distress, help me to know that you truly hear me. Be my strength when I am weak and my shield when I am vulnerable. Teach my heart to trust in you more deeply with each passing day. Transform my anxious cries into songs of praise, and let my joy in your deliverance overflow to those around me. Through Jesus Christ, my ultimate refuge and strength. Amen.

ASCRIBING GLORY

Ascribe to the LORD *the glory due his name; worship the* LORD *in the splendor of his holiness* (Psalm 29:2).

The opening verses of Psalm 29 transport us into a divine assembly, a heavenly court where the celestial beings gather before the throne of God. Yet this psalm, composed perhaps during the monarchy or exilic period, speaks not merely to angelic worship but also calls us, earthly creatures, into that same exalted space. The second verse issues a commanding imperative that stands at the heart of biblical worship: "Ascribe to the LORD the glory due his name; worship the LORD in the splendor of his holiness."

The Hebrew word *kabod*, translated as "glory," carries profound weight throughout Scripture. Literally meaning "weight" or "heaviness," it conveys the substantial reality of God's character: his power, majesty, and overwhelming presence. When we ascribe *kabod* to the Lord, we are not conferring upon him something he lacks. Rather, we are acknowledging and declaring what already belongs to him by virtue of his nature and his deeds. The phrase "glory due his name" suggests a debt we owe, an obligation arising from a covenant relationship. God has revealed himself through his name, through his character as creator, sustainer, and redeemer. Our ascription of glory is the proper response to this self-disclosure.

The verse's parallel structure presents two closely related imperatives: "Ascribe" and "worship." The verb "to give" or "to ascribe" pairs with "to bow down" or "to worship." This parallelism reveals the integrated nature of biblical worship. Ascription involves both vocal declaration and bodily posture, as well as intellectual acknowledgment and physical submission. We cannot truly ascribe glory to God while remaining aloof or detached. Genuine worship demands our whole selves: heart, mind, will, and body in unified response to God's majesty.

The phrase "splendor of his holiness" deserves careful attention. The Hebrew word suggests brightness, beauty, and adornment, the visual splendor that radiates from God's presence. This is not mere aesthetic beauty, though it certainly includes that. Rather, it is the terrible, awesome beauty of holiness itself. The holiness of God, his fundamental separateness, and moral perfection create an aesthetic that transcends human categories. When Isaiah encountered God "high and lifted up" in the temple, the seraphim cried out, "Holy, holy, holy is the Lord of hosts; the whole earth is full of his glory" (Isaiah 6:3). That same overwhelming holiness permeates Psalm 29.

Historically, scholars have debated the background of Psalm 29. Some argue it draws upon Canaanite hymnic traditions, perhaps originally addressed to Baal before being recontextualized for Yahweh worship. The psalm's vivid descriptions of the voice of the Lord thundering over the waters and the wilderness of Kadesh certainly evoke storm theophany language familiar from ancient Near Eastern religious literature. Yet the psalm's present form is thoroughly Yahwistic, affirming that the God of Israel alone possesses the power and majesty that lesser gods falsely claimed. The opening call to ascribe glory exclusively to the Lord serves as a corrective against syncretism and a declaration of monotheistic faith.

For contemporary worshippers, this verse invites us to consider what we truly ascribe glory to in our lives. Our actions and priorities reveal what we genuinely honor. Do we ascribe glory to God through our stewardship of resources? Through our treatment of the vulnerable? Through our pursuit of justice and mercy? Ascribing glory is not merely a liturgical act; it is a lifestyle that recognizes God's rightful place at the center of all things.

The call to worship "in the splendor of his holiness" also reminds us that worship is not casual or generic. We do not approach God as we might a friend or colleague, with comfortable familiarity. We come into the presence of one whose holiness is at once attractive and terrifying, beautiful and morally demanding. This is worship that humbles us, that calls us to account, that transforms us. It is worship that acknowledges we are creatures before our Creator, sinners before our judge, beloved children before our Father.

As we meditate on this verse, we are summoned into that heavenly assembly where the ancient words continue to echo: Ascribe to the Lord the glory due his name. This is the perennial call of the people of God across the centuries, to recognize, acknowledge, and declare the majesty of our King.

PRAYER

Eternal God, whose glory fills heaven and earth, we come before you in humble acknowledgment of your majesty and holiness. Teach us to ascribe to your name the honor and worship due to you alone. Transform our hearts that we might worship not merely with our lips but with our whole lives. May our daily choices reflect our conviction that you alone are worthy of glory, that your holiness calls us to justice, mercy, and truth. Draw us ever deeper into that splendor of your presence until we, too, join the eternal chorus of praise. In the name of Jesus Christ, your Son and our Savior, we pray. Amen.

THE DAWN OF GOD'S FAITHFULNESS

Sing the praises of the LORD, you his faithful people; praise his holy name. For his anger lasts only a moment, but his favor lasts a lifetime; weeping may stay for the night, but rejoicing comes in the morning (Psalm 30:4–5).

There is something profound about the rhythm of night and day that speaks to the deepest patterns of human experience. We know instinctively that darkness does not last forever, that morning always comes. Yet when we are in the midst of our own midnight hours, those seasons of grief, disappointment, or struggle, it can feel like dawn will never break. Psalm 30:4–5 offers us a word of hope that transforms our understanding of both our suffering and our God.

David begins with a call to praise, inviting God's faithful people to sing and celebrate his holy name. This is not a mere religious routine or empty obligation. The invitation to praise emerges from a deep truth about God's character: his anger is momentary, but his favor is lifelong. This striking contrast reveals something essential about who God is and how he relates to his people.

When Scripture speaks of God's anger, it describes his righteous response to sin and rebellion. God's holiness cannot coexist comfortably with evil; his justice demands a response to wrongdoing. Yet David tells us this anger "lasts only a moment." The Hebrew word suggests something fleeting, a brief instant. God's wrath, though real, is not his default posture toward his children. It is not where he dwells or what defines his relationship with those who belong to him.

Contrast this with God's favor, which "lasts a lifetime." The span could not be more different. Where anger is momentary, favor endures. Where discipline is brief, blessing extends across all our days.

This is the God we serve, one whose fundamental disposition toward his people is grace, whose lovingkindness does not flicker with our failures but remains steady through every season of life.

The second half of verse five brings this principle into the terrain of our lived experience: "Weeping may stay for the night, but rejoicing comes in the morning." Here is where theology becomes deeply personal. David is not denying the reality of sorrow. He does not minimize our pain or suggest we should not grieve. Weeping is acknowledged, even expected. There are nights in our lives, sometimes long, dark nights, when tears are our only language.

But notice the time limit David places on sorrow: it may stay "for the night." Not forever. Not even for many nights, in the scope of eternity. The weeping has a season, but it is not the final season. Joy, on the other hand, comes with the morning, and morning always comes. This is God's promise to his people: sorrow is the visitor, but joy is the inheritance.

This pattern reflects the very nature of redemption. Jesus spoke of a woman in labor whose anguish gives way to joy when her child is born, so that she forgets the pain (John 16:21). The night of Christ's crucifixion, the darkest in human history, gave way to resurrection morning. Peter tells us that we may suffer grief in various trials "for a little while," but these light and momentary troubles are achieving for us an eternal weight of glory (1 Peter 1:6; 2 Corinthians 4:17).

Living in light of this truth changes everything. It does not remove us from the night seasons; we still walk through valleys, still experience loss, still face trials that bring us to tears. But it gives us hope that transforms how we endure. We can weep without despair, grieve without hopelessness, and struggle without surrendering to cynicism. We know the story's ending. We know that God's favor outlasts his discipline, that morning outlasts night, that joy outlasts sorrow.

This is why David begins with a call to praise. Praise is not denial of our present pain; it is defiance against the lie that pain is permanent. It is choosing to rehearse God's faithfulness when circumstances tempt us to doubt it. It is lighting a candle in the darkness, not because we pretend the darkness is not real, but because we know light is stronger.

So today, whatever night you are walking through, remember this: joy comes in the morning. Your weeping has a season, but it is not the final word. God's anger toward sin lasted a moment at the cross; his favor toward you will last forever. The dawn is coming. In fact, for those who are in Christ, the dawn has already broken, and we are simply waiting for our eyes to fully adjust to its light.

PRAYER

Faithful God, help me trust your rhythm when I am in the night. When tears are my companion, remind me that morning is coming. Let me praise you not only in my joy but also in my sorrow, knowing that your favor toward me is unending. Thank you that weeping is only for a season, but your faithfulness is forever. In Jesus' name, Amen.

FINDING GOD IN OUR DISTRESS

Be merciful to me, LORD, for I am in distress; my eyes grow weak with sorrow, my soul and body with grief. My life is consumed by anguish and my years by groaning; my strength fails because of my affliction (Psalm 31:9–10).

The psalmist's cry pierces through the centuries with raw, unfiltered honesty: "Be merciful to me, LORD, for I am in distress." These words from Psalm 31 do not tiptoe around suffering or dress it up in spiritual language. They present grief in its totality: eyes weakened by weeping, a soul wrung out by sorrow, a body that aches with the physical weight of emotional pain, strength depleted by affliction. This is suffering that has moved in and taken up residence, consuming life itself and turning years into groaning.

We live in a culture that often expects us to maintain composure, to "stay strong," to find the silver lining quickly. Even within faith communities, there can be an unspoken pressure to demonstrate unwavering confidence or to wrap up our pain with a tidy bow of spiritual victory. Yet here in Scripture, we find permission to acknowledge when we are undone. The psalmist models something profoundly important: bringing our whole, broken selves to God without pretense or performance.

Notice that this prayer does not begin with explanation or justification. It does not start with "I know I should not feel this way, but . . ." or "I am trying to trust you, however . . ." It simply begins with need: "Be merciful to me, LORD." There is a beautiful directness here, a recognition that God does not require us to sanitize our suffering before we approach him. The psalmist understands what we often forget: that God is big enough to handle our reality, including the parts that feel too dark or too overwhelming to share with anyone else.

The cascade of distress described in these verses, from eyes to soul to body to life itself, reminds us that suffering is rarely compartmentalized. When we grieve deeply, whether from loss, disappointment, chronic pain, broken relationships, or the accumulation of life's burdens, it affects every dimension of our being. We cannot simply think our way out of grief, nor can we pray it away as though it were a minor inconvenience. The psalmist's honesty validates what many of us experience but hesitate to admit: sometimes our affliction does fail our strength. Sometimes the groaning does seem to consume our years.

Yet even in this darkness, notice where the psalmist directs his plea. Not into the void. Not to friends who might offer platitudes or solutions. He turns to the Lord. This is the heart of biblical lament; it is a complaint directed Godward, a protest offered in relationship rather than in abandonment of faith. The very act of crying out to God is itself an act of faith, a stubborn insistence that God is still there, still listening, still capable of mercy even when we cannot feel or see it.

The request for mercy is particularly significant. The psalmist does not ask first for deliverance or for circumstances to change, though those desires are surely present. He asks for mercy, for God's compassionate presence in the midst of distress, for grace that meets him where he is rather than where he wishes he could be. This is the mercy that does not demand we pull ourselves together first, the mercy that sits with us in our weakness rather than waiting for us to manufacture strength.

For those walking through their own valleys, these verses offer profound companionship. Your tears are not a sign of failed faith. Your physical exhaustion from emotional burden is not a weakness of character. Your feeling that life is consumed by anguish does not mean you have lost your way. The psalmist's words give us language for what cannot be spoken, permission to name our reality before God without shame.

What is remarkable about Psalm 31 is that this raw lament does not represent the psalmist's final word. Later in the same psalm, he will declare trust and praise. But he does not skip over the grief to get there. He walks through it, bringing God into the darkest rooms of his experience. This is the path of faith, not denying our distress, but refusing to face it alone. We serve a God who is not frightened by our frailty, who draws near to the brokenhearted, who collects our tears as treasures.

PRAYER

Merciful Lord, meet me in my distress. When my strength fails, and my tears will not stop, when the grief feels like it will consume me entirely, help me remember that you are still here. Give me the courage to bring you my whole truth: the exhaustion, the anguish, the groaning. Hold me in my weakness, and let your mercy be enough for this moment. Amen.

PSALM 32

THE HEALING POWER OF CONFESSION

Then I acknowledged my sin to you and did not cover up my iniquity. I said, "I will confess my transgressions to the LORD." And you forgave the guilt of my sin (Psalm 32:5).

The fifth verse of Psalm 32 stands as one of Scripture's most luminous passages on the transformative grace of confession. The psalmist moves from the silence and burden of hidden sin into the liberating clarity of full disclosure before God. In doing so, David articulates a spiritual principle that reverberates throughout the entire biblical narrative: acknowledgment of wrongdoing becomes the indispensable gateway to divine forgiveness and restoration.

The opening phrase, "Then I acknowledged my sin to you," marks a decisive turning point. The word "acknowledged" carries the sense of intimate knowing and recognition. This is not mere intellectual assent to one's failure, but rather a profound, emotional, and spiritual reckoning with the reality of one's transgression. The psalmist does not rationalize, minimize, or deflect blame. Instead, he confronts the stark truth of his own culpability before the God who sees all things. This acknowledgment represents a break from the deception that characterized the preceding verses, where the poet described the devastating consequences of silence: "When I kept silent, my bones wasted away through my groaning all day long" (verse 3).

The second clause deepens this confession: "and did not cover up my iniquity." The word "cover" evokes the very language of the Fall narrative, where Adam and Eve attempt to conceal their nakedness and shame after eating the forbidden fruit. In every age, human beings instinctively seek to hide their moral failures. We construct elaborate narratives to justify our actions, we confess to others but not to God, or we simply push our guilt into the recesses of consciousness, hoping that silence will somehow erase the offense. The psalmist categorically rejects this universal impulse. He declares that he will no longer participate in the futile project of concealment.

What follows is particularly striking in its directness: "I said, 'I will confess my transgressions to the LORD.'" Here we encounter three distinct Hebrew terms for sin, each adding nuance to the theological vocabulary of wrongdoing. In Hebrew, the word "transgressions" denotes rebellion or violation of boundaries, the deliberate stepping over of divine boundaries. This is not accidental stumbling but willful transgression. By choosing such a robust term, the psalmist takes full responsibility for volitional wrongdoing rather than claiming weakness or circumstance as an excuse.

The remarkable promise embedded in this verse's conclusion, "And you forgave the guilt of my sin," unveils the divine response to genuine confession. In Hebrew, the word "forgave" literally means "to bear away" or "to lift up and carry away." God does not merely overlook the sin; rather, God actively removes it from the psalmist's account. The phrase "the guilt of my sin" refers not merely to the act of transgression but to the liability, culpability, and shame that cling to the guilty party. What has been acknowledged and confessed is now lifted away entirely.

This theological sequence offers profound instruction for contemporary spiritual practice. In our modern context, we tend to compartmentalize confession into categorical forms: psychological therapy addresses emotional damage, reconciliation programs address relational harm, and religious confession addresses spiritual standing. Yet Psalm 32 insists on an integrative understanding of confession as encompassing the totality of human experience before God. The psalmist moves from physical manifestation of guilt ("bones wasted away") through emotional suppression and spiritual deadness, toward comprehensive wholeness through honest acknowledgment.

The pastoral implication here cannot be overstated. How many believers remain imprisoned in cycles of guilt, anxiety, and spiritual paralysis because they have never fully articulated their failures before God? The Psalmist's experience testifies that the pathway from bondage to freedom runs necessarily through the vulnerable act of confession. This is not confession as a mere religious obligation, but rather as an indispensable condition of spiritual transformation.

Significantly, the logic of Psalm 32:5 resists the notion that God's forgiveness depends upon anything other than honest confession. There is no elaborate penance, no merit-based system of restoration. The divine response to genuine acknowledgment is immediate and complete forgiveness. This stands as revolutionary good news to all who have carried the weight of unconfessed sin.

PRAYER

Eternal and gracious God, grant me the courage to acknowledge before you all that I have hidden in the shadows of my heart. Release me from the illusion that silence can conceal what your eyes already know. Give me the humility to confess my transgressions without excuse or rationalization. As I lay bare my failures before your throne, grant me faith to receive the forgiveness you freely offer through Christ Jesus. Transform my confession into liberation and restore to me the joy of my salvation. Amen.

PSALM 33

WAITING IN HOPE

We wait in hope for the LORD; he is our help and our shield. In him our hearts rejoice, for we trust in his holy name. May your unfailing love be with us, LORD, even as we put our hope in you (Psalm 33:20–22).

There is something profoundly countercultural about waiting. In a world that prizes immediate results, instant gratification, and constant forward motion, the psalmist invites us into a different rhythm entirely: "We wait in hope for the LORD." This is not the passive waiting of resignation or the anxious waiting of uncertainty. This is active, expectant, hope-filled waiting, the kind that rests on the character of God himself.

The psalmist presents us with a paradox that defines the Christian life. We wait, yet we rejoice. We hope for what we do not yet see, yet our hearts are already full of gladness. How can both be true simultaneously? The answer lies in understanding who it is we are waiting for. We wait for the Lord who is already "our help and our shield." Our hope is not placed in an unknown deity or an uncertain future, but in the God who has already proven himself faithful, who has already demonstrated his protective care.

Consider the image of a shield. In ancient warfare, a shield was not merely defensive equipment; it was a soldier's confidence in battle. With a sturdy shield, a warrior could advance toward danger, knowing protection was close at hand. When we call God our shield, we acknowledge that life's battles are real: the arrows fly, the threats are genuine, but we are not exposed or vulnerable. Our trust is in the One who stands between us and every force that would seek to destroy us.

Yet the psalmist does not stop with protection. God is also "our help." He is not distant or detached, merely warding off blows from afar. He actively aids, strengthens, and empowers us on our journey. This dual nature of God's care, both shielding and helping, reminds us that faith is not about avoiding difficulty but about facing it with divine assistance. We are neither abandoned to fight alone nor left passive in our own defense.

The heart of this passage pulses with joy: "In him our hearts rejoice." Notice where the joy is located, not in our circumstances, not in what we can see or control, but "in him." This is the secret to rejoicing while waiting. Our gladness is not contingent on answered prayers arriving on our timeline or trials ending when we would prefer. Our joy springs from the unchanging reality of who God is. We trust "in his holy name," in his character, his nature, his very essence. The name of God represents everything he has revealed about himself: his faithfulness, his love, his power, his wisdom, his goodness.

Trust, the psalmist teaches us, is not blind optimism or wishful thinking. Biblical trust is built on knowledge. We trust in God's "holy name" because we know what that name represents. We have seen his faithfulness in the grand narrative of Scripture. We have experienced his presence in our own stories. We have witnessed his work in the lives of others. This accumulated evidence forms the foundation upon which our hope securely rests.

The psalm concludes with a beautiful prayer that we can make our own: "May your unfailing love be with us, LORD, even as we put our hope in you." Notice the phrase "unfailing love." God's covenant love, his loyal, steadfast, unwavering commitment to his people. This is not a love that ebbs and flows with our performance or wavers when we stumble. It is unfailing precisely because it depends on God's character, not ours.

The final phrase creates a profound connection: "even as we put our hope in you." Our hope and God's love are intertwined. As we choose to place our confidence in him, we experience the reality of his love more fully. This is not transactional; God's love does not increase because we hope in him. Rather, our hope opens our eyes and hearts to perceive and receive the love that has been there all along.

Waiting in hope, then, becomes not a burden but a gift. It is the sacred space where our hearts learn to rejoice not in outcomes but in God himself. It is where we discover that the one we are waiting for is already with us, already helping us, already shielding us with his unfailing love. In a world obsessed with arrival, the psalmist reminds us that the journey itself, lived in hope and trust, is where we encounter the very heart of God.

PRAYER

Lord, teach us to wait with hope rather than anxiety, to trust in your holy name rather than our own understanding. Be our help in times of trouble and our shield in every battle. Fill our hearts with joy that springs from knowing you, and may your unfailing love surround us as we place all our hope in you. In your faithful name we pray, Amen.

CRYING OUT TO GOD

This poor man called, and the LORD heard him; he saved him out of all his troubles. The angel of the LORD encamps around those who fear him, and he delivers them (Psalm 34:6–7).

Among the Psalms of David, few passages offer such comfort to the afflicted as these two verses from Psalm 34. The psalmist declares with confidence: "This poor man called, and the LORD heard him; he saved him out of all his troubles. The angel of the LORD encamps around those who fear him, and he delivers them." These words bridge the gap between human desperation and divine compassion, reminding us that our cries reach God's ear and that his protection surrounds those who commit their lives to him.

The Hebrew word for "poor" in verse 6 carries connotations beyond mere economic poverty. It speaks to weakness, helplessness, and vulnerability in the face of overwhelming circumstances. The psalmist does not hide behind pretense; he openly acknowledges his dire condition. The verb translated "called" means to cry out, to summon, to call with urgency and intensity. This is not a quiet whisper; it is a desperate cry from the depths. Yet the most remarkable word in this verse is "heard." To hear in Hebrew is not merely to perceive sound with the ear; it is to listen with understanding, to attend to, to respond to with action. God heard not just the noise of the psalmist's cry but the desperation within it, and he responded.

The second part of verse 6 promises rescue. The Hebrew verb translated "save" means to deliver and bring to safety. Significantly, the text says he saved him from "all his troubles," not merely some of them. This suggests a comprehensive deliverance that addresses the full scope of the sufferer's distress. It is a total rescue, not a partial relief.

Verse 7 shifts from the psalmist's experience to a universal promise. The angel of the Lord encamps around those who fear God. The word "camps" suggests a military encampment, protective fortifications surrounding the vulnerable. This is not distant protection but an intimate, immediate defense. The angel does not stand guard from a distance but "encamps around," meaning the protection completely surrounds and encompasses those under its care. Those who are encompassed by this divine protection are those who fear the Lord. The fear of God is not cowardly terror but reverence, respect, and commitment, a recognition of God's greatness and a dedication to honor him.

What comfort these verses offer to us in our modern struggles! We live in an age of anxiety, where unprecedented challenges assault us from every direction. Yet this ancient song reassures us that our cries are not lost in the void. God hears not with indifference but with active, saving love. His protection is not theoretical but concrete, surrounding those who commit themselves to him. When we feel weak, when circumstances seem overwhelming, we may take courage from these words.

PRAYER

O God of compassion, we come before you today acknowledging our weakness and our need. We cry out from the depths of our troubles, some of which seem overwhelming in their intensity. Hear us, we pray, as you heard the poor man of old. Let not our voices be lost in the vastness of creation, but let them reach your ear and stir your saving love. Deliver us, we beseech you, from all our troubles. And as we commit ourselves to fear and revere you, surround us with your protective presence. Let your angels encamp around us, that we might walk through this world not in terror but in confidence, secure in the knowledge of your steadfast love. We thank you for these precious words and for the assurance they bring to our hearts. In the name of Jesus Christ, our Savior and Lord, we pray. Amen.

WHEN GOD FIGHTS OUR BATTLES

Contend, LORD, with those who contend with me; fight against those who fight against me (Psalm 35:1).

David's opening words in Psalm 35 strike us with their raw honesty. Here is a man under attack, besieged by enemies, and his first instinct is not to mount his own defense but to call upon God to enter the battle on his behalf. This cry reveals something profound about the nature of faith when we find ourselves in conflict.

The psalm was likely written during one of the many periods when David faced opposition, perhaps from Saul's pursuit or later conspiracies within his own kingdom. What matters most is not the historical context but the spiritual principle David demonstrates: when wrongfully attacked, our primary response should be to invite God into our struggle rather than relying solely on our own strength or schemes.

Notice the verbs David uses: "contend" and "fight." These are legal and military terms that portray God as both an advocate and a warrior. In ancient Israel, to contend meant to present one's case in court, to argue on behalf of the accused. David is not asking God to rubber-stamp his own revenge fantasies. He is asking the righteous judge to take up his case, examine the evidence, and render justice. This is a crucial distinction. David surrenders the outcome to God's wisdom rather than insisting on his own vindication.

We live in an age that encourages self-advocacy at every turn. When we are wronged, our culture tells us to fight back immediately, to defend ourselves on social media, to never let an offense go unanswered. But David models something countercultural: the discipline of stepping back and allowing God to be our defender. This does not mean we become doormats or ignore injustice. Rather, it means we refuse to let bitterness and vengeance consume us while we trust God to work on our behalf.

The request for God to "fight against those who fight against me" acknowledges a spiritual reality we often forget: our struggles are rarely merely human conflicts. Behind visible opposition often lie spiritual forces that require divine intervention. When we face attacks on our character, our faith, or our calling, we are dealing with battles too great for human weapons alone. Paul would later echo this truth when he reminded the Ephesians that "our struggle is not against flesh and blood" (Ephesians 6:12).

But perhaps the most liberating aspect of David's prayer is what it frees us from. When we genuinely place our battles in God's hands, we are released from the exhausting burden of orchestrating our own vindication. We do not have to spend sleepless nights plotting responses or obsessively rehearsing arguments. We do not have to manipulate situations or people to ensure we come out on top. Instead, we can rest in the confidence that God sees, God knows, and God acts in perfect justice and perfect timing.

This does not mean victory comes quickly or in the form we expect. Sometimes God fights for us by changing our circumstances. Other times, he fights by changing us, giving us supernatural peace and wisdom amid ongoing difficulty. He may vindicate us publicly, or he may do his deepest work in the hidden places of our hearts where only he can see. The key is trusting that his methods are better than ours.

David's prayer also reminds us that it is okay to bring our pain and anger to God. He does not demand that we arrive in his presence with perfectly sanitized emotions. He invites us to be honest about our hurt, our sense of injustice, our desire for things to be made right. The psalms give us permission to lament, to question, to cry out. What matters is that we bring these feelings to God rather than allowing them to drive us toward sin.

When you find yourself under attack today, whether from obvious enemies or subtle undermining, remember David's wisdom. Resist the urge to fight every battle with your own strength. Instead, follow the psalmist's example: present your case to the judge of all the earth. Ask him to contend on your behalf. Trust him to fight your battles. And then rest in the freedom that comes from knowing the outcome is in the hands of a far more capable person than your own.

PRAYER

Lord, I bring my battles to you today. Where I face opposition or injustice, I ask you to be my defender and advocate. Give me the wisdom to know when to speak and when to remain silent, trusting you to contend on my behalf. Fight for me where I cannot fight for myself, and grant me peace as I rest in your sovereign care. Amen.

THE FOUNTAIN OF LIFE

For with you is the fountain of life; in your light we see light
(Psalm 36:9).

In the middle of Psalm 36, nestled between David's observations about human wickedness and his plea for God's continued protection, we encounter one of Scripture's most luminous declarations: "For with you is the fountain of life; in your light we see light." This verse does not merely describe God's attributes; it reveals the fundamental nature of our existence and the source from which all meaning flows.

The image of a fountain is striking in its vitality. Unlike a cistern that holds stagnant water, a fountain bubbles up continuously, fresh and life-giving. In the ancient Near East, where water determined survival, a reliable fountain meant the difference between flourishing and perishing. David understood this reality intimately from his years in the wilderness, and he applies it to spiritual truth: God himself is not merely a source of life but *the* fountain from which all life springs. Everything that truly lives does so because it draws from him.

This is not abstract theology; it is the daily reality of our existence. We wake each morning sustained by a heartbeat we did not initiate, breathing air we did not create, animated by a consciousness we cannot fully explain. Every moment of genuine joy, every experience of authentic love, every instance of beauty that catches our breath, these are drops of water from the eternal fountain. We live and move and have our being in him, whether we acknowledge it or not.

But David does not stop with the fountain image. He adds another metaphor that deepens our understanding: "in your light we see light." This second phrase unlocks something profound about how we perceive reality itself. Light not only allows us to see, but it also transforms what we see. The same room looks entirely different in candlelight, fluorescent glare, or golden sunrise. Similarly, God's light does not just illuminate objects; it changes how we understand everything.

Consider how many people search for meaning in achievement, relationships, possessions, or experiences, only to find these things strangely hollow when obtained. Why? Because they are examining life by the wrong light. Apart from God's illumination, we fundamentally misunderstand what we are looking at. We mistake shadows for substance, temporary pleasures for lasting joy, and self-assertion for true strength. We are like people trying to appreciate a masterpiece painting in a darkened gallery, fumbling to make sense of shapes we can barely perceive.

In God's light, everything becomes clear. Suffering reveals its capacity to refine rather than merely destroy. Humility appears as strength rather than weakness. Service to others becomes freedom rather than bondage. Death itself, that darkest of all human realities, transforms into a doorway rather than a wall. None of these truths is visible by the dim lights of human wisdom alone; they require divine illumination.

This explains why Scripture speaks so often about spiritual blindness. It is not that unbelievers lack intelligence or perception, but that they operate under inadequate light. Paul describes people whose "foolish hearts were darkened," and Jesus speaks of those who "seeing do not see." The tragedy is not a lack of information but a lack of illumination, the inability to perceive what the available information actually means.

For believers, this verse offers both comfort and challenge. The comfort is knowing that we do not have to generate our own life or manufacture our own understanding. We can come to the fountain daily, confident that it will never run dry. We can ask for light, trusting that God delights in revealing truth to those who seek him. The spiritual life is not about achieving but receiving, not about climbing to God but opening ourselves to what he freely offers.

The challenge, however, is equally clear: Are we actually drinking from the fountain, or are we trying to survive on what our own efforts can produce? Are we truly seeing by God's light, or are we still squinting in the darkness of cultural assumptions, personal preferences, and comfortable illusions? The fountain is available, the light is shining, but we must choose to approach and allow our eyes to adjust to truths that may initially seem strange or difficult.

Today, you stand at a choice point. Will you return to the fountain? Will you ask for eyes to see by divine light rather than human wisdom? The invitation stands open, as fresh this morning as it was when David first penned these words three thousand years ago.

PRAYER

Father, you are the fountain of life, and apart from you, we have nothing that lasts. Forgive us for the countless times we have sought satisfaction in broken cisterns of our own making. Today, we come to you thirsty. Illuminate our minds with your truth, that in your light we might see everything: our joys and sorrows, our relationships and responsibilities, our past and our future, as they truly are. Give us eyes to see and hearts to receive. Amen.

THE INTEGRATION OF TRUST AND DELIGHT

Trust in the LORD and do good; dwell in the land and enjoy safe pasture. Take delight in the LORD, and he will give you the desires of your heart (Psalm 37:3–4).

The opening verses of Psalm 37 establish a fundamental theological principle that has sustained God's people through centuries of uncertainty and distress. At their heart lies a paradox that challenges our modern sensibilities: to abandon our anxious striving and instead embrace a posture of trust that paradoxically leads to the fulfillment of our deepest longings. The psalmist addresses an audience struggling with the apparent triumph of the wicked and the suffering of the righteous, a struggle as ancient as faith itself.

The Hebrew word translated as "trust" conveys confidence, refuge, and security. It is not a mere intellectual assent to God's existence but rather a relational commitment rooted in the conviction that God is fundamentally trustworthy and reliable. The parallelism that follows, "and do good," is instructive. Trust is never meant to be passive resignation. Rather, it is an active engagement with righteousness and ethical living. The righteous person who trusts God is precisely the person who "does good," demonstrating through conduct the reality of their faith commitment. This integration of faith and works characterizes biblical wisdom literature.

The command to "dwell in the land" recalls the Abrahamic covenant and Israel's inheritance of Canaan as a gift from God. Yet this is not merely about geographical tenure. The expression, "to dwell," suggests a stable, secure habitation, a dwelling in peace and belonging. For the ancient Israelite, land represented security, inheritance, and God's covenantal promise made concrete. For the contemporary believer, this resonates spiritually: those who trust God inhabit a land of stability that transcends external circumstances. We "dwell" in God's care, secure in his provision.

The phrase "enjoy safe pasture," which translates the Hebrew expression "pasture faithfulness," presents a striking image. The righteous one grazes not in dangerous terrain but in a protected, verdant space. This is the theology of the Good Shepherd, reaching its fullest expression in Psalm 23. The metaphor conveys not merely provision but protection, not merely sustenance but security. The psalmist insists that the trusting person inhabits a realm where legitimate needs are met, and genuine safety is assured.

The second verse pivots to the affective dimension of faith. "Take delight in the LORD" moves beyond compliance or dutiful obedience to embrace joy and pleasure in God himself. This expression suggests enjoyment and emotional satisfaction. The psalmist is not counseling a grim, joyless submission. Rather, he invites us to find our deepest pleasure in a relationship with God. This is countercultural in any era. Our consumer culture promises satisfaction through acquisitions and achievements. The psalmist redirects our desire itself toward its proper object.

Here we encounter one of Scripture's most challenging promises: "and he will give you the desires of your heart." How shall we understand this? Does God grant us whatever we want? The answer lies in understanding the theology of desire that underwrites the promise. When our fundamental delight is in God, our desires are reformed and reoriented. We come to want what God wants for us. We desire righteous living, spiritual growth, reconciliation, justice, and mercy. These are the desires God grants, often abundantly and surprisingly. The promise is not that God becomes our cosmic vending machine; rather, it is that as we delight in God, our hearts are transformed so that our desires increasingly align with his will and character.

The promise also acknowledges God's generous nature. The God who created us with the capacity for longing and desire does not abandon that dimension of our humanity. Rather, he fulfills it through a relationship with himself and through the life of faith. The righteous person who delights in God discovers that genuine satisfaction comes not through the frantic pursuit of substitutes but through primary allegiance to the living God.

This passage addresses the psalmist's original audience, who are anxious about the apparent success of the wicked. The invitation is radical: cease your anxious calculations about justice and equity. Instead, trust God, do what is right, find your joy in God himself, and allow him to fulfill your deepest needs and longings. This is the gift of Psalm 37, not the elimination of difficulty, but the reorientation of our hearts toward the one who is altogether trustworthy.

PRAYER

Eternal God, you alone are worthy of our trust and delight. We confess that we often place our confidence in circumstances, achievements, and possessions that ultimately disappoint. Grant us grace to redirect our hearts toward you. Teach us to find our deepest joy in your presence and our most genuine security in your unfailing care. Transform our desires so that we long for what truly satisfies. May we dwell in the security of your promise and graze in the safe pasture of your providence. As we trust you and commit ourselves to doing good, fulfill the longings of our hearts according to your wisdom and love. In Christ, our Lord and Shepherd, we pray. Amen.

A CRY FOR GOD'S NEARNESS

LORD, do not forsake me; do not be far from me, my God. Come quickly to help me, my Lord and my Savior (Psalm 38:21–22).

The psalmist's plea in Psalm 38:21–22 emerges from a place of profound anguish. These are not the polished words of someone whose spiritual life feels tidy and ordered. This is raw desperation, the kind that strips away pretense and leaves only the honest cry of a soul that feels utterly alone. "LORD, do not forsake me; do not be far from me, my God. Come quickly to help me, my LORD and my Savior."

What makes this passage so powerful is its universal resonance. We have all experienced seasons when God feels distant, when our prayers seem to bounce off the ceiling, when circumstances press in from every side, and heaven appears silent. The psalmist gives voice to what many of us fear to admit: that we sometimes feel abandoned by the very One we need most.

The context of Psalm 38 reveals a man weighed down by multiple burdens. Physical suffering ravages his body. Friends and loved ones have withdrawn, keeping their distance as though his troubles might be contagious. Enemies circle like vultures, exploiting his weakness. And beneath it all lies the crushing awareness of his own sin, the recognition that some of his suffering stems from his own failures and foolish choices.

Yet notice how the psalmist responds. He does not turn away from God in his pain; he turns toward him. Even in his desperation, even when he feels forsaken, he still addresses God with covenant language: "my God," "my Lord," "my Savior." These possessive pronouns reveal a relationship that suffering has not destroyed. The very act of crying out to God demonstrates faith that God can hear, help, and still care.

This teaches us something crucial about authentic faith. Mature spirituality is not about maintaining constant emotional certainty of God's presence. It is about choosing to seek God even when we cannot feel him, about calling out to him especially when he seems distant. The psalmist models for us a faith that persists through doubt, that clings to God even as we wrestle with the feeling of divine absence.

The threefold repetition in these verses intensifies the urgency: "do not forsake me," "do not be far from me," "come quickly to help me." This is not casual prayer. This is a man on the edge, understanding that without divine intervention, he will be utterly undone. Sometimes we need to pray with this same intensity, abandoning our carefully crafted religious language and simply begging God to show up.

There is also profound honesty in acknowledging that we need God to "come quickly." The psalmist does not pretend he can wait patiently for years while God works in mysterious ways. He needs help now. And God honors such honesty. Throughout Scripture, we see God responding to desperate prayers, meeting people in their moments of greatest need. He is not offended by our urgency; he invites it.

For those walking through their own valleys, these verses offer both permission and hope. Permission to admit when faith feels hard, when God seems absent, when the weight of life threatens to crush us. And hope that crying out to God is never futile, that our desperate prayers reach his ears even when we cannot sense his nearness.

The Christian journey includes both mountaintop experiences of God's tangible presence and valley experiences in which we must walk by faith rather than by feeling. The psalmist's prayer reminds us that God remains our God, our Lord, our Savior, even and especially in the valleys. His character does not change based on our fluctuating feelings. His commitment to us does not waver when our circumstances darken

Perhaps you are in a season where God feels far away. Perhaps you are battling physical illness, relational brokenness, financial stress, or the heavy burden of your own failures. The psalmist's prayer becomes yours: do not abandon me, do not stay distant, come quickly. This is not weak faith; this is honest faith. And the God who inspired these words to be preserved in Scripture clearly values such authenticity.

The beauty of this passage is that it does not end in despair. It ends in petition, which itself is an act of hope. By asking God to come near, the psalmist demonstrates his belief that God can and will respond. May we carry this same conviction into our own times of trouble.

PRAYER

Lord, in seasons when you feel far away, teach us to cry out to you with the psalmist's honest desperation. Come near to us in our pain, meet us in our loneliness, and remind us that you are always our God, our Lord, our Savior, even when we cannot feel your presence. Come quickly to help us. Amen.

UNDERSTANDING OUR FLEETING DAYS

Show me, LORD, my life's end and the number of my days; let me know how fleeting my life is (Psalm 39:4).

When David penned these words in Psalm 39, he was not asking God to reveal the exact date of his death. Rather, he was asking for something far more transformative: the wisdom to grasp the brevity of life itself. In a moment of profound spiritual clarity, David understood that acknowledging our mortality is not morbid; it is essential to living well.

We live in a culture that does everything possible to avoid thinking about death. We pursue youth through countless means, speak of the deceased in hushed tones, and plan our lives as though we have unlimited time. Yet David's prayer cuts against this grain. He asks God to make him aware of life's fleeting nature, suggesting that this awareness is actually a gift we should seek.

Consider the context of this psalm. David had been silent, holding back his words even as his heart burned within him. When he finally spoke, these verses emerged, a meditation on the temporary nature of human existence. He recognized that each person is "but a breath," that our busy pursuits are often "mere phantoms," and that we accumulate things without knowing who will ultimately get them. This is not pessimism; it is realism infused with faith.

The wisdom David sought transforms how we approach our days. When we truly understand that our time is limited, we become more intentional about how we spend it. Petty grievances lose their grip. Procrastination on what truly matters becomes less appealing. The courage to love deeply, forgive quickly, and pursue our calling with urgency increases. Time becomes not just a commodity but a sacred trust.

This awareness also reshapes our priorities. How many of us fill our calendars with activities that do not align with our deepest values? We tell ourselves we will get to what really matters later, spending meaningful time with family, pursuing our God-given purpose, investing in relationships, or growing spiritually. But David's prayer reminds us that "later" is not guaranteed. Understanding our fleeting days helps us distinguish between the urgent and the important, between what merely demands our attention and what truly deserves it.

There is also profound humility in this prayer. David, the mighty king, acknowledges that he needs God to show him what he cannot fully grasp on his own. We might intellectually know that life is short, but spiritual understanding requires divine illumination. It is one thing to know we are mortal; it is another to live with that reality informing our choices daily. This kind of wisdom does not come naturally; it is a gift we must seek.

Paradoxically, meditating on life's brevity does not lead to despair but to hope. When David acknowledges his fleeting days, he immediately turns to God as his only hope (Psalm 39:7). Recognizing our temporal limitations points us toward the eternal. Our days may be numbered, but we serve a God who exists outside of time, whose love endures forever, and who offers us life that transcends our earthly years.

This verse also calls us to hold our plans and possessions lightly. If our days are fleeting, then clinging too tightly to our agendas, our stuff, or our status makes little sense. It frees us to be generous, to take risks for God's kingdom, and to invest in what will last beyond our lifetime. The fleeting nature of life becomes not a reason for anxiety but for liberation from the tyranny of temporary things.

Living with this awareness does not mean becoming reckless or fatalistic. Rather, it means living with intentionality and gratitude. Each day becomes a gift to be received with thanksgiving rather than a right to be demanded. Each relationship becomes an opportunity to love well rather than something to take for granted. Each moment becomes precious rather than disposable.

David's prayer is one we would do well to make our own. In asking God to show us the brevity of our days, we are not seeking to live in fear but to live in wisdom. We are asking for the grace to number our days rightly so that we might gain hearts of wisdom (Psalm 90:12). We are seeking the perspective that allows us to live fully, love deeply, and finish well.

PRAYER

Lord, like David, I ask you to give me a true understanding of how brief my life is. Help me not to waste my days on things that do not matter while neglecting what does. Teach me to live with urgency but not anxiety, with intentionality but not rigidity. May the awareness of my mortality drive me closer to you, the eternal God who holds all my days in your hands. Give me wisdom to invest my time in what will last beyond this life. In Jesus' name, Amen.

THE POWER OF PRAISE

He put a new song in my mouth, a hymn of praise to our God.
Many will see and fear the LORD and put their trust in him
(Psalm 40:3).

When David penned these words in Psalm 40, he was reflecting on a profound personal transformation. The verses preceding this declaration paint a picture of desperate waiting, of being lifted from a "slimy pit" and set upon solid ground. But notice what God does next: he does not merely rescue David and leave him standing in silence. He puts a new song in his mouth, a hymn of praise that would echo far beyond David's own experience.

This is the remarkable nature of divine deliverance. God does not just change our circumstances; he changes our very voice. The song he gives is not one we manufacture through willpower or religious duty. It is genuinely new, fresh, spontaneous, and born from the authentic experience of his faithfulness. Before our rescue, we might have sung songs of desperation or lament. Afterward, God himself composes a melody of praise within us, one that flows naturally from hearts that have known his saving power.

Consider the significance of this new song being placed specifically in our mouths. Our mouths are instruments of tremendous power; they can bless or curse, encourage or destroy, speak truth or deception. When God takes possession of this instrument and fills it with praise, he reorients our entire being toward worship. The song becomes our testimony, our witness, and our offering all at once. It is not hidden away in our hearts alone but given voice for others to hear.

This is where the second part of the verse becomes crucial: "Many will see and fear the LORD and put their trust in him." Our transformed lives and our songs of praise are never meant to be private affairs. They exist in the economy of God's kingdom as invitations to others. When people witness genuine transformation, when they see someone who was once stuck in despair now singing with authentic joy, it creates what we might call holy curiosity. They do not just hear about God's power; they see its effects in living color.

The word "fear" here should not conjure images of terror but rather of reverent awe. When observers witness what God has done in our lives, they are confronted with his reality and power. This healthy fear is the beginning of wisdom, the foundation upon which trust is built. Our praise becomes a bridge that others can walk across from doubt to faith, from distance to intimacy with God.

Think about the chain reaction David describes: deliverance leads to a new song, the song leads to others seeing, seeing leads to fearing, and fearing leads to trusting. This is the ripple effect of one life touched by God. Your transformation is not just about you. The song God gives you is not solely for your own comfort. It is part of a larger symphony he is conducting to draw all people to himself.

This truth should profoundly affect how we view our testimonies and our worship. Every time we gather with other believers to sing praises, every time we share what God has done in our lives, every time we choose thanksgiving over complaint, we are participating in this divine strategy for reaching the lost. Our praise is evangelistic. Our joy is apologetic. Our songs are sermons that need no translation.

But what if you feel like you are still in the pit, waiting to be lifted out? Remember that this psalm begins with the words "I waited patiently for the LORD." David's song did not come instantly. There was a season of waiting, of darkness, of uncertainty. Yet he trusted that deliverance would come, and when it did, it was so complete that it demanded a new song. Your rescue is coming, and with it will come a melody you have never sung before.

In our culture of curated image and performed authenticity, the church desperately needs people singing new songs, real testimonies of real transformation by a real God. Not polished performances, but honest expressions of what it means to be lifted from the mire and given solid ground. These are the songs that will cause many to see, fear, and trust.

So sing your new song boldly. Let it be heard. Tell what God has done. Your deliverance story might be exactly what someone else needs to hear to begin their own journey of trust.

PRAYER

Lord, thank you for lifting me from the pit and placing my feet on solid ground. Give me a new song today, one that genuinely reflects your faithfulness in my life. Help me to sing it boldly, knowing that my praise might be the invitation someone else needs to trust in you. May my life be a testimony that draws many to fear you and put their trust in your unfailing love. In Jesus' name, Amen.

THE BLESSING OF COMPASSION

Blessed are those who have regard for the weak; the LORD delivers them in times of trouble. The LORD protects and preserves them—they are counted among the blessed in the land—he does not give them over to the desire of their foes (Psalm 41:1–2).

When we think about what makes a blessed life, our minds often drift toward personal prosperity, security, or success. We imagine blessings as things that flow *to* us: good health, financial stability, loving relationships. But Psalm 41 opens with a startling inversion of this expectation: blessing comes not from what we receive, but from how we regard those who have nothing to give us in return.

"Blessed are those who have regard for the weak," the psalmist declares. The Hebrew word translated here as "regard" carries rich meaning; it suggests thoughtful consideration, discernment, and active attention. This is not merely noticing the vulnerable or feeling a passing sympathy. It is a deliberate turning of our hearts and minds toward those whom society overlooks, taking time to understand their circumstances, and choosing to engage with wisdom and compassion.

The weak, the poor, the marginalized, these are the people who cannot advance our careers, boost our social standing, or repay our kindness with material benefits. Yet God places them at the very center of what it means to live a blessed life. This divine mathematics confounds worldly logic. We invest in those who can help us climb; God asks us to kneel beside those who are falling. We network upward; God directs our attention downward and outward.

What follows in this psalm is remarkable: a cascade of divine promises for those who live with this countercultural orientation. "The LORD delivers them in times of trouble." Notice the connection: those who deliver others from their troubles will themselves be delivered. There is a beautiful reciprocity here, not of human transaction but of divine faithfulness. When we embody God's compassion toward the vulnerable, we position ourselves to experience God's compassion toward us.

The promises continue: protection, preservation, blessing in the land. These are not arbitrary rewards, as if God is simply incentivizing good behavior. Rather, they reveal a fundamental spiritual principle woven into the fabric of creation. When we align ourselves with God's heart for the weak, we align ourselves with the flow of God's providential care. We become participants in the divine work of restoration and, in doing so, open ourselves to God's restorative power in our own lives.

"He does not give them over to the desire of their foes." This final promise carries particular weight. Our enemies, whether spiritual, relational, or circumstantial, desire our destruction or downfall. But God becomes our defender when we have been defenders of the defenseless. There is an echo here of Jesus' teaching in the Sermon on the Mount: "Blessed are the merciful, for they will be shown mercy" (Matthew 5:7).

Living with regard for the weak transforms us. It softens hearts that the world hardens. It opens eyes that privilege blinds. It redirects love that self-interest hoards. When we pause to see the struggling single mother, the isolated elderly neighbor, the immigrant family navigating a foreign land, the colleague everyone avoids, when we truly regard them with God's eyes, we become different people. We become conduits of grace rather than consumers of blessing.

This psalm challenges our natural tendency toward self-preservation and self-advancement. It asks us to consider: Who are the weak in our sphere of influence? Who needs our thoughtful attention, our time, our resources, our advocacy? The answers will differ for each of us, but the call remains the same: to see, to consider, to act.

Perhaps most beautifully, this passage reminds us that God is watching not just what we do, but where our attention goes. He notices the direction of our regard. He sees when we slow down for the person others rush past, when we dignify the person others dismiss, when we invest in the person others ignore. And in those moments, we discover that blessing is not just something we might receive in the future; it is something we experience in the very act of giving ourselves away.

The blessed life, it turns out, is not found in accumulating more for ourselves but in having regard for those who have less. In caring for the weak, we find ourselves held by him who is strong. In protecting the vulnerable, we discover we are preserved by the Almighty. This is the upside-down kingdom Jesus proclaimed, and it begins with where we choose to direct our attention today.

PRAYER

Loving God, open my eyes to see the weak and vulnerable in my life, those you are calling me to regard with compassion. Soften my heart toward those I might overlook or avoid. Give me wisdom to help in ways that truly serve, and courage to act even when it is inconvenient. Thank you for your promise to deliver, protect, and preserve those who live with hearts turned toward others. May I trust your faithfulness as I seek to reflect your love. In Jesus' name, Amen.

THE SACRED THIRST FOR GOD

As the deer pants for streams of water, so my soul pants for you,
my God. My soul thirsts for God, for the living God. When can
I go and meet with God? (Psalm 42:1–2).

There is a specific kind of silence found in the wilderness: a heavy, expectant quiet that precedes a breaking point. It is in this landscape that the sons of Korah begin Psalm 42, not with a theological treatise, but with a visceral cry of biological necessity: "As the deer pants for streams of water, so my soul pants for you, my God."

To understand the depth of this metaphor, we have to look past the serene, precious moments imagery often associated with this verse. In the arid climate of the Near East, a deer "panting" is not just slightly thirsty; it is likely fleeing a predator or enduring a grueling drought. Its sides are heaving, its tongue is parched, and its very survival depends on finding a source of water that has not dried up under the relentless sun.

The psalmist is telling us something profound about the human condition: Our need for God is not a hobby; it is a hunger. It is not a preference; it is a prerequisite for life.

The text shifts from the physical image of a deer to the spiritual reality of the "living God." This distinction is vital. In the ancient world, the hills were crawling with idols, stone statues, and wooden carvings that looked impressive but remained static. You could carry a stone god, but it could never carry you.

When the psalmist cries out for the *living* God, he is seeking a dynamic, responsive presence. He is not looking for a philosophy to study or a ritual to perform; he is looking for a person to encounter.

The most piercing part of this passage is the question: "When can I go and meet with God?" This is the language of exile. Whether the psalmist was physically barred from the Temple or spiritually feeling a "dark night of the soul," the pain is the same. It is the agony of remembered intimacy. He remembers the "shouts of joy and praise" (v. 4), which makes his current isolation feel even more hollow.

Perhaps you are in that season right now. You look at your Bible, and it feels like paper and ink. You pray, and the words seem to bounce off the ceiling. You see others experiencing "spiritual highs," while you feel like you are wandering in a canyon of echoes.

The encouragement here is surprising: The very fact that you feel the thirst is proof that your soul is alive. A dead person does not thirst. If you are "panting" for God, if you feel the ache of his perceived absence, it is because your spirit knows what it was made for. Your soul recognizes that nothing in this material world, whether it be success, relationships, or comfort, can satisfy a thirst that was designed for the infinite.

We often try to quench our souls' thirst with distractions. We scroll through feeds, overwork, or seek validation from others. But these are "broken cisterns" (Jeremiah 2:13) that cannot hold water.

Meeting with God does not always require a grand pilgrimage or a perfect emotional state. Sometimes it looks like honesty. It looks like the psalmist's raw transparency, admitting, "I am thirsty, and I am not okay." When we stop pretending we are full, we finally make room for the "living water" to flow in.

God does not mock the thirsty. He invited us through Christ, who stood and cried out, "Let anyone who is thirsty come to me and drink" (John 7:37). The stream is not a reward for those who have it all together; it is a rescue for those who are running out of breath.

There is also a discipline embedded within the psalm's structure that we dare not overlook: the psalmist preaches to himself. Three times the refrain returns, "Why, my soul, are you downcast? Why so disturbed within me? Put your hope in God" (vv. 5, 11). This is not spiritual denial, pretending the pain is not real. Rather, it is the act of anchoring one's feelings to a truth that is larger than feelings. The psalmist does not silence his sorrow, but he refuses to let sorrow have the final word. In our age of emotional authenticity, this distinction is crucial: we can be honest about the dark without being ruled by it.

Ultimately, Psalm 42 is not a map out of suffering but a companion through it. It does not promise that the drought will end tomorrow, or that the tears will stop flowing, or that the questions will resolve into neat answers. What it does promise is that thirst itself is a form of prayer, and that the God who is called "living" is also the God who is listening. The deer panting in the wilderness does not yet see the stream — but the stream exists. And the One who placed that longing in the deer's chest is the very One who knows where every hidden water runs. If you find yourself in the valley today, panting and desperate, know this: your longing is not a sign that God has forgotten you. It is the sound your soul makes when it is being drawn, by grace, toward the source of everything it was created to need.

PRAYER

Heavenly Father, I admit that my soul is parched. I have tried to quench my thirst at wells that have run dry, seeking peace in places where it cannot be found. Today, I bring my "panting" soul to you. I thank you that even in the desert, you are the living God who hears my cry. Grant me the grace to wait for you with hope. Refresh my spirit with the reality of your presence, and remind me that my deep longing is simply a homing signal for your heart. I do not just want your blessings; I want you. Meet me in this quiet moment. In Jesus' name, Amen.

LEARNING HOPE IN THE DEPTHS

Why, my soul, are you downcast? Why so disturbed within me?
Put your hope in God, for I will yet praise him, my Savior and
my God (Psalm 43:5).

The concluding verse of Psalm 43 presents one of Scripture's most poignant moments of spiritual reorientation. The psalmist has just traversed a landscape of lament, confusion, and desperate petition, yet arrives at this remarkable declaration: "Why, my soul, are you downcast? Why so disturbed within me? Put your hope in God, for I will yet praise him, my Savior and my God." The word *yet*, that small but mighty conjunction, transforms this verse from mere resignation into authentic hope forged in the furnace of suffering.

The form of this verse deserves careful attention. The psalmist addresses his own soul, engaging in what we might call theological self-exhortation. This is not passive acceptance but active resistance against despair. The word "downcast" suggests a bowing down, a pressing into the earth, as though the weight of circumstances threatens to bury the speaker entirely. The parallel construction "disturbed within me" conveys tumultuous agitation, the roiling chaos of a soul in torment. These are not gentle emotional fluctuations but profound interior disturbances.

What makes this moment remarkable is that the psalmist does not deny these feelings. He does not pretend they do not exist or minimize their reality. Instead, he confronts them directly, speaking to his own soul with the tone of one addressing a wayward companion. There is neither self-recrimination nor despair in this address; rather, there is the tone of a faithful friend reminding another friend of what they already know to be true but have temporarily forgotten. This is the genius of the command: "Put your hope in God." It is not framed as a discovery but as a reorientation toward what has always been real. The Hebrew word translated "put your hope," carries the sense of waiting expectantly, of patient endurance mixed with confident anticipation. It is not merely optimism or positive thinking. Rather, it represents a deliberate turning of the entire person toward the God who has proven faithful. The object of hope matters immensely. The psalmist does not place hope in changing circumstances, in human intervention, or in personal resourcefulness. The hope is placed entirely in God, the covenant partner who has established a relationship with the people of faith across generations.

Yet the most transformative word in this verse may be that single syllable: *yet*. In Hebrew, this word means "still," "again," or "yet." It opens the door to future praise even in present darkness. The psalmist does not claim to be praising God at this exact moment; he is in too much distress for that false cheerfulness. Instead, he prophesies over his own future: "I will yet praise him." This is not wishful thinking; it is confidence grounded in God's character. The psalmist knows from his own experience and from the traditions of faith that God is worthy of praise, and he commits himself in advance to render that praise when the darkness lifts.

Notice that the verse concludes with a double designation: "my Savior and my God." This possessive language, *my* Savior, *my* God, personalizes the faith affirmation. This is not abstract theology but an intimate relationship. The God who saves and who is utterly transcendent is the very one who has established a covenant relationship with this particular worshiper. The tension between transcendence and intimacy in these dual titles reflects the fullness of biblical faith: God is infinitely beyond us, yet personally present to us.

For those who struggle with depression, anxiety, or the weight of circumstances, this verse offers neither false comfort nor denial of pain. Instead, it models a way forward: the deliberate practice of reminding our souls of what we know to be true about God, even when our circumstances scream otherwise. This is the discipline of faith, not feeling our way into trust, but choosing trust and allowing our feelings to follow eventually.

The verse invites us into a practice that has sustained God's people across millennia. When your soul is downcast, speak to it. Remind it of God's character. Commit yourself to praise, not because you feel like it now, but because you know God is worthy and because you have learned that praise has a way of transforming the one who praises.

PRAYER

Eternal God, source of all hope and author of our salvation: I come before you today with a soul that is often downcast, a spirit that knows too well the weight of this world's sorrows. Yet I hear in these ancient words the voice of faith speaking to my own hesitation, reminding me of what I know but sometimes forget. Help me to speak truth to my own soul, to turn my face toward you even when darkness surrounds me. Grant me the grace to believe not in the changing of my circumstances, but in your unchanging character. And give me courage to declare, with the psalmist of old: I will yet praise you, my Savior and my God. Amen.

PSALM 44

THE GIFT OF SACRED STORIES

We have heard it with our ears, O God; our ancestors have told us what you did in their days, in days long ago (Psalm 44:1).

There is something profoundly human about gathering around a story. Whether it is children begging for "just one more" bedtime story or adults lingering over coffee to share memories, we are a people shaped by narrative. The psalmist understood this deeply when he wrote, "We have heard it with our ears, O God; our ancestors have told us what you did in their days, in days long ago."

This opening line of Psalm 44 celebrates the sacred practice of passing down faith from one generation to the next. It is a reminder that our relationship with God is built not solely on our personal experience but also on the testimonies of those who walked before us. Faith has always been a relay race, with each generation carrying the baton of God's faithfulness forward.

Notice the intimacy in that phrase: "we have heard it with our ears." This is not secondhand information from a dusty book or abstract theological concepts debated in a classroom. These are stories heard directly from beloved voices: grandparents who spoke with trembling reverence about answered prayers, parents who recounted God's provision in difficult times, and mentors who shared how God transformed their brokenness into beauty. Faith was transmitted through relationships, through the warmth of presence and the power of personal testimony.

In our modern age of digital connection and instant information, we risk losing this vital practice. We can access countless sermons, podcasts, and devotionals with a tap of our phones, yet something irreplaceable is lost when we do not sit face-to-face with those who have walked with God through decades of joy and suffering. The wrinkles around their eyes as they describe God's faithfulness, the catch in their voice when remembering how prayer sustained them through loss; these details carry a weight that no blog post can replicate.

But this verse also confronts us with a sobering question: What stories are we telling? What will the next generation hear with their ears about what God has done in our days? Are we actively cultivating a testimony worth passing down, or have we become so consumed with the present moment that we have forgotten to notice God's movement in our lives?

The psalmist's ancestors told stories of God's mighty acts: deliverance, provision, miraculous intervention. They did not sanitize their history or pretend the journey was easy. They were honest about the struggles while remaining anchored in God's proven character. This is the kind of faith testimony that shapes generations: authentic, specific, and centered on God's faithfulness rather than human achievement.

There is also deep wisdom in recognizing that our faith does not begin with us. We stand on the shoulders of countless believers who chose faithfulness when it cost them everything. They prayed when prayer seemed futile, worshiped when circumstances warranted despair, and trusted when trust made no logical sense. Their stories are our inheritance, a reminder that God has been faithful through wars and famines, persecution and plague, personal tragedy and national upheaval. If he carries them through, he will carry us.

This intergenerational transfer of faith also protects us from the dangerous myth that each generation must reinvent Christianity from scratch. We do not need to discover God's character on our own through trial and error alone. The faithful who came before us have already learned crucial lessons, and their wisdom can spare us unnecessary pain while deepening our understanding of who God is.

So how do we honor this sacred practice today? We make time to listen to the testimonies of older believers, asking them to share not just their successes but the moments when God met them in their darkest valleys. We create spaces around our own tables where stories of God's faithfulness can be shared, with our children, yes, but also with friends, neighbors, and anyone willing to listen. We become intentional historians of God's work in our own lives, noting the answers to prayer, the unexpected provisions, the moments of divine intervention that might otherwise slip through the cracks of our busy lives.

Most importantly, we live in a way that makes stories worth telling. We take risks of faith that will become testimonies. We trust God in our present challenges so that future generations might hear with their ears what God did in our days.

PRAYER

Gracious God, thank you for the faithful witnesses who have gone before us, whose stories have shaped our faith and reminded us of your unchanging character. Help us to listen well to the testimonies of those who have walked with you through many seasons. Give us eyes to see your work in our own lives and the courage to share those stories with the generation coming behind us. May our lives become testimonies of your faithfulness that will strengthen others long after we are gone. In Jesus' name, Amen.

THE THRONE THAT ENDURES

Your throne, O God, will last for ever and ever; a scepter of justice will be the scepter of your kingdom (Psalm 45:6).

The throne room of heaven presents a peculiar tension that runs throughout Scripture and Christian theology. On one hand, we encounter the majesty of divine rule, a cosmic monarchy that transcends time itself. On the other hand, we discover something startling about the nature of this reign: it is fundamentally rooted in justice rather than mere power. Psalm 45:6 invites us into this paradox, declaring both the eternal stability of God's throne and the moral character that sustains it.

The Hebrew word for throne carries implications far deeper than a mere seat of authority. In ancient Near Eastern contexts, the throne represented the nexus point between heaven and earth, between the divine realm and human affairs. To speak of God's throne was to affirm divine governance not as abstract metaphysics but as active, immediate rule over creation. The psalmist addresses the divine king directly, "Your throne, O God," using the word *Elohim*, the general designation for divinity that emphasizes power and majesty. This is not an intimate address to a trusted friend but a formal recognition of transcendent authority.

Yet the temporal dimension demands our attention. The phrase "will last for ever and ever" translates the Hebrew construction that literally "eternity and eternity," a doubled expression that intensifies the concept of endless duration. This is not merely perpetual; it is doubly eternal, emphasizing a permanence that surpasses human comprehension. In an ancient world where dynasties fell, and kingdoms crumbled, where political power seemed as ephemeral as morning mist, the psalmist makes an audacious claim: God's rule is immune to the forces that topple human governments.

The second half of the verse introduces the remarkable specification: "a scepter of justice will be the scepter of your kingdom." Here, the Hebrew word typically rendered as "justice" or "righteousness" appears alongside the instrument of royal power. The scepter itself, the ancient symbol of monarchy, is not simply an emblem of force but an implement of moral governance. This is deeply countercultural, both in the ancient world and in our own. We might imagine a throne secured by military might, economic leverage, or political cunning. The psalmist instead envisions a kingdom sustained by justice.

The doubling of "scepter" in the Hebrew text creates a poetic emphasis that our English translations often compress. The redundancy is intentional; the psalmist wishes to hammer home this truth: justice is not merely an appendage to power; it is the very substance of the scepter itself. To rule the kingdom, God wields an instrument of righteousness.

This becomes profoundly consequential for faith. If God's throne rested on capricious power alone, we would have reason to fear divine authority. If divine rule were simply the triumph of the strong over the weak, we would find no refuge there. But a throne established in justice transforms our relationship with God entirely. We approach not with terror but with trust, not expecting arbitrary judgment but righteous governance.

The Christian tradition has long recognized Christological implications in this psalm. The New Testament writers, particularly the author of Hebrews, understood Psalm 45:6 as pointing to Jesus Christ, the one who inherits the throne of David and establishes a kingdom in which justice finally reigns without compromise. In Christ, we witness the convergence of the eternal and justice dimensions. His throne, established through resurrection and ascension, manifests a kingship where mercy and justice kiss one another (Psalm 85:10).

Yet the devotional application extends beyond doctrinal affirmation. In our daily experience of injustice, whether personal betrayal, systemic oppression, or the seemingly random cruelty of circumstance, this verse speaks a word of hope. The universe is not ruled by chance or chaos. The forces that currently seem to reign with impunity are not ultimate. Above all the thrones of earth, with their compromised justice and corrupted power, stands the throne of God, established forever and sustained by righteousness. Our task is not to secure justice ourselves through vengeance or desperation but to align ourselves with the justice that sustains the eternal throne.

As we live beneath this throne, we are invited to reflect its justice in our own spheres of influence: in our families, our workplaces, our communities. We become, as it were, extensions of the scepter of justice in this world, working toward the day when God's kingdom comes in its fullness.

PRAYER

Eternal God, whose throne stands secure beyond all time and whose scepter rules through perfect justice, we offer you our reverence and our trust. May our hearts find peace in knowing that the universe is governed not by chance or cruelty but by your righteous hand. Grant us wisdom to see your justice at work, even when the world seems dark. And make us instruments of your justice in our own time, reflecting the character of your eternal kingdom. In the name of Christ, the heir of your throne, we pray. Amen.

PSALM 46

OUR REFUGE AND STRENGTH

God is our refuge and strength, an ever-present help in trouble. Therefore we will not fear, though the earth give way and the mountains fall into the heart of the sea (Psalm 46:1–2).

There are moments in life when the ground beneath us seems to dissolve. A sudden loss, an illness without a clear path to recovery, a crisis that arrives without warning and swallows the stability we thought we had carefully built. In those moments, the world stops making sense, and we search desperately for something, anything, solid enough to hold onto. Psalm 46 was written for exactly those moments. It is not a psalm of leisurely reflection or quiet praise on a peaceful afternoon. It is a declaration forged in the heat of instability, a bold confession of trust made precisely when trust feels most difficult.

The psalmist opens not with a question or a hope, but with a declaration. There is no tentative wishing here, no "we pray that God might become our refuge." The language is declarative and absolute: *God is* our refuge and strength. This is not something the psalmist is asking God to become. It is something already known to be true. And that knowledge, the psalmist insists, changes everything about how we face the worst that life can bring.

To call God a "refuge" is to invoke the image of a shelter, a place of safety one runs to when danger draws near. Picture a fortress carved into the side of a mountain, impervious to the storms raging across the plains below. But the psalmist does not stop there. A crucial word is added: *strength*. God is not merely a place we hide. God is the very power that sustains us while we are sheltered. The refuge does not simply shield us from harm; it equips us to endure it. This pairing, protection and power form the foundation upon which the psalm's remarkable courage is built.

And then comes the word "therefore." It is one of the most significant words in Scripture because it reveals how faith translates into lived experience. *Because* God is our refuge and strength, *therefore* we will not fear. The fearlessness that follows is not reckless or naive. The psalmist is not pretending that trouble does not exist. The very next breath imagines the most catastrophic scenario conceivable: the earth itself giving way, the mountains, those ancient, immovable, seemingly eternal landmarks, crumbling and plunging into the heart of the sea. This is not a passing storm. This is the total unraveling of the created order as we know it. And still, the psalmist declares: we will not fear.

This is where the psalm becomes genuinely radical. Most of us operate on a quiet, unexamined assumption that our sense of peace depends on our circumstances being under control. We believe, deep down, that if the external world remains stable, we too can be stable. Psalm 46 dismantles that assumption entirely. It places the believer in the most unstable scenario imaginable and then declares that peace is still possible. Not because the chaos has been resolved, but because the one who stands above all chaos remains entirely unchanged. God's presence does not waver when the mountains fall. His strength does not diminish when the earth trembles. And so the one who has truly found refuge in him does not need the mountains to remain standing in order to stand himself.

This does not mean we are to be indifferent to suffering, or that we should dismiss the real weight of a crisis. The psalmist is not offering emotional detachment. What is being offered is a reorientation, a turning of the heart toward a source of security that no earthquake, no grief, no catastrophe can touch. It is the quiet, stubborn conviction that beneath the chaos of this world, there is a foundation that holds. And that foundation is not our own strength, our own plans, or our own understanding of how things should unfold. It is God.

In our own lives, the "earth giving way" may never take the form of a literal earthquake. It may be a marriage crumbling, a career collapsing, a medical diagnosis that rearranges everything we believed about the future. Whatever form it takes, the invitation of Psalm 46 remains the same: do not anchor your peace in what is shaking. Anchor it in the One who is not.

PRAYER

Lord, we confess that we so often place our trust in what we can see and control: in our plans, in stability, in our own ability to keep the ground firm beneath our feet. When the trembling comes, remind us of what is true: that you are our refuge, that your strength does not fail, and that in you we may find peace even when everything around us is falling away. Teach us not merely to believe this, but to live it, with calm hearts and steady hands. Amen.

A CALL TO UNIVERSAL PRAISE

*Clap your hands, all you nations; shout to God with cries of joy.
For the LORD Most High is awesome, the great King over all
the earth* (Psalm 47:1–2).

There is something extraordinary happening in Psalm 47. The psalmist
is not addressing Israel alone, nor is he calling merely to the faithful
remnant or the temple worshipers. Instead, these opening verses burst
forth with a radical invitation: "Clap your hands, *all you nations*; shout
to God with cries of joy."

This is worship without borders.

In the ancient Near East, each nation claimed its own gods, its own
localized deities who supposedly governed their particular territories
and peoples. But Psalm 47 shatters this compartmentalized worldview.
The God of Israel is not simply one god among many, nor is he merely
the tribal god of a small nation. He is "the great King over all the
earth," a stunning declaration that refuses to let God be domesticated,
reduced, or confined.

Notice the physical, embodied nature of this worship. We are called to
clap our hands and shout, not to maintain quiet reverence or
whispered piety. There is a time for silence before God, certainly, but
there is also a time for exuberant, full-throated celebration. The kind
of joy that cannot be contained in polite nods or subdued smiles. The
kind of joy that makes your hands come together in rhythmic
celebration, that opens your mouth in unrestrained praise.

Why such enthusiasm? Because "the LORD Most High is awesome."
The Hebrew word here carries connotations of fearsome power, of
majesty that inspires awe. This is not the casual "awesome" we use to

describe a good sandwich or a pleasant sunset. This is the awesome that makes mountains melt, that causes the earth to tremble, that silences all other claims to ultimate authority.

And here is what makes this psalm so relevant for us today: it envisions a worship that transcends every human division. All nations. Every tribe, tongue, and people group. The wealthy and the poor. The powerful and the marginalized. Those who have known God for generations and those just discovering his greatness. In God's presence, our typical categories dissolve. We are human beings responding to divine majesty.

This universal call to worship also carries profound implications for our understanding of God's kingdom. If the Lord is King over all the earth, then no corner of creation falls outside his concern. No nation operates beyond his authority. No political power, economic system, or cultural force stands independent of his sovereign rule. This should humble us when we are tempted to assume God is primarily concerned with our particular group, our nation, our way of doing things.

The psalm also reminds us that true worship is inherently joyful. Notice it does not say, "Drag yourselves before God with resigned obligation." It calls for cries of joy, for celebration. Yes, worship involves reverence and sometimes repentance, but at its core, encountering the living God should produce joy. When we truly grasp who God is, his power, his goodness, his sovereignty, the natural response is delight.

Perhaps you are reading this, and joy feels distant. Maybe worship feels like a duty rather than a celebration. The psalmist's invitation still stands. Sometimes joy begins not as a feeling but as an act of obedience: we clap our hands, we lift our voices, and in the doing, something shifts within us. We remember who God is. We recall his faithfulness. We recognize his authority over everything that troubles us.

The call to "all nations" also challenges us to consider who is missing from our worship. Whose voices are not being heard? The vision of Psalm 47 will not be fully realized until that day when people from every nation, tribe, and language stand before God's throne. But we can begin living into that reality now, ensuring that our worship communities reflect the diversity of God's kingdom and welcome all who would join in praising the great King.

Ultimately, Psalm 47 reminds us that worship is not about us. It is about the One who deserves all praise, the awesome Lord Most High, the King whose reign extends over all the earth. And in recognizing his supremacy, we find our proper place, not as isolated individuals or competing factions, but as a chorus of humanity united in celebration of the One who made us, sustains us, and reigns over us all.

PRAYER

Lord Most High, you are the great King over all the earth, and we join our voices with all creation in praising you. Awaken joy within us, not the shallow happiness that depends on circumstances, but the deep delight that comes from knowing you reign. Help us to worship with our whole selves, holding nothing back. And expand our vision to embrace your global kingdom, welcoming all who would join in celebrating your awesome majesty. In Jesus' name, Amen.

OUR GOD, OUR GUIDE, FOREVER

For this God is our God for ever and ever; he will be our guide even to the end (Psalm 48:14).

The concluding verse of Psalm 48 resounds with a confidence that transcends the particular historical circumstances of Jerusalem's deliverance. What begins as a celebration of divine protection, the God who defended the city against impossible odds, becomes a timeless proclamation about the nature of God's relationship with his people. The Hebrew text presents a masterfully constructed theological statement that merits careful examination.

The opening phrase literally reads in the Hebrew text as "for this [is] God, our God." The demonstrative pronoun "this" is particularly significant. Rather than simply stating "God is our God," the psalmist employs a gesture of personal recognition and assurance. It conveys something akin to "this God here, the one we have just witnessed, he is our God." The redundancy of the divine name, moving from the indefinite to the possessive construction, emphasizes both God's character and the covenant relationship between God and Israel. We are not merely subjects of a distant god; we belong to this God, and he belongs to us in a mutual relationship.

The temporal designation "forever and ever" extends this relationship beyond the immediate crisis into perpetuity. The doubled form intensifies the concept of eternity, suggesting not merely a long time but genuine timelessness. This is not a promise contingent upon future circumstances or conditional upon Israel's faithfulness. Rather, it speaks to the unchanging nature of God's commitment. Where political alliances falter, human strength wanes, and earthly powers collapse, the relationship established by God persists eternally.

The second half of the verse introduces perhaps the most personally comforting element: "He will be our guide even to the end." The verb "to guide" carries rich associations throughout Scripture. This is the God who guided Israel through the wilderness, who led Abraham to an unknown land, and who directs the righteous in paths of righteousness. The guide knows the terrain, anticipates danger, and possesses intimate knowledge of the destination. A guide is not merely a figurehead but a companion, one who walks alongside, adjusts the pace, and provides direction when the path becomes unclear.

The phrase "even to the end" translates the Hebrew expression "even unto death," which, more broadly, means "even unto our final end, our completion, our ultimate destination." This is not a journey of a few miles or a few years. It is the entire pilgrimage of life, from our beginning to our final breath and beyond. It promises that the God who claims us eternally will not abandon us mid-journey. He will guide us not merely through youth and strength but through old age, infirmity, sorrow, and approaching mortality.

For the contemporary believer, this verse addresses one of our deepest anxieties: the fear of being lost, of facing life without direction or purpose. We live in an age of bewildering choices, competing philosophies, and cultural disorientation. The psalmist offers a radical counterpoint. The God revealed in Israel's history, the God who established a covenant, delivered from bondage, and protected his people, offers himself as our personal guide, not as a distant cosmic force but as an intimate companion willing to shepherd us through every circumstance.

Yet the verse requires more than intellectual assent. It demands that we actively recognize this God as "our God" and accept his guidance. This involves trust that may seem foolish to the world. It means relinquishing the illusion that we fully comprehend the map of our lives. It requires yielding to guidance that may lead us through valleys rather than along mountaintops. But it also promises that we will never navigate these valleys alone.

The beauty of concluding the psalm with this assurance is that it transforms particular historical memory into universal spiritual truth. The God who defended Jerusalem against the Assyrian threat is the same God who guides the faithful through the perplexities of modern existence. The promise made in ancient Zion extends to believers across centuries and continents. Whatever our circumstance, whether we experience the city's safety or wander in figurative wilderness, we possess access to this God and his guidance.

This is the extraordinary claim of verse 14: your journey through life, extending to its ultimate terminus, is not random or abandoned. It unfolds under the attentive direction of the God who established a covenant with his people and sealed it eternally. Such a promise invites both profound gratitude and complete surrender.

PRAYER

Eternal God, we acknowledge that you are our God, sealed in relationship through covenant love that transcends time itself. We confess our tendency to imagine we must navigate our days through our own wisdom and strength. Grant us grace to recognize your guidance in both the clarity of open roads and the bewilderment of shadowed paths. As we journey from this moment toward our ultimate end, hold us in your care. Transform our anxiety into trust, our questioning into faith. Guide us not only through the easy seasons of our lives but especially through their difficulties, knowing that you will not abandon us. Make us faithful companions to fellow pilgrims, that we might reflect your guidance toward them. We offer our gratitude for the promise that the same God who protected your ancient people will grant us safe passage. In the name of Jesus, we pray. Amen.

PSALM 49

FROM DEATH TO LIFE

But God will redeem me from the realm of the dead; he will surely take me to himself (Psalm 49:15).

In the middle of a psalm dedicated to examining life's greatest questions about wealth, power, and mortality, we encounter a sudden burst of light. The psalmist paints a sobering picture of human limitation, describing how the rich and powerful cannot ransom themselves from death, how wisdom cannot save us from the grave, and how all people, regardless of status, face the same mortal end. Then comes this remarkable declaration: "But God will redeem me from the realm of the dead; he will surely take me to himself."

That word "but" changes everything.

Throughout Psalm 49, the writer observes that wealthy people trust in their riches and boast in their abundance, yet they cannot escape death's grip. No amount of money can purchase immortality. The grave claims both the wise and the foolish, the rich and the poor alike. This is the human condition in its starkest reality. Yet in verse 15, the psalmist pivots from despair to hope, from human impossibility to divine possibility.

The word "redeem" carries profound meaning. In ancient Israel, redemption referred to the act of buying back something or someone that had been lost or sold. A kinsman-redeemer could purchase a relative's freedom from slavery or buy back family land that had been forfeited. The psalmist is saying that God will act as his redeemer, paying the price to rescue him from death's dominion. What no human wealth can accomplish, God's power will achieve.

This verse represents one of the earliest expressions of hope in the Old Testament for life beyond death. While much of ancient Israelite thought focused on life in this world, here we glimpse a dawning awareness that God's love and power extend even beyond the grave. The psalmist is not merely hoping to avoid death for a while longer; he is expressing confidence that God will bring him through death and into divine presence.

Notice the personal nature of this faith: "God will redeem *me.*" This is not abstract theological speculation; it is an intimate trust. After observing the fate of those who trust in wealth, the psalmist declares where his own trust lies: not in what he possesses, but in who possesses him. The contrast is striking: while the wealthy fool dies and leaves everything behind, the faithful person is *taken up* by God.

The phrase "he will surely take me to himself" echoes another significant biblical moment. The Hebrew verb used here is the same one used to describe how God "took" Enoch in Genesis 5:24. It suggests not merely survival but intimate divine encounter. God does not just rescue us from something; he draws us toward someone. The ultimate destination of redemption is not simply escape from death; it is a union with God himself.

For Christians reading this ancient psalm, the promise resonates with special force. We see in Jesus Christ the ultimate fulfillment of this prophetic hope. In his death and resurrection, Christ has indeed redeemed us from the realm of the dead. He has paid the ransom we could never pay, accomplishing what human wealth and wisdom could never do. The resurrection of Jesus transforms this psalmist's hope into historical reality and future certainty.

This verse also speaks to our present moment. We live in a culture obsessed with accumulation and preservation, accumulating wealth, preserving youth, and extending life by any means possible. Like the people described in Psalm 49, we can easily fall into the trap of thinking that our security comes from what we build, earn, or control.

This verse reminds us that our true security rests in God's redemptive power alone.

The promise here is not that we will avoid suffering or escape physical death. Rather, death will not have the final word. The one who created us loves us too much to let death separate us from him permanently. Where the grave seems to be an ending, God sees a transition. Where we see loss, God promises presence.

Living in light of this promise changes how we face each day. When we know that God will redeem us and take us to himself, we are freed from the anxious grasping that characterizes so much of human existence. We can hold possessions lightly, face mortality honestly, and invest our lives in what truly matters: loving God and loving others.

PRAYER

Gracious God, our redeemer, thank you for the promise that death is not the end. When I am tempted to find security in temporary things, remind me that you alone can redeem me from death's power. Help me live today with the confidence that I belong to you, now and forever. Through Christ, who conquered death, Amen.

WHEN GRATITUDE BECOMES WORSHIP

Sacrifice thank offerings to God, fulfill your vows to the Most High, and call on me in the day of trouble; I will deliver you, and you will honor me (Psalm 50:14–15).

In Psalm 50, God speaks through Asaph with startling directness. The Almighty, who "summons the earth from the rising of the sun to where it sets," does not need our religious performances. He owns the cattle on a thousand hills. Yet in verses 14–15, he makes a profound request: offer thanks, keep your promises, and call on him in trouble. This simple triad reveals the heart of what God truly desires from his people.

"Sacrifice thank offerings to God." The Hebrew word for "thank offerings" carries the weight of public acknowledgment. This was not meant to be a private sentiment whispered in quiet moments, though those have their place. God calls us to express our gratitude actively, vocally, and visibly. In ancient Israel, a thank offering was a communal celebration where the worshiper shared their sacrifice with family and friends, telling the story of God's faithfulness. It was gratitude made tangible, thanksgiving that drew others into the narrative of God's goodness.

How easily we forget this in our modern pursuit of private spirituality. We consume God's blessings like we consume everything else, individually, privately, moving quickly to the next thing. Yet God designed thanksgiving to be declarative. When we sacrifice thank offerings, we interrupt our own narratives of self-sufficiency. We acknowledge out loud that every good gift flows from the Father of lights. This kind of gratitude costs us something: our pride, our illusion of control, our carefully maintained image of independence.

"Fulfill your vows to the Most High." Here God moves from gratitude to integrity. The vows he speaks of are not casual promises but sacred commitments made in desperate moments or seasons of devotion. How many of us have bargained with God in our extremity? How many promises have we made in the valley that we conveniently forgot on the mountaintop?

God does not need our promises, but we need to keep them. Our integrity before God shapes our integrity before everyone else. When we follow through on what we have committed to the Most High, we are training our souls in faithfulness. We are learning that our words matter, that covenant-keeping is the bedrock of relationship, that God takes our promises as seriously as he takes his own. This is not legalism; it is the practice of becoming people whose yes means yes and whose no means no.

"Call on me in the day of trouble; I will deliver you." What remarkable condescension. The God who needs nothing invites us to need him. He does not promise to eliminate trouble from our lives; that would rob us of opportunities to know him as deliverer. Instead, he promises to meet us in our trouble, to respond when we cry out, to demonstrate his power in our weakness.

Notice the economy of this exchange. We call; he delivers. There is no complicated formula, no prerequisite worthiness, no ritual to perform first, just honest, desperate prayer. God loves to be needed. He is not offended by our dependence; he is offended by our pretense of self-sufficiency. The day of trouble is not evidence of God's absence but an invitation to experience his presence in new ways.

"And you will honor me." Here, the circle completes itself. We give thanks, keep our vows, call on God in trouble, experience his deliverance, and then honor him, which leads us back to thanksgiving. This is the rhythm of faithful living: gratitude, integrity, dependence, deliverance, worship, and gratitude again. It is an upward spiral, each revolution drawing us deeper into a relationship with the One who needs nothing yet desires everything from us.

God is not impressed by the size of our religious activities. He is looking for an authentic relationship expressed through grateful hearts, faithful lives, and humble dependence. When we offer thanks, keep our promises, and cry out to him in our need, we give him what religious ritual never can: our real selves, in our actual circumstances, trusting his actual character.

The question for us today is simple: Will we trade the performance of religion for the practice of relationship? Will we make gratitude our worship, integrity our witness, and dependence our strength?

PRAYER

Father, you who own everything yet desire our hearts, teach us the sacrifice of thanksgiving. Help us keep the promises we have made to you, even when no one else is watching. When trouble comes, and it will come, give us the faith to call on you, trusting that you hear and you will deliver. May our lives honor you not through empty ritual but through a grateful, faithful, dependent relationship. In Jesus' name, Amen.

PSALM 51

A PLEA FOR MERCY AND RESTORATION

*Have mercy on me, O God, according to your unfailing love;
according to your great compassion blot out my transgressions.
Wash away all my iniquity and cleanse me from my sin* (Psalm
51:1–2).

The opening verses of Psalm 51 confront us with one of the most profound expressions of human need in the entire scriptural corpus. Whether we accept the traditional superscription attributing this psalm to David in the aftermath of his sin with Bathsheba or whether we view it as a liturgical composition for communal confession, the psalm speaks to a universal human condition: the desperate recognition of wrongdoing and the urgent plea for divine mercy. In these two verses, the psalmist employs multiple Hebrew terms for transgression and purification, each word choice revealing layers of theological meaning that transform a personal lament into a timeless meditation on repentance and restoration.

The psalm begins with an urgent imperative: "Have mercy on me, O God." The Hebrew verb means to "show favor," "be gracious." This is not a casual request but a desperate cry. The verb form demands immediate attention, and the directness of address, simply "O God," strips away all pretense and ceremony. The psalmist stands before the divine presence with nothing to offer but vulnerability. The Hebrew verb carries connotations not merely of pity but of undeserved favor, an action that flows from the benefactor's character rather than the recipient's merit. This distinction is crucial: the psalmist does not appeal to his own righteousness or any compensation he might offer. Instead, he appeals exclusively to God's nature.

The first verse provides the grounds for this petition through two parallel phrases that deepen our understanding of divine mercy.

"According to your unfailing love" invokes *hesed*, the magnificent Hebrew concept that encompasses covenant loyalty, steadfast love, and gracious commitment. The word *hesed* describes God's refusal to abandon the covenant relationship despite human failure. It is not conditional on human worthiness but flows from God's character and commitment. The parallel phrase, "according to your great compassion," employs a word derived from the Hebrew word for womb. This term suggests an almost maternal compassion, an instinctive, tender response that arises from the very depths of divine nature. Together, these two phrases paint a portrait of God whose essential character is oriented toward mercy and restoration rather than punishment and abandonment.

The second verse shifts from petition to urgent request, introducing three Hebrew terms for human wrongdoing, each with distinct nuances. "Blot out my transgressions" uses the verb "to wipe away" or "obliterate," creating an almost physical image of cleansing from rebellion. The Hebrew word means willful transgression against known authority. The psalmist then requests, "Wash away all my iniquity," employing the verb for washing clothes, suggesting a thorough cleansing from iniquity. The Hebrew word for iniquity means the twisting or perversion of proper order and relationship. Finally, the verse concludes with "cleanse me from my sin," using the term for ritual purification and the Hebrew word for "missing the mark." This threefold terminology, rebellion, distortion, and failure, encompasses the full spectrum of human moral failure.

What makes this expression of confession particularly powerful is that the psalmist does not merely request forgiveness in the abstract sense of non-punishment. Rather, he asks for active transformation: blotting out, washing away, cleansing. These are not passive states but dynamic divine actions that restore the person to wholeness and right relationship. The progression moves from the external act of obliteration to washing, then to the internal state of ritual purity. The psalmist understands that genuine restoration requires not merely the remission of guilt but the renewal of one's standing in relationship with God and the community of faith.

We encounter in these verses a theology of repentance that remains breathtakingly contemporary. In our modern context, where shame often silences confession and where we sometimes attempt to manage our guilt through minimization or excuse-making, Psalm 51:1–2 calls us to radical honesty. The psalmist does not negotiate, does not offer excuses, does not attempt to earn his way back into divine favor. He simply stands before God, acknowledging his need and appealing to God's nature as his only ground for hope.

The pastoral significance of these verses cannot be overstated. Whether we face devastating moral failure, chronic patterns of sin, or simply the accumulated weight of human limitation, these words give us language for an authentic encounter with the God who desires our restoration more than our punishment. They teach us that mercy is not the absence of moral seriousness but rather God's serious commitment to our transformation and renewal.

PRAYER

Eternal God, grant us the courage of this psalmist to acknowledge our need for your mercy. Wash away the denial and defensiveness that prevent genuine transformation. Blot out the rebellion within us, not through our effort but through your unfailing love and great compassion. Cleanse us from the patterns of sin that entangle us, and restore us to right relationship with you and with one another. We appeal not to our own worthiness but to your gracious character. Transform us, we pray, into vessels fit for your use and your glory. Amen.

ROOTED IN THE HOUSE OF GOD

But I am like an olive tree flourishing in the house of God; I trust in God's unfailing love for ever and ever (Psalm 52:8).

The olive tree stands as one of the ancient world's most remarkable symbols of endurance and vitality. Unlike many plants that demand ideal conditions, the olive tree thrives in rocky, difficult soil. It withstands scorching heat and extended drought. Its roots dig deep, sometimes penetrating fifteen feet into the earth, drawing sustenance from hidden sources. And perhaps most remarkably, an olive tree can live for thousands of years, continuing to bear fruit even in old age.

When David declares, "But I am like an olive tree flourishing in the house of God," he is making a profound statement about the nature of spiritual vitality. This verse appears at the conclusion of Psalm 52, a psalm written in response to Doeg the Edomite's betrayal. David has just described the fate of those who trust in their own strength and wealth rather than God. In contrast, he positions himself not as self-sufficient, but as deeply rooted in God's presence.

Notice the location David emphasizes: "in the house of God." The olive tree does not flourish in isolation or by its own merit. Its vitality comes from being planted in the right place. For David, writing before the temple was built, the house of God represented wherever God's presence dwelt. For us today, this means living in continuous communion with God, dwelling in his presence through prayer, worship, and obedience.

The imagery of flourishing carries tremendous weight. This is not mere survival or barely getting by spiritually. The Hebrew word suggests greenness, freshness, and verdancy. It speaks of a life marked by spiritual health and productivity. Just as the olive tree produces oil for light, healing, and consecration, believers rooted in God's presence produce the fruit that brings light to dark places and healing to broken people.

But David does not claim this flourishing comes from his own efforts or righteousness. Instead, he immediately points to the true source: "I trust in God's unfailing love for ever and ever." The foundation of spiritual vitality is not our strength, wisdom, or determination. It is trust in God's *hesed*, that covenant love that never wavers, never diminishes, and never runs out.

This unfailing love provides what the olive tree's deep roots provide: a constant, reliable source of life. When circumstances become difficult, when the heat of trials beats down, when the soil of our situation seems impossibly hard, God's love remains. We do not flourish because life is easy or because we are exceptionally strong. We flourish because we are connected to an inexhaustible source.

The phrase "for ever and ever" extends this trust beyond temporary relief or short-term solutions. David is not trusting God's love just for today's crisis or this season's challenge. He is anchoring his entire existence, present and future, in the eternal constancy of God's character. This is the kind of trust that transforms how we face uncertainty, endure hardship, and maintain hope when circumstances suggest despair.

Consider what this means practically. The olive tree does not panic during drought because its roots reach water that the surface never sees. Similarly, when our visible circumstances look barren, our trust in God's unfailing love allows us to draw from resources the world cannot perceive. We have access to peace that transcends understanding, joy that exists independent of circumstances, and strength that comes not from ourselves but from the Lord.

Furthermore, olive trees become more valuable with age. Their wood grows harder, more beautiful, and more useful. Their oil production often continues for centuries. This challenges our culture's obsession with youth and immediate results. Spiritual maturity is not about instant transformation but about steady, patient growth in the house of God. The longer we are rooted in his presence, trusting in his unfailing love, the more fruit we bear and the more stable we become.

Today, wherever you find yourself, whether in seasons of abundance or scarcity, certainty or confusion, you have the same invitation David embraced. You can choose to be like an olive tree flourishing in the house of God. Not by your own strength, but by sinking your roots deep into the soil of his presence. Not by trusting in what you can see or control, but by trusting in his unfailing love that endures forever.

PRAYER

Faithful God, plant me deeply in your presence. Let my roots grow down into the soil of your unfailing love. In seasons of drought and difficulty, help me trust that you are my constant source of life. Make me fruitful not by my own effort but by my connection to you. May my life flourish to your glory, today and always. Amen.

THE SILENT REBELLION

The fool says in his heart, 'There is no God.' They are corrupt, and their ways are vile; there is no one who does good (Psalm 53:1).

In the quiet chambers of the human heart, a conversation is constantly taking place. It is not always a conversation of words, but of inclinations, desires, and fundamental assumptions. Psalm 53:1 pierces through the noise of our daily lives to address the most dangerous whisper of all: "The fool says in his heart, 'There is no God.'"

To understand this verse, we must first redefine what it means to be a "fool." In the biblical context, folly is not a lack of intellectual horsepower or a low IQ. Rather, it is a moral and spiritual orientation. The Hebrew word used here, *nabal*, describes someone who is spiritually insensitive, someone who lives as if they are the ultimate authority over their own life. This "practical atheism" is often more common than the intellectual variety. It is the lifestyle of those who may acknowledge God with their lips on Sunday but dismiss his sovereignty in their business dealings, their relationships, or their private thoughts on Monday.

Notice that the fool makes this claim "in his heart." This is a deliberate choice. The heart, in Scripture, is the seat of the will and the emotions. By denying God in the heart, the individual is attempting to evict the ultimate landlord. If there is no God, there is no ultimate judge; if there is no judge, there is no objective moral law; and if there is no law, one is free to pursue one's own desires without the "inconvenience" of divine accountability.

The psalmist immediately links this internal denial to external decay: "They are corrupt, and their ways are vile; there is no one who does good." This is the inevitable trajectory of a life lived outside the light of the Creator. When we remove the sun from the center of our solar system, the planets do not just find a new rhythm; they fly off into the dark, chaotic void. Similarly, when we remove God from the center of our internal world, our character begins to erode. Our "goodness" becomes a matter of convenience or social performance rather than a reflection of God's holiness.

It is tempting to read Psalm 53:1 and point a finger at the "villains" of the world, the staunch mockers or the notoriously wicked. However, the Apostle Paul quotes this very passage in Romans 3 (Romans 3:12) to remind us that we all carry a bit of this "foolishness" within us. We are all prone to moments where we act as if God is absent, invisible, or indifferent.

The "vile ways" mentioned are not always grand crimes; they are the subtle corruptions of pride, the hardening of our hearts toward the suffering of others, and the pursuit of self-glory. When we claim to be the masters of our own fate, we are, in that moment, playing the fool.

The beauty of the Psalms is that they do not leave us in the wreckage of our own folly. By identifying the problem, the denial of God's presence, the psalmist points us toward the solution: surrender.

To cease being a fool is to stop whispering "There is no God" and to start shouting "he is here." It is an invitation to bring God back into the "heart," the center of our decision-making and our secret thoughts. When we acknowledge him, the corruption begins to clear. Our ways, once vile and self-serving, are slowly transformed by his grace into paths of righteousness.

The pursuit of "doing good" is not a ladder we climb to reach God; it is the natural fruit of a heart that has finally admitted that he is exactly who he says he is.

Consider for a moment the areas of your own life where God has been quietly pushed to the margins. Perhaps it is your finances, where anxiety drives every decision and prayer is an afterthought. Perhaps it is your relationships, where pride and self-protection have crowded out humility and grace. The "fool" of Psalm 53 is rarely a dramatic villain; he is often simply a busy, well-intentioned person who has grown accustomed to making plans without consulting the One who holds every plan in his hands. Recognizing this tendency in ourselves is not cause for despair; it is the first act of wisdom.

True wisdom, then, begins the moment we stop rehearsing our own sufficiency and start resting in his. This is not passivity; it is the most courageous act a human being can perform. To say "God, you are here, and I need you" in a culture that prizes self-reliance is a quiet act of rebellion against the spirit of the age. The psalmist does not write as someone standing above the fray; he writes as someone who has seen what happens when the heart goes dark and has chosen, by grace, to let the light back in. That same choice is available to you and me, not once, but every single morning.

PRAYER

Heavenly Father, search my heart today. I confess that there are moments when I live as if you do not exist, when I lean on my own understanding and seek my own glory. Forgive me for the "practical atheism" that creeps into my thoughts and actions. Soften my spirit where it has become corrupt or indifferent. I acknowledge you as the sovereign king of my life. May my heart no longer whisper denials, but instead sing of your presence and your goodness. Guide my steps today, that I might do what is right in your sight. In the name of Jesus, Amen.

FINDING HELP

Surely God is my help; the Lord is the one who sustains me
(Psalm 54:4).

The psalmist's declaration in Psalm 54:4 strikes at the very heart of what it means to trust God in the face of adversity. "Surely God is my help; the Lord is the one who sustains me." These words are not mere platitudes uttered in a moment of comfort. Rather, they represent a deliberate affirmation of faith spoken in the context of genuine peril. To understand this verse, we must first recognize the circumstances that prompted it.

Psalm 54 appears to have been written during a time when the psalmist faced enemies who sought his life. The superscription suggests a connection to David's flight from Saul, when he took refuge among the Ziphites, who betrayed him to his pursuer. Whether this historical context is accurate or not, the psalm clearly addresses a situation of vulnerability and threat. The psalmist begins by crying out: "Save me, O God, by your name, and vindicate me by your strength" (Psalm 54:1). The enemies are described as those who "pay no regard to God" (Psalm 54:3). Into this crucible of fear and danger comes the remarkable confession of verse 4.

The Hebrew word translated "help" carries the sense of aid or assistance. It is the same word used to describe how God helped the Israelites in Egypt, delivering them from bondage. But notice what makes this particularly striking: the help the psalmist speaks of is not primarily military strength or material resources. Rather, it is the direct intervention of God himself. The psalmist does not say, "Surely I have friends to help me," or "Surely I have wealth to sustain me." Instead, he places his ultimate confidence in God as his helper.

The second part of the verse deepens this affirmation: "the Lord is the one who sustains me." The word "sustains" comes from a Hebrew word which literally means "to support" or "to uphold." It depicts someone or something providing stability, maintaining it, and keeping it alive. In ancient Israel, this was the language used to describe how God sustained the people in the wilderness with manna from heaven (Exodus 16). It speaks of ongoing, moment-by-moment provision and care.

What makes this confession so powerful is its radical simplicity and exclusivity. In a moment of crisis when the psalmist might have been tempted to seek help through deception, compromise, or strategic alliance with the enemies of his enemies, he instead looks directly to the Lord. He places his dependence entirely upon God, with no contingency plans and no backup strategies.

This kind of faith is not naïve or foolish. Rather, it reflects a mature understanding of where true security lies. The psalmist has learned through experience that human help, while sometimes valuable, is ultimately insufficient and unreliable. Only God possesses the power to sustain us through genuine trials. Moreover, only God possesses perfect wisdom to know what we truly need, rather than what we merely think we need.

The structure of the psalm bears this out. After making his confession of faith in verse 4, the psalmist goes on to express confidence that God will repay his enemies for their evil (verses 5–7). Significantly, the psalmist does not himself take vengeance. Rather, he entrusts his cause to God. This demonstrates that his trust in God's help and sustenance is not merely emotional comfort; it translates into concrete action, the willingness to refrain from self-help measures and to allow God to work on his behalf.

For us as contemporary believers, this verse offers profound reassurance. We, too, face enemies, not always physical adversaries, but spiritual opponents and the circumstances of a broken world that can overwhelm us. We face situations of loss, illness, betrayal, and uncertainty. In such moments, the psalmist's confession becomes our own: "Surely God is my help; the Lord is the one who sustains me."

This affirmation does not guarantee that our trials will end or that our enemies will be defeated immediately. Rather, it promises that we will not face these trials alone, and that God will provide us with the spiritual resources to endure them and ultimately to overcome them. As we learn to trust in God's help and sustenance, we discover that our greatest security does not lie in the absence of trouble but in the presence of our faithful God.

PRAYER

Eternal God, we come before you acknowledging that our ultimate help and sustenance come from you alone. In moments of fear and uncertainty, help us to remember the psalmist's confession and to place our trust wholly in your care. Grant us the courage to release our anxieties into your hands and the faith to believe that you will uphold us through every trial. We thank you for your constant presence and your unfailing love. May we grow ever more confident in your help as we walk with you through all the seasons of our lives. In the name of Jesus Christ, our Lord and our hope, we pray. Amen.

FINDING GOD IN EVERY HOUR

As for me, I call to God, and the LORD saves me. Evening, morning and noon I cry out in distress, and he hears my voice (Psalm 55:16–17).

There is something profoundly human about the rhythm David describes in Psalm 55:16–17. Evening, morning, and noon, three distinct moments marking the arc of each day, and in each one, a cry to God. This is not the polished prayer of a saint who has it all together. This is the desperate, daily practice of someone who knows where his help comes from.

David wrote these words during one of his darkest seasons. Betrayed by a close friend, surrounded by enemies, feeling the weight of isolation and danger, he could have given up on prayer altogether. After all, when life falls apart, it is tempting to wonder if God is listening at all. Yet David's response to the crisis was not to abandon his faith but to intensify it. He established a rhythm of return, a pattern of crying out that structured his entire day around God's presence.

What strikes me most about these verses is their honest simplicity. David does not claim that praying three times daily solves all his problems instantly. He says he cries out "in distress," and God "hears" his voice. There's a gap between the crying and the deliverance, between the prayer and the answer. But in that gap, something vital happens: God listens. God is present. And somehow, that presence becomes the lifeline David needs to make it through.

The three-times-daily rhythm is not arbitrary. It sanctifies the full cycle of human experience. Evening prayer meets us when we are exhausted, reviewing the day's failures and frustrations. Morning prayer catches us in our anxiety about what lies ahead, when the day feels too heavy to lift. Noon prayer interrupts us in the midst of chaos, reminding us that we do not have to wait until we are depleted to reconnect with God.

This rhythm teaches us that prayer is not reserved for emergencies or scheduled only for calm, contemplative moments. It is woven into the fabric of ordinary time. David did not wait until he felt spiritual or composed. He cried out in distress, bringing his raw, unfiltered self to God repeatedly throughout each day. There is freedom in this; we do not have to clean ourselves up before approaching God. We can come as we are, as often as we need to.

In our distracted age, establishing such a rhythm feels countercultural. We are conditioned to solve problems through endless productivity, to manage stress through entertainment, and to numb pain rather than voice it. The idea of pausing three times daily to cry out to God can seem impractical, even impossible. Yet David's practice suggests that this consistent return to God is not a luxury for the spiritually advanced; it is a necessity for anyone who wants to survive life's storms with their soul intact.

What transforms this practice from ritual into relationship is David's confidence: "The LORD saves me." Not "maybe the LORD will save me" or "I hope God is paying attention." David speaks with the assurance of someone who has tested this pattern and found it trustworthy. His evening, morning, and noon prayers are not shots in the dark; they are conversations with a God who has proven faithful.

This does not mean David's life became easy or that his problems vanished. The psalm itself reveals ongoing struggle. But through the rhythm of prayer, David discovered something more sustaining than quick fixes: he found that God's attentive presence could carry him through whatever he faced. The Lord hears. The Lord saves. And that is enough.

For us, the invitation is clear. We do not need to manufacture a crisis to pray, nor do we need to wait for perfect peace. We simply need to begin establishing our own rhythm of return, whatever that looks like in our context. Maybe it is three specific times, like David. Maybe it is bookending each day with prayer and finding one midday moment to pause. The specific form matters less than the consistent practice of bringing our whole selves, distress and all, to the God who listens.

In a world that constantly demands our attention and fragments our focus, the ancient rhythm of prayer becomes an anchor. Evening, morning, and noon, we are reminded that we are not alone, that someone hears, and that crying out in our need is not weakness but wisdom.

PRAYER

Lord, teach me the rhythm of returning to you. In my evening weariness, morning anxiety, and midday chaos, help me remember to cry out. Thank you for hearing every prayer, for not letting my distress drive you away, and for your saving presence always near. Give me the faith to trust you in the gap between my crying and your deliverance. Amen.

WHEN FEAR MEETS TRUST

When I am afraid, I put my trust in you. In God, whose word I praise— in God I trust and am not afraid. What can mere mortals do to me? (Psalm 56:3–4).

The superscript of Psalm 56 tells us that David composed this psalm when the Philistines seized him in Gath. We can imagine the terror of his situation: alone, far from home, surrounded by enemies who would gladly see him dead. Yet from this crucible of fear emerges one of Scripture's most profound statements about the relationship between fear and faith. These two verses form the emotional and theological heart of the psalm, and they speak directly to our contemporary struggles with anxiety and trust.

The Hebrew structure of verse 3 reveals something remarkable about the proper place of fear in the spiritual life. The opening Hebrew word typically means "when" or "if," but in this context, it means "at the time when," not "if" but "when." David does not promise a life without fear. Rather, he acknowledges fear as an inevitable human experience. Then comes the crucial pivot: "I put my trust in you." The Hebrew verb carries the idea of placing one's complete confidence in another, of leaning one's full weight upon someone or something. It is not a tentative hope; it is a decisive act of the will. When fear arrives, and it will, we deliberately redirect our weight, our trust, our vulnerability toward God.

This framing is radically different from much modern spirituality, which often teaches that faith eliminates fear. Scripture offers something more honest and profound: faith acknowledges fear and responds to it with intentional trust. David does not say "I am not afraid"; he says "when I am afraid, I trust." Fear and faith are not opposites but rather two responses that must be negotiated in the human heart. The person of faith is not the one who never experiences fear but rather the one who, when fear comes, consciously chooses to place their trust in God.

Verse 4 expands and deepens this conviction through parallel construction and escalation. "In God, whose word I praise" contains a significant textual note. The psalmist's trust rests not on his own words or efforts but on God's word. The Hebrew term for word encompasses both the spoken word and the event that fulfills it. God's word is not mere language; it is effective, performative, reality-creating. When we place our trust in God, whose word we praise, we are trusting in a God whose promises have demonstrable power.

The doubling of "In God I trust" in the second half of verse 4 intensifies the commitment. The Hebrew form of the verb here signals a completed action with lasting effects: "I have placed my trust and continue to place my trust." This is not wishy-washy faith but resolute confidence.

Then comes perhaps the most audacious statement: "and am not afraid. What can mere mortals do to me?" The conjunction is emphatic: "and I will not fear." The shift from past to future tense is significant. David moves from his present state ("I am afraid, I put my trust") to his achieved condition ("I will not fear"). This is not yet realized in his experience; he is still a fugitive in enemy territory, but it is realized through trust. Trust repositions our fear.

The final rhetorical question, "What can mere mortals do to me?" deliberately uses a Hebrew word that emphasizes human weakness and mortality. Yes, mortals can wound us, imprison us, even kill us. David knew this danger intimately. But mortals cannot touch the deepest part of our identity, the part that is eternally connected to God. We are not ultimately vulnerable to human power because our essential security rests in God alone.

This psalm speaks powerfully to our contemporary anxieties. We face economic uncertainties, health crises, relational conflicts, and the erosion of stability we once took for granted. The culture around us offers various remedies: self-sufficiency, positive thinking, soothing medications, and distraction through entertainment. These may have their place, but Psalm 56 offers something deeper: the possibility that fear, when brought into relationship with trust in God, becomes the occasion for genuine faith rather than its contradiction.

The invitation of this psalm is to stop trying to eliminate fear and start learning to trust when afraid. That is the hard, true, liberating path of genuine faith.

PRAYER

O God, whose word we praise, we confess that fear often overwhelms us. We fear for our safety, our futures, our loved ones. We fear our own inadequacy and the instability of this world. Yet you invite us to bring our fear into the presence of your trustworthiness. Grant us the grace to place our weight upon you, not denying fear but responding to it with active trust. Help us remember that we rest not in human power but in the eternal reality of your word and your faithfulness. In our trembling, give us your strength. Amen.

FINDING REFUGE IN THE STORM

Have mercy on me, my God, have mercy on me, for in you I take refuge. I will take refuge in the shadow of your wings until the disaster has passed (Psalm 57:1).

There is something profoundly human about the cry that opens Psalm 57. "Have mercy on me, my God, have mercy on me." The repetition is not redundant; it is the sound of a soul in genuine distress, reaching out with both hands to grasp hold of God. David wrote these words while hiding in a cave, pursued by King Saul, who sought his life. The historical context matters because it reminds us that this is not abstract theology; it is a prayer forged in the furnace of real fear.

What strikes me most about this verse is how David moves so quickly from a desperate plea to a confident declaration. In the same breath that he begs for mercy, he announces his decision: "in you I take refuge." This is not wishful thinking or passive hope. The Hebrew word for "take refuge" carries the sense of actively fleeing to a place of safety, of making a deliberate choice about where to run when danger threatens. David does not merely wish he could find refuge in God; he plants himself there with intention.

The image David chooses is tender and surprising. He speaks of hiding "in the shadow of your wings." In ancient Near Eastern thought, this metaphor would have evoked both the protective wings of a mother bird sheltering her young and the wings of the cherubim that overshadowed the mercy seat in the tabernacle, the place where God's presence dwelt among his people. David says that the safest place in the universe, when disaster looms, is not a fortified city or a powerful army. It is being pressed close to the heart of God.

But notice what David does not promise himself: he does not claim that the disaster will be removed immediately. Instead, he takes refuge "until the disaster has passed." There is a realism here that speaks to anyone who has ever waited in the dark. Faith does not always mean instant deliverance. Sometimes it means enduring the storm while sheltered in God's presence, trusting that morning will come even when the night feels endless. David is not denying the reality of his circumstances. Saul really is hunting him, and the danger is genuine, but he is choosing to interpret his situation through the lens of God's character rather than the intensity of his circumstances.

This verse teaches us something crucial about the nature of refuge. When we take shelter in God, we are not hiding from reality; we are finding the truest reality. The shadow of God's wings is more substantial than the cave walls around David, more protective than any human stronghold. Our modern tendency is to seek refuge in control, in contingency plans, in our ability to manage outcomes. But David shows us a different way: acknowledging our complete vulnerability while simultaneously claiming complete safety in God's care.

The double cry for mercy also reminds us that coming to God in our weakness is not a failure of faith; it is the pathway to faith. God does not need us to have it all together before we approach him. He invites our desperate prayers, our repeated pleas, our honest fear. The repetition in David's prayer is not evidence of doubt; it is evidence of relationship. We repeat ourselves to the people we trust, to those we believe are truly listening.

For those of us navigating our own disasters, whether they are external threats or internal turmoil, sudden crises or slow-burning anxieties, this verse offers both comfort and challenge. The comfort is that God's wings are extended, his refuge is available, and his mercy is real. The challenge is that we must actively choose to run to him rather than to lesser shelters. We must decide to wait in his presence "until the disaster has passed" rather than demanding immediate resolution.

David would eventually emerge from that cave. Saul's pursuit would end. But the deeper truth David learned in the darkness would sustain him for the rest of his life: that God's protective presence is more reliable than any favorable circumstance, and his mercy is the only foundation secure enough to build a life upon.

PRAYER

Merciful God, we come to you in our need, as David did. When disasters threaten and fear overwhelms, help us remember that the safest place is close to your heart. Teach us to take refuge in you not only when we have no other options but as our first and constant choice. Shelter us in the shadow of your wings, and give us faith to wait there until the storm passes, trusting in your perfect timing and unfailing love. Amen.

DIVINE JUSTICE VINDICATED

*Then people will say, "Surely the righteous still are rewarded;
surely there is a God who judges the earth"* (Psalm 58:11).

The concluding verse of Psalm 58 offers profound affirmation in the face of widespread injustice. The psalmist has spent the entire prayer lamenting the corruption of judges and the prosperity of the wicked, describing them with vivid imagery as venomous serpents and roaring lions. Yet here, at the culmination, we encounter not despair but confident proclamation. The "then" marks a decisive turning point, signaling not merely temporal sequence but the assured arrival of divine judgment that will vindicate the righteous and expose the futility of wickedness.

The twofold declaration that closes this psalm deserves careful attention. First, the psalmist affirms that "the righteous still are rewarded" or, more literally, "there is a fruit to the righteous." This is not naive optimism but theological conviction rooted in the character of God. The concept of reward or recompense suggests a restoration of balance, a making whole of what has been fractured by injustice. The psalmist asserts that despite appearances to the contrary, those who walk in covenant faithfulness with God will ultimately discover that their righteousness is not meaningless. This vindication may not arrive on our timeline or according to our expectations, but it will arrive.

The second affirmation, "surely there is a God who judges the earth," carries connotations not merely of judgment but also of governance and restoration. This is the God who sits on the divine throne, seeing all things, weighing all actions, and ultimately setting things right. The certainty expressed here through the emphatic double assurance ("Surely . . . surely") reflects the psalmist's unshakable conviction that

God is not indifferent to the suffering of the innocent or the arrogance of the wicked.

What is particularly striking about this verse is its communal dimension. The statement begins with "people will say." This suggests that the vindication of the righteous and the execution of judgment will be so apparent, so unmistakable, that even ordinary people, those not privy to special revelation, will openly acknowledge it. The justice of God will not be a matter of private faith alone but will become publicly evident. This echoes the promise that God's name and character will ultimately be recognized and praised among all peoples.

For contemporary readers, Psalm 58:11 addresses a persistent spiritual struggle: How do we maintain faith in God's justice when the wicked prosper, and the righteous suffer? We live in an age of institutional corruption, when judges and leaders frequently abuse their power. The gap between what should be and what is can seem unbridgeable. The psalmist neither offers easy solutions nor denies the reality of injustice. Rather, the psalmist calls us to transcend the limited perspective of the present moment and to trust in the ultimate purposes of a God whose justice encompasses all time and eternity.

This trust is not passive resignation. The entire context of Psalm 58 demonstrates that faith in God's justice motivates the psalmist to cry out, to bring the injustice before God in prayer, to petition the divine judge to act. We are called to do likewise: to work for justice in our own contexts while maintaining ultimate confidence that God is the final judge of all things.

The promise embedded in this verse also addresses the deepest anxieties of faith. Does my righteousness matter? Does my faithfulness count for anything in a world that often rewards cunning and cruelty? The psalmist responds with unequivocal affirmation: yes. Your righteousness will be rewarded. Not because the universe operates on mechanical principles of karma, but because you serve a God who is attentive, who sees, who judges, and who loves righteousness. The reward consists ultimately not in material prosperity but in restored relationship with God, in peace of conscience, in the knowledge that we have aligned ourselves with the purposes of the divine judge. As we meditate on this verse, we are invited into deeper trust. The injustices that trouble us so deeply have not escaped God's notice. The God who judges the earth will ultimately vindicate those whose trust is placed in him, and all people will come to acknowledge the reality of divine justice.

PRAYER

Eternal God and judge of all the earth, we confess our struggle to trust in your justice when injustice surrounds us. We see the wicked prosper; we witness the righteous suffer. Yet you call us to maintain faith in your righteous judgment that encompasses all time and all eternity. Grant us the courage to pursue justice in our own spheres while entrusting ultimate vindication to you. Strengthen our conviction that righteousness is never meaningless in your eyes, that our faithfulness matters eternally. Help us to live as those who have seen your justice vindicated, confident that your name will be praised among all peoples. Amen.

PSALM 59

A MORNING SONG OF STRENGTH

But I will sing of your strength, in the morning I will sing of your love; for you are my fortress, my refuge in times of trouble (Psalm 59:16).

The ancient city gates are shut tight. Enemy soldiers circle the walls, waiting for dawn to attack. Inside, a man sits awake through the long night, acutely aware of the danger surrounding him. Yet as darkness begins to yield to the first light of morning, he does not cry out in fear; he sings.

This is the context of Psalm 59:16, a verse born not from comfort but from crisis. David penned these words when King Saul's men surrounded his house, intent on killing him. The threat was real, immediate, and terrifying. Yet David's response reveals a profound spiritual truth: the darkest nights can give birth to the most beautiful songs of faith.

Notice that David does not sing *because* his circumstances have changed. The danger remains. The soldiers still lurk. His life is still at stake. What transforms David's response from fear to worship is not the absence of trouble but the awareness of God's presence within it. He chooses to sing "of your strength" and "of your love," making God himself, rather than his deliverance, the subject of his praise.

This distinction matters greatly for our own spiritual lives. How often do we wait for problems to resolve before lifting our voices in gratitude? How often do we withhold our worship until we receive the answer we are seeking? David shows us a different way. He teaches us that worship is not the reward we offer God after deliverance; it is the weapon we wield in the midst of battle.

The timing of David's song is equally significant: "in the morning I will sing." Morning represents new beginnings, fresh mercies, and renewed hope. After a long night of danger and fear, David greets the dawn with a song. This is more than poetic imagery; it is a deliberate spiritual discipline. David chooses to begin his day not by rehearsing his problems but by remembering God's character. Before the day's anxieties can take root, he plants seeds of praise.

We live in an age of morning anxiety, where countless people wake up and immediately scroll through news feeds filled with trouble, checking messages loaded with stress, mentally cataloging everything that could go wrong in the hours ahead. David offers us an alternative rhythm: begin with a song. Start with strength, God's strength. Open your eyes to love, God's love. Before the fortress of your heart is assaulted by the day's demands, remind yourself who your true fortress is.

This brings us to the heart of the verse: "you are my fortress, my refuge in times of trouble." David uses military language to describe his relationship with God. A fortress is not a pleasant vacation spot; it is a stronghold you run to when under attack. A refuge is not where you go when life is easy; it is where you flee when pursued. These are crisis words, emergency words, words that acknowledge life's brutal realities while simultaneously declaring that we are not defenseless against them.

The beauty of God as our fortress is that he is both strong enough to protect us and personal enough to care for us. Unlike stone walls or human armies that can fail, God's protection is certain. Unlike cold shelters that offer safety without comfort, God's refuge is warm with love. He does not merely defend us from danger; he surrounds us with his presence, sings over us with his delight, and holds us through our fear.

Living in this truth transforms how we face our troubles. When God is our fortress, we stop building walls around our hearts to keep pain out. When God is our refuge, we stop running to lesser comforts that numb but never heal. We learn, like David, that the safest place in a dangerous world is not a life free from trouble but a life hidden in God.

We join David's song. Even before our feet hit the floor, we choose to sing of the strength we did not manufacture and the love we did not earn. We make our mouths a fortress against despair by filling them with praise. We make our hearts a refuge for hope by remembering whose we are. And we discover that the song we sing in faith often becomes the testimony we share in victory.

PRAYER

Lord, you are my fortress and my refuge. As this new day begins, I choose to sing of your strength and your love, not because my circumstances are easy, but because you are faithful. When trouble surrounds me, remind me to run to you. When fear whispers lies, let me answer with songs of truth. Be my strong tower today, my safe place, my unchanging rock. In Jesus' name, Amen.

THE RIGHT HAND OF DELIVERANCE

Save us and help us with your right hand, that those you love may be delivered (Psalm 60:5).

There is something profoundly human about the desperate plea that echoes through Psalm 60:5: "Save us and help us with your right hand, that those you love may be delivered." This is not the calm, measured prayer of a quiet morning devotional. This is the raw cry of people who know they are in over their heads and recognize that, without divine intervention, they are finished.

The context matters here. Psalm 60 emerges from a moment of military crisis in David's reign. The superscription tells us it was written when David was fighting on multiple fronts, and Edom had attacked from an unexpected direction. His forces were stretched thin, his people vulnerable, and the situation dire. In that moment of national emergency, David does not turn to a better strategy or more soldiers. He turns to God's right hand.

In ancient Near Eastern culture, the right hand symbolized power, authority, and favor. Kings extended their right hands to bless, warriors wielded swords in their right hands, and covenant agreements were sealed by clasping right hands. When the psalmist appeals to God's right hand, he's asking for the fullness of divine power to intervene in an impossible situation. He's not asking for a gentle touch or a word of encouragement. He is asking God to roll up his sleeves and enter the battle.

But notice the beautiful progression in this verse. It moves from "save us" to "help us" to "those you love may be delivered." The prayer begins with an urgent need: save us now, immediately, from the present danger. It continues with a request for ongoing assistance: help us, not just in this moment but through whatever comes next. And then it concludes with the ultimate purpose: the deliverance of God's beloved.

That final phrase should stop us in our tracks. "Those you love." Not "those who love you," though that is true as well. Not "those who deserve it" or "those who have earned it." Simply those you love. The foundation of our deliverance is not our affection for God, our spiritual resume, or our track record of faithfulness. It is his love for us.

This is where many of us miss the point when we face our own battles. We come to God with our crisis, yes, but often with an underlying anxiety about whether we have qualified for his help. Have we prayed enough? Been faithful enough? Sinned too much lately? But the psalmist understands something crucial: deliverance flows from God's love, not our worthiness. We appeal to his character, not our credentials.

The right hand of God has been extended throughout history. It parted the Red Sea when Israel was trapped between Pharaoh's army and the water. It brought down the walls of Jericho when the military situation seemed hopeless. It delivered David from Goliath, Daniel from the lions, and the three Hebrew young men from the furnace. And supremely, God's right hand raised Jesus from the dead, breaking the power of sin and death once and for all.

For us today, this psalm speaks into every impossible situation we face. Maybe it is not a military crisis, but the battles are no less real. Financial disaster. Broken relationships. Chronic illness. Mental health struggles. Addiction. The loss of someone we love. Circumstances in which we have exhausted our options and realized we cannot save ourselves.

In these moments, Psalm 60:5 gives us permission to cry out with urgency and honesty. We do not have to sanitize our desperation or pretend we are fine. We can come before God and say, "I need your right hand. I need your power. I need you to do what I cannot do." And we can anchor that plea in the most solid foundation available: not our love for him, but his love for us.

The right hand of God is still extended. Still powerful. Still ready to save, help, and deliver. And that hand reaches toward us not because we have done everything right, but because we are loved with an everlasting love.

PRAYER

Father, we lift our eyes to you in this moment, acknowledging that we need your right hand of deliverance. Our resources are insufficient, our strength inadequate, our wisdom limited. Save us and help us, Lord, not because we deserve it, but because you love us. Extend your mighty hand into our impossible situations and do what only you can do. We trust not in our own efforts but in your unfailing love and power. In Jesus' name, Amen.

WHEN YOUR HEART GROWS FAINT

Hear my cry, O God; listen to my prayer. From the ends of the earth I call to you, I call as my heart grows faint; lead me to the rock that is higher than I (Psalm 61:1–2).

There is something profoundly human about David's cry in Psalm 61. He does not approach God with carefully crafted theology or polished religious language. Instead, he comes with raw honesty: "my heart grows faint." These words capture a universal experience: those moments when strength abandons us, when the ground beneath our feet feels unsteady, when we are not sure we can take another step forward.

David identifies himself as calling "from the ends of the earth." This phrase suggests more than geographical distance. It speaks to emotional and spiritual isolation, to that feeling of being far removed from safety, comfort, and stability. Perhaps you know this place. It might be a hospital room where you have received devastating news, a relationship that is crumbling despite your best efforts, or the quiet desperation of financial ruin. The "ends of the earth" is wherever we find ourselves utterly depleted, feeling as though we are on the furthest edge of our capacity to endure.

What is remarkable about this psalm is not just David's honesty about his weakness, but his instinct in the midst of it. When his heart grows faint, he does not first draw on his own resources or summon his inner strength. He does not pretend to be okay or minimize his struggle. Instead, his first impulse is to cry out to God. This is the reflexive faith of someone who has learned where true help comes from.

Notice what David asks for: "lead me to the rock that is higher than I." He is not asking God to remove his circumstances or eliminate his problems immediately. He is asking to be led to a place of stability, perspective, and security that transcends his current situation. The rock higher than himself represents a vantage point he cannot reach on his own, a place where he can see beyond the overwhelming immediacy of his crisis, where he can stand on something more solid than his fluctuating feelings or faltering strength.

This imagery of the rock appears throughout Scripture as a symbol of God's unchanging nature and steadfast reliability. When everything else shifts and crumbles, God remains. When our hearts grow faint, and they will, we need something outside ourselves to anchor to. Our own willpower, positive thinking, or determination will eventually run dry. We need the Rock.

There is beautiful wisdom in recognizing we need to be led to this rock. David does not claim he can climb there himself or that he knows the way. He acknowledges his need for divine guidance even to find refuge. How often do we exhaust ourselves trying to manufacture our own stability, create our own peace, or conjure our own strength? David teaches us that sometimes the most spiritual thing we can do is admit we do not know the way and ask God to lead us.

The psalm also reminds us that God hears our cries from wherever we are. The ends of the earth are not too far from his attention. Your darkest valley is not beyond his reach. Your most overwhelming circumstance does not muffle your voice to his ears. "Hear my cry, O God; listen to my prayer." These are not wishful requests; they are confident appeals based on the character of a God who has shown himself attentive to his children's needs.

When your heart grows faint today, you have permission to acknowledge it. You do not need to pretend you are stronger than you are or spiritualize your struggles into neat packages. Instead, follow David's pattern: cry out honestly to God and ask him to lead you to stability beyond yourself. The Rock is always there, always higher than your circumstances, always more solid than your feelings. Your responsibility is not to climb it alone but to call out and let yourself be led.

This is the paradox of faith: we are strongest when we acknowledge our weakness and look beyond ourselves. We find stability not by standing firm in our own power but by being led to a rock higher than we could ever reach on our own.

PRAYER

Lord, I come to you with a heart that grows faint. Lead me to the Rock that is higher than I am, higher than my circumstances, higher than my fears, higher than my limited perspective. Help me trust that you hear me even from the ends of the earth, and that you are faithful to guide me to the stability and refuge I cannot find on my own. In my weakness, be my strength. Amen.

PSALM 62

FINDING REST IN THE UNSHAKEABLE

Truly my soul finds rest in God; my salvation comes from him.
Truly he is my rock and my salvation; he is my fortress, I will
never be shaken (Psalm 62:1–2).

There is a particular exhaustion that comes not from physical labor but from the soul, a weariness that sleep cannot cure and vacation cannot touch. It is the fatigue of striving, of carrying burdens we were never meant to bear, of building our lives on foundations that shift beneath our feet. Into this universal human condition, David speaks words that echo across millennia: "Truly my soul finds rest in God."

Notice the emphasis. David does not merely say his soul finds rest; he says "truly" it does, as if convincing himself, as if pushing back against every voice that suggests otherwise. This repetition of "truly" at the beginning of both verses is not accidental. It is the language of someone who has tested other sources of security and found them wanting. It is the declaration of someone who has learned, perhaps through painful experience, where genuine rest can and cannot be found.

The rest David describes is not the absence of activity but the presence of peace amid it all. It is not about escaping life's demands but about facing them from a place of deep settledness. When he says his soul finds rest in God, he is speaking of that profound stillness that lies beneath the surface turbulence of daily life, the kind of rest that remains even when circumstances do not change.

This rest flows directly from a stunning reality: "my salvation comes from him." Salvation here encompasses more than a ticket to heaven. In Hebrew thought, salvation means deliverance, rescue, safety, wholeness. It is the assurance that we do not have to be our own saviors, that we do not have to manufacture our own security or orchestrate our own rescue from life's predicaments. The burden of self-salvation is perhaps the heaviest weight we carry, and David names the liberating truth that this burden belongs to God alone.

Then David shifts his metaphor: "Truly he is my rock and my salvation; he is my fortress." These are not decorative images but survival language. In ancient Israel, rocks provided shade in scorching heat and shelter from storms. Fortresses meant protection from enemies, thick walls between you and destruction. David knew both literally; he had hidden in caves and taken refuge in strongholds when Saul hunted him. But he had learned that even these physical refuges were only shadows of what God himself provided.

The beauty of calling God our rock is that rocks do not shift, do not bend to public opinion, do not change with circumstances. In a world of constant flux, where today's certainties become tomorrow's questions, God remains. Our feelings vacillate. Our circumstances pivot. Our relationships evolve. Our bodies age. But the rock remains.

The final declaration carries defiant confidence: "I will never be shaken." This is not naive optimism or denial of life's hardships. David wrote many psalms from places of deep distress. He was not claiming immunity from difficulty but asserting something more profound: when your foundation is God himself, the shaking around you does not have to become shaking within you. The storms may rage, but the anchored ship, though tossed, does not capsize.

This is a countercultural truth. Our culture suggests that security comes from bank accounts, credentials, relationships, or achievements, all good things, but terrible foundations. These can be lost, can fail, can prove insufficient. David points us to the only foundation that cannot be moved because it is not subject to the forces that move everything else.

But here is the practical question: How do we actually experience this? How does our soul find rest in God? It begins with the act of turning, deliberately shifting our attention from all the places we instinctively look for security and consciously placing our weight on God. It is a daily, sometimes moment-by-moment practice of remembering where our salvation truly comes from. It is cultivating an interior life that returns again and again to the rock, the fortress, the unmovable foundation.

The invitation of Psalm 62 is to stop trying to be our own rock and instead to stand on the Rock that does not shift. To let our striving cease, to release our white-knuckled grip on control, and to discover that underneath everything, God holds us.

PRAYER

God, teach my restless soul to find its rest in you alone. When I am tempted to build my life on shifting foundations, on my own strength, on others' approval, or on circumstances that change, anchor me to the unshakeable rock of your presence. Be my fortress when life feels overwhelming and my salvation when I cannot save myself. Help me live today from a place of deep settledness, knowing that because you are my foundation, I will never ultimately be shaken. Amen.

PSALM 63

A LIFELONG COMMITMENT TO WORSHIP

I will bless you as long as I live; I will lift up my hands and call
on your name (Psalm 63:4).

In the heart of Psalm 63, we encounter David's profound declaration of unwavering devotion to God. This verse stands as a testament to the enduring nature of authentic worship, not merely as an occasional religious exercise, but as the fundamental orientation of a life lived in relationship with God.

The psalmist's promise, "as long as I live," encompasses the entirety of human existence. This is not worship confined to sanctuary walls or festival seasons, but a comprehensive life posture. David understands that blessing God, acknowledging his goodness, power, and faithfulness, must permeate every season of life: in abundance and in want, in triumph and in trial, in youth's vigor and age's frailty.

The physical gesture of lifting hands reveals worship as an embodied practice. In ancient Near Eastern culture, raised hands symbolized both surrender and supplication, acknowledging God's sovereignty while expressing complete dependence upon him. This posture suggests vulnerability: hands lifted cannot simultaneously grasp for control or self-protection. It is the stance of one who has learned that true security comes not from what we can hold onto, but from the One to whom we surrender.

Calling "on your name" signifies the covenant relationship between God and his people. In Hebrew thought, a name reflects a person's character and authority. To call upon God's name is to appeal to his revealed nature: his mercy, justice, faithfulness, and love. It recognizes that our relationship with God is grounded in his self-disclosure throughout history.

The structure of this verse reveals the progression of worship: from internal disposition ("I will bless") to physical expression ("lift up my hands") to vocal declaration ("call on your name"). True devotion engages the whole person, heart, body, and voice, in unified response to God's grace.

This commitment takes on deeper meaning when we consider the context of Psalm 63, traditionally associated with David's wilderness experience. Even in circumstances of physical hardship and spiritual dryness, the psalmist commits to a life of worship. This teaches us that blessing God is not contingent upon favorable circumstances, but rather flows from recognizing who God is, regardless of our situation.

For believers today, this verse challenges our tendency toward conditional worship: blessing God when life goes well, falling silent when it does not. David's example calls us to a more mature faith that recognizes God's worthiness of praise as an unchanging reality, not dependent on our changing circumstances.

The phrase also speaks to the perseverance required in spiritual life. Worship is not sustained by emotional highs or mystical experiences alone, but by the deliberate choice to honor God through all of life's seasons. This is worship as a spiritual discipline, a regular practice that shapes character and sustains faith through both desert and promised-land experiences.

Moreover, this verse reminds us that worship is fundamentally relational. We do not merely observe religious rituals; we engage with a personal God who knows our name and calls us by name. The intimacy suggested by calling upon God's name reflects the covenant relationship that makes such a bold approach possible.

As we reflect on these words, we are invited to examine our own commitment to lifelong worship. Will we bless God only when it is convenient, or will our praise transcend circumstances? Will our worship engage our whole being, or remain merely intellectual? Will we call upon his name with the confidence of those who know they are known and loved?David's declaration in Psalm 63:4 stands as both inspiration and challenge: a reminder that authentic faith expresses itself in whole-life, whole-person worship that endures as long as breath remains.

Perhaps the most striking aspect of Psalm 63:4 is its location within the wilderness narrative. David does not wait for deliverance before he worships; he worships in the waiting. This transforms our understanding of prayer itself. We are not called to come before God only when we have something to celebrate, but to approach him in the full honesty of our longing, our weariness, and our unresolved questions. It is precisely in those unresolved spaces that lifting our hands becomes most countercultural, most courageous, and most transformative. When we choose to call upon God's name not because our circumstances have changed but because we trust that he does not change, our worship becomes a school of faith that shapes us from the inside out.

PRAYER

Gracious God, like the psalmist, we commit ourselves to blessing you as long as we live. May our worship not be confined to moments of comfort but extend through every season of our journey. Help us to lift our hands in surrender, trusting in your sovereign care even when we cannot see the way forward. Teach us to call upon your name with confidence, knowing that you are faithful to your promises. Shape us into people whose lives are living hymns of praise, reflecting your goodness to a watching world. Through all our days, may our hearts, hands, and voices unite in worship of you alone. In Christ's name we pray. Amen.

FINDING REFUGE IN RIGHTEOUSNESS

Let the righteous rejoice in the LORD and take refuge in him; let all the upright in heart praise him (Psalm 64:10).

Psalm 64 concludes with a triumphant declaration that stands in stark contrast to the anxiety and fear that permeate its opening verses. David begins this psalm as a man under siege, pleading for protection from the "conspiracy of the wicked" and the "plots of evildoers" (v. 2). Yet by verse 10, we encounter not cowering fear but confident celebration. This dramatic shift reveals a fundamental truth about the nature of divine justice and the believer's response to God's faithfulness.

The Hebrew word for "rejoice" carries connotations of exultation and gladness that go beyond mere happiness. It suggests a deep, abiding joy rooted not in circumstances but in the character of God himself. This rejoicing is specifically "in the LORD," indicating that the source and object of this joy is the covenant God of Israel. The righteous are those who live in alignment with God's moral order, not through perfect performance but through faith that seeks to honor God's ways.

The parallel structure of this verse reveals two complementary responses to God's faithfulness: taking refuge and offering praise. The image of refuge evokes the ancient Near Eastern practice of seeking sanctuary in a temple or with a powerful protector. In the Psalms, this metaphor frequently describes the security found in God's presence and protection. Unlike human refuges that can fail, divine refuge provides absolute security because it rests on God's unchanging character and unlimited power.

The "upright in heart" are distinguished not merely by external religious observance but by internal moral integrity. In Hebrew thought, the heart encompasses not just emotions but the entire inner life, including mind, will, and moral center. Those who are upright in heart have allowed God's truth to penetrate and transform their deepest motivations and desires.

What makes this verse particularly striking is its context within Psalm 64. David has just described God's decisive judgment against the wicked, noting how their own schemes have become their downfall (vv. 7–8). The psalm suggests that divine justice, though sometimes delayed, is ultimately certain. The righteous can rejoice not in vindictive triumph over enemies, but in the vindication of God's moral order and the security this provides for all who trust in him.

This verse also carries eschatological implications. While the righteous experience God's protection in the present age, the ultimate fulfillment of this promise awaits the full establishment of God's kingdom. The praise and refuge described here anticipate the eternal worship and perfect security that characterize the age to come.

For today's believers, Psalm 64:10 offers both comfort and challenge. It reminds us that our joy is not dependent on favorable circumstances but on God's unchanging faithfulness. Even when facing opposition, betrayal, or injustice, we can find refuge in the One whose justice will ultimately prevail. Yet this verse also challenges us to examine whether we are truly among the "righteous" and "upright in heart," not through self-righteous confidence, but through humble dependence on God's grace and a sincere desire to live according to his ways.

The call to praise that concludes this verse is not merely a suggestion but an imperative. Praise is the natural response of those who have experienced God's protection and witnessed his justice. It declares to ourselves, to others, and to the spiritual realm that God alone is worthy of worship and trust.

The communal dimension of this closing verse deserves careful attention. David does not speak of the righteous individual alone, but of a company of the faithful who together rejoice and praise. This corporate aspect of worship reflects a pattern woven throughout the Psalter: the believer who has experienced God's deliverance does not retreat into private gratitude but gathers with the assembly to declare what God has done. The congregation becomes both the audience and the amplifier of praise, as each testimony of divine faithfulness strengthens the faith of those who hear it. In this sense, the final verse of Psalm 64 is not merely a personal confession but an invitation extended to all who will join their voices in the worship of the living God.

Ultimately, Psalm 64:10 confronts us with a choice that every generation must make: will we define our lives by the dangers that surround us, or by the God who surrounds those dangers? The wicked in this psalm were consumed by their own schemes precisely because they built their world around the power of human words and human plans. The righteous, by contrast, build their world around the character and promises of the One whose word called creation into being and whose justice governs its course. To rejoice in the Lord and take refuge in him is therefore not a passive retreat from reality; it is the most clear-eyed and courageous response available to the human heart, a declaration that the last word belongs not to the counsel of the wicked, but to the Lord who reigns in righteousness forever.

PRAYER

Gracious Lord, we thank you that you are our refuge and strength, a very present help in our time of trouble. Please help us to be counted among the righteous who find their joy in you, not in the temporary securities of this world. Purify our hearts so that we might be truly upright before you, and fill our mouths with praise for your faithfulness. When we face opposition or injustice, remind us that you see all things and that your justice will ultimately prevail. May our lives testify to your goodness, and may our praise encourage others to seek refuge in you as well. In your holy name we pray. Amen.

THE UNIVERSAL CALL TO PRAYER

O you who hear prayer, to you all people will come (Psalm 65:2).

In this simple yet profound verse, the psalmist captures one of the most beautiful truths about the nature of God and humanity's deepest longing. David presents God not merely as one who can hear, but as "you who hear prayer," making the act of listening to human hearts a defining characteristic of God.

The Hebrew word for "hear" implies not just auditory reception but active, attentive listening with the intent to respond. This is not a distant God who occasionally tunes in to human concerns, but one whose very nature is oriented toward receiving the cries, whispers, and longings of creation. God is presented as eternally available, perpetually attentive, and consistently responsive to those who call upon his name.

What strikes us immediately is the universal scope of this promise: "all people will come." The psalmist envisions not just the covenant people of Israel, but all humanity eventually recognizing their need for divine connection. This is remarkable considering the ancient Near Eastern context, where gods were typically viewed as territorial or tribal. Here, David glimpses a truth that would later be fully revealed in the New Testament, that God's heart encompasses every nation, tribe, and tongue.

The phrase suggests both inevitability and invitation. "Will come" carries the weight of prophecy: there is something in the human heart that inevitably seeks the transcendent, that recognizes its need for connection with something greater than itself. Yet it also extends an open invitation, suggesting that the door to divine communion stands perpetually open for any who would approach

This verse speaks to the universal human experience of prayer, regardless of religious tradition or cultural background. Across history and geography, people have lifted their voices, hearts, and hands toward heaven. From the parent beside a sick child's bed to the refugee fleeing violence, from the student facing an exam to the elderly person facing mortality, prayer emerges naturally from the human condition. The psalmist suggests this is not coincidental but intentional, reflecting our created design to commune with our Creator.

The positioning of this verse within Psalm 65 is significant. It appears in a psalm celebrating God's provision, forgiveness, and the abundance of creation. The psalmist has just acknowledged human sinfulness and God's gracious atonement, and then immediately declares God to be the one who hears prayer. This sequence suggests that our ability to approach God in prayer is not based on our righteousness but on his grace and mercy.

For believers today, this verse offers profound comfort and challenge. The comfort lies in the assurance that our prayers are truly heard by the One who not only can respond but whose nature compels him to listen attentively. No prayer is too small, no concern too insignificant, no person too marginalized to capture God's attention. The challenge comes in the universal scope: if God hears all people, then our prayers should reflect his heart for all people, not just our immediate circle.

This verse also provides perspective during seasons when God seems silent. The promise is not that God will answer according to our timeline or preferences, but that he hears. Sometimes the most profound response to prayer is the assurance that we have been truly heard by the One who understands us completely and loves us perfectly.

In our fragmented world, where division often seems stronger than unity, Psalm 65:2 points to a fundamental human commonality: our need for divine connection. It suggests that beneath our surface differences lies a shared spiritual hunger that ultimately draws all people toward the same source of hope and help.

Ultimately, Psalm 65:2 invites us to reimagine prayer not as a religious duty or a last resort in times of crisis, but as the natural breath of the soul in communion with its Maker. Just as creation itself continually declares God's glory, so too are we designed to live in an ongoing conversation with the One who formed us. To pray is to step into our truest identity as creatures made for relationship with the living God, and to discover that in every season and circumstance, the ear of heaven is already inclined toward us.

PRAYER

Gracious God, you who hear prayer, we thank you that your ears are always open to our cries and that your heart is moved by our needs. Help us to approach you with confidence, knowing that you welcome all who come to you in sincerity. Expand our hearts to pray not only for ourselves and our loved ones, but for all people everywhere who are seeking you, that they might find in you the hope, healing, and home their souls long for. May our lives reflect your welcoming nature to all who seek you. In your holy name we pray, Amen.

THE FAITHFULNESS OF GOD

Praise be to God, who has not rejected my prayer or withheld his love from me (Psalm 66:20).

In this triumphant declaration that concludes Psalm 66, the psalmist bears witness to two fundamental realities of God's character: his attentiveness to prayer and his unwavering love. These words emerge not from theoretical theology but from lived experience, the testimony of one who has walked through dark valleys and emerged with deeper knowledge of God's faithfulness.

The Hebrew word for "rejected" carries the force of spurning or casting away with contempt. When the psalmist declares that God has not rejected his prayer, he is celebrating something profound: the Almighty, who dwells in unapproachable light, has chosen to incline his ear to human petition. This is not mere religious optimism but a bold assertion rooted in a covenant relationship. God's willingness to receive our prayers reveals his character as *El Shaddai*, the God who is both transcendent and intimately present.

The parallel structure of Hebrew poetry links God's receptiveness to prayer with his steadfast love. This term, often translated as "loving-kindness" or "faithful love," represents one of the most significant theological concepts in the Old Testament. God's love is not merely emotional affection but covenant loyalty, God's binding commitment to his people that endures through circumstances, seasons, and even human unfaithfulness.

For the Christian reader, this covenant love finds its fullest expression in the person of Jesus Christ. What the psalmist celebrated as God's unwithheld love becomes, in the New Testament, the astonishing reality of the incarnation: God himself entering human history to ensure that no barrier, not sin, not death, not the full weight of our brokenness, could ultimately separate his people from his love (Romans 8:38–39). The cross is the definitive answer to every fear that God might one day turn away. When we pray in Christ's name, we do so with a confidence even greater than the psalmist's, for we stand on this side of Calvary, where love was not merely declared but demonstrated at infinite cost.

The context of Psalm 66 deepens our understanding of this verse. Earlier, the psalmist acknowledges that God has tested his people "as silver is tested" (v. 10) and brought them through fire and water. Yet even in seasons of divine discipline and refinement, God's faithful love remains unwithheld. This teaches us that God's love is not contingent upon our circumstances or even our spiritual performance, but flows from his unchanging nature.

Notice the psalmist's confidence: he does not say "I hope God will hear" or "perhaps God loves me," but declares with certainty what God has already done and continues to do. This assurance emerges from a relationship, from a history of walking with God through both triumph and trial. It reflects the kind of mature faith that recognizes God's faithfulness not despite difficulties but often through them.

For us today, this verse offers both comfort and challenge. It comforts us with the assurance that our prayers matter to God, that the Creator of the universe genuinely desires communion with his creatures. Our petitions are not lost in cosmic indifference but received by a loving Father who delights in relationship with his children.

Yet this verse also challenges us to examine our prayer lives. Do we approach God with the confidence of the psalmist, or do we harbor secret doubts about his willingness to hear us? Do we recognize that even when prayers seem unanswered, God's love remains constant? The psalmist's testimony invites us into deeper trust, acknowledging that God's ways of answering prayer may exceed our understanding while his love remains our unshakeable foundation.

There is also a communal dimension to the psalmist's witness that we should not overlook. He does not offer his testimony in isolation but before the assembly, inviting others to hear what God has done for his soul (v. 16). In the same way, our experience of answered prayer and received love is not meant to remain a private treasure. When we share the stories of God's faithfulness, in conversations, in worship, in the simple act of encouraging a struggling brother or sister, we become living echoes of this psalm. The testimony of God's unfailing love multiplies its power as it passes from one life to another, building a community of people who know, by experience and not merely by doctrine, that God hears and that God loves.

As we meditate on these words, we join our voices with the psalmist in praise. We celebrate not only God's mighty acts in history but his personal involvement in our daily lives. We acknowledge that every breath we draw, every moment of joy we experience, every strength we find in weakness, bears witness to God's unrestricted love and his attentive ear.

PRAYER

Gracious God, we join the psalmist in praising you for your faithfulness to hear our prayers and your steadfast love that never fails. Thank you that our cries do not fall upon deaf ears, and that your love is not dependent upon our circumstances or our worthiness. Help us to approach you with the confidence that comes from knowing your character, and may our lives bear witness to your unfailing goodness. In seasons of joy and seasons of testing, may we remember that you have not rejected our prayers nor withheld your love from us. We offer this prayer in grateful trust. Amen.

A LIFETIME OF PRAISE

I will bless you as long as I live; I will lift up my hands and call on your name (Psalm 63:4).

David's words in Psalm 63 emerge from the wilderness, both literally and spiritually. Traditionally associated with his flight from Absalom or his exile in the Judean desert, this psalm captures the heart of someone who has discovered that God's presence transcends circumstances. In verse 4, we encounter a remarkable declaration of lifelong devotion that reveals the transformative power of divine encounter.

What makes David's devotion all the more striking is the context in which it was forged. Wilderness seasons, whether geographic, relational, or spiritual, have a way of stripping away the comfortable supports on which we so often lean. It is in these stripped-down places that faith either deepens into bedrock trust or quietly erodes. For David, the desert did not diminish his longing for God; it intensified it. The absence of the temple, of community worship, of familiar rhythms only sharpened his hunger for the One who could not be left behind. His praise in the wilderness reminds us that genuine devotion is not the product of comfortable circumstances but is revealed precisely when circumstances are anything but comfortable.

The phrase "as long as I live" carries profound theological weight. The Hebrew word encompasses not merely biological existence but the fullness of life itself. David is not offering a temporary commitment contingent on favorable conditions, but rather pledging his entire life to blessing God. This echoes the Shema's (Deuteronomy 6:4–9) call to love God with all one's heart, soul, and strength, a total orientation of being toward God.

The physical gesture of lifting hands connects us to ancient Israel's worship practices, where raised hands signified both surrender and reaching toward heaven. Archaeological evidence from the ancient Near East reveals that this posture was universally recognized as an attitude of prayer and worship. Yet David's gesture moves beyond mere ritual; it becomes the embodiment of his inner disposition. The lifting of hands represents the lifting of his entire being toward God.

"Calling on your name" invokes the rich biblical tradition of the divine name as revelation of character and presence. To call upon God's name is to appeal to God's revealed nature, the One who is faithful, merciful, and present with the covenant people. David's commitment to bless and call upon God's name throughout his lifetime reflects his understanding that worship is not episodic but integral to faithful living.

This verse stands in beautiful tension with human frailty. While we often struggle to maintain consistency in our spiritual disciplines, David models what it means to anchor one's life in worship that transcends momentary feelings or circumstances. His example challenges us to consider whether our praise of God depends on favorable conditions or flows from a deeper recognition of God's unchanging character.

There is also a communal dimension to this act of praise that deserves our attention. While David speaks in the first person, his words emerge from a tradition of corporate worship deeply embedded in Israel's identity. To bless God and call upon the divine name was never meant to be an entirely solitary exercise. The gathered community of faith has always served as a school of praise, the place where wavering hearts are steadied by the witness of those who have praised through harder trials than our own. When our individual devotion falters, we are sustained by those who stand beside us, still lifting their hands. This is why the rhythms of communal worship, however imperfect the gathering may be, remain an irreplaceable gift rather than an optional supplement to personal faith.

The structure of David's commitment, blessing, lifting hands, and calling on God's name suggests a rhythm of worship that engages mind, body, and voice. This holistic approach to devotion reminds us that faith involves our entire being, not merely intellectual assent or emotional response. True worship integrates our thoughts, physical presence, and spoken words in a unified offering to God.

In our contemporary context, David's lifetime pledge offers both inspiration and challenge. In a culture of temporary commitments and conditional relationships, the psalmist's unwavering devotion stands as a counter-narrative. His words invite us to consider what it might mean to orient our entire lives around blessing God, regardless of the wilderness seasons we may face.

The beauty of this verse lies not in its demand for perfect consistency, which none of us can achieve, but in its vision of life lived in conscious relationship with God. David's commitment models a spirituality rooted not in performance but in recognition of God's worthiness of lifelong praise. Even when we fail to maintain such consistency, God's faithfulness remains constant, inviting us back into the rhythm of worship that brings life and meaning to our days.

PRAYER

Gracious God, like David in the wilderness, we come before you with the desire to bless your name throughout our lives. Help us to lift not only our hands but our hearts, our hopes, and our whole selves toward you each day. When circumstances challenge our devotion and when our consistency wavers, remind us of your unchanging faithfulness. Grant us grace to make worship not merely an event but a way of life, calling upon your name in both triumph and trial. May our lives become a continuous offering of praise to you, who are worthy of all honor and glory. Amen.

REJOICING IN GOD

May the righteous be glad and rejoice before God; may they be happy and joyful (Psalm 68:3).

In a world often marked by struggle, uncertainty, and sorrow, Psalm 68:3 rings out like a bell of hope, calling God's people to something beautiful and profound: joy. This verse does not merely suggest that the righteous might find happiness; it declares with confident expectation that they should be glad, should rejoice, should overflow with happiness and joy in God's presence.

The Hebrew words used here paint a vivid picture of celebration. The word "glad" suggests deep satisfaction and contentment, while "rejoice" conveys a sense of spinning or whirling with delight, the kind of uninhibited joy we see in children at play. The doubled emphasis on happiness and joy reinforces the idea that this is not a fleeting emotion but a settled state of the heart that finds its source in God himself.

What makes this joy distinctly different from the world's pursuit of happiness is its location: "before God." This joy is not dependent on circumstances, achievements, or the fulfillment of our desires. Instead, it flows from being in the presence of God, from knowing that we stand accepted and beloved before the Creator of the universe. When we truly grasp what it means to be righteous, not through our own efforts but through God's grace, joy becomes the natural response of our hearts.

The psalmist's use of "may" is significant. This is not a command forcing artificial cheerfulness but a blessing, a prayer, a hopeful declaration of what should characterize those who walk with God. It acknowledges that joy might not always come easily or naturally, especially in seasons of trial, but it affirms that joy is our inheritance as God's children.

This verse also reveals something beautiful about God's heart. He does not desire his people to live in perpetual solemnity or fear. Instead, he delights in their delight. Just as earthly parents find joy in their children's laughter, our heavenly Father wants his children to experience the fullness of joy that comes from knowing him. This joy is not selfish or superficial; it is rooted in the profound reality of God's love, mercy, and faithfulness.

In our daily lives, this verse challenges us to examine the sources of our joy. Are we seeking happiness in temporary things that will ultimately disappoint, or are we learning to find our deepest satisfaction in God himself? When we face difficulties, do we remember that our joy is anchored in unchanging truths about God's character and promises? The righteous can be joyful even in hardship because their joy is not circumstantial but relational; it is found in communion with the God who never changes.

This joy also has the power to witness. In a world filled with anxiety and despair, the genuine joy of God's people serves as a beacon of hope. It testifies to the reality that there is something beyond this world that satisfies the deepest longings of the human heart. Our joy becomes an invitation to others to taste and see that the Lord is good.

As we meditate on this verse, let us ask God to cultivate in us this deep, abiding joy. Let us learn to rejoice not just when things go well, but because we are his. Let our gladness before God become so genuine and infectious that it draws others to wonder at the source of such lasting happiness.

PRAYER

Heavenly Father, thank you for calling us to joy and gladness in your presence. Forgive us when we seek happiness in things that cannot truly satisfy, and help us to find our deepest delight in you alone. Fill our hearts with the joy that comes from knowing we are loved, forgiven, and accepted by you. May our gladness serve as a testimony to your goodness and draw others to experience the same joy we have found in you. In Jesus' name, Amen.

PRAISE IN THE MIDST OF PAIN

I will praise God's name in song and glorify him with thanksgiving (Psalm 69:30).

This remarkable declaration emerges from one of the most emotionally raw psalms in the entire Psalter. Psalm 69 is a lament that pulls no punches: David cries out about sinking in deep mire, about waters closing over his head, about enemies who hate him without cause. The imagery is visceral and desperate: "I am weary with my crying; my throat is parched. My eyes fail while I wait for my God" (v. 3). Yet from this valley of despair comes one of Scripture's most profound statements of faith.

The Hebrew word for "praise" here is *halal*, from which we derive "hallelujah." It conveys a sense of boasting or enthusiastic celebration. David is not offering grudging acknowledgment or resigned acceptance; he is choosing exuberant praise. The parallel verb "glorify" means to magnify or make great, suggesting that David's response will actually enhance God's reputation before others.

What makes this verse extraordinary is its context. David has not been rescued yet. The enemies still surround him, the mire still threatens to swallow him, and his prayers seem to echo in an empty sky. This is not praise *after* deliverance; it is praise *in anticipation* of deliverance. It represents a profound act of faith that refuses to let present circumstances dictate spiritual response.

The structure of the verse itself teaches us something crucial about worship. David moves from the personal ("I will praise") to the communal ("with thanksgiving"), from the individual expression of faith to corporate acknowledgment of God's goodness. True praise rarely remains private; it spills over into testimony that encourages others and builds up the community of faith.

This verse also reveals the anatomy of biblical praise. It combines *song* (emotional, artistic expression) with *thanksgiving* (cognitive recognition of God's benefits). Authentic worship engages both heart and mind, emotion and reason. David does not separate feeling from thinking or artistic expression from theological reflection. His praise is holistic, engaging his entire being in worship.

It is worth pausing to consider how this integrated praise is cultivated in practical terms. David's ability to sing in the middle of suffering was not accidental; it grew from a sustained discipline of remembrance. Throughout the psalms, he repeatedly rehearses the mighty acts of God, the exodus, the covenant, the provision in the wilderness, as the foundation for present trust. When we feed our minds on the record of God's faithfulness and train our voices to articulate what we believe rather than only what we feel, we build the spiritual muscle memory that makes praise possible in the hardest seasons. The practice of praise in good times is the school in which we learn to praise in desperate times.

The theological implications are staggering. If David can praise God while drowning in trouble, what does that say about the nature of God himself? It suggests that God's worthiness of praise is not contingent on our circumstances. His character remains constant whether we are walking through valleys or standing on mountaintops. This kind of praise becomes a declaration of God's essential goodness that transcends temporal experience.

For contemporary believers, Psalm 69:30 offers both challenge and comfort. It challenges us to examine whether our praise is conditional, tied to good times and easy seasons, or unconditional, rooted in who God is rather than in what he does for us in any given moment. It comforts us with the assurance that we can worship meaningfully even when life feels overwhelming, that praise can coexist with pain, and that thanksgiving can emerge from the darkest nights of the soul.

This verse ultimately points us toward the cross, where another son of David would cry out from even deeper waters, experiencing abandonment we will never know, yet maintaining perfect trust in his Father's plan. Jesus embodied the spirit of Psalm 69:30, offering himself as the ultimate sacrifice of praise even as he bore the weight of human sin and divine wrath.

Yet the story does not end at Golgotha. The Resurrection stands as God's thunderous vindication of every act of praise offered in darkness. When Christ rose from the dead, he confirmed that no depth of suffering has the final word, and that the voice of faith lifted in anguish is never swallowed by silence. For the believer, this means that praise in affliction is not a desperate gamble but a confident wager on the resurrection principle woven into the very fabric of redemptive history. Every "I will praise" spoken from the pit of suffering is an echo of Easter morning, a declaration that life and light always outlast the tomb.

PRAYER

Lord God, help us to learn the secret David discovered in his darkest hour, that you are worthy of praise not because of our circumstances, but because of who you are. When we find ourselves sinking in deep waters, teach us to lift our voices in song. When despair threatens to overwhelm us, remind us of your unfailing goodness. Give us hearts that can offer thanksgiving even before we see your deliverance, trusting that you are working all things together for our good and your glory. May our praise, like David's, become a testimony to others of your faithfulness, and may it join the eternal chorus of heaven that proclaims your worthiness forever and ever. Amen.

FINDING JOY IN SEEKING GOD

*May all who seek you rejoice and be glad in you; may those who
long for your saving help always say, "The Lord is great"*
(Psalm 70:4)

In this brief but powerful verse, David paints a beautiful picture of
what it means to live in a relationship with God. The psalmist's words
reveal two fundamental truths about the spiritual life: the joy found in
seeking God and the natural response of praise that flows from
experiencing his salvation.

The first part of this verse speaks to those "who seek you." Seeking
God is not a passive endeavor but an active pursuit that requires
intentionality, persistence, and desire. Yet David does not describe this
seeking as burdensome or sorrowful. Instead, he envisions those who
seek God as people who "rejoice and be glad." This challenges our
natural tendency to view spiritual discipline as a duty rather than a
delight. When we truly understand who God is, his goodness, his
faithfulness, his love, the very act of seeking him becomes a source of
joy rather than obligation.

The Hebrew word for "rejoice" here carries the idea of spinning
around with joy, like a child celebrating. This suggests that seeking
God should fill us with childlike wonder and enthusiasm. Too often,
we approach our relationship with God with grim determination rather
than eager anticipation. David reminds us that God delights in being
found by those who seek him, and he rewards their search with
genuine happiness and contentment.

It is also worth noting that Psalm 70 is a psalm of urgent petition. The
opening cry, "Hasten, O God, to save me" (v. 1), reflects a soul pressed
by real distress, and the whole psalm is saturated with the language of

desperate need. This context makes verse 4 all the more remarkable. David does not wait until deliverance is complete before calling on the community to rejoice. He summons praise in the very midst of trouble, trusting that God's character is sufficient grounds for joy even before the answer arrives. This teaches us that biblical joy is not the absence of difficulty but a confidence in who God is that transcends present circumstances

The second half of the verse shifts focus to "those who long for your saving help." This phrase acknowledges that many who seek God do so from places of need, desperation, or trouble. Yet even in these circumstances, David envisions a community of believers who consistently declare, "The Lord is great!" The word "always" is significant here: not just when life is easy, not just when prayers are answered quickly, but always.

This consistent praise does not come from denying difficulties or from superficial optimism. Rather, it springs from a deep understanding of God's character and his proven faithfulness. Those who have experienced God's saving help, whether deliverance from external enemies, internal struggles, or spiritual bondage, cannot help but proclaim his greatness. Their testimony serves as an encouragement to others who are still waiting for their breakthrough.

The verse also creates a beautiful picture of community. David uses plural pronouns throughout: "all who seek," "those who long," suggesting that the life of faith is not meant to be lived in isolation. When believers gather to seek God and share their testimonies of his saving power, their collective joy and praise create an atmosphere that draws others to experience God's goodness firsthand.

There is also a cyclical nature to this verse that reflects the rhythm of spiritual life. Seeking leads to gladness, which leads to praise, which inspires continued seeking. Those who are currently longing for God's help are encouraged by the joy of those who have found him, while those who are rejoicing remember their own seasons of longing and offer hope to others.

For us today, this verse challenges us to examine both our motivation for seeking God and our response to his faithfulness. Are we approaching God with expectant joy, or have we reduced our faith to mere religious routine? When we experience God's help and intervention in our lives, do we consistently give him credit and praise, or do we quickly forget his goodness when new challenges arise?

David's vision reminds us that a life centered on seeking God and acknowledging his greatness is a life filled with genuine joy and hope. In a world that often feels chaotic and uncertain, we can find stability in the unchanging character of God and community with others who share this same pursuit.

PRAYER

Lord, help us seek you with joy and expectation, not out of duty but out of a genuine desire for your presence. For those who are longing for your saving help today, we ask that you meet them in their need and remind them of your faithfulness. May our hearts always be quick to declare your greatness, and may our praise encourage others to seek you as well. Seeking you is not a burden but a delight. Thank you for rewarding those who earnestly seek you. In Jesus' name, Amen.

THE RIGHTEOUSNESS OF GOD

Your righteousness, God, reaches to the heavens, you who have done great things. Who is like you, God? (Psalm 71:19).

In the twilight of life, when the weight of years presses upon the soul and the shadows of mortality grow long, the psalmist lifts his voice in a declaration that transcends human experience: "Your righteousness, God, reaches to the heavens, you who have done great things. Who is like you, God?" These words, born from a lifetime of wrestling with both divine faithfulness and human frailty, offer us one of Scripture's most profound meditations on the incomparability of God.

The psalmist's declaration that God's righteousness "reaches to the heavens" employs the ancient Near Eastern understanding of the cosmos as a way of expressing the infinite. In Hebrew thought, the heavens represented the ultimate boundary of human perception and experience. To say that God's righteousness reaches to the heavens is to declare that it extends beyond all human measure and comprehension. This is not merely a statement about God's moral perfection, but about the cosmic scope of divine justice and covenant faithfulness.

The Hebrew word for righteousness here encompasses far more than our modern legal understanding of the term. It speaks to God's covenant faithfulness, his commitment to act in accordance with his promises, and his unwavering dedication to setting all things right. When the psalmist contemplates this divine righteousness, he reflects on a lifetime of witnessing God's faithfulness, through seasons of blessing and trial, youth and old age, national triumph and personal struggle.

The phrase "you who have done great things" serves as the evidence for this cosmic righteousness. The psalmist speaks from experience, having witnessed great, magnificent acts that only God can perform. These are not merely impressive displays of power, but demonstrations of God's character worked out in the theater of human history. Each generation discovers anew that the God who split the sea, who raised the dead, who turns hearts of stone to flesh, continues to work with the same magnificent power and unchanging character.

The rhetorical question "Who is like you, God?" echoes throughout Scripture as a fundamental confession of monotheistic faith. It is the question that Moses and Miriam sang at the Red Sea, that Hannah proclaimed in her prayer, and that the prophets hurled as a challenge to the nations and their idols. This is not merely a comparison between competing deities, but a recognition that God exists in a category entirely his own. The question itself contains its answer: no one and nothing can be compared to the Lord.

For the believer walking through the complexities of modern life, this ancient confession offers profound comfort and perspective. In a world where moral relativism clouds our understanding of justice and human institutions often fail to deliver righteousness, the psalmist's words remind us that there is a righteousness that transcends human limitations and reaches to the very heights of creation. This righteousness is not distant or abstract, but personally engaged with our lives through the great things God continues to do.

The elderly psalmist, looking back over decades of divine faithfulness, models for us the kind of perspective that comes only through long obedience in the same direction. His confession emerges not from naive optimism but from tested faith. He has seen enough of God's great works to know that this righteousness, which reaches to the heavens, is not merely a theological concept but a lived reality that sustains the faithful through every season of life.

In our own moments of uncertainty, when the headlines proclaim injustice and our personal circumstances seem to mock any notion of divine righteousness, we are called to lift our eyes beyond the immediate horizon. The righteousness that reaches to the heavens remains unchanged, and the God who has done great things continues his work of setting all things right, often in ways we cannot yet perceive or understand.

PRAYER

Almighty God, whose righteousness reaches beyond our highest thoughts and deepest understanding, we thank you for the great things you have done and continue to do. When our vision is clouded by present circumstances and our faith is tested by delayed justice, help us to remember that you alone are God, incomparable in your faithfulness and unmatched in your power to make all things right. Grant us eyes to see your great works in our own lives and hearts that trust in your righteousness, even when we cannot trace your ways. Through Christ our Lord, Amen.

PRAYING FOR OUR LEADERS

Endow the king with your justice, O God, the royal son with your righteousness (Psalm 72:1).

Psalm 72 opens with one of the most profound prayers for leadership found anywhere in Scripture. As we encounter these words, traditionally attributed to Solomon, we witness a father's heart cry for divine wisdom to rest upon his son's reign. Yet this verse transcends its historical context, offering timeless insight into what godly leadership should embody and what we should earnestly seek for those in authority over us.

The Hebrew word for "endow" here means giving or placing something upon another. It is not a casual request but an urgent plea for God to actively invest his character into human leadership. The psalmist understands something crucial: justice and righteousness are not merely human constructs or political ideals; they are divine attributes that must be imparted from above. No leader, regardless of their wisdom or good intentions, possesses these qualities inherently or sufficiently.

Notice the parallel structure: "your justice" and "your righteousness." These are not abstract concepts but living expressions of God's character. Justice speaks to the fair and equitable treatment of all people, particularly those who are vulnerable or marginalized. Righteousness encompasses both moral integrity and the active pursuit of what is right and good. Together, they form the foundation of leadership that reflects God's heart.

The distinction between "the king" and "the royal son" may suggest both present and future leadership, or it may simply be a Hebrew poetic parallelism that emphasizes the same truth. Either way, the prayer acknowledges that righteous leadership is not a one-time gift but an ongoing need that spans generations. Each leader, whether seasoned or new to authority, requires fresh endowments of divine wisdom and character.

This verse challenges our contemporary understanding of leadership and power. In a world where leadership is often pursued for personal gain, prestige, or the ability to impose one's will, Psalm 72:1 presents a radically different vision. Authentic leadership, according to this prayer, is about being a conduit for God's justice and righteousness. It is about stewarding authority in a way that reflects heaven's values rather than earth's ambitions.

The implications extend far beyond ancient monarchies or modern political systems. Whether we are parents guiding children, managers overseeing teams, pastors shepherding congregations, or citizens participating in democracy, this prayer shapes how we should approach both exercising and responding to authority. We are called to pray earnestly for those in leadership positions, asking God to endow them with His wisdom and character.

Perhaps most importantly, this verse reminds us that lasting positive change in society flows from hearts transformed by divine grace. Laws and policies matter, but they are only as effective as the character of those who create and enforce them. When leaders are endowed with God's justice and righteousness, their decisions naturally protect the vulnerable, promote fairness, and pursue the common good.

As we reflect on this opening verse of Psalm 72, we are invited to examine our own hearts. In whatever spheres of influence we occupy, do we seek God's justice and righteousness to guide our choices? Are we praying faithfully for those in authority over us, asking God to endow them with his character rather than simply hoping they will advance our preferred policies?

The prayer of Psalm 72:1 remains as relevant today as it was three millennia ago. In a world crying out for authentic leadership, we find hope not in human wisdom or strength, but in God's willingness to endow earthly leaders with heavenly virtues.

PRAYER

Heavenly Father, we echo the prayer of the psalmist today. We ask that you would endow our leaders, in government, in our communities, in our churches, and in our families, with your justice and righteousness. Help them see through your eyes, love with your heart, and lead with your wisdom. Where leadership has failed or fallen short, bring renewal and transformation. And Lord, endow us as well with these same qualities in whatever spheres of influence you have placed us. May your kingdom come and your will be done through those who bear the responsibility of leadership. In Jesus' name, Amen.

WHEN FLESH FAILS, GOD REMAINS

My flesh and my heart may fail, but God is the strength of my heart and my portion forever (Psalm 73:26).

Asaph's words in Psalm 73:26 emerge from the depths of a profoundly honest spiritual struggle. The psalmist has just worked through one of the most challenging theological questions that believers face: the apparent prosperity of the wicked while the righteous suffer. Yet here, in this climactic verse, Asaph moves beyond his initial envy and confusion to embrace a truth that transcends circumstances: God himself is enough.

The psalm opens with a declaration that functions almost as a creed: "Surely God is good to Israel, to those who are pure in heart" (v. 1). Yet the very next verse reveals how tenuous that confession had become: "But as for me, my feet had almost stumbled, my steps had nearly slipped" (v. 2). The Hebrew verb translated "slipped" carries the image of a traveler losing his footing on treacherous ground, an image that captures with remarkable precision the experience of faith under assault. Asaph does not merely report a momentary doubt; he describes a near-total collapse of his theological footing. The juxtaposition of these two verses is itself a pastoral confession: a person can hold an orthodox creed in the mind while the heart is simultaneously being dragged toward abandonment by what the eyes observe.

What triggered this spiritual crisis was not tragedy or personal suffering, but envy: "I was envious of the arrogant when I saw the prosperity of the wicked" (v. 3). Asaph surveys the wicked and catalogues their advantages with painful detail through verses 4 through 12—their bodies are fat and sleek, they escape the troubles that afflict ordinary people, their pride is worn like a necklace, and they mock heaven itself without consequence. The believer who prays faithfully, maintains integrity, and endures suffering begins to wonder whether God's covenant faithfulness is merely an illusion. This is the theological vertigo that Asaph names with unflinching honesty, and it is the same vertigo that every serious believer eventually confronts when the evidence of daily experience seems to contradict the promises of God. The Hebrew word for "fail" carries the sense of being consumed, exhausted, or coming to an end. Asaph acknowledges what every honest believer must eventually confront: our physical bodies will deteriorate, our emotional reserves will be depleted, and our human capacity will reach its limits. The parallel structure emphasizes the totality of human frailty; both flesh and heart represent the complete person, body and inner being alike.

This is not a moment of despair, however, but of profound theological insight. The conjunction "but" marks a decisive turn from human limitation to divine sufficiency. When Asaph declares that God is "the strength of my heart," he employs the image of God as a rock or fortress, the same metaphor David used throughout his psalms to describe God's unchanging reliability. The word "rock" suggests not merely strength, but permanence and immovability in contrast to human instability.

The phrase "my portion" draws from Israel's inheritance theology. Just as the Levites received no territorial inheritance because "the Lord is their portion" (Numbers 18:20), Asaph recognizes that God himself constitutes his true inheritance. This is not compensation for earthly losses, but the discovery of what was always the highest good. The temporal prosperity of the wicked, which so troubled the psalmist earlier, pales in comparison to this eternal inheritance.

The word "forever" seals this confession with permanence. While flesh fails and hearts give out, God's strength and his relationship with his people endure beyond the temporal realm. This perspective transforms Asaph's entire worldview; he moves from envying the temporary success of the ungodly to treasuring an eternal relationship with the living God.

For believers today, this verse offers profound comfort in seasons of physical decline, emotional exhaustion, or spiritual dryness. It reminds us that our ultimate security does not rest in our own resilience or resources, but in the unchanging character of God. When health fails, when strength ebbs, when circumstances overwhelm us, we discover, perhaps for the first time, that God himself is sufficient.

This is particularly relevant in a culture that often equates human worth with productivity, strength, and independence. Asaph's confession challenges us to find our identity not in what we can accomplish or endure, but in whose we are. The God who is our portion does not love us less when we are weak; indeed, it is often in our weakness that we most clearly perceive his strength.

The verse also speaks to the universal human experience of aging and mortality. Rather than denying these realities or viewing them as failures of faith, Psalm 73:26 invites us to see them as opportunities to discover God's all-sufficiency. The faithful who have walked with God for decades often testify that their greatest spiritual growth came not in their years of strength, but in their seasons of dependence.

PRAYER

Eternal God, we thank you that when our bodies grow weary and our hearts feel overwhelmed, you remain our unshakeable foundation. Help us to find our security not in our own strength, but in your faithful love. When we face limitations, remind us that you are limitless. When we confront our mortality, assure us of your eternal nature. May we learn to treasure you as our true portion, finding in you what no earthly blessing could provide. Through seasons of strength and seasons of weakness, be our constant refuge and our everlasting inheritance. In your holy name we pray, Amen.

GOD IS MY KING FROM LONG AGO

God is my King from long ago; he brings salvation on the earth
(Psalm 74:12).

The psalmist's declaration in Psalm 74:12 arrives not at a moment of triumph, but amid profound distress. This prayer of lament begins with the cry, "Why have you rejected us forever, O God?" (74:1) and proceeds through vivid descriptions of the desecration of the sanctuary, the destruction wrought by enemies, and the apparent abandonment of God's people. Yet precisely at this nadir of despair, the worshiper pivots toward affirmation: "God is my King from long ago; he brings salvation on the earth." This sudden shift from lamentation to declaration deserves our careful attention, for it reveals something fundamental about faith in the midst of suffering.

The Hebrew phrase translated "from long ago," emphasizes antiquity and enduring reality. The preposition 'from' combined with "long ago" creates a sense of something stretching backward through the centuries, something established in the distant past and therefore reliable in the present crisis. The psalmist is not asserting that God has only recently become king; such a claim would ring hollow given the immediate circumstances. Rather, the affirmation reaches backward through Israel's entire history: the deliverance from Egypt, the guidance through the wilderness, the establishment of the Davidic kingdom, and countless smaller mercies. God's kingship is not new; it is ancient, tested, and proven across generations.

This perspective proves essential for faith during suffering. The psalmist does not claim that God is presently acting with visible power, nor does the prayer pretend that enemies are not destroying the sanctuary or that the people are not experiencing abandonment. Instead, the worshiper appeals to memory, the collective memory of a people who have witnessed God's kingly rule across time. This memory becomes an anchor when present circumstances seem to contradict the reality of divine care. The psalmist effectively argues: "I may not understand what is happening now, but I remember who God is. I have the testimony of my ancestors. This kingship is old, established, and therefore trustworthy."

The second part of our verse extends this affirmation outward: "he brings salvation on the earth." The Hebrew verb, meaning "to save, to deliver," appears throughout the Psalter and throughout Israel's story. The parallel construction suggests that God's kingship is not abstract or merely heavenly, but concrete and earthly in its effects. God's rule manifests itself in salvation: in rescue, deliverance, and the restoration of justice. The phrase "on the earth" emphasizes that God's sovereignty extends into the material world, into history, into the actual circumstances of suffering people. This is no distant deity presiding over a heavenly realm while earth suffers abandonment. This is a King who acts, who saves, who brings deliverance into concrete human experience.

For contemporary believers facing our own trials, this verse addresses a critical spiritual question: How do we maintain trust in God when circumstances contradict the promises we have received? The answer the psalmist models is neither denial nor blind optimism, but rather a grounding in historical remembrance and theological conviction. Our faith rests not on the favorable circumstances of any particular moment, but on the demonstrated character of God across time. We are invited to recall not only biblical history but our own personal and communal histories, the times we have experienced God's faithfulness, the moments when deliverance came in unexpected ways, and the seasons when God sustained us through darkness.

Moreover, the affirmation that God "brings salvation on the earth" reminds us that faith is not merely about personal spiritual comfort. God's rule extends to justice, to the healing of communities, to the transformation of social structures. Even when individual circumstances remain difficult, we can trust that God's ultimate purpose is to establish salvation throughout creation. This perspective relativizes our personal suffering without invalidating it. The lament of Psalm 74 remains authentic; God's people did experience destruction and abandonment. Yet the acknowledgment of God's ancient kingship and saving power prevents despair from becoming final.

The movement from lamentation to affirmation in this verse models a mature faith, not the faith that denies suffering or manufactures false joy, but the faith that remembers God's character and commits itself to trusting that character even when immediate evidence seems sparse. It is the faith of one who has prayed honestly about pain, yet who still chooses to confess: "God is my King from long ago; he brings salvation on the earth."

PRAYER

Eternal God and King, we come before you as the psalmist came, sometimes in confusion and pain, yet seeking to remember your faithfulness across generations. We confess that you have been our God from ancient times, that your character has been proven through countless deliverances and mercies. When our circumstances tempt us toward despair, teach us to remember your acts, to trust your kingship, and to wait for your salvation. Grant us the courage to pray honestly about our pain, and the grace to affirm your rule even in darkness. Make us instruments of your salvation on the earth, witnesses to your justice and mercy, until your kingdom is fully established and all creation knows your peace. In the name of Christ, our Savior and King, we pray. Amen.

THE NEARNESS OF GOD'S NAME

*We praise you, God, we praise you, for your Name is near;
people tell of your wonderful deeds* (Psalm 75:1).

There is something profoundly comforting about repetition in praise. When the psalmist declares, "We praise you, God, we praise you," the echo is not redundant; it is emphatic. It is the sound of a heart so full of gratitude that one acknowledgment is not enough. This doubled praise reminds us that worship is not a checkbox on our spiritual to-do list; it is the overflow of recognizing who God is and what he has done.

But what makes this particular praise so compelling is the reason given: "for your Name is near." In ancient Hebrew culture, a name represented far more than a label. It embodied character, reputation, and presence. God's name carries his very nature: his holiness, his power, his covenant faithfulness. To say his name is near is to declare that God himself is accessible, not distant or removed from our daily lives.

Think about what nearness means in human relationships. When someone is near, they are available. They can hear you. They can respond. The psalmist is not praising a deity who dwells in remote abstraction, ruling from an unreachable throne. This is praise directed toward a God who draws close, who makes himself known, who invites relationship. In a world where we often feel alone even in crowded rooms, the nearness of God's name offers profound hope.

This nearness is not just a personal, private experience. The verse continues: "people tell of your wonderful deeds." The Hebrew word for "wonderful" here refers to things that inspire awe, acts that defy ordinary explanation. God's wonderful deeds are not hidden mysteries kept secret from the masses; they are testified to, shared, and proclaimed. Throughout Scripture, we see this pattern: God acts, and his people respond by telling the story.

Think of the Israelites recounting their deliverance from Egypt, generation after generation. Consider the woman at the well who ran to tell her whole town about Jesus, or the formerly blind man who simply could not stop talking about the One who gave him sight. When God moves in our lives, silence becomes impossible. His wonderful deeds create storytellers.

This presents us with a beautiful cycle: God draws near, he acts on our behalf, we experience his goodness, and in response, we tell others, which leads to more praise. Our testimonies become invitations for others to discover his nearness for themselves. Every story of provision, healing, guidance, or transformation becomes evidence that God's name is indeed near, not just to ancient Israel, but to us today.

Yet we live in an age of silence about the sacred. Many of us have grown uncomfortable sharing what God has done. Perhaps we fear seeming overly religious or worry that our stories are not dramatic enough. But Psalm 75:1 suggests that telling of God's wonderful deeds is the natural response to experiencing his nearness. When we withhold our testimonies, we rob others of encouragement and rob ourselves of the joy that comes from remembering God's faithfulness.

What wonderful deeds has God done in your life? Maybe he has sustained you through a season you thought would break you. Perhaps he has provided in unexpected ways, opened doors that seemed permanently closed, or brought healing to broken relationships. Maybe his wonderful deed was simply meeting you in your loneliness on an ordinary Tuesday, making his presence known in a moment of prayer or through a verse that seemed written just for you.

These stories matter. They are not boasting about ourselves; they are bearing witness to a God whose name is near. When we tell of his wonderful deeds, we participate in something larger than ourselves. We join the chorus of praise that has echoed through the ages, from the psalmist's time to our own.

The call of Psalm 75:1 is both personal and communal. Individually, we are invited to recognize and rejoice in God's nearness. Corporately, we are commissioned to keep telling the stories, to ensure that knowledge of his wonderful deeds passes from one generation to the next, from one conversation to the next.

So today, let this verse reorient your heart. God's name is near. He is not far off, disinterested, or unavailable. And because he is near, because he acts, because he is worthy, we praise him. We praise him again. And then we tell the story.

PRAYER

Father, we praise you. We praise you for drawing near to us, for making your name and your nature known. Thank you for your wonderful deeds: those you have already done and those you are doing even now. Give us bold and grateful hearts to tell others what you have accomplished. May our lives be testimonies to your nearness, and may our stories point others to you. In Jesus' name, Amen.

THE SACRED WEIGHT OF OUR PROMISES

Make vows to the LORD your God and fulfill them; let all the neighboring lands bring gifts to the One to be feared (Psalm 76:11).

There is something profoundly countercultural about the idea of making vows. In our contemporary world, we have grown comfortable with flexibility, with keeping our options open, with the unspoken understanding that our commitments come with invisible escape clauses. We say "I will try" when we mean "probably not," and "let me think about it" when we mean "no." Against this backdrop, Psalm 76:11 rings out with startling clarity: "Make vows to the LORD your God and fulfill them."

The psalmist is not merely suggesting that we keep our promises to God. He calls us to something far more radical: to deliberately make vows and willingly bind ourselves to sacred obligations. This seems almost reckless to our modern sensibilities. Why would we voluntarily limit our freedom? Why lock ourselves into commitments we might later regret?

Yet the wisdom here runs deeper than our initial resistance suggests. The act of making vows to God is fundamentally an act of trust. When we make a vow, we are declaring that we believe God is worthy of our wholehearted commitment, that his character is so reliable we can safely stake our future on our relationship with him. We are saying that we trust him enough to let go of our carefully maintained control over our own lives.

Consider what happens in the space between making a vow and fulfilling it. Life intervenes. Circumstances change. Our emotions fluctuate. The enthusiasm we felt when we made our promise fades, leaving us with the harder work of following through when it is no longer convenient or exciting. This is precisely where transformation occurs. Keeping our vows when it costs us something shapes us into people of integrity, whose word actually means something, and who reflect the unchanging faithfulness of God himself.

The second part of this verse shifts our perspective outward: "let all the neighboring lands bring gifts to the One to be feared." This is not about a God who demands tribute out of insecurity or vanity. Rather, it is about the appropriate human response to encountering genuine holiness. The "fear" spoken of here is that profound reverence that overtakes us when we glimpse something infinitely greater than ourselves, not terror, but awe that transforms how we live.

Notice the connection the psalmist makes between our personal vows and this universal worship. Our faithfulness in keeping our promises to God becomes a testimony that draws others to him. When people see that we are different, that our yes means yes and our no means no, that we honor our commitments even when they are difficult, that we worship a God who is actually worth organizing our lives around, they begin to ask questions. Our fulfilled vows become an invitation to the watching world.

This has practical implications for how we live. It means we should be careful about the promises we make, knowing that each vow we take seriously either builds or diminishes our witness. It means that the commitments we make in seasons of spiritual fervor, to pray daily, to give generously, to serve faithfully, to forgive completely, are not just momentary emotional responses but sacred obligations we carry forward into ordinary time.

It also means recognizing that every broken promise to God matters, not because he is keeping score to punish us, but because each unfulfilled vow slightly erodes our own integrity and dims the light we are meant to shine in the world. The good news is that God's grace covers our failures, but grace is not meant to make us casual about our commitments. Rather, it should free us to take them even more seriously, knowing that our standing before God does not depend on perfect performance but on his perfect love.

Living this way, making vows carefully and keeping them faithfully, will set us apart. In a world of broken promises and abandoned commitments, people who actually do what they say they will do become living testimonies to a God who never wavers. Our faithfulness, imperfect as it is, points beyond itself to his perfect faithfulness.

PRAYER

Lord God, you who are always faithful, help me to make my promises carefully and keep them faithfully. Give me wisdom to know what vows to make, and give me strength to follow through when keeping them costs me something. Shape me into a person of integrity whose life draws others to your trustworthy character. May my small faithfulness point to your perfect faithfulness. Amen.

THE GOD OF MIRACLES AMONG US

You are the God who performs miracles; you display your power among the peoples (Psalm 77:14).

In the midst of deep distress, Asaph the psalmist makes a stunning declaration: "You are the God who performs miracles; you display your power among the peoples." These words emerge not from a place of triumph but from the depths of a troubled soul. Earlier in this psalm, Asaph describes sleepless nights, a spirit too troubled to speak, and hands outstretched in prayer that seem to find no comfort. Yet from this darkness comes one of Scripture's most powerful affirmations of God's miraculous nature.

What transforms Asaph's perspective? He deliberately turns his gaze backward, choosing to remember God's deeds of old. This is not mere nostalgia but a spiritual discipline: meditation on God's character revealed through his mighty acts. The word "miracles" here carries the sense of wonders that inspire awe, acts that transcend natural explanation and point unmistakably to divine intervention. Asaph recalls the exodus, the parting of the Red Sea, and the provision in the wilderness. These were not just historical events; they were revelations of who God is.

The second part of this verse adds a crucial dimension: God displays his power "among the peoples." The miracles of God are never merely private affairs or abstract demonstrations of omnipotence. They occur in the public square of human history, witnessed by nations, transforming communities, and reshaping humanity's story. When God delivered Israel from Egypt, Pharaoh and all Egypt saw it. When he parted the Red Sea, both the Israelites and their pursuers witnessed his power. The miracle was inseparable from the testimony.

This public nature of God's miracles speaks to his desire to be known. He does not work in secretive ways that leave us guessing whether he acted at all. Throughout Scripture, God performs wonders that leave no doubt about his presence and power. He heals the sick where crowds can see, raises the dead with witnesses present, and feeds thousands on a hillside. Even Jesus' resurrection, the ultimate miracle, was confirmed by hundreds of witnesses who saw, touched, and ate with the risen Christ.

For us today, this verse offers profound encouragement. When we find ourselves in Asaph's position, troubled, questioning, searching for God in the darkness, we can follow his example. We remember. We rehearse God's faithfulness in Scripture and in our own stories. Every answered prayer, every unexpected provision, every moment when God's presence became undeniable, these become stepping stones back to faith.

But Asaph's declaration also challenges us. Do we live with expectancy for God to work miraculously? Or have we become so accustomed to natural explanations that we have lost our capacity for wonder? The God who parted the Red Sea has not changed. He remains the God who performs miracles, who intervenes in human affairs, who displays his power for all to see.

This does not mean we should seek signs and wonders for their own sake or manufacture false testimonies to prove God's activity. Rather, it means we should keep our eyes open and our hearts ready to recognize when God moves. Sometimes his miracles are dramatic: healing, provision, deliverance. Other times, they are quieter: a changed heart, restored relationship, unexpected peace in suffering. All reveal the same truth: God is actively at work among his people.

The verse also reminds us that God's miracles serve a purpose beyond our personal blessing. When God displays his power among the peoples, he is making himself known to a watching world. Our testimonies of his faithfulness become part of how he reveals himself to others. The miracle in your life may be the very thing that draws someone else to faith.

As we navigate our own seasons of difficulty, uncertainty, or doubt, let us anchor ourselves in this truth: we serve the God who performs miracles. He has not retired from supernatural intervention. He has not become distant or passive. He remains actively engaged with his creation, working in ways beyond our understanding, displaying his power so that all peoples might know him, trust him, and worship him.

PRAYER

Gracious God, you are the God who performs miracles. When my faith wavers and darkness surrounds me, remind me of your mighty acts, both in Scripture and in my own life. Open my eyes to see your hand at work, give me courage to trust in your power, and use my story to display your glory among all peoples. May my life be a testimony to your faithfulness and your miraculous presence. In Jesus' name, Amen.

THE CALL TO LISTEN

My people, hear my teaching; listen to the words of my mouth
(Psalm 78:1).

The opening line of Psalm 78 issues an invitation that reverberates across the centuries, a summons to listen. This wisdom psalm, attributed to Asaph, begins not with praise or lament, but with a call to attention. Before the psalmist recounts Israel's history, before he rehearses God's mighty acts and the people's repeated failures, he first asks for ears willing to hear.

The dual command, "hear" and "listen," is no mere redundancy. In Hebrew thought, hearing implies more than auditory reception. The Hebrew word *shema* carries the weight of obedience, comprehension, and response. To hear is to heed. To listen is to lean in with the whole self. The psalmist understands what we so often forget: transformation begins not with speaking but with listening.

Notice the intimacy embedded in this verse. The psalmist addresses "my people," a phrase that assumes a relationship and a sense of belonging. This is not instruction shouted to strangers, but wisdom shared within the covenant community. The teacher speaks as one who stands among the people, not above them. His words come "from my mouth," emphasizing the personal, oral tradition through which faith was transmitted from one generation to the next. This is the language of family, of elders gathering children around the fire to tell the old, old story.

Yet there is an urgency here, too. The imperative mood presses upon us. In a world clamoring for our attention, where countless voices compete for our ears, the call to listen becomes an act of spiritual discipline. We live in an age of constant noise: notifications, news cycles, streaming content, and endless chatter. The psalmist's opening words challenge us to create space for sacred listening, to silence the static so we might hear what God is saying through Scripture, through the witness of those who have gone before us, through the still, small voice of the Spirit.

What follows in Psalm 78 demonstrates why listening matters. The psalmist will recount Israel's history: the exodus, the wilderness wandering, and the cycle of rebellion and rescue. He tells this story so that future generations might learn, might remember, might not repeat the tragic pattern of forgetting God's faithfulness. But none of these instructions can take root in hearts that refuse to listen. The most profound truths fall on deaf ears when we are too distracted, too proud, or too hurried to attend to them.

This opening verse also reminds us that teaching and learning are central to the life of faith. The psalmist does not merely expect people to absorb faith by osmosis. He actively teaches, and he expects active listening in return. In our individualistic age, we sometimes imagine that spiritual growth is a private endeavor, something between "me and God." But the Psalms paint a different picture, one of communal worship, shared wisdom, and intergenerational transmission of faith. We need teachers, and we need to be teachable.

Perhaps most challenging is the self-examination this verse demands. Are we truly listening? Do we approach Scripture with ears eager to hear, or do we skim passages looking for quick inspiration? When we gather for worship, do we lean in with expectancy, or do we passively consume? When wise counsel comes from fellow believers, do we receive it with humility, or do we dismiss what does not immediately align with our preferences?

The call to listen is a call to humility. It acknowledges that we do not know everything, that we need instruction, that God speaks through means beyond our own limited understanding. It requires us to be present, attentive, and open, postures that do not come naturally in our age of distraction. As we begin our journey through this historical psalm, we are reminded that everything depends on this first step: the willingness to hear.

Without it, even God's most powerful acts of deliverance become footnotes in history rather than living testimonies that shape our present and future. May we cultivate ears that hear and hearts that heed.

PRAYER

Gracious God, quiet the noise that drowns out your voice. Open our ears to hear your teaching and our hearts to receive your word. Make us attentive students of your truth, humble enough to learn and wise enough to apply what we hear. Speak, Lord, for your servants are listening. Through Christ our Lord, Amen.

PSALM 79

A CRY FROM THE RUINS

Help us, God our Savior, for the glory of your name; deliver us and forgive our sins for your name's sake (Psalm 79:9).

In the shadowed aftermath of the catastrophe, when the walls of Jerusalem lay crumbled and the sanctuary desecrated, the psalmist lifted a raw, unfiltered plea to the heavens. Psalm 79, a communal lament attributed to Asaph, paints a grim picture of what happened: enemies have poured out the blood of God's servants like water, leaving their bodies unburied as carrion for the birds, and the nations mock, "Where is their God?" (v. 10).

It is into this vortex of grief and outrage that verse 9 erupts like a thunderclap of desperate faith: "Help us, God our Savior, for the glory of your name; deliver us and forgive our sins for your name's sake." This verse is no polite petition; it is a gut-wrenching cry from a people stripped bare, clinging to the only anchor they know: God's own character.

In our own fractured world, where personal betrayals, global unrest, and inner turmoil echo ancient despairs, this cry invites us to reorient our prayers not around our worthiness, but around his glory. At its heart, the plea begins with a bold address: "Help us, God our Savior." The psalmist does not grovel in anonymity but names God as the divine Rescuer, the One who parted seas and toppled tyrants. This is not a generic god, distant and indifferent; it is the covenant God whose history is etched with acts of salvation: from the Exodus to the whispers of restoration in exile.

Yet the call for help is communal, "us," not "me," reminding us that our struggles are rarely solitary. In a culture obsessed with individualism, where social media amplifies solo victories and silences shared sorrows, Psalm 79 urges us to pray as a body. Think of the church today, battered by division or the wider world reeling from pandemics, wars, and moral erosion. Who among us has not whispered, "Help us," in boardrooms turned battlegrounds or hospital waiting rooms?

The psalmist models vulnerability: help is not a sign of weakness but the gateway to divine strength. As Isaiah would later echo, "In repentance and rest is your salvation" (Isaiah 30:15). To cry for help is to step into the current of God's saving power, trusting that the Savior who calmed storms for one fisherman will steady the collective ship of his people. But notice what the psalmist says: this help is sought "for the glory of your name." Here lies the radical humility that transforms a selfish whine into a symphony of worship. The psalmist's motivation is not personal vindication or national pride; it is the radiant display of God's holiness amid the rubble.

In ancient Near Eastern thought, a god's "name" encapsulated their essence, reputation, and authority, like a royal seal on a decree. When enemies desecrated the temple, they did not merely assault stone and wood; they impugned God's sovereignty, implying he was powerless or uncaring. The psalmist's prayer flips the script: deliver us, not because we deserve it, but because your undelivered people make you look small.

When we pray in God's name, we align with his eternal plan, where every salvation story directs praise back to him. The verse reaches a peak with two requests: "deliver us and forgive our sins." Without forgiveness, deliverance is superficial; it is just surviving within a cycle of self-harm. The psalmist admits collective guilt, idolatry, and injustice, sins that called for judgment (v. 8), but still pleads for mercy and grace. The phrase "for your name's sake" highlights that forgiveness depends not only on our repentance but also on God's unwavering faithfulness.

This is gospel foreshadowed: the cross, where Christ bore our sins to vindicate God's righteous name. John writes, "If we confess our sins, he is faithful and just to forgive us our sins" (1 John 1:9). For the believer today, this verse is a lifeline in the grind of habitual failures. Struggling with anger that flares like Jerusalem's flames? Addictions that chain like exile's bonds? National sins that mock our witness? Cry out: deliver and forgive, not for my spotless record, but for your spotless name.

In that surrender, we taste freedom: chains loosened, hearts mended, communities revived. God's glory, once dimmed by our shadows, blazes forth in redeemed lives. Let Psalm 79:9 linger as a reminder that our deepest needs find their deepest answer in the One whose name is above every name. In a world that glorifies self, may we learn to plead for his splendor, knowing that in lifting his fame, we find our salvation.

PRAYER

Heavenly Father, our Savior and Redeemer, we echo the ancient cry: help us for the glory of your name. Deliver us from the ruins of our making, sins that entangle, fears that paralyze, and forgive us freely, that your mercy might echo through our lives. May every rescue, every pardon, magnify your holy name. In Jesus' name, Amen.

RESTORE US

Restore us, God Almighty; make your face shine on us, that we may be saved (Psalm 80:7).

There is something achingly honest about a prayer that begins with need. No preamble, no lengthy catalog of credentials, no attempt to earn what is being asked. Just a soul, or in this case, an entire people, turning toward God with outstretched hands and a single, desperate petition: *Restore us.* The writer of Psalm 80 does not arrive before God in triumph. He arrives in ruin, and he knows exactly where the only help can be found.

Psalm 80 is a communal lament, likely written during a period of devastating national loss, possibly the fall of the Northern Kingdom of Israel, possibly the exile, possibly some other catastrophe whose weight we can only imagine from across the centuries. Three times in the psalm, this refrain surfaces like a cry that cannot be suppressed: *Restore us, O God. Make your face shine on us, that we may be saved.* It is a liturgy of desperation. And yet, paradoxically, it is also a liturgy of extraordinary faith.

Consider what the prayer assumes. To ask God to *restore* something is to believe that there was once wholeness, and that wholeness is possible again. The Hebrew word translated "restore" carries the idea of turning, bringing back, or reversing direction. The people are not asking God to build something entirely new from scratch. They are asking him to return them to what they were made to be. Embedded in the very grammar of the prayer is a theology of hope: what God has made, God can remake. What has been broken by sin and suffering and the long wearing-down of time is not beyond his ability to mend.

Then there is that beautiful, ancient phrase: *make your face shine on us.* It echoes the Aaronic blessing of Numbers 6, where God instructs the priests to bless the people with nearly identical words: "The LORD make his face shine on you and be gracious to you." In the ancient world, the shining of a king's face meant favor, warmth, and access. To be in the light of a ruler's countenance was to be safe, seen, and welcomed. To have that face turned away was to be in darkness, cut off, vulnerable to every enemy. The psalmist is not reaching for metaphor as literary decoration. He is reaching for his life. *Look at us, God. Turn toward us. Let us feel the warmth of your regard again.*

There is something profoundly personal here, even within a communal prayer. Most of us know what it feels like to move through seasons when God seems distant, when prayers feel like words dissolving in empty air, when the distance between who we are and who we long to be feels unbridgeable. Restoration is not an abstract theological concept in those moments. It is the one thing the heart cannot stop wanting. We want to be returned to ourselves and returned to God.

The final phrase anchors everything: *that we may be saved.* The psalmist knows that restoration is not ultimately about comfort or national pride or the return of better circumstances. It is about salvation. The shining of God's face is not merely pleasant; it is life-giving. Without it, there is no rescue. With it, no enemy, no exile, no darkness is the final word.

What makes this verse so enduringly powerful is its refusal to be sophisticated about its need. The people do not offer a plan for their own restoration. They do not propose reforms or strategies. They simply confess that they cannot restore themselves, and that only the face of God, turned toward them in grace, can save them. It is, in the truest sense, an act of faith to pray this prayer. It is the admission that our best efforts at self-restoration have limits, and the conviction that God's grace does not.

If you find yourself in a season of spiritual dryness, of failure, of loss, or of that quiet despair that has no single name, this verse is your permission to pray without pretense. *Restore me, God Almighty. Let me feel your nearness again. Save me.* God does not turn away from that prayer. He never has.

PRAYER

Father, we come to you not with polished words but with honest need. Restore what has been broken in us: our faith, our joy, our sense of your nearness. Turn your face toward us today, not because we have earned it, but because you are gracious and because your mercy is the only hope we have. Shine on us, Lord. Save us. Amen.

THE STRENGTH BEHIND OUR SONG

Sing for joy to God our strength; shout aloud to the God of Jacob
(Psalm 81:1).

There is something profoundly counterintuitive about the opening verse of Psalm 81. "Sing for joy to God our strength; shout aloud to the God of Jacob." The psalmist does not whisper a timid prayer or offer a subdued acknowledgment. Instead, he calls us to sing, to shout, to make joyful noise. But notice what comes immediately after that command: "to God our strength."

This pairing reveals a vital truth about the nature of worship and the character of God. We sing not because we are strong, but because he is. We shout not from our own abundance, but because of his inexhaustible power. The very act of worship is an admission of our need and a celebration of his sufficiency.

Consider how often we approach life from the opposite direction. We wait until we feel strong to take action. We postpone joy until circumstances improve. We reserve our celebrations for moments when we have achieved something worthy of praise. But the psalmist flips this script entirely. He commands us to sing to the One who is our strength precisely because we need strength. The song comes first; the strength follows.

This is the paradox at the heart of biblical worship. When we feel weakest, when circumstances press in from every side, when our own resources have run dry, these are the very moments when we are called to lift our voices. Not because we are pretending everything is fine, but because we acknowledge that our security has never rested on our own capabilities. God is our strength, whether we feel strong or not.

The reference to "the God of Jacob" deepens this truth. Jacob was not a hero of unwavering faith. He was a schemer, a deceiver, a man who wrestled with God and with his own limitations throughout his life.

Yet God met him repeatedly, transformed him, and made him into a patriarch of faith. When we shout to "the God of Jacob," we acknowledge that God works with flawed people, that his strength is made perfect in our weakness, and that his faithfulness does not depend on our perfection.

There is also something communal embedded in this verse. The psalmist uses plural pronouns throughout: "our strength," inviting us into corporate worship. We do sing alone; we sing together. When one person's voice falters, another's rises. When you cannot find words, the person beside you carries the melody. The strength we find in God is both personal and collective, and our worship reflects this reality.

But why joy? Why not simply dutiful obedience or resigned acceptance? Because joy is the natural response to recognizing who God is and what he has done. It is the emotional overflow of understanding that we are not alone, that we are not relying on our own meager resources, that the One who created mountains and oceans and galaxies has become our personal fortress. Joy does not mean the absence of struggle; it means the presence of hope even in the midst of difficulty.

The command to "shout aloud" is equally significant. This is not quiet, controlled, respectable worship. It is exuberant, unrestrained, and even disruptive. Sometimes our praise needs to break through the ceiling of our circumstances, to drown out the voice of fear, to declare with volume what our hearts know to be true, even when our feelings lag behind.

In our contemporary context, where strength is often equated with self-sufficiency and independence, this verse offers a radically different vision. True strength comes from recognizing our dependence on

God. True joy emerges not from controlling our circumstances but from trusting the One who holds us steady through every storm. True worship happens when we stop trying to manage our image and simply respond to God's character with honest, wholehearted praise.

So today, whether you feel strong or weak, whether circumstances are favorable or challenging, whether your faith feels rock-solid or paper-thin, the invitation remains the same: sing for joy. Shout aloud. Not because you have it all together, but because God is your strength. Not because you have arrived, but because he is faithful. Let your voice join the chorus of those who have discovered that the greatest power comes not from standing on our own but from standing on the foundation of God's unchanging love.

PRAYER

Lord, you are our strength when we have none of our own. Teach us to sing even when our hearts feel heavy, to shout your praises even when doubt whispers in our ears. Help us remember that our joy rests not in our circumstances but in your faithfulness. May our worship today be honest, exuberant, and rooted in the truth of who you are. Amen.

PSALM 82

A CALL TO JUSTICE

Defend the weak and the fatherless; uphold the cause of the poor and the oppressed (Psalm 82:3).

The psalmist's words cut through the centuries with remarkable clarity. They speak to a timeless principle embedded within the character of God himself. When the writer of Psalm 82 addresses those in positions of authority, whether judges, leaders, or anyone wielding influence, the command is unambiguous: defend the vulnerable. This is not a suggestion for the spiritually ambitious or a challenge for the exceptionally charitable. It is a fundamental obligation for all who claim to follow the God of Israel.

The context of Psalm 82 reveals God standing in the divine assembly, passing judgment on those who have neglected their sacred duty to care for the marginalized. "How long will you defend the unjust and show partiality to the wicked?" God asks (v. 2). The answer is clear: the time for evasion has ended. Justice delayed is justice denied, and those who hold power bear responsibility before Almighty God for how they exercise it.

Three groups are highlighted in this verse: the weak, the fatherless, and the poor and oppressed. Each designation carries profound theological weight in the Hebrew scriptures. The weak, those lacking strength, resources, or influence, required protection because they could not protect themselves. The fatherless held a particular status in ancient Israel, representing not merely those without paternal guidance but those entirely bereft of a male protector in a patriarchal society. Without a father, brother, or kinsman redeemer, orphans stood at the mercy of systemic indifference. The poor and oppressed encompassed those crushed by economic injustice and those actively victimized by the powerful.

What makes this command remarkable is its theological foundation. The God of Israel does not issue this decree as a mere ethical preference. Rather, God repeatedly demonstrates in Scripture that defending the vulnerable reflects the very nature of the divine character. When God acts, God acts on behalf of the enslaved, the displaced, the hungry, and the abandoned. The exodus itself was fundamentally an act of divine justice: God coming down to liberate the oppressed from Egyptian bondage. The psalms repeatedly celebrate this reality: "For the LORD watches over the way of the righteous, but the way of the wicked leads to destruction" (Psalm 1:6). Justice is not peripheral to God's character; it is central to it.

In our contemporary context, this ancient command resonates with even greater urgency. We live in a world of staggering inequality. The weak are still with us: those suffering from poverty, homelessness, and disease. The fatherless remain: children growing up without stable families, without mentors, without advocates. The oppressed are everywhere: those marginalized by systemic injustice, discrimination, and exploitation. The psalmist's demand that we defend these vulnerable populations is not a suggestion for denominational charity committees. It is a summons addressed to every follower of Christ.

Consider what this defense entails. It requires more than pity or sympathy. Defending the weak means taking action, using whatever resources, influence, and position we possess to create protection and opportunity for those who lack them. It means speaking when the weak have no voice, standing when they cannot stand on their own, and intervening when society overlooks their suffering. For some, this may mean direct service in homeless shelters, food banks, or advocacy organizations. For others, it may mean using professional expertise to reform unjust systems. For many, it means simply refusing to remain silent in the presence of injustice.

The beauty of Psalm 82:3 lies in its universal applicability. You need not hold formal office or wield governmental power to obey this command. Parents defend their weak children. Employers can defend vulnerable workers from exploitation. Teachers can defend struggling students. Neighbors can defend vulnerable neighbors. Every person occupies some sphere of influence, some context where power operates, and in each of those places, we are called to defend the vulnerable.

Yet this command also carries a warning. The verses surrounding it make clear that those who ignore this duty face God's judgment: "'Because the poor are plundered and the needy groan, I will now arise,' says the LORD" (Psalm 12:5). The God who commands justice is also the God who will execute it. We cannot claim faith in this God while remaining indifferent to the suffering of the vulnerable.

As you reflect on this verse today, consider: Where do you encounter the weak, the fatherless, the poor, or the oppressed? What resources, time, money, skills, and influence has God given you? How might you more faithfully answer the psalmist's call to defend them?

PRAYER

O God of justice and mercy, forgive us for our indifference to the suffering of the vulnerable. Open our eyes to see those around us who lack protection, resources, and hope. Grant us courage to speak for those without a voice, strength to stand for those who cannot stand, and wisdom to work toward systems that reflect your justice rather than perpetuate oppression. Make us defenders of the weak, advocates for the fatherless, champions of the poor. Transform our comfortable faith into active compassion. We pray in the name of Jesus, who came that the captives might be freed and the oppressed might be released. Amen.

THE CRY FOR GOD'S PRESENCE

O God, do not remain silent; do not turn a deaf ear, do not stand aloof, O God (Psalm 83:1).

The opening verse of Psalm 83 presents one of the most poignant and urgent cries in the entire Psalter. The psalmist's words burst forth with an almost desperate intensity: "O God, do not remain silent; do not turn a deaf ear, do not stand aloof, O God." In these opening lines, we encounter the fundamental human fear that God has abandoned us, that our prayers fall on deaf ears, and that the Almighty remains indifferent to our suffering. Yet this verse, situated at the beginning of a corporate lament, invites us to examine what it truly means to cry out to God in our darkest moments and how such vulnerability can become the pathway to renewed faith.

The structure of this verse reveals the psalmist's escalating concern. The repetition of imperatives, "do not remain silent," "do not turn a deaf ear," "do not stand aloof," creates a rhythmic intensity that mirrors the urgency of the psalmist's need. Each prohibition builds upon the previous one, moving from cosmic silence to deliberate avoidance. The psalmist fears not merely that God cannot hear but that God will not hear, that divine attention is being deliberately withheld. This distinction matters profoundly. It suggests that the crisis facing the community is not merely one of circumstance but of perceived abandonment.

The phrase "remain silent" speaks to God's role as a responding judge and king. Throughout the Scriptures, God's silence often marks judgment or withdrawal of favor. When God speaks, mountains tremble, and nations are established. When God is silent, the righteous question whether divine justice still operates in the world. The psalmist's plea here assumes that God's voice is the solution to whatever crisis threatens the community. Only when God breaks the silence can order be restored and justice established.

To "turn a deaf ear" suggests something more than mere inattention; it implies a deliberate closing off of divine perception. The psalmist recognizes that God possesses both the power to hear and the freedom to choose whether to listen. This acknowledgment positions us in a place of radical dependence. We cannot compel God's attention through the force of our need alone. We can only appeal, petition, and implore. The verb forms used here are pleas rather than demands, revealing the appropriate posture of the creature before the Creator.

The final phrase, "do not stand aloof," conveys the sense of God withdrawing into the distance, becoming a neutral observer rather than an active participant in human affairs. To stand aloof is to refuse involvement, to maintain detachment from our suffering. The psalmist's fear is that God has become an unconcerned spectator to the troubles facing God's people. This fear resonates across the centuries with all who have questioned why God seems distant during our seasons of greatest need.

Yet there is profound spiritual wisdom in bringing such fears before God rather than suppressing them. By voicing this dread directly to God, the psalmist does not abandon faith; rather, the psalmist exercises faith. To cry out to God, even with accusations of silence or indifference, is to affirm that God alone can address the situation. The very act of prayer becomes a declaration that we still believe God is listening, even as we plead for God to prove it.

The context of Psalm 83 reveals that this opening cry precedes a description of enemies gathering against God's people. The community faces external threats and perhaps internal confusion about divine protection. In such moments, the silence of God becomes intolerable. The psalmist needs reassurance that the Almighty still champions the cause of the vulnerable and still judges those who oppose God's covenant people.

In our contemporary context, this verse speaks to experiences common to all believers. We face seasons when prayer echoes in empty chambers. We struggle through circumstances where God's guidance feels absent and divine intervention seems nowhere to be found. In these moments, Psalm 83:1 gives us permission to voice our concerns, cry out in our anguish, and demand that God act. Such cries are not unfaithful; they are expressions of faith that assume God remains responsive to covenant prayers.

The devotional power of this verse lies in its honesty and its hope. The honesty acknowledges that silence from God is one of our deepest spiritual fears. The hope rests in the conviction that God will not ultimately remain unmoved by the cries of the faithful. By bringing our most desperate questions before the throne of grace, we position ourselves to hear God's response, to experience renewed assurance of divine presence, and to discover that God was never truly silent; we simply needed to quiet ourselves enough to listen.

PRAYER

O God, we come before you with the same urgency as the psalmist of old. We confess our fear that you may have grown silent in our lives, that perhaps you have turned away from our struggles. Yet even as we voice these fears, we affirm our trust that you remain the God who hears, the God who acts, and the God who will not ultimately abandon those who call upon your name. Grant us grace to wait for your response, wisdom to discern your subtle movements, and faith to believe that your silence is never the final word. In the name of Christ our Lord, we pray. Amen.

THE SOUL'S DEEP LONGING

My soul yearns, even faints, for the courts of the LORD; my heart and my flesh cry out for the living God (Psalm 84:2).

There is a hunger built into the human heart that nothing earthly can satisfy. The psalmist captures this profound truth with visceral language that speaks to our deepest experience. He does not merely say he wants to go to the temple or that he thinks worship is important. He uses words like "yearns," "faints," and "cry out," the vocabulary of desperate need, not casual preference.

This verse reveals three dimensions of spiritual longing that resonate across the centuries to our own souls today.

First, notice the intensity of the desire. The soul does not just want or wish; it yearns. This is the language of aching, of being stretched toward something just beyond reach. The Hebrew word suggests a longing so intense it causes physical weakness, even to the point of fainting. Have you ever wanted something so badly that it left you breathless? This is how the psalmist describes his longing for God's presence.

We live in an age of casual spirituality, where faith is often reduced to a lifestyle accessory or a source of occasional inspiration. But the psalmist reminds us that a true relationship with God engages us at the deepest level. It is not about fitting God into our schedule or adding religious practices to our routine. It is about recognizing that our souls were made for him and cannot rest until they rest in him.

Second, observe the completeness of the longing. The psalmist says both his heart and his flesh cry out. This is not merely intellectual assent or emotional sentiment; it is a whole-person response. Our minds may engage theological concepts, our emotions may respond to worship, but there is something more profound happening here. The "flesh" crying out suggests that even our physical bodies are attuned to this spiritual reality. We are integrated beings, and our longing for God involves every part of who we are.

This challenges the false division between the spiritual and physical aspects of life. The psalmist does not apologize for the bodily dimension of worship or try to spiritualize it away. Instead, he embraces it. When we gather for worship, when we lift our hands, when we kneel in prayer, when we fast or feast in celebration, these physical acts matter because we are embodied souls. Our whole selves were designed to connect with our creator.

Third, consider the object of this longing: "the living God." Not an idea, not a philosophy, not even a set of religious practices, but a living, personal God. The psalmist yearns for the courts of the Lord because that is where God's presence dwells. The temple, the tabernacle, the gathered assembly, these were not ends in themselves but gateways to encountering the One who is alive and active.

This phrase "the living God" distinguished Israel's faith from the surrounding cultures with their lifeless idols. Those gods of wood and stone could neither hear nor respond. But the God of Israel is dynamic, personal, and present. He sees, hears, acts, and relates. This is why the psalmist's longing makes sense: you can have a relationship with a living God in ways that are impossible with mere religious concepts.

For us today, this verse poses a challenging question: do we share this intensity of longing? In our world of endless entertainment and comfortable religion, have we lost touch with this deep hunger? Or have we perhaps tried to satisfy it with substitutes, with religious activity instead of relationship, with theological knowledge instead of transformative encounter, with the trappings of faith instead of the living God himself?

The beautiful truth is that this yearning, when we feel it, is itself a gift from God. Augustine famously prayed, "You have made us for yourself, and our hearts are restless until they rest in you." That restlessness, that ache, that sense of something missing, these are not problems to be solved but invitations to be accepted. God has placed eternity in our hearts, and he alone can fill that God-shaped void within us.

If you have lost that longing, ask God to reawaken it. If you feel it now, lean into it. Let your soul yearn. Let your heart and flesh cry out. This is not weakness but wisdom, the recognition of our deepest need and the one who alone can meet it.

PRAYER

Living God, awaken in us a holy hunger for your presence. When our souls grow cold and our hearts become complacent, stir within us that deep yearning that can only be satisfied by you. Draw us into your courts not out of duty but out of desperate desire. May our whole selves, heart, soul, mind, and strength cry out for you, the only one who can truly satisfy the longing you yourself have placed within us. In Jesus' name, Amen.

PSALM 85

LOVE AND FAITHFULNESS
MEET TOGETHER

*Love and faithfulness meet together; righteousness and peace kiss
each other* (Psalm 85:10).

Few verses in Scripture capture the reconciliation between God's
seemingly divergent attributes as beautifully as Psalm 85:10. This verse
presents a theological portrait of divine harmony, the meeting of
mercy and truth, justice and peace, in a way that speaks to both the
contemplative mind and the longing heart. To understand this verse,
we must first situate ourselves within the psalm's context and then
allow its profound implications to reshape our understanding of God
and his work in our lives.

Psalm 85 belongs to a collection of psalms addressing national
restoration. The community faces displacement or judgment, and the
psalmist cries out for divine favor and restoration. The earlier verses
(1–7) rehearse God's past faithfulness: "You showed favor to your
land, O LORD; you restored the fortunes of Jacob." Yet the psalm
transitions to lament, acknowledging that Israel has provoked God's
anger through sin. By verse 10, however, the tone shifts. The psalmist
perceives a turning point, a moment where God's redemptive
purposes converge.

The verse employs personification to describe four divine attributes
meeting as if they were persons greeting or embracing one another.
Love and faithfulness meet together. Righteousness and peace kiss
each other. This is no accident of poetic language; it is a profound
theological assertion that God's character is fundamentally unified,
despite what our circumstances might suggest.

When we experience God's justice without mercy, we may conclude that God is harsh. When we encounter grace without accountability, we might imagine God is indifferent to moral order. The psalmist reminds us that this is an incomplete picture. God does not compartmentalize his attributes. His love never operates apart from his faithfulness to keep his word. His righteousness never excludes his desire for our peace. In the economy of God's kingdom, these attributes do not conflict; they converge in perfect harmony.

Consider the cross of Christ, where this convergence reaches its apex. At Calvary, God's justice demanded payment for sin, yet his mercy provided the payment through his own Son. Righteousness and peace kissed each other at the empty tomb. The resurrection vindicated God's commitment to both moral order and redemptive restoration. We are justified (declared righteous through Christ) yet transformed into peacemakers and bearers of God's peace. The meeting place of these divine attributes is Jesus himself.

For those of us walking in seasons of uncertainty, this verse offers profound comfort. We may find ourselves in circumstances where justice seems distant, where we cry out for God to act righteously on our behalf. We may also wonder whether God's mercy covers our own failings and shortcomings. Psalm 85:10 assures us that these concerns need not be in tension. God will vindicate his purposes, and in that vindication, his mercy will shine forth. His faithfulness to his promises means that he will complete the redemptive work he has begun in us.

The verse also calls us to embody this convergence in our own lives. As followers of Christ, we are called to reflect his character. How often do we err by emphasizing either justice or mercy in isolation? In our churches, we may focus so intently on doctrinal precision (righteousness) that we lose our capacity for compassion (love). Conversely, we may pursue hospitality and inclusion (peace) while neglecting the hard work of maintaining integrity and accountability (faithfulness). The psalmist invites us into a more mature spirituality, one where these virtues dance together rather than compete.

In our personal relationships, the convergence of these attributes transforms how we relate to one another. When we must address someone's wrongdoing, we can speak the truth in love, combining righteousness with mercy. When we extend forgiveness, we do so not by pretending the wrong never occurred (which would deny righteousness) but by releasing our need for retribution while maintaining appropriate boundaries. We are called to be agents of peacemaking, but never at the expense of truth.

Finally, this verse invites us to trust in God's character during seasons when restoration feels impossible. If you find yourself in a spiritual winter, when judgment or consequence feels heavy, remember that love and faithfulness still meet together in God's heart. If you wonder whether you are worthy of grace, remember that righteousness and peace still kiss in God's redemptive purposes. The meeting place of these attributes is where God always works.

PRAYER

Eternal God, we thank you for the mystery and majesty of your character. We confess that we often struggle to hold together your justice and your mercy, your truth and your compassion. Yet you have revealed in Christ that these attributes need not be in tension: they converge in perfect harmony within your redemptive work. Grant us grace to live in light of this convergence, reflecting in our own lives your commitment to both righteousness and peace, love and faithfulness. Transform our hearts that we might be agents of this same reconciliation in a fractured world. Amen.

AN UNDIVIDED HEART

Teach me your way, LORD, *that I may rely on your faithfulness; give me an undivided heart, that I may fear your name* (Psalm 86:11).

In Psalm 86:11, David makes a request that cuts to the very heart of spiritual life: "Teach me your way, LORD, that I may rely on your faithfulness; give me an undivided heart, that I may fear your name." This single verse contains a profound progression, from learning to trusting to experiencing the transformation of our inner being.

David begins with a posture of humility: "Teach me your way, LORD." Here is a king, a man after God's own heart, acknowledging that he still needs instruction. The prayer recognizes that God's ways are not our ways by instinct. We need divine teaching to understand how to walk the path that leads to life. This teaching is not merely intellectual knowledge about God, but experiential wisdom gained through a relationship with him. God's way encompasses his character, his purposes, his commandments, and the manner in which he operates in the world. To learn God's way is to learn God himself.

But David does not stop at knowledge. He connects teaching to trust: "that I may rely on your faithfulness." The purpose of learning God's way is not to accumulate religious information but to deepen our dependence on his unchanging character. God's faithfulness is the bedrock upon which our spiritual lives are built. When we truly understand his ways, when we see how he has kept his promises throughout history and in our own lives, we naturally lean into his reliability. Reliance is not passive; it is the active choice to stake our lives on God's trustworthy nature, even when circumstances seem uncertain.

The second half of the verse introduces David's most vulnerable request: "give me an undivided heart, that I may fear your name." Here, David acknowledges a fundamental human struggle: the tendency toward internal division. The Hebrew word translated "undivided" carries the sense of being unified or made one. David is asking God to heal the fractures within him, to gather all the scattered pieces of his affection, attention, and will, and to direct them toward a single point: the reverence and worship of God alone.

An undivided heart stands in stark contrast to the duplicity that so easily besets us. We live in an age of fragmented attention, where our hearts are pulled in countless directions: toward comfort, success, approval, security, pleasure, and a thousand lesser gods. We often attempt to serve God while keeping one foot planted in other kingdoms. We worship on Sunday while bowing to other altars the rest of the week. David's prayer recognizes that this division weakens us spiritually and prevents us from experiencing the fullness of life with God.

The fear of God's name that David seeks is not terror but reverent awe, the proper response to encountering the holy, the recognition of God's supreme worth and authority. This fear is the beginning of wisdom, the foundation of authentic worship. But such fear requires wholeness of heart. We cannot truly fear God's name, cannot properly revere and honor him, when our hearts are divided among competing loyalties.

Notice the order of David's requests. He asks first to be taught God's way so he can rely on God's faithfulness, and this foundation enables him to ask for an undivided heart. This progression matters. We cannot manufacture wholehearted devotion through sheer willpower. An undivided heart is God's gift, granted as we grow in our understanding of his ways and our trust in his character. As we learn who God truly is and experience his faithfulness again and again, our hearts are slowly drawn away from lesser things and unified in devotion to him.

This prayer is one we might return to throughout our lives, because the journey toward an undivided heart is ongoing. Even as we grow spiritually, new divisions can emerge: new distractions, new fears, new idols. We need God's continual teaching, his faithfulness to lean upon, and his unifying work in our hearts. The beautiful truth is that God delights to answer this prayer. He desires our wholehearted love even more than we desire to give it. When we ask him to unify our hearts, we are asking for something he is already at work to accomplish.

PRAYER

Father, teach me your way. Show me who you truly are and how you work in this world. Help me to rely completely on your faithfulness, which never fails. I confess the divisions within my own heart, the scattered affections and competing loyalties that pull me away from wholehearted devotion to you. Give me an undivided heart, Lord. Gather all that I am and direct it toward the reverence and worship of your holy name. May I fear you rightly and love you completely, all the days of my life. In Jesus' name, Amen.

THE CITIZENSHIP OF FAITH

The LORD *will write in the register of the peoples: "This one was born in Zion." As they make music they will sing, "All my fountains are in you"* (Psalm 87:6–7).

The promise embedded in these two verses from Psalm 87 speaks to one of the deepest longings of the human heart: the assurance of belonging. To be written in a register, to have one's name recorded in an official document, means to be recognized as legitimate, as claimed, as belonging to a particular people. When the psalmist declares that the Lord will write the names of believers in the register of the peoples with the notation "This one was born in Zion," we encounter a profound statement about spiritual citizenship and divine adoption that transcends national boundaries and ethnic limitations.

The context of Psalm 87 places Zion, Jerusalem, the city of God, not merely as a geographic location but as a spiritual reality. Throughout the Psalms, Zion represents the dwelling place of God, the center of divine presence and blessing. What makes this psalm remarkable is its insistent universalism. The preceding verses celebrate how God has established Zion as a foundation city, and then the psalmist lists various nations, Rahab (Egypt), Babylon, Philistia, Tyre, and Cush (Ethiopia), declaring that these peoples will be considered as "born there." This is revolutionary language. Despite their geographic distance from Jerusalem, despite their historical enmity toward Israel, and despite their pagan origins, these nations are invited into a spiritual citizenship that transcends human categories of inclusion and exclusion.

The image of registration appears significant throughout Scripture. Moses writes the names of the faithful in a book (Exodus 32:32). Daniel speaks of names written in the book of life (Daniel 12:1).

Revelation employs this same metaphor repeatedly. Names written in God's register carry weight beyond mere documentation; they signify permanence, value, and an unbreakable claim upon God's attention and care. When God writes our names in the register of the peoples with the designation "born in Zion," God declares us members of God's own household, citizens of the spiritual commonwealth whose foundation is God's holiness and whose walls are God's saving grace.

The second verse shifts from registration to celebration. "As they make music they will sing, 'All my fountains are in you.'" Here, the psalmist envisions the peoples of earth joining in corporate worship, their musical praise acknowledging that all their sources of life, nourishment, and renewal flow from God alone. The image of fountains evokes artesian springs that gush up from deep within the earth, providing water when the surface would otherwise be dry. In an ancient Near Eastern context, where water determined survival, the metaphor carried visceral power. To declare that all one's fountains are in God is to acknowledge absolute dependence upon divine provision.

What transforms these verses from mere poetry into spiritual truth is their application to Christian believers. Through Jesus Christ, we who come from every nation and language have been granted access to spiritual citizenship in Zion. Our birth certificate in God's kingdom does not depend upon our ancestry, our accomplishments, or our worthiness. Rather, it rests entirely upon God's sovereign grace. The blood of Christ has written our names in the register, has adopted us into the household of faith, has granted us the status of those "born in Zion."

The invitation to join the music and sing that all our fountains are in God calls us to a profound reorientation of our lives. We live in a world that teaches us to trust in our own resources: our talents, our income, our networks, our physical strength. We construct elaborate systems of self-sufficiency and independence. Yet the psalmist invites us to sing a counternarrative: all our true sources of life and sustenance flow from God. Our creativity comes from the creator. Our security rests in God's faithfulness. Our hope springs from God's promises. Our joy bubbles up from God's presence.

This psalm calls us to move from isolation to community, from anonymous existence to named belonging. It invites us to recognize that our registration in God's book makes us part of a vast company of saints across all nations and all ages. We are not alone; we belong to the people of God. And it summons us to join the music, to add our voice to the chorus of those who have discovered that every fountain of blessing in their lives flows from the God who has written them into the register of the peoples, marking them as belonging forever to Zion.

PRAYER

O God of all peoples, I thank you that my name is written in your register, that you have claimed me as one born in Zion through the grace of Jesus Christ. Forgive me for the countless times I have sought sustenance from broken cisterns when all my fountains are in you. Teach me today to trust more deeply in your provision, to rest more completely in your care, and to sing more joyfully that you are the source of all that matters. Draw me closer into the communion of saints across all nations, and grant me a glad heart as I add my voice to their praise. Amen.

WHEN PRAYER FEELS LIKE CRYING

LORD, you are the God who saves me; day and night I cry out to you. May my prayer come before you; turn your ear to my cry (Psalm 88:1–2).

There are seasons in life when prayer does not feel like a peaceful conversation with God, but more like a cry of desperation. Psalm 88 gives voice to this raw, unfiltered kind of faith, the kind that shows up day and night, even when the heavens seem silent. The psalmist does not begin with praise or thanksgiving but with an urgent, almost desperate appeal: "LORD, you are the God who saves me; day and night I cry out to you."

What strikes us immediately is the tension in these opening verses. The psalmist affirms God as "the God who saves me" while simultaneously crying out for that very salvation. This is faith in its most honest form: believing in God's character while wrestling with present circumstances that seem to contradict everything we know to be true about him. It is the faith of someone who clings to theology when experience offers little comfort.

The phrase "day and night" reveals the relentless nature of this person's suffering. This is not a momentary difficulty or a passing trial. The psalmist's pain has become the rhythm of his life, marking both his waking hours and his sleepless nights. Yet remarkably, this same phrase also describes the persistence of his prayer. His suffering is constant, but so is his crying out to God. He has not given up. He has not turned away. Even in profound darkness, he continues to direct his anguish toward the One who can save.

This teaches us something vital about prayer: it does not always have to be eloquent, composed, or full of faith-filled declarations.

Sometimes prayer is simply showing up before God with our pain and refusing to go anywhere else with it. The psalmist models for us that bringing our complaints to God is itself an act of faith. To cry out to God in our darkest moments is to affirm that he is still there, still listening, still capable of responding, even when we cannot feel his presence or see his hand at work.

Notice the plea: "May my prayer come before you; turn your ear to my cry." The psalmist asks for God's attention, for his attentiveness. This request acknowledges a fundamental truth about our relationship with God: we need him to hear us, to incline himself toward us, to bridge the gap between heaven and earth. We cannot manufacture his presence or force his response, but we can persistently place ourselves before him, trusting that our prayers matter to him.

What makes Psalm 88 so unusual, and so honest, is that it ends without resolution. Unlike most psalms that move from lament to praise, from complaint to confidence, Psalm 88 concludes in darkness. Yet its inclusion in Scripture is itself a profound message: God welcomes our unresolved grief. He does not require us to tie everything up with a neat bow before we come to him. He receives our midnight cries, our desperate pleas, our faith that wavers but does not quit.

In our contemporary Christian culture, we sometimes feel pressure to always be victorious, always full of joy, always testifying to a breakthrough. But Psalm 88 gives us permission to simply be honest. It tells us that persevering faith is not always about feeling strong or declaring victory; sometimes it is about continuing to cry out to the God who saves us, even when the salvation we are crying for has not yet arrived.

The psalmist's example challenges us to examine where we take our deepest pain. Do we numb it, distract ourselves from it, or complain about it to everyone except God? Or do we follow this ancient model of relentless, honest prayer that refuses to seek comfort anywhere but in the presence of the one who saves?

Perhaps you are in your own season of crying out day and night. Perhaps your prayers feel like they are bouncing off the ceiling, and you wonder if God is listening at all. Let Psalm 88 encourage you: your persistent crying out is itself a profound expression of faith. Keep showing up before God. Keep turning your ear toward him even as you ask him to turn his ear toward you. The God who saves is the God who hears, and even our midnight cries reach his attentive heart.

PRAYER

Lord, you are the God who saves me. In this moment, I bring before you everything that weighs heavily on my heart. Hear my cry, O God, and turn your ear to my prayer. Even when I cannot feel your presence, help me to persist in faith, trusting that you receive every honest word I bring before you. Give me grace to wait for your salvation, even when the darkness feels overwhelming. Amen.

PSALM 89

A SONG OF ETERNAL COVENANT

I will sing of the LORD's great love forever; with my mouth I will make your faithfulness known through all generations. I will declare that your love stands firm forever, that you have established your faithfulness in heaven itself (Psalm 89:1–2).

The opening verses of Psalm 89 deliver a bold and confident declaration of faith that resonates powerfully, especially when considering the deep spiritual crisis that occurs later in the same psalm. The psalmist begins with an unequivocal pledge to proclaim the Lord's steadfast love and faithfulness, vowing to recall these divine qualities across all generations. However, beneath this uplifting declaration lies a significant theological tension that challenges us to reflect on both the foundation of our faith and the difficulties that test it.

The Hebrew verb translated as "sing" carries rich connotations in Hebrew poetry. To sing is not merely to produce pleasant sounds, but to declare solemnly, to proclaim with the voice, to testify publicly. The psalmist employs the imperfect tense, suggesting not a single act of singing but a habitual, ongoing commitment. This is a vow, an intentional, deliberate decision to proclaim the Lord's lovingkindness the defining characteristic of one's life and ministry. The use of "forever" emphasizes the enduring, perpetual nature of this commitment. The psalmist is not promising a temporary enthusiasm but a lifetime dedication to articulating God's covenant love.

The term "great love" translates the Hebrew *hesed*, one of the most theologically rich words in the Old Testament lexicon. *Hesed* encompasses covenant loyalty, steadfast love, mercy, and grace. It refers not to emotional sentiment but to God's binding commitment to his people, rooted in the covenant relationship established at Sinai. By declaring that he will sing of God's *hesed* "forever," the psalmist affirms his conviction that this covenant love is the fundamental reality underlying all existence and all history.

The second verse intensifies this declaration through a different but complementary approach. Where verse one emphasizes the public proclamation of God's love, verse two focuses on the theological affirmation of God's faithfulness, or more precisely, God's truth. The psalmist declares that this divine attribute does not merely exist in historical time but is established "in heaven itself," which points to the cosmic, transcendent dimension of God's reliability. God's faithfulness is not subject to the vicissitudes of human affairs or the mutations of earthly circumstance; it is anchored in the eternal realm beyond our temporal limitations.

The promise to make God's faithfulness "known through all generations" reflects the psalmist's understanding of a corporate responsibility to transmit theological truth and covenantal memory across time. In ancient Israelite thought, each generation bore responsibility for rehearsing and preserving the mighty acts of God, ensuring that the knowledge of God's character and covenant remained alive in communal memory and religious practice. This reflects the instruction in Deuteronomy 6, in which parents are commanded to teach God's ordinances diligently to their children, speaking of them continually.

The phrase "your love stands firm forever" represents an emphatic affirmation of permanence. The Hebrew structure suggests not merely that love exists perpetually, but that it is established, fixed, immovable, like a foundation stone upon which all else rests. In a world characterized by change, uncertainty, and the seeming fragility of human purposes, the psalmist anchors faith in something absolute and eternal.

What makes these verses particularly poignant is that they introduce a psalm that ultimately becomes a profound lament. By verse 38, the psalmist cries out in anguish, questioning whether God has rejected his anointed and cast off his people. The temple lies in ruins; the Davidic monarchy has collapsed. The confident proclamation of verses 1 and 2 thus stands in stark relief against the pain and perplexity that follow. Yet therein lies the profound truth these verses encapsulate: authentic faith does not depend upon favorable circumstances or visible evidence of divine favor. The commitment to sing of God's love and to proclaim his faithfulness persists even when experience contradicts expectation.

For contemporary believers, Psalm 89:1–2 calls us to examine the foundation of our own faith. Do we sing of God's steadfast love only when circumstances favor it, or do we commit ourselves to this proclamation regardless of circumstance? Do we truly believe that God's faithfulness is established in heaven itself, transcending the tribulations of earthly life? These verses invite us to join with the psalmist in a deliberate, covenantal commitment to make known the character of God across generations, maintaining faith not because all is well, but because God remains faithful regardless of how our sight might deceive us.

PRAYER

Eternal God, we praise you for your steadfast love that endures beyond the comprehension of mortal minds. Grant us the courage and conviction of the psalmist, that we might proclaim your faithfulness not only in seasons of abundance and joy, but also in times of darkness and doubt. Help us anchor our faith in your eternal character rather than in the fluctuating circumstances of our lives. May we faithfully transmit knowledge of your covenant love to generations yet unborn. In Jesus Christ our Lord, we pray. Amen.

THE GIFT OF NUMBERED DAYS

Teach us to number our days, that we may gain a heart of wisdom
(Psalm 90:12).

In the rush of modern life, we often live as though we have an endless supply of tomorrows. We defer difficult conversations, postpone meaningful pursuits, and accumulate regrets like loose change in our pockets. But Psalm 90:12 confronts us with a profound truth: our days are numbered, and recognizing this reality is the doorway to wisdom.

Moses, the author of this psalm, understood impermanence intimately. He had watched an entire generation perish in the wilderness, their numbered days complete before entering the Promised Land. He had seen the fragility of human life set against the backdrop of God's eternality. The psalm opens with a stark contrast: "Before the mountains were born or you brought forth the whole world, from everlasting to everlasting you are God." Against this infinite canvas, human life appears as brief as grass that flourishes in the morning and withers by evening.

Yet Moses does not pray for God to extend our days or reverse mortality's clock. Instead, he asks for something far more valuable: that God would teach us to number our days. This is a curious request. We already know, intellectually, that our time is finite. We mark birthdays, watch our children grow, and notice the silver threading through our hair. But there is a vast difference between knowing we will die someday and truly numbering our days, between acknowledging mortality as an abstract concept and allowing it to shape how we live each irreplaceable moment.

To number our days is to live with intentionality rather than passivity. It means recognizing that every morning is a gift, not a guarantee.

When we truly grasp this, our priorities clarify remarkably quickly. The petty grievances that consume our emotional energy shrink in significance. The relationships we have been taking for granted suddenly demand our attention and care. The dreams we have been deferring reveal themselves as now-or-never propositions.

This awareness cultivates what Moses calls "a heart of wisdom." Biblical wisdom is not merely intellectual knowledge or the accumulation of facts. It is the art of living well, of aligning our brief existence with what truly matters. A wise heart recognizes that while we cannot control the length of our days, we absolutely can influence their depth, their richness, their meaning.

Consider how differently we would live if we truly believed our days were numbered. Would we spend hours nursing resentment toward a family member? Would we postpone telling people we love them? Would we invest so much energy in accumulating possessions that will outlast us but never satisfy us? The numbering of our days burns away the trivial and illuminates the essential.

Yet this meditation on mortality need not lead to morbidity or despair. On the contrary, it can infuse our lives with urgency and purpose. When we number our days, ordinary moments become sacred. A shared meal, a child's laughter, the quiet companionship of an old friend; these are not just pleasant diversions but the very substance of a life well-lived. We stop waiting for some future moment when life will "really begin" and recognize that life is happening right now, in these numbered, precious days.

The psalm also reminds us that numbering our days draws us closer to God. When we acknowledge our mortality, we confront our profound need for something, someone, beyond ourselves. Our fragility points us toward God's permanence. Our limitations highlight God's limitlessness. In recognizing that our days are numbered by One who holds all time in his hands, we find both humility and hope.

This is perhaps the deepest wisdom: that our numbered days are held within God's eternal purpose. We are not cosmic accidents, our brief lives meaningless flickers in an indifferent universe. Rather, each of our days was ordained before one of them came to be. Our lives, though finite, are infinitely meaningful because they are lived in relationship with an infinite God.

Moses' prayer, then, is not just a request for awareness but for transformation. He asks that the recognition of our mortality would produce in us a wisdom that reshapes how we love, how we serve, how we spend the currency of our hours. May we have the courage to ask the same.

PRAYER

Lord, teach us to number our days with honesty and hope. Help us to live with the wisdom that comes from knowing our time is precious and limited. Give us courage to love deeply, forgive quickly, and pursue what truly matters. May we steward our numbered days in ways that honor you and bless others, knowing that our brief lives are held secure in your eternal hands. Amen.

THE SHELTER OF THE ALMIGHTY

Whoever dwells in the shelter of the Most High will rest in the shadow of the Almighty (Psalm 91:1).

The opening verse of Psalm 91 invites us into one of Scripture's most comforting theological spaces: the shelter of the Most High. "Whoever dwells in the shelter of the Most High will rest in the shadow of the Almighty. These words have consoled countless believers throughout the centuries, offering assurance in times of uncertainty, fear, and trial. Yet to fully appreciate their depth, we must consider what it means to "dwell" and to "rest," and what security truly looks like in a world fraught with danger and unpredictability.

The psalmist employs two complementary metaphors: shelter and shadow. The shelter speaks of a place of concealment and protection, much like the inner sanctuary of a fortress where one is hidden from enemies. The shadow evokes the protection of a shade tree on a scorching day, offering respite and relief from the intense heat. Both images suggest a God who actively interposes himself between his people and the threats they face. This is not distant, abstract protection, but intimate, encompassing security, the kind experienced by one who takes refuge directly beneath divine wings.

What is particularly striking about this verse is the word "dwells." This is not a momentary seeking of refuge, nor is it merely a turn toward God in crisis. The Hebrew verb carries the sense of remaining, abiding, settling into residence. The psalmist envisions not a fleeting transaction but an ongoing habitation. One does not simply pray a quick prayer and then leave the shelter; rather, one makes one's home there, establishes one's life within that protective space. This suggests a fundamental posture toward God and life: a commitment to remain in conscious relationship with the Almighty, to order one's existence around this central reality of divine protection.

The parallel phrase "will rest in the shadow" reinforces this theme of permanence and peace. The Hebrew verb translated "rest" suggests not merely resting but lodging, remaining overnight, being secure enough to fall asleep. It speaks to the peace that permits vulnerability, the kind of rest that only comes when one is utterly convinced of one's safety. In the ancient world, to sleep soundly while enemies prowled outside one's dwelling was the ultimate testimony to trustworthy protection. The psalmist is saying that those who dwell in God's presence can experience a peace so profound that they can rest, truly rest, in an otherwise hostile world.

This distinction between the outer world and the inner shelter deserves our attention. The psalm does not deny that dangers exist; indeed, the verses that follow make abundantly clear that pestilence, terror, and countless threats are real. Rather, the psalm affirms that while these dangers may surround us, they need not penetrate the protective space we occupy in God's presence. The shelter is real. The shadow is real. And the safety they offer is both genuine and transformative.

The phrase "Most High" and "the Almighty" reinforce God's sovereignty and supreme authority. The Most High emphasizes God's exaltation above all powers and forces in creation; the Almighty emphasizes divine sufficiency and might. Together, they affirm that the God offering this shelter is no small deity, no limited power, but the one who stands above all creation. Our security, therefore, rests not in our own strength or cunning, but in alignment with the most powerful reality in existence.

For those who read this verse in our modern age, it speaks to a perennial human need. We face different dangers than the ancient Israelites, not wild beasts and foreign armies, perhaps, but anxiety, despair, isolation, and the overwhelming sense that circumstances are beyond our control. Psalm 91:1 addresses this existential vulnerability by pointing us to a reality that transcends circumstance: the possibility of genuine safety and rest in relationship with God. It is not a promise that difficulties will vanish, but rather an invitation to a transformed way of being within those difficulties, life lived not in fear but in shelter, not in exhaustion but in rest.

The question this verse places before us is not merely theological but profoundly personal: Do we dwell in this shelter? Have we made God's presence the center of our habitation, the place where we genuinely live? Or do we merely visit God in moments of crisis, then venture back into the exposed places of our lives?

PRAYER

Most High and Almighty God, I come to you acknowledging my need for shelter and safety. Teach me what it means to dwell in your presence, not as a passing visitor but as one who makes my home in your protective embrace. Grant me the courage to trust in your sovereignty and the peace to rest in your shadow, even when dangers surround me. Transform my anxious heart into one that dwells securely in relationship with you. Amen.

PSALM 92

MORNING AND EVENING

It is good to praise the Lord and make music to your name, O Most High, proclaiming your love in the morning and your faithfulness at night (Psalm 92:1–2).

There is something profoundly countercultural about beginning and ending each day with praise. In a world that teaches us to start our mornings scrolling through news feeds and to end our nights reviewing our anxieties, Psalm 92 invites us into a different rhythm entirely. The psalmist declares it is "good," not merely dutiful, but genuinely good for our souls, to bookend our days with worship.

Notice the psalmist does not say it is *necessary* or *required* to praise the Lord, though both would be true. He says it is *good*. This is the language of delight, of something that nourishes and satisfies. Like a meal shared with dear friends or the warmth of sunlight after winter, praising God is good for us. It realigns our perspective, recalibrates our hearts, and reminds us of what is true when everything else feels uncertain.

The structure of this verse reveals a beautiful pattern for daily life. In the morning, we proclaim God's love, his *hesed*, that steadfast, covenant-keeping, relentless affection that pursues us before we have accomplished anything for the day. Before we have checked a single item off our to-do list, before we have succeeded or failed at anything, we wake to the reality that we are loved. This is not a love we earn through productivity or performance. It simply *is*, as constant as the sunrise itself.

What would change in our lives if we truly began each day anchored in this truth? Instead of waking to worry about all we must do, we could wake to wonder at all God has already done. The morning proclamation of God's love sets the tone for everything that follows.

It means we do not have to prove our worth today; we can simply live from the worth already given to us.

Then, as day yields to darkness, we proclaim God's faithfulness at night. This is the wisdom of looking back on the hours we have lived and recognizing that God has been present through it all. In the moments we noticed him and the moments we did not. In our successes and our stumbles. In what went according to plan and what fell apart. His faithfulness does not depend on our circumstances; it undergirds them.

The nighttime reflection on God's faithfulness is an act of remembering. We are prone to spiritual amnesia, forgetting by evening what we knew with certainty in the morning. But when we pause before sleep to recount the ways God has been faithful, the grace that met us in a difficult conversation, the strength that sustained us through a tedious task, the peace that steadied us when anxiety threatened, we build a memorial of his goodness. These memories become the foundation of our trust when the next trial comes.

The psalmist's call to "make music" reminds us that worship is meant to engage our whole being. Music involves breath and body, melody and emotion. It is active, not passive. Whether we sing audibly or let our hearts hum with gratitude, we are participating in something that touches every part of us. This is worship that moves beyond mere intellectual assent to full-bodied celebration.

Perhaps most striking is that this psalm was written as a song for the Sabbath day. The rhythm of morning praise and evening reflection is not meant to be exhausting; it is meant to be restorative. It creates a holy structure that holds our days, a framework of worship that transforms ordinary time into sacred time. We are not adding one more obligation to our already packed schedules; we are discovering the pattern that makes everything else fall into place.

When we live between the morning proclamation of God's love and the evening recounting of his faithfulness, we find ourselves held by something larger than our own efforts. We begin to see our days not as isolated units we must somehow survive, but as chapters in a larger story that God is faithfully writing. The praise that frames our days becomes the lens through which we see everything else.

It is good, deeply, nourish-your-soul good, to live this way. Not because God needs our praise, but because we need to give it. In praising him, we remember who he is and who we are. We realign with reality. We come home to ourselves.

PRAYER

Lord Most High, teach us the goodness of beginning and ending our days with you. May your love be the first truth we proclaim each morning, and may your faithfulness be the last word we speak each night. Let our lives become songs of worship, and our days a testimony to your unending grace. In Jesus' name, Amen.

THE REIGN OF MAJESTY

The LORD reigns, he is robed in majesty; the LORD is robed in majesty and armed with strength; indeed, the world is established, firm and secure (Psalm 93:1).

The opening declaration of Psalm 93 confronts us with a fundamental theological reality that ancient Israel understood but that modern readers often overlook: the God of Israel does not merely exist at a distance in the cosmos, withdrawn from creation. Rather, the psalmist proclaims with unmistakable clarity that "the LORD reigns." This is not a tentative suggestion or a hope for future vindication. It is a present declaration of divine sovereignty that establishes the very foundation upon which all reality stands.

The Hebrew verb "reigns" carries the weight of active kingship. This is not passive, theoretical rulership but a dynamic, governing presence. When the psalmist declares that Yahweh reigns, he announces that God actively exercises dominion over all creation. In the ancient Near Eastern context where this psalm was composed and sung, such a declaration would have resonated powerfully. Other gods claimed dominion: the storm god Baal, the high god El, yet Israel's faith confessed that above all these competing claims stood the one true God whose reign was absolute and unquestionable.

The second element in this verse focuses our attention on the *manner* of God's reign: "he is robed in majesty." The image of royal vestments appears throughout Scripture as a symbol of authority and power. When a king dressed himself in purple robes and regalia, he was not merely adorning himself; he was visibly displaying his authority and right to rule. God, the psalmist tells us, is clothed in majesty, not casually wearing it like an outer garment that might be removed, but so thoroughly identified with majesty that it constitutes his very appearance and essence.

The Hebrew word for majesty here encompasses not only splendor and beauty but also honor, glory, and majesty in the sense of dignified power. When we encounter this term elsewhere in the Psalter and in prophetic literature, it describes the ineffable quality of God that commands respect and reverence. This is not an abstract theological concept but an overwhelming reality: the visible manifestation of God's transcendent authority. The repeated phrase "robed in majesty" (appearing twice in our verse) emphasizes that this is not incidental to God's nature but constitutes his very identity and presentation to creation.

Yet the psalmist immediately moves beyond mere splendor to emphasize practical power: "armed with strength." Here we encounter one of Scripture's most compelling tensions: God is simultaneously beautiful and terrible, majestic and mighty. The image of armament suggests preparedness, capability, and defensive or executive power. While majesty describes God's appearance and presence, strength speaks to God's capacity and actual power to enforce his will. The God who reigns is not an ornamental deity relegated to ceremonial functions but a God whose majesty is backed by unstoppable strength.

These truths about God's reign and character are not presented as abstract theological claims but as the secure foundation for all reality: "indeed, the world is established, firm and secure." The Hebrew word suggests stability, firmness, and security. The world is not in chaos or flux. It is not suspended precariously over an abyss of uncertainty. Rather, God's reign, manifested in his majesty and armed with his strength, establishes creation itself in stable, firm security.

This threefold movement in the verse is theologically crucial. The psalmist begins with God's reign (sovereignty), describes God's appearance (majesty), acknowledges God's power (strength), and then draws the inevitable conclusion (cosmic stability). There is a logical progression here that ancient Israel would have found deeply comforting. If the Lord reigns, if his majesty is manifest, if his strength is real, then creation itself is secure. The universe is not wobbling toward destruction. It is not subject to the capricious whims of competing deities. It stands firm because God, majestic and mighty, reigns over it absolutely. For those of us who read this psalm in our own age of uncertainty and change, this declaration strikes with unusual power. We live in times when the permanence of institutions, systems, and even planetary stability seems questionable. The psalmist invites us to remember that beneath all earthly instability stands the unchanging reality of God's reign. Our security is not ultimately rooted in economic systems, political structures, or technological advancement, but in the majesty and strength of the God who reigns over all things.

PRAYER

Gracious and sovereign Lord, we confess that you alone reign in majesty and strength. When our hearts are troubled by the uncertainties of our age, remind us that you have established the world with firm and secure foundations. Grant us faith to trust in your reign, reverence to respond to your majesty, and peace to rest in your strength. In Jesus's name, Amen.

FINDING REFUGE

The LORD has become my fortress, and my God the rock in whom I take refuge (Psalm 94:22).

In a world that shifts beneath our feet like sand, the psalmist offers us an image of breathtaking stability: God as fortress, God as rock. Psalm 94:22 emerges from a context of profound distress: the writer has witnessed injustice, seen the wicked prosper, and felt what feels like God's absence. Yet precisely in this crucible of doubt and difficulty, a declaration breaks forth: "The LORD has become my fortress, and my God the rock in whom I take refuge."

Notice the personal nature of this confession. The psalmist does not merely acknowledge that God *is* a fortress in some abstract, theological sense. Rather, he testifies that the Lord "has become" his fortress, a lived reality forged through experience. This is the language of relationship, of testing, of discovering God's faithfulness through the very trials that threatened to undo him. The fortress was not just there; it became his shelter through the act of running to it.

The imagery here is deliberately military. Ancient fortresses were massive stone structures built on high ground, designed to withstand prolonged sieges. Their thick walls, strategic positions, and reliable water sources made them places of last resort when enemies threatened. To say God is our fortress is to acknowledge that life brings genuine threats: emotional, spiritual, relational, and sometimes physical. The Christian life is not lived in a world without danger. But it is lived in the presence of an impregnable refuge.

Paired with the fortress is the image of rock. While a fortress suggests protection from external enemies, a rock speaks to something even more fundamental: solid ground beneath us when everything else proves unstable. When employment fails, when relationships fracture, when health deteriorates, when our own sense of identity crumbles, we discover whether we have built our lives on sand or on stone. The psalmist has learned through hard experience that God alone provides the immovable foundation that holds when all else gives way.

But here is what makes this verse so powerful: the act of taking refuge is something we must do. God does not force us into his fortress. The protection is available, the rock is solid, but we must run to it. We must choose, especially in our panic and pain, to turn toward God rather than away from him. How often do we instead seek refuge in lesser things: in the numbing comfort of distraction, in the false security of control, in the temporary relief of escape? These refuges promise much but crumble under pressure. They are fortresses made of wishes, rocks built on rationalizations.

Taking refuge in God looks like bringing our honest fears to him in prayer, even when prayer feels empty. It looks like choosing to remember his past faithfulness when present circumstances scream of his absence. It looks like sitting with Scripture, letting ancient promises anchor us when modern chaos threatens to sweep us away. It looks like remaining in community with God's people when isolation seems easier. It looks like the simple, stubborn act of returning to him again and again, even when we have run everywhere else first.

The psalmist's testimony also reminds us that God proves himself through our trials, not necessarily by removing them. The fortress became real to him not because God eliminated every enemy, but because God provided shelter while the battle raged. The rock revealed its solidity not by preventing the earthquake, but by standing firm through it. Sometimes God's greatest gift is not the removal of our difficulty but his sustaining presence within it, transforming our understanding of what it means to be safe.

In our deepest moments of need, we discover whether our theology is merely intellectual or truly personal. When we cry out "my God" rather than just "God," we are claiming the relationship, staking our lives on the reality that this fortress is not just available but accessible, not just strong but one that specifically shelters us. This is the faith that sustains: not a vague belief in divine power somewhere out there, but a lived confidence in a personal God who has proven himself faithful and who invites us, again and again, to run to him for refuge.

PRAYER

Lord, you are my fortress and my rock. When life feels unstable, and threats surround me, teach me to run to you first, not last. Help me trust that your protection is enough, even when storms still rage around me. When I am tempted to seek refuge in lesser things, draw me back to the only shelter that holds. Thank you for being not just strong, but near. Not just powerful, but personal. In your name I find my safety. Amen.

BOWING BEFORE OUR SHEPHERD

Come, let us bow down in worship, let us kneel before the LORD
*our Maker; for he is our God and we are the people of his
pasture, the flock under his care* (Psalm 95:6–7).

The psalmist invites us into a posture that our modern world increasingly resists. "Come, let us bow down in worship, let us kneel before the LORD our Maker." These words from Psalm 95:6–7 call us away from the casual stance we often adopt toward the divine and into a physical, emotional, and spiritual position of profound submission. Yet within this call to humility lies one of Scripture's most tender affirmations: we are not slaves before a distant tyrant, but rather the beloved flock of a caring Shepherd.

The Hebrew word for "bow down" carries the sense of prostration, of making oneself low before another. It appears throughout the Old Testament in contexts ranging from respectful greeting to religious devotion. When used in religious contexts, as here, it denotes the complete surrender of one's will and pride before the Almighty. The accompanying phrase "kneel before" reinforces this imagery of physical submission. The psalmist is not merely suggesting an internal attitude; he is calling for an external, bodily act that mirrors the internal disposition of the heart. There is wisdom in this integration of body and spirit. When we assume the kneeling posture, something shifts within us. Our knees become hinges upon which our pride swings open, and our bodies become instruments of confession that we are not in control.

But notice what follows, and this is crucial. The psalmist provides the *reason* for this submission: "for he is our God and we are the people of his pasture, the flock under his care." The Hebrew word for "pasture" evokes the shepherd metaphor that threads through Scripture like a golden thread. Our God is not merely powerful; he is attentive. He is not simply to be feared; he is to be followed as sheep follow their shepherd. And we, flawed, wandering, sometimes lost, are described not as servants (though we are), but as the flock under his care. This phrase suggests active, vigilant care. The shepherd does not merely own his flock; he watches over it, guides it to green pastures, and protects it from danger.

The tension between these two images is beautiful and instructive. We are called to bow in worship before our maker, to acknowledge his majesty, his power, his worthiness of absolute obedience. Yet simultaneously, we are invited into the tender relationship of sheep and shepherd, where our submission is not the fearful compliance of servants to a demanding master, but the trusting dependence of vulnerable creatures upon one whose very nature is to care for them. This is the gospel in miniature: the God who is infinitely transcendent is also intimately immanent.

In our contemporary context, where so much of life operates on the assumption that we must grasp for control, assert our independence, and refuse to kneel before anything or anyone, these verses offer a radically countercultural invitation. To bow before God is to acknowledge a fundamental truth about our existence: we are not self-sustaining. We did not create ourselves, and we cannot shepherd our own lives. The illusion of autonomy that our culture cherishes so dearly is precisely that, an illusion that leaves us anxious, exhausted, and ultimately alone.

But the psalmist calls us to something far better. When we kneel before the Lord our maker, we are not diminishing ourselves; we are finding our truest identity. We are not surrendering our humanity; we are embracing it fully. For we are made in the image of God, and it is in acknowledging his lordship that we become most fully human. And because he is not a distant, uncaring deity but a shepherd who knows each member of his flock by name, our submission is an act not of desperation but of faith.

Moreover, the plural pronouns throughout this verse, "let us bow down," "we are the people of his pasture," remind us that this is not a solitary act. We bow together, as God's gathered people. Our submission is corporate. We kneel alongside countless others throughout history and across the globe who have recognized the same truth: that to fall before God is to rise into our true destiny as his beloved flock.

As you reflect on these verses today, consider: What would change in your life if you truly embraced this dual reality: the majesty before which we bow, and the shepherd whose care sustains us?

PRAYER

Almighty God, you who formed the heavens and the earth and set in motion all things seen and unseen, we come before you in humility and awe. We confess that we have so often lived as though we were our own masters, forging our own paths and defending our own kingdoms. Forgive us. Help us to kneel before you, not out of fear, but out of the grateful recognition that you are our maker and our shepherd. Grant us the grace to surrender our illusions of control and to rest, like your flock, in your faithful care. May our bowing before you be an act of worship that overflows into every corner of our lives, and may we truly know ourselves as the people of your pasture, held secure in your everlasting arms. Amen.

PSALM 96

A NEW SONG FOR ALL THE EARTH

Sing to the LORD *a new song; sing to the* LORD, *all the earth. Sing to the* LORD, *praise his name; proclaim his salvation day after day. Declare his glory among the nations, his marvelous deeds among all peoples* (Psalm 96:1–3).

There is something profoundly stirring about the opening words of Psalm 96: "Sing to the LORD a new song." The psalmist does not merely suggest we sing; he commands it with urgency and joy. But why a *new* song? The old songs were enough once. Our ancestors taught us how to praise God, and we praised him well. Must we now sing new songs?

The call to newness here is not about discarding what came before, but about recognizing that God's mercies are new every morning. Each dawn brings fresh reasons to worship, new evidence of God's faithfulness, and unprecedented ways in which he is working in our lives and in the world. A new song reflects a living faith, one that encounters God not merely in memory but in the present moment. When we sing a new song, we testify that our relationship with the Lord is vibrant and ongoing, not confined to past experiences or inherited traditions.

Notice also the scope of this worship: "all the earth." This is not music for the spiritually elite or the geographically privileged. The psalmist envisions a global chorus, every tribe and language lifting their voices in unified praise. Written during a time when Israel might have seen itself as God's exclusive people, these words break through narrow boundaries. The God of Israel is the God of all creation, and every person, regardless of origin, status, or history, is invited into this symphony of worship

285

The psalm then shifts from singing *to* the Lord to singing *about* the Lord: "proclaim his salvation day after day." Worship and witness become inseparable. True praise cannot remain private; it overflows into proclamation. When we have genuinely encountered God's saving power, silence becomes impossible. We become like the healed blind man in John's Gospel who, when questioned about his transformation, could only reply, "One thing I know: I was blind but now I see!" Our songs naturally become testimonies.

"Day after day" captures the rhythm of faithful witness. Proclaiming God's salvation is not a one-time event or an occasional duty; it is a daily practice, as regular as breathing. In a world of constantly shifting narratives and competing voices, we are called to be consistent witnesses to the unchanging goodness of God. Some days our proclamation might be bold and public; other days it might be a quiet word of encouragement or a simple act of kindness that points others toward divine love. But every day offers new opportunities to make his salvation known.

The psalm reaches its crescendo with a missionary vision: "Declare his glory among the nations, his marvelous deeds among all peoples." Here, we see that worship is not meant to be confined to temple walls or church buildings. The glory of God is too magnificent to be kept secret, his deeds too marvelous to be enjoyed by only a select few. We are commissioned as heralds, carrying the news of God's character and actions to every corner of creation.

What are these "marvelous deeds" we are to declare? They include creation itself, the intricate design of a universe that reveals its maker. They include the redemptive acts throughout history, culminating in Christ's incarnation, death, and resurrection. They include the personal testimonies of transformation: the addict set free, the broken heart mended, the purposeless life given meaning, the guilty conscience cleansed. Every act of divine intervention, every answered prayer, every moment of unexpected grace qualifies as a marvelous deed worth declaring.

For us today, living between Christ's first and second comings, this psalm takes on even deeper meaning. We sing our new songs knowing that the ultimate new song awaits us in Revelation, where every nation and language will worship before God's throne. Our current worship is both genuine and anticipatory, authentic praise that also longs for the day when every knee will bow and every tongue confess.

The challenge before us is clear: Have we allowed our worship to grow stale? Are we singing songs that reflect our ongoing experience of God's faithfulness? Are we proclaiming his salvation beyond our comfortable circles? Are we declaring his glory to those who do not yet know him? The invitation stands: Join the global chorus. Lift your voice. Tell what God has done. And in doing so, discover that worship itself becomes the oxygen of a thriving faith.

PRAYER

Lord, put a new song in our hearts, a song born from fresh encounters with your goodness. Help us not merely to sing to you, but to proclaim your salvation boldly to those around us. Give us courage to declare your marvelous deeds among all peoples, and let our lives be living testimonies to your glory. May our worship overflow into witness, and our witness back into worship, until that day when all the earth joins in perfect harmony before your throne. In Jesus' name, Amen.

PSALM 97

A LOVE THAT HATES EVIL

Let those who love the LORD hate evil, for he guards the lives of his faithful ones and delivers them from the hand of the wicked (Psalm 97:10).

The psalmist presents us with a profound paradox embedded in this verse. The command to love God is inseparably linked with the command to hate evil. These are not separate impulses competing within the human heart; rather, they flow from a single, unified source. When we truly love the Lord with the fullness of our being, hatred of evil becomes not an optional disposition but an inevitable consequence of that primary allegiance.

The Hebrew word for "hate" in this context carries the weight of active opposition rather than mere passive dislike. To hate evil as the psalmist means to stand against it, to refuse it, to recoil from it with the same intensity that characterizes our love for God. In our contemporary culture, we have domesticated the concept of disliking evil. We treat it as a personal preference, something akin to declining a particular food. But biblical hatred of evil involves conviction, decision, and commitment. It requires us to examine our lives, our choices, our entertainment, our speech, and our work, asking whether they align with God's character or resist it.

Yet notice how the psalmist frames the motivation for this hatred of evil: not primarily fear, not guilt, not self-improvement, but the promise of divine protection. "He guards the lives of his faithful ones and delivers them from the hand of the wicked." Here lies the remarkable comfort in the psalm. Our commitment to righteousness is not an isolated personal struggle; it is met with God's active guardianship. The one who loves the Lord and refuses evil does not stand alone against the forces of wickedness in this world.

The promise of deliverance from "the hand of the wicked" acknowledges the real and present threat of evil in our world. The psalmist does not offer false comfort by suggesting that hatred of evil will eliminate all difficulty or suffering. Rather, he affirms that in the cosmic conflict between God and evil, those who align themselves with God, who love him and therefore hate what he hates, are placed under his protection.

The promise contained in Psalm 97:10 offers us both challenge and encouragement. The challenge is to examine whether our love for God is genuine and formative, producing in us the fruit of righteousness and the courage to stand against evil in all its manifestations. The encouragement is that such faithfulness does not go unnoticed by God. He guards those who love him. He delivers those whose hatred of evil flows from a sincere devotion to his kingdom. As we meditate on the psalmist's words, let us consider one area of our lives where a deeper hatred of evil might strengthen our love for God. What compromise have we tolerated? What half-truth have we permitted? What injustice have we overlooked because it seemed convenient to do so? In hating evil, we demonstrate that we love the Lord.

PRAYER

Almighty God, strengthen within me a love for your name that is accompanied by a genuine hatred of evil. Give me courage to stand against what is wrong, wisdom to discern your truth in a world of deception, and confidence in your promise that you guard the lives of those who love you. Deliver me from the compromises that diminish my devotion and from the fear that prevents me from speaking truth. Keep me always under your protective hand. Amen.

PSALM 98

SING SOMETHING NEW

Sing to the LORD *a new song, for he has done marvelous things;*
his right hand and his holy arm have worked salvation for him
(Psalm 98:1).

There is a moment in the life of every believer when the old words simply are not enough. Not because they are untrue, the ancient hymns and inherited prayers remain as faithful as the God they address, but because something has happened. Something so immediate, so personal, so undeniably fresh that it demands a fresh expression. The psalmist understood this well. His opening command in Psalm 98 is not merely a musical instruction; it is a theological declaration: the God who acts deserves a song that rises to meet the moment.

"Sing to the LORD a new song." The Hebrew word for "new" carries the sense of something freshly made, recently revealed, not yet worn smooth by repetition. It is the same word used when God promises through the prophet Isaiah, "Behold, I am doing a new thing" (Isaiah 43:19). The psalmist is not asking us to abandon the old songs of faith. He is asking us to open our eyes to what God is doing right now and to let that vision reshape our worship.

The reason for the new song is immediately given: "for he has done marvelous things." The Hebrew word translated as "marvelous" is a word reserved in Scripture for acts so extraordinary, so beyond human capacity, that they can only be attributed to God. It is the word used of the wonders at the Red Sea, the manna in the desert, the walls of Jericho crumbling at a shout. These were not lucky turns of history. They were the fingerprints of a God who refuses to be absent from the story of his people.

And yet the psalmist does not leave salvation as a vague cosmic event. He makes it strikingly personal: "his right hand and his holy arm have worked salvation for him." In ancient Near Eastern imagery, the "right hand" was the seat of power, the arm of a warrior raised in battle.

When Scripture speaks of God's "holy arm," it pictures divine strength personally extended, not a distant deity setting the universe in motion and then retreating, but a God who rolls up his sleeves and intervenes. The salvation here is not theoretical. It is fought for. It is won.

The psalmist's imagery draws upon the deep memory of Israel's exodus. The "right hand" of God is celebrated in the Song of the Sea: "Your right hand, O LORD, is majestic in power; your right hand, O LORD, shatters the enemy" (Exodus 15:6). For the original singers of Psalm 98, this language was not metaphor alone but the accumulated testimony of generations who had watched God act on their behalf. To call for a "new song" was to place one's own experience of God's faithfulness in the same unbroken line as the Passover and the crossing of the sea. Every fresh act of divine deliverance becomes, in the psalmist's theology, an extension of that original saving event, proof that the God of the exodus is still the same God today.

Christians reading this psalm cannot help but hear in these words a foreshadowing of the cross. The ultimate "marvelous thing" is the incarnation itself: God taking on flesh, entering our story, and extending not merely a metaphorical arm but real, nail-scarred hands to work our salvation. The resurrection of Jesus Christ is the great new thing, the event so unprecedented, so world-altering, that it has been generating new songs ever since. Every hymn written in the last two thousand years is, in some sense, an attempt to answer the psalmist's call.

But this psalm also speaks to the present tense. God is still doing marvelous things: in your life, in your family, in your community, in the world. Healings that confound, provisions that arrive at the last moment, prodigals who return, hearts that soften against all expectation. Each of these is a reason to sing something new. The danger of a long faith is not that we stop believing, but that we stop marveling. We can accumulate a vast storehouse of theological knowledge and still lose the capacity for wonder. Psalm 98 is a call to recover it.

It is worth noting that Psalm 98 does not limit the singing to Israel alone. Verses 4 through 9 summon the whole earth, every nation, the sea and all that fills it, the rivers and the hills, to join in this chorus of praise. The new song is not a private lyric sung in the corner of a single heart; it is a cosmic anthem. This universalizing impulse reminds us that the salvation God works is never merely personal in its scope, even when it is deeply personal in its touch. When God acts on behalf of one person, one family, one congregation, he is writing a verse in a song that the whole creation will one day sing together before the throne. Your fresh experience of his grace is not yours alone to keep; it is a contribution to the larger choir

PRAYER

Lord God, forgive me for the times I have grown so familiar with your goodness that I have ceased to be astonished by it. You are a God of marvelous things. Your right hand has never been shortened; your holy arm has never grown weary. Open my eyes today to see the ways you are at work in and around my life, and loosen my lips to praise you for them. Give me a new song, not because the old truths have failed, but because you are a living God whose mercies are new every morning. May my worship rise to match the greatness of what you have done, and may it always begin and end with you. In the name of Jesus, who is himself your greatest marvel, Amen.

WHEN THE EARTH SHAKES

The LORD reigns, let the nations tremble; he sits enthroned between the cherubim, let the earth shake (Psalm 99:1).

There is a particular kind of silence that falls over a room when someone truly powerful enters it. Conversation stops. Posture straightens. The air itself seems to reorganize. We recognize authority intuitively, in our bones, before our minds have time to process it. The psalmist opens Psalm 99 with a declaration that is meant to produce exactly that effect, not in a room, but across the entire earth, among every nation, in every trembling heart: *The LORD reigns.*

Two words in Hebrew. Absolute in their confidence. There is no argument offered, no evidence presented, no diplomacy attempted. The psalmist does not say "the LORD reigns in our community" or "the LORD reigns over those who believe." The declaration is cosmic and unconditional. Every nation, every government, every throne built by human ambition exists within the shadow of this single truth. And the appropriate response, the psalmist insists, is trembling.

We live in an age that is deeply uncomfortable with trembling before anything. We are taught from childhood to stand tall, to advocate for ourselves, to refuse to be diminished. These are not entirely bad lessons. But they can quietly cultivate a posture of the soul that becomes resistant to awe, a kind of inner stiffness that makes it difficult to bow, even before the One before whom all bowing is right and good. The nations tremble in this verse not because God is a tyrant, but because they are standing in the presence of reality itself. To tremble before the Lord is not weakness. It is the first movement of wisdom.

Then the image deepens: *he sits enthroned between the cherubim.* This is the language of the Ark of the Covenant, the sacred chest that sat at the center of Israel's worship life, overshadowed by two golden angelic figures with wings outstretched. The space between those wings was understood to be the mercy seat, the place where God's presence dwelt among his people. It was so holy that only the High Priest could approach it, and only once a year, and only with blood. The psalmist is telling us something extraordinary: the God who makes nations tremble and shakes the foundations of the earth has chosen to dwell in a specific place, among a specific people, in intimate and terrifying nearness.

This is the great tension that runs through all of Scripture, and it runs straight through this single verse. He is transcendent enough to make the earth shake, yet personal enough to sit enthroned in a tent among wandering shepherds and former slaves. He is the Lord of all nations and the God who called Abraham by name. His power is not cold or distant; it is the power of a father who is also King, a Shepherd who is also Lord of Hosts. The shaking of the earth and the nearness of the mercy seat belong together. You cannot fully understand his tenderness without grasping his majesty, and you cannot fully grasp his majesty without being undone by his tenderness.

Perhaps this is why so many of us live with an anemic sense of God's presence. We have settled on a deity who is manageable and approachable, certainly, but not particularly overwhelming. We have kept the mercy seat and quietly removed the cherubim. We have wanted the comfort of his nearness without the disruption of his glory. But the psalmist will not allow us that convenience. He insists that the God who is near enough to dwell among us is simultaneously powerful enough to make the whole earth tremble, and that both truths must be held at once if we are to know him at all.

To sit with Psalm 99:1 is to be invited into a recalibration of the soul. It is an invitation to let the earth shake a little beneath our feet, to release our grip on the illusion that we are the ones holding things together. The Lord reigns. That was true before you woke up this morning. It will be true long after this day ends. Your anxieties, your uncertainties, your seasons of confusion, all of them exist inside a universe that has a throne at its center, and that throne is occupied.Let the nations tremble. Let the earth shake. And let your heart, at last, be still.

PRAYER

 Lord, you reign over everything I can see and everything I cannot. Forgive me for the ways I have reduced you to something manageable, something that fits neatly inside my understanding. Today, let me tremble rightly before your majesty, and in that trembling, find the strange and solid peace that only comes from knowing the earth is in your hands. Amen.

THE ENDURING FOUNDATION

The LORD is good and his love endures forever; his faithfulness continues through all generations (Psalm 100:5).

In a world characterized by constant change and uncertainty, Psalm 100:5 offers us an anchor for the soul. This single verse contains three profound declarations about God's character that have sustained believers for millennia: his goodness, his enduring love, and his faithfulness across generations. These are not merely poetic sentiments; they represent the bedrock truths upon which we can build our entire lives.

"The LORD is good." This opening statement is deceptively simple, yet it addresses one of humanity's deepest questions: What is God really like? The psalmist does not hedge or qualify this declaration. God's goodness is not conditional, fluctuating with our circumstances, or dependent on our perception. It is intrinsic to his nature. When we look at creation, we see evidence of this goodness in the beauty of a sunset, the intricacy of a newborn's fingers, and the provision of food and water. When we look at redemption, we see his goodness in sending Christ to rescue us from sin and death. God's goodness means that everything he does flows from a heart that desires our ultimate well-being, even when his ways confound our understanding.

The second phrase, "his love endures forever," takes us even deeper. The Hebrew word translated as "love" here is *hesed*, a rich term that encompasses steadfast love, loyal kindness, and covenant faithfulness. This is not the fickle affection that evaporates when someone disappoints us. This is the kind of love that pursues us in our rebellion, that remains constant through our failures, that never gives up on us even when we have given up on ourselves. The phrase "endures forever" stretches our minds toward eternity. There will never be a moment, in this life or the next, when God's love for his people runs out or grows cold. His love is not exhaustible; it has no limit or expiration date.

Consider what this means practically. When you wake in the middle of the night gripped by anxiety, God's love is present. When you have made the same mistake for the hundredth time and wonder if you have finally exhausted his patience, his love endures. When you stand at a graveside or receive a devastating diagnosis, his love has not diminished by even a fraction. This truth does not erase our pain, but it ensures we never face our struggles alone or unloved.

The final phrase, "his faithfulness continues through all generations," extends God's character beyond our individual lives into the sweep of human history. Our grandparents knew the same faithful God we serve today. Our great-great-grandchildren, should the Lord tarry, will depend on that same faithfulness. This generational continuity matters profoundly. It means that God does not change his mind about his promises. The commitments he made to Abraham, David, and the prophets remain in force. The new covenant established through Christ's blood is as secure today as it was two thousand years ago.

This generational faithfulness also calls us to a responsibility. We are links in a chain, recipients of a faith passed down and trustees of truth to pass forward. The God who sustained our ancestors through persecution, poverty, and pain is the same God available to us today. And we have the privilege of testifying to the next generation that yes, he is still good, his love still endures, and his faithfulness still holds.

In our therapeutic age, we are often encouraged to look inward for strength and validation. But Psalm 100:5 invites us to look upward instead. Our foundation is not our own resilience or positive thinking; it is the unchanging character of God. When our emotions tell us we are unloved, this verse speaks truth. When circumstances suggest God has abandoned us, this verse corrects our vision. When we wonder if faith is worth passing to our children, this verse reminds us that countless generations have staked their lives on these truths and found them sufficient.

The beauty of this verse is that it does not require us to muster up feelings or manufacture faith. It simply asks us to recognize what is objectively true about God. He is good. His love endures forever. His faithfulness continues through all generations. These realities existed before we believed them and will continue after we are gone. Our invitation is simply to rest in them, to build our lives upon them, and to let them shape how we face each day.

PRAYER

Faithful God, we praise you for your unchanging goodness. Thank you for your love for us that does not depend on our performance but flows from your perfect nature. Help us rest in your faithfulness, especially when circumstances tempt us to doubt. May we pass this confidence to the next generation, that they, too, might know the God who endures forever. Amen.

A SONG OF DEVOTION AND INTEGRITY

I will sing of your love and justice; to you, LORD, I will sing praise. I will be careful to lead a blameless life (Psalm 101:1–2a).

The psalmist opens Psalm 101 with a ringing declaration of intention: "I will sing of your love and justice; to you, LORD, I will sing praise. I will be careful to lead a blameless life." These opening lines establish the thematic tension that governs the entire psalm: the commitment to align one's public and private conduct with the character of God. This is not merely a song; it is a covenant of the heart, a solemn vow made before the divine audience.

The Hebrew word for "love" here is *hesed*, that magnificent term that encompasses covenant loyalty, steadfast love, and mercy. It is not emotional sentimentality but rather the binding commitment that God makes to his people, which they reciprocate. When the psalmist promises to sing of *hesed*, he is celebrating the foundational reality of his relationship with God: that he is loved not because of his merit but because of God's faithful commitment. This love is not abstract; it reveals itself supremely in God's justice. The psalmist couples love with justice, understanding that a God who indulged his people's failings would not truly love them. Justice without love becomes tyranny; love without justice becomes indulgence. The psalmist celebrates their integration in God's character and commits to reflecting both in his own life.

The commitment to sing praise, or more literally, to "make music," indicates that this is not a grudging obligation but a joyful overflow. The psalmist will respond to God's love and justice with the full expression of his being: his voice, his heart, his deliberate choice to honor God. This is worship as a covenant response, the proper reply of the creature to the creator who has revealed both mercy and righteousness.

Yet immediately, the psalmist pivots to a startling promise: "I will be careful to lead a blameless life." In Hebrew, this statement literally says: "I will understand/be prudent regarding the way of wholeness/integrity." In Hebrew, the word translated "blameless" conveys the idea of completeness, wholeness, and integrity, not sinlessness in an absolute sense, but rather a deliberate orientation toward righteousness. The verb "be careful" suggests thoughtful deliberation; this will not be an accidental achievement but the fruit of conscious intention. There is something almost austere about this vow. The psalmist is saying, in effect: "Because you are loving and just, I commit myself to a life of integrity."

This connection between worship and conduct reveals something profound about biblical piety. Singing praise and living blamelessly are not separate compartments of the spiritual life; they are intimately woven together. One cannot authentically celebrate God's justice while personally practicing injustice. One cannot genuinely proclaim God's love while allowing one's own life to contradict that proclamation. The psalmist understands that worship must overflow into ethics, that our choices must back our songs.

The psalm, which continues with the psalmist's description of his household standards and his rejection of wickedness, makes clear that he understands his personal integrity as a reflection of his vocation before God. If he has been given authority, whether as a king (the psalm is often interpreted as a royal psalm) or more broadly as one called to lead, then that authority must be exercised in alignment with God's character. The personal commitments he outlines are not ascetic practices designed to earn divine favor; rather, they are the necessary expression of one who has truly grasped God's love and justice.

For modern readers, this psalm invites us to examine our own relationship between worship and witness. Do our songs of praise align with the patterns of our choices? Do we truly grasp that God's love and justice are inseparable, and that our commitment to both must inform the way we navigate daily relationships and decisions? The psalmist's careful promise to lead a blameless life is not about perfection but about the conscious alignment of our whole selves: our worship, our words, and our works with the character of the God we claim to honor.

PRAYER

Gracious God, you who are both infinitely loving and perfectly just, grant us the courage of this psalmist. Teach us to sing your praise not merely with our voices but with the integrity of our lives. Where we have allowed our conduct to contradict our confession, grant us repentance and renewal. Give us wisdom to understand the paths of wholeness, and strengthen us to walk them with deliberate faithfulness. May our worship be authentic, our witness consistent, and our lives a living song of gratitude for your steadfast love. In Christ we pray. Amen.

WHEN GOD SEEMS SILENT

Hear my prayer, LORD; let my cry for help come to you. Do not hide your face from me when I am in distress. Turn your ear to me; when I call, answer me quickly (Psalm 102:1–2).

There are moments in life when our prayers feel like they are echoing into an empty sky. We cry out to God, and the silence that follows can be deafening. The psalmist captures this raw human experience in Psalm 102, pleading with God not to hide his face, begging him to answer quickly. These are not the polite, measured prayers we often think we are supposed to pray. This is desperation laid bare.

What strikes me most about these verses is their unflinching honesty. The psalmist does not begin with gratitude or praise, and does not apologize for the urgency of his plea. He simply cries out: *Hear me. Do not hide from me. Answer me quickly.* There is something profoundly liberating in this kind of prayer. It reminds us that God does not need us to dress up our pain in pretty language or wait until we have achieved the proper spiritual posture before approaching him. He invites us to come exactly as we are, even when what we are is desperate and afraid.

The phrase "do not hide your face from me" carries deep significance in the Hebrew tradition. God's face represents his presence, his favor, his attention turned toward us. To have God hide his face meant experiencing his absence, feeling cut off from the source of life and hope. The psalmist fears this more than the distress itself. It is not just that life is hard; it is that God seems distant amid the hardship. This is often the deeper wound: not our circumstances alone, but the sense that we face them alone.

Yet even in this plea, there is an implicit faith. The psalmist is crying out *to* God, not *about* God. He is directing his complaint to the one person who can actually do something about it. This is the paradox of lament: it sounds like doubt, but it is actually a form of trust. The psalmist believes God is listening even while he begs God to listen. He believes God can answer even as he pleads for an answer. His very act of prayer contradicts his fear of abandonment.

We live in a culture that often confuses positive thinking with faith. We are told to "claim our blessings" and "speak things into existence," as if acknowledging pain were itself a failure of belief. But the Psalms offer us a different model. They show us that faith is not the absence of struggle; it is knowing where to take our struggle. It is not pretending everything is fine; it is bringing everything that is broken to the one who can heal.

When the psalmist asks God to "answer me quickly," he is acknowledging his limitations. We do not have unlimited reserves of strength. We cannot endure forever on our own. There is a timeline to our resilience, and God knows this. Jesus himself, in his humanity, experienced this urgency in the Garden of Gethsemane, praying so intensely that his sweat became like drops of blood. Our desperation does not surprise God or disappoint him. He made us with both our strength and our frailty.

The beautiful truth woven through this psalm, and indeed through all of Scripture, is that God does not hide his face forever. The same psalm that begins with this desperate plea ends with confidence in God's faithfulness to future generations. The psalmist's circumstances may not change immediately, but his perspective shifts as he remembers who God is. This is often how God answers us: not by removing our trials instantly, but by meeting us in the middle of them, reminding us we are not alone.

If you are in a season where God feels distant, where your prayers seem to disappear into silence, these verses give you permission to be honest about it. Bring your desperation to God. Tell him you need him to answer quickly because you do not know how much longer you can hold on. He can handle your raw honesty far better than your pretended piety.

And then, having poured out your heart, wait. Not passively, but expectantly. Because the God who invites our desperate prayers is also the God who promises that he will never leave us or forsake us. He may not answer in the way we expect or on our preferred timeline, but he always answers. And sometimes, the answer begins the moment we dare to cry out.

PRAYER

Lord, hear my prayer today. When I am in distress, and you seem far away, remind me that you are near. Help me to bring my honest heart to you, my fears, my desperation, my questions. Teach me to trust you even in the silence, knowing that you never truly hide your face from those who seek you. Answer me, Lord, in your perfect timing and in your perfect way. Amen.

THE COMPASSION OF OUR GOD

The LORD *is compassionate and gracious, slow to anger, abounding in love* (Psalm 103:8).

When the psalmist declares that "The LORD is compassionate and gracious, slow to anger, abounding in love," he offers us one of the most reassuring theological statements in all of Scripture. This verse, nestled within the grateful exaltation of Psalm 103, provides the theological foundation for understanding God's character, a foundation that transforms how we approach both our daily struggles and our relationship with the Divine.

The Hebrew word translated here as "compassionate" is derived from another Hebrew term meaning "womb." This etymology is not incidental to the meaning; it carries the profound implication that God's compassion flows from the deepest place of creative care and intimate concern. A mother's protective instinct toward her child captures something of what the psalmist means. God's compassion is not a distant, intellectual benevolence; it is visceral, embodied, and rooted in the very nature of God as creator. When we say that God is compassionate, we confess that our ultimate Creator regards us with the tender, protective concern a mother holds for her child.

Paired with this is the word "gracious." This term speaks of God's willingness to bestow favor upon those who do not deserve it. Grace, by definition, cannot be earned or demanded; it must be given freely. The juxtaposition of compassion and graciousness tells us something vital: God does not merely feel for our suffering; God actively responds with unmerited favor. God sees our condition and reaches toward us, not because we have satisfied some cosmic obligation, but because grace is fundamental to God's nature.

The phrase "slow to anger" appears throughout the Hebrew Bible as a refrain describing God's character, particularly in passages dealing with God's response to human rebellion and failure. In Exodus 34:6, immediately following Israel's catastrophic sin with the golden calf, God reveals himself to Moses with precisely these words: "The LORD, the LORD, a God compassionate and gracious, slow to anger, abounding in love and faithfulness." This is not meant to suggest that God is indifferent to sin or moral failure. Rather, it reveals that God's patience far exceeds God's judgment. God does not wait eagerly for an occasion to punish; instead, God extends opportunity after opportunity for repentance and restoration.

Consider the weight of this truth in your own life. How many times have you stumbled into the same sin, the same failure, the same spiritual lethargy? The revelation that God is slow to anger means you do not face a cosmic accountant waiting to strike you down. Instead, you face a God whose inclination toward patience and restoration vastly outpaces the divine wrath. This does not eliminate God's judgment. Scripture makes clear that consequences are real, but it positions judgment as a final resort rather than a first response.

The concluding phrase, "abounding in love," employs the word *hesed*, perhaps the richest term in biblical vocabulary. *Hesed* encompasses loyalty, mercy, covenant faithfulness, and steadfast love. It is the word used to describe God's commitment to the covenants God makes. When God abounds in *hesed*, it means that God's love is not merely sufficient; it overflows. It supersedes our deserving. It covers our inadequacy. The psalmist uses the imagery of abundance, not just love, but love in abundance, love in excess, love that pours out beyond what we could calculate or repay.

This verse appears in a context in which the psalmist has just called his own soul to praise the Lord and remember "all his benefits" (verse 2). The gratitude of the psalmist is rooted in the character of God. We praise God not primarily for what God does, though God's actions are worthy of praise, but for who God is. God's character is the foundation upon which all divine action rests.

In the midst of your struggles, whether they arise from personal failure, unresolved grief, persistent temptation, or the weight of uncertain circumstances, this verse invites you to reconsider the nature of the God you serve. The God revealed in Scripture is neither a distant God who created the universe and turned away, nor a capricious tyrant delighting in human suffering. The God of the psalms is compassionate, moved by the plight of those created in God's image; gracious, extending undeserved favor; slow to anger, patient beyond measure; and abounding in love, offering mercy in overwhelming abundance.

This is the God who invites your trust. This is the God who offers your weary soul genuine hope.

PRAYER

Eternal God, I confess that I often doubt your compassion and question your willingness to forgive me. Teach me to rest in the truth that you are slow to anger and abounding in love. Help me to receive your grace not as something I must earn, but as the free gift of your heart toward me. Transform my understanding of who you are, and in that transformation, reshape how I relate to you and to those around me. Amen.

THE JOY OF PERPETUAL PRAISE

I will sing to the LORD *all my life; I will sing praise to my God as long as I live. May my meditation be pleasing to him, as I rejoice in the* LORD (Psalm 104:33–34).

There is something profoundly beautiful about a promise that spans a lifetime. When the psalmist declares, "I will sing to the LORD all my life; I will sing praise to my God as long as I live," he is not speaking of a momentary emotion or a Sunday morning commitment. He is articulating a fundamental orientation of the soul, a decision to make praise the soundtrack of his existence, regardless of what melodies or discords life might bring.

This commitment to lifelong worship emerges from Psalm 104, a magnificent meditation on God's creative power and sustaining presence. The psalmist has just finished surveying the wonders of creation: from the waters above the heavens to the creatures of the deep, from the wine that gladdens human hearts to the stork making her home in the junipers. Having witnessed God's fingerprints across the canvas of creation, the only fitting response is perpetual praise. The psalmist's worship is not manufactured or forced; it flows naturally from eyes that have learned to see.

But notice the realism in this vow. The psalmist does not promise to sing only when life is easy, only when prayers are answered as hoped, only when the path is clear. He promises to sing "all my life" and "as long as I live," through every season, every circumstance, every joy and sorrow that the years might hold. This is worship that transcends feelings, a praise rooted not in our changing circumstances but in God's unchanging character.

What sustains such lifelong worship? The answer lies in the second part of our passage: "May my meditation be pleasing to him, as I rejoice in the LORD." The psalmist understands that outward praise flows from inward meditation. Our songs are only as deep as our thoughts of God. Meditation here is not empty mysticism but a focused dwelling on who God is and what he has done. It is the practice of letting truth sink from our heads into our hearts, allowing God's character and works to marinate in our minds until they transform our affections.

The psalmist's concern that his meditation be "pleasing" to God reveals something beautiful about the nature of worship. He is not simply trying to feel better or manufacture positive emotions. He genuinely cares whether his inner life honors the One he adores. This is the heart of authentic devotion: wanting not just to experience God's blessings but to bring him pleasure, to offer him something worthy of his attention and delight.

And then comes that remarkable phrase: "as I rejoice in the LORD." Here is the secret to sustained worship across a lifetime. The psalmist does not rejoice in his circumstances, his achievements, or even his own spiritual discipline. He rejoices in the Lord himself. When God becomes our joy rather than merely our helper, when he becomes our treasure rather than simply our problem-solver, then praise becomes as natural as breathing. We are no longer singing because we should, but because we cannot help it.

This kind of rejoicing transforms everything. It does not mean pretending difficulties do not exist or plastering on artificial happiness. Rather, it means discovering a joy that runs deeper than our troubles, a gladness rooted in the bedrock reality of God's goodness, presence, and faithfulness. It is the joy of a child held securely in a parent's arms, even when the storm rages outside.

The challenge for us today is to embrace this same lifelong commitment. In a culture of fleeting commitments and momentary enthusiasms, we are called to a worship that endures. This requires cultivating the discipline of meditation, creating space in our overstimulated lives to dwell deeply on God's character and works. It means choosing praise even when our hearts feel dry, trusting that faithfulness in the valley prepares us for authenticity on the mountaintop.

As we age, as life brings its inevitable disappointments and losses, the temptation is to let our songs fade, to allow cynicism or weariness to silence our praise. But the psalmist shows us another way: a worship that grows richer and deeper with time, a meditation that becomes sweeter as we accumulate years of witnessing God's faithfulness, a joy that persists because it is anchored not in what changes but in the one who remains the same yesterday, today, and forever.

PRAYER

Lord, give me grace to make the psalmist's vow my own. Teach me to sing to you not just in seasons of blessing, but all my life, as long as I live. Deepen my meditation on who you are until my thoughts of you become pleasing in your sight. And let my joy be rooted in you alone, so that nothing in this world can silence my song. Amen.

SEEKING THE FACE OF GOD ALWAYS

Look to the LORD and his strength; seek his face always
(Psalm 105:4).

The psalmist issues a double imperative in verse 4 of Psalm 105, calling us to both "look to the LORD and his strength" and to "seek his face always." These twin commands work together as a comprehensive invitation into a life of intentional devotion, transforming how we navigate the demands and uncertainties of our daily existence. To understand what the psalmist means, we must examine both the context of this verse and the profound spiritual reality it invokes.

Psalm 105 is a psalm of praise that recounts God's mighty deeds throughout Israel's history. The psalmist rehearses the covenant with Abraham, the miracles in Egypt, the wilderness wanderings, and the conquest of Canaan. This historical narrative forms the essential backdrop for verse 4. The command to "look to the LORD and his strength" does not emerge from philosophical abstraction but from historical memory. The congregation is invited to remember what God has already done and, on that foundation, to direct their gaze toward him in the present moment.

The word "look" carries more weight than casual observation. In Hebrew, the concept involves focusing one's attention, deliberately turning one's gaze toward a particular object or person. We are not simply to acknowledge God's existence; we are to focus our attention upon him with intentionality. This looking is not a passive but an active spiritual discipline that requires our conscious participation. In a world that relentlessly demands our attention through endless distractions, the psalmist calls us to reclaim our capacity to look toward God. This act of looking becomes a form of worship, a statement that God is worthy of our focus and allegiance.

The phrase "his strength" reveals what specifically we are to contemplate. God's strength is not abstract power divorced from our circumstances. Throughout Psalm 105, God's strength manifests in concrete ways: defeating Pharaoh, guiding Israel through the wilderness, and giving them the land. When we look to the Lord and his strength, we are remembering that the one who sustained our spiritual ancestors remains the same God who sustains us. His strength is not diminished by the passage of time or the complexity of our modern challenges. This looking to God's strength becomes an antidote to fear, a remedy for anxiety, and a source of confidence in circumstances that might otherwise overwhelm us.

The second imperative parallels and extends the first: "Seek his face always." To seek God's face is to pursue an intimate relationship with him. In biblical language, "the face of God" represents his direct presence and favor. This seeking is not occasional but habitual. The word "always" indicates that this is to become the orientation of our entire existence. We do not seek God's face only when crisis compels us or when convenient seasons of life permit. Rather, we are called to establish a perpetual posture of seeking, a continuous turning toward God that characterizes our days, whether we experience blessing or suffering, plenty or want.

The pairing of these two commands suggests an important spiritual truth. We cannot sustain authentic seeking of God's face apart from confidence in his strength. Conversely, merely acknowledging God's strength without seeking his face reduces him to an impersonal force rather than inviting us into the covenant relationship he offers. The two imperatives work together to form a complete spirituality: we ground ourselves in the reality of God's mighty power, and from that grounding we pursue the intimate presence of the one who possesses that power.

In our contemporary context, this verse challenges us to establish spiritual practices that embody these commands. What does it mean for us to "look to the LORD and his strength"? Perhaps it means beginning our day by deliberately remembering God's past faithfulness before we face present challenges. It might involve reading Scripture, studying God's historical acts of deliverance, and allowing these accounts to reorient our perspective. Seeking God's face might always manifest in regular prayer, in silence and listening, and in corporate worship with others who share our faith.

The promise embedded within these commands deserves our attention. When we look to the LORD and his strength, when we persistently seek his face, we position ourselves to receive what our souls desperately need. We find guidance for decisions we must make, comfort in losses we must bear, and strength for the journey ahead. We discover that the God we remember in history is the God who meets us in the present and will sustain us into the future.

As you move through this day, consider where your gaze is fixed. What captures your attention and concern? The psalmist lovingly redirects us: Look to the Lord and his strength. Seek his face always. This is not a burden imposed from without but an invitation to the deepest satisfaction our hearts can know.

PRAYER

Eternal God, our ancestors looked upon your mighty deeds and found their faith strengthened. Grant us the grace to fix our attention upon you and your strength. When distractions clamor for our focus, redirect our gaze toward you. Teach us to seek your face not as an occasional discipline but as the constant orientation of our hearts. Make us people who remember your faithfulness and from that memory draw confidence for each new day. We offer these prayers through Jesus Christ, our Lord. Amen.

THE ENDURING FOUNDATION

Give thanks to the LORD, for he is good; his love endures forever
(Psalm 106:1).

"Give thanks to the LORD, for he is good; his love endures forever."
These words from Psalm 106:1 echo throughout Scripture like a
refrain that never grows old. We find nearly identical language in
Psalms 107, 118, and 136, in the songs of Israel's worship, and in the
thanksgiving offerings of God's people across generations. This
repetition is no accident. Some truths are so fundamental, so essential
to our spiritual lives, that they must be proclaimed again and again until
they shape the very rhythm of our hearts.

The psalmist begins with a command: "give thanks." Not "consider
giving thanks" or "give thanks when you feel like it," but simply "give
thanks." Gratitude, in the biblical worldview, is not primarily an
emotion that wells up spontaneously when circumstances align in our
favor. It is an act of the will, a deliberate choice to acknowledge who
God is and what he has done. The psalmist calls us to thanksgiving
because our natural tendency is to forget, to take for granted, to allow
the extraordinary to become ordinary in our eyes.

But notice the foundation of this thanksgiving: "for he is good." Our
gratitude rests not on our circumstances but on God's character. The
Hebrew word translated "good" here carries rich meaning: it speaks of
beauty, excellence, and moral perfection. God's goodness is not merely
the absence of evil; it is the fullness of everything right, true, and lovely.
When we give thanks for God's goodness, we are acknowledging that
at the center of the universe beats a heart of perfect love and wisdom.

This is profoundly countercultural. Our world teaches us to measure
goodness by outcomes, to judge reliability by consistency with our

preferences. But biblical thanksgiving transcends circumstance. Psalm 106 itself, immediately after this opening verse of praise, launches into a lengthy recounting of Israel's repeated failures and God's persistent faithfulness. The Israelites grumbled in the wilderness, worshiped the golden calf, rejected the Promised Land, and continually turned away from God. Yet the psalm begins and ends with praise because God's goodness is not contingent on our faithfulness; it flows from his nature.

The second half of the verse adds an eternal dimension: "his love endures forever." The Hebrew word for "love" here is *hesed*, that magnificent term that English struggles to capture in a single word. It encompasses steadfast love, loyal devotion, covenant faithfulness, and unfailing mercy all at once. This is not the fickle affection that waxes and wanes with mood or circumstance. This is the love that keeps its promises, that remains constant through betrayal, that pursues the wanderer and restores the broken.

"Forever" is not hyperbole; it is reality. God's love has no expiration date, no conditions under which it will be withdrawn, no limit to its patience or extent. When you were formed in your mother's womb, God's love was already ancient and will outlast the stars. When you stumble today, his love does not diminish. When you doubt tomorrow, his love remains unchanged. This enduring quality of divine love is the anchor for our souls in every storm.

Living in light of these truths transforms us. When we internalize that God is good, truly, perfectly, unchangeably good, we stop demanding that he prove himself according to our limited understanding. When we grasp that his love endures forever, we find the courage to trust him in seasons of confusion and pain. Thanksgiving becomes not a fair-weather practice but the deep conviction that shapes how we interpret every chapter of our story.

The call to give thanks is also an invitation to join the great chorus of God's people across time and space. When we speak these words, we add our voices to those of ancient Israel, to the early church, and to centuries of saints who have found this verse to be true in their own lives. We are not alone in our gratitude, and our thanksgiving today strengthens the faith of those who will come after us.

Let this verse become a daily declaration in your life. In moments of joy, let it give voice to your celebration. In times of sorrow, let it anchor you to what remains true even when feelings fail. For the Lord is good, not was, not will be, but is, right now, in this very moment. And his love, that magnificent, unshakeable *hesed*, endures forever.

PRAYER

Lord, we give you thanks, for you are good. Your love endures forever. When our circumstances confuse us and our feelings mislead us, anchor us in these eternal truths. Teach us to give thanks not as a ritual but as the overflow of hearts that truly know you. May gratitude shape our perspective, our prayers, and our daily walk. In Jesus' name, Amen.

TELLING OUR STORY

Let the redeemed of the LORD *tell their story* (Psalm 107:2).

The opening verse of Psalm 107 rings with an imperative that cuts through the centuries to reach our modern ears with surprising directness. The psalmist does not gently suggest that the redeemed might consider sharing their experiences. Instead, he commands them, us, to speak. This is not a timid invitation but a clarion call: tell your story. Let it be known what the LORD has done.

The very first word, "let," immediately establishes the psalmist's purpose. This is not poetry written merely for aesthetic appreciation. It is a summons to testimony, a public declaration of what redemption looks like in human experience. The Hebrew verb here, "let them recount," carries the sense of narrative, not abstract theological propositions, but the concrete, lived reality of God's saving work in individual lives. This matters profoundly for us as believers living in an age of skepticism and competing worldviews.

We live in a culture that has grown weary of grand proclamations and institutional claims. Yet people are far from weary of authentic human stories. They hunger for narratives that ring true, that acknowledge struggle and complexity while pointing toward genuine transformation. When we, the redeemed of the Lord, step into this role as storytellers, we offer something the world desperately needs: a counter-narrative to despair, a lived testimony to redemption that cannot be argued away in abstract debate.

The phrase "redeemed of the LORD" deserves our careful attention. In the Hebrew scriptures, redemption carries legal and relational weight. It speaks of being bought back, recovered from bondage, and restored to a covenant relationship. The redeemed are those who have been claimed by God, those whose fundamental condition has been transformed through divine intervention. This is not sentimentality. This is the language of liberation, of restoration, of a relationship restored against the odds.

Yet consider what the psalmist asks us to do with this redemption: tell the story. Share it. Make it public. Throughout Psalm 107, this structure repeats with remarkable clarity. Four times we encounter different circumstances: those lost in the wilderness, those imprisoned in darkness, those made fools by their rebellion, and those nearly destroyed by storms. And each time, in their distress, they cry out to the Lord, and each time they are delivered. Each deliverance prompts the refrain: "Let them give thanks to the LORD for his unfailing love and his wonderful deeds for mankind" (verses 8, 15, 21, 31).

The pattern is unmistakable: deliverance calls for declaration. Redemption demands testimony. We are not saved in isolation; we are saved into a community of witnesses who bear testimony to what God has accomplished. When we remain silent about our redemption, we participate in a kind of theft; we withhold from others the very hope and encouragement they may desperately need.

This raises uncomfortable questions for many of us. What is our story? Can we point to moments where we have experienced genuine redemption, times when we were lost, broken, imprisoned by circumstances or our own choices, only to find ourselves claimed and restored by God's gracious action? Many of us can. We have known deliverance from addiction, from despair, from broken relationships, from the spiritual wilderness. We have experienced the uncanny providence of God working through circumstances we could not have engineered ourselves.

But perhaps we are hesitant to speak these stories aloud. We worry about overstepping, appearing self-righteous, or simplifying complex experiences into neat spiritual narratives. These concerns are not entirely misplaced. Yet the psalmist's command suggests that such hesitation may itself be a form of disobedience. If God has genuinely redeemed us, does silence honor that redemption or diminish it? The call to "tell your story" is fundamentally a call to gratitude made visible and to worship made accessible. When we articulate what God has done in our lives, we do not diminish the sacred mystery of his work. Rather, we illuminate it for those who stumble in darkness, searching for evidence that redemption is possible.

As you reflect on this verse today, consider: What is your story of redemption? Where have you experienced God's saving grace? And who needs to hear it?

PRAYER

Gracious God, you have redeemed us at infinite cost and claimed us as your own. Yet we confess our hesitation to speak boldly of what you have done. Free us from false modesty and self-protective silence. Give us courage to tell our stories, not to boast, but to bear witness. Let our words kindle hope in those who wander in darkness, who cry out from their own wildernesses and imprisonments. And may our testimonies always point beyond ourselves to your faithfulness, your love, your power to restore. In Jesus' name, we pray. Amen.

THE STEADFAST HEART

My heart, O God, is steadfast; I will sing and make music with all my soul (Psalm 108:1).

"My heart, O God, is steadfast; I will sing and make music with all my soul." These words from Psalm 108:1 ring with a confidence that seems almost defiant in its certainty. David speaks not of a heart that hopes to become steadfast or struggles toward steadfastness, but of a heart that already is. This is the language of settled conviction, of a soul that has found its anchor.

The Hebrew word translated as "steadfast" carries the sense of being firmly established, fixed, or prepared. It is the opposite of wavering, the antithesis of doubt. But here is what strikes me most powerfully about this declaration: it comes not from a life of ease, but from a man who knew betrayal, exile, warfare, and profound loss. David's steadfastness was not born in a sanctuary of safety but forged in the crucible of real struggle.

We live in an age that seems designed to unsettle us. News cycles spin faster than our capacity to process them. Relationships fracture under the weight of misunderstanding. Financial pressures mount. Health concerns emerge without warning. The very ground beneath our feet can feel uncertain, shifting with every tremor of circumstance. In such a world, how do we cultivate steadfastness?

David gives us a clue in the very structure of his declaration. Notice that steadfastness is not something he manufactures through willpower alone. His heart is steadfast toward God, not simply steadfast in general. This is the crucial distinction. We cannot white-knuckle our way into stability. We cannot think positive thoughts and expect our inner worlds to stop trembling. True steadfastness comes from being anchored to something, to someone, outside ourselves, something immovable when everything else shifts.

The response to this steadfastness is equally instructive: "I will sing and make music with all my soul." David does not retreat into stoic silence. His stability does not express itself as grim determination or joyless duty. Instead, it bursts forth in song. This is the paradox of biblical faith: the more firmly we are rooted in God, the more freely we can express ourselves. Constraint leads to freedom. Surrender leads to song.

Consider what it means to sing "with all my soul." This is not half-hearted humming or distracted mumblings. This is total engagement, full-throated praise that involves the whole person. When our hearts are truly steadfast in God, worship stops being an obligation and becomes an overflow. We do not sing because we must, but because we cannot help it. The steadfast heart naturally makes music.

There is something else here worth noting: David says "I will sing," using the language of decision and commitment. Even steadfast hearts must choose their expression. Even settled souls must determine how they will respond to God's faithfulness. Praise is not merely an emotional reaction that happens to us; it is a deliberate act we offer. On days when feelings fail and circumstances conspire against us, we can still choose to sing. We can still decide to make music. The steadfast heart has learned this secret: worship is not dependent on our circumstances but on God's character.

This psalm invites us to examine the state of our own hearts. Are we steadfast, or are we tossed about by every wind of change? Do we have an anchor that holds, or are we drifting? And when we consider God's faithfulness to us, his love that endures, his presence that sustains, his promises that never fail, does our response rise to the level of song?

Perhaps today you feel anything but steadfast. Perhaps your heart is troubled, anxious, or heavy. Take comfort in this: steadfastness is not the absence of struggle but the presence of God in the midst of it. You do not need to manufacture confidence or fake joy. You need only to turn your unsteady heart toward the One who never wavers, and let him be your firm foundation. From that place of being held, you may find that song rises naturally, even in surprising circumstances. The steadfast heart sings not because everything is perfect, but because God is faithful. And that makes all the difference.

PRAYER

Lord God, establish my heart in you. When circumstances shift and troubles rise, be my anchor and my stability. Teach me to find my steadfastness not in my own strength but in your unchanging character. And from that place of being held by you, let my soul overflow with songs of praise. May my worship be wholehearted, my trust unwavering, and my joy rooted in your faithfulness. In Jesus' name, Amen.

THE ADVOCATE FOR THE VULNERABLE

With my mouth I will greatly extol the LORD*; in the great throng of worshipers I will praise him. For he stands at the right hand of the needy, to save their lives from those who would condemn them* (Psalm 109:30–31).

The final verses of Psalm 109 offer a striking contrast to the bitter lament that precedes them. After many words of desperate pleas against enemies and requests for divine vengeance, the psalmist suddenly shifts from anguish to exultation, from complaint to confident praise. This tonal transformation teaches us something profound about the nature of faith: our worship is not dependent upon the resolution of our circumstances but upon our unshakeable conviction that God stands with the vulnerable and defenseless.

To understand these verses, we must recognize them within the larger context of Psalm 109. The psalmist has suffered deeply: attacked by enemies, maligned by false witnesses, stripped of dignity. Yet amid this suffering, the psalmist experiences a spiritual awakening. Despite the ongoing reality of opposition and injustice, despite the fact that enemies have not vanished and suffering has not ceased, the psalmist chooses praise. This is not the shallow optimism of someone whose problems have been resolved. Rather, it is the profound confidence of one who has encountered the God who sees, who remembers, and who acts on behalf of the oppressed.

The first clause, "With my mouth I will greatly extol the LORD," emphasizes vocal, visible, communal praise. The Hebrew verb here conveys not merely quiet devotion but bold proclamation. The psalmist intends to declare God's greatness openly, enthusiastically, without apology. This is significant for those who suffer. We often feel pressure to hide our pain, to appear composed, to keep our struggles private. Yet the psalmist demonstrates that authentic worship sometimes means speaking our praise despite our pain. The mouth that has cried out in lament becomes the instrument of exaltation.

The phrase "in the great throng of worshipers" adds another crucial dimension. The psalmist's praise is not solitary but communal. Individual believers gather together in worship, and their collective voice rises to heaven. For those of us who have felt isolated by suffering, who have wondered whether anyone understands our struggles, this communal context offers comfort. We praise God not alone in our pain but surrounded by others who worship the same God, who celebrate the same convictions about divine character and divine justice.

The second verse provides the theological foundation for this praise: "For he stands at the right hand of the needy, to save their lives from those who would condemn them." The image of God standing at the right hand is rich with meaning. In the ancient world, the right hand symbolized power, protection, and honor. When God stands at the right hand of the needy, God assumes the role of advocate, defender, and protector. This is not a distant God who observes human suffering from afar. This is an intimate God who positions himself alongside the vulnerable.

The Hebrew word for "needy" here encompasses the poor, the defenseless, those without resources or power to defend themselves. It describes the widow, the orphan, the immigrant, those whom ancient Near Eastern law codes explicitly protected because they had no other recourse. God becomes their champion, their legal defender, their refuge. When society condemns them, when the powerful exploit them, when justice seems unavailable, God intervenes.

The verb "to save their lives" suggests deliverance from mortal danger. The psalmist speaks of life-and-death stakes. These are not abstract principles about divine benevolence but concrete assurances about divine action. God does not merely sympathize with the oppressed;

God saves them. God does not passively observe injustice; God acts against those who would destroy the vulnerable.

For those of us who serve as spiritual leaders and teachers, these verses challenge us to examine our theology and our practice. Do we truly believe that God stands at the right hand of the needy? How do our churches reflect this conviction? Are we advocating for the vulnerable, or have we become comfortable with unjust systems? Are we using our voices, our platforms, our influence, our authority, to amplify the cries of those whom society marginalizes?

Yet the primary message of these verses is personal and pastoral. Whatever adversity we face, whatever enemies assail us, whatever injustice threatens us, we can declare with confidence: God stands at my right hand. God has not abandoned me. My circumstances do not determine my faith; my God does. Therefore, I will praise him, loudly and publicly, in the fellowship of God's people, knowing that the God of justice is my defender.

PRAYER

Eternal God, I praise you because you stand at the right hand of the vulnerable and the weak. Forgive me for the times I have remained silent in the face of injustice, for moments I have prioritized comfort over courage. Give me a voice that speaks your truth boldly and a heart that champions those whom the world condemns. Help me to praise you not when all my circumstances are resolved but because of who you are: the God of justice, the defender of the defenseless, the advocate for the vulnerable. May my worship, spoken in the great throng of believers, testify to your faithfulness and your power. In Christ's name, Amen.

PSALM 110

ENTHRONED IN VICTORY

The LORD says to my lord: "Sit at my right hand until I make your enemies a footstool for your feet" (Psalm 110:1).

Psalm 110:1 opens with a remarkable conversation overheard by the psalmist: "The LORD says to my lord: 'Sit at my right hand until I make your enemies a footstool for your feet.'" In these few words, we encounter one of the most quoted verses in the New Testament and a passage that has captivated believers for millennia.

The imagery is striking. To sit at someone's right hand in the ancient world signified the highest honor, the place of authority and intimate access. When God invites this figure to sit at his right hand, he is conferring upon him unparalleled dignity and power. This is not a temporary appointment or a ceremonial gesture but an enthronement that speaks of permanent authority and sovereign rule.

Yet the command contains a curious element: "until I make your enemies a footstool for your feet." The posture is one of rest, of confident waiting. The king sits while God subdues his enemies. Ancient Near Eastern kings would literally place their feet on the necks of conquered enemies as a sign of total victory. Here, God promises to arrange all opposition under the feet of this enthroned lord. The victory is certain, but there is a period of waiting, a time when the king reigns while the final subjugation of enemies unfolds.

For David to call anyone "my lord" was extraordinary. As Israel's anointed king, few could claim authority over him. Yet David recognized someone greater than himself, a future king whose reign would transcend his own. The early church saw in these words a prophecy of the Messiah, and Jesus himself pointed to this psalm when challenging the religious leaders about the identity of the Christ. Peter proclaimed on Pentecost that these words found their fulfillment in Jesus, who was exalted to God's right hand after his resurrection.

This verse invites us to consider what kind of kingdom we serve. Christ's enthronement at the Father's right hand is not merely a future hope but a present reality. He reigns now, even as we live in the tension of the "already but not yet." His enemies have not yet been fully vanquished, evil still prowls, suffering persists, and death continues its work. Yet the outcome is never in doubt. The king is seated, and the Father is actively bringing all things under his feet.

What does it mean for us to live in this in-between time? We are citizens of a kingdom whose King is enthroned but whose final victory is still unfolding. We are called to faithfulness in a world where darkness has not yet been banished, where the footstool is still being arranged. This requires patience, the same patience displayed by the King who sits and waits for the Father's timing.

There is profound comfort here. When we face opposition, when the enemies of our souls seem overwhelming, when circumstances appear to contradict God's promises, we remember that our King sits at the Father's right hand. He is not anxious or uncertain. He does not wring his hands at the strength of his foes. He sits in confidence because the battle belongs to the Lord, and the victory is assured.

This psalm also challenges our understanding of power. The world's kingdoms are built on force, on the immediate crushing of opponents, on displays of domination. But God's kingdom operates differently. The King sits. He waits. He trusts the Father to accomplish what has been promised. This is not weakness but the ultimate expression of faith and authority.

As we walk through our days, facing personal battles and witnessing the struggles of a broken world, Psalm 110:1 anchors us in a stunning reality: Jesus Christ reigns now, seated in the place of highest honor, and every enemy will ultimately bow before him. Our calling is to live as faithful subjects of this king, proclaiming his lordship, extending his kingdom through love and service, and waiting with confident hope for the day when every knee will bow and every tongue confess that he is Lord.

PRAYER

Lord Jesus, you are seated at the right hand of the Father, enthroned in glory and power. Help us to live each day in light of your victory, trusting that you are working all things according to your purposes. When we grow weary in the waiting, remind us that you are king, that your triumph is certain, and that we serve a kingdom that cannot be shaken. May we rest in your sovereign rule and proclaim your lordship with boldness and joy. Amen.

WHERE WISDOM BEGINS

The fear of the LORD is the beginning of wisdom; all who follow his precepts have good understanding. To him belongs eternal praise (Psalm 111:10).

The climactic verse of Psalm 111 presents one of Scripture's most profound theological statements: "The fear of the LORD is the beginning of wisdom; all who follow his precepts have good understanding. To him belongs eternal praise." This declaration, echoing throughout the wisdom literature of the Old Testament, invites us to reconsider what it truly means to be wise, not in the manner of the world, but in the way of God.

The psalmist has spent the previous nine verses recounting God's magnificent works and faithful character. He has celebrated the Lord's righteousness, justice, and eternal covenant with Israel. Then, having established this foundation of divine majesty and covenant reliability, the author distills all his observations into a single, startling assertion: wisdom begins with fear. This is not the timid, cowering fear that one experiences before a tyrant. Rather, the Hebrew word translated "fear" encompasses reverence, awe, respect, and wonder. It is the appropriate response of a creature standing before the Creator, of a finite being confronting infinite majesty.

This concept represents a direct challenge to contemporary culture. Our world values a different kind of wisdom: the accumulation of degrees, the gathering of information, the cultivation of intellectual prowess. We celebrate those who question everything, who doubt authority, who build their understanding upon skepticism. Yet the psalmist suggests that true wisdom has its foundation not in doubt but in reverence. Before we can genuinely understand God, his purposes, and his ways, we must first bow before his majesty and acknowledge his supremacy.

Consider what this fear accomplishes. The psalmist immediately connects it to understanding: "all who follow his precepts have good understanding." There is no contradiction between fearing God and understanding him. Rather, the fear of the Lord actually opens our minds to deeper comprehension. When we approach Scripture with reverent awe rather than detached analysis, when we read not merely as scholars seeking intellectual mastery but as servants seeking to know our master, something transformative occurs. The text speaks differently to us. We perceive layers of meaning that cold scholarship might miss.

The relationship between fear and precepts is equally significant. The precepts of God, his commandments, his teachings, his instructions, become not burdensome restrictions but precious guides. They are the articulation of God's wisdom for human flourishing. When we fear the Lord, we desire to follow his precepts not from obligation or legal compulsion but from genuine love and reverence. We recognize that his commandments are for our good, that they reflect his character and his desire for our wholeness.

Furthermore, the psalmist declares that to God belongs eternal praise. This is the natural outpouring of one who has begun the journey of wisdom through the fear of the Lord. Praise flows from recognition: recognition of who God is, what he has done, and what he continues to accomplish. When fear of the Lord produces understanding, and understanding leads us to follow his precepts, praise becomes inevitable. It is not manufactured or forced; it emerges organically from a heart that genuinely perceives God's glory.

Yet we must ask ourselves: What does this look like in our own lives? How do we cultivate the fear of the Lord in an age of presumption? It begins with intentional reflection on God's greatness. We read the Psalms not as ancient literature but as invitations to encounter the living God. We contemplate his creation, recognizing the fingerprints of infinite wisdom and power. We meditate on his redemptive history, observing how he has acted on behalf of his people across the centuries. We confess our own smallness and limitations, acknowledging that we are dependent upon God for every breath.

This fear also manifests practically. The fear of the Lord leads us to examine our lives against his standard, to repent of our rebellion, and to submit our wills to his. It prompts us to take his word seriously, to believe what he has promised, and to obey what he has commanded, not begrudgingly, but with the joy of those who recognize that his way is always the better way.

As we proceed through life, let us remember that the beginning of true wisdom is not in ourselves but in God. It is not in our achievements or our accumulation of knowledge, but in our reverent acknowledgment of his supremacy. When we begin here, with fear, with awe, with genuine respect for the Almighty, everything else follows naturally. Our understanding deepens, our obedience becomes joyful, and our praise rises continually toward him who alone is worthy.

PRAYER

Almighty God, we bow before your majesty and acknowledge your infinite greatness. Forgive us for the arrogance that so often characterizes our approach to knowledge and understanding. Teach us to fear you, not with trembling terror, but with reverent awe that recognizes your sovereignty and goodness. Grant us the wisdom that comes only through reverential trust in you. Help us to embrace your precepts with joy and gladness, knowing that your commands reflect your perfect character. And may our lives become a song of eternal praise to your holy name. In Jesus Christ, our Lord and Savior, we pray. Amen.

FINDING JOY IN REVERENCE

Blessed are those who fear the LORD, who find great delight in his commands (Psalm 112:1).

At first glance, the opening verse of Psalm 112 appears to present a paradox. How can fear and delight coexist? We typically think of fear as something that repels us, while delight draws us near. Yet the psalmist boldly declares that true blessing belongs to those who simultaneously fear the Lord and find great delight in his commands. Understanding this tension unlocks one of the most profound truths about the Christian life.

The "fear of the LORD" that Scripture commends is not the cowering terror of a slave before a tyrant, but rather the awe-filled reverence of a child before a loving yet majestic father. It is the recognition that we stand before the Creator of the universe, the One who spoke galaxies into existence and who knows the number of hairs on our heads. This fear involves a healthy awareness of God's holiness, power, and justice. It means taking him seriously, recognizing that his words carry weight and his character demands our respect.

When we properly fear God, we understand that his commands are not arbitrary rules designed to restrict our freedom, but rather loving boundaries established by infinite wisdom. A child who fears disappointing a beloved parent does not feel oppressed by that parent's guidance; rather, that healthy respect becomes the foundation for a deeper relationship. Similarly, our reverence for God creates the space where genuine delight can flourish.

The delight mentioned in this verse is no mild preference or dutiful acceptance. The Hebrew word suggests intense pleasure and satisfaction. These are people who do not merely tolerate God's commands; they treasure them. They meditate on his words not out of obligation but because they have discovered something precious. Like the psalmist who wrote, "Oh, how I love your law! I meditate on it all day long" (Psalm 119:97), they have tasted and seen that the Lord's ways are good.

This delight grows from understanding the heart behind the commands. God's laws reflect his character and his desire for our flourishing. When he commands us to love our neighbors, he is not imposing arbitrary social requirements; he is inviting us into the life-giving practice of other-centered love that mirrors his own nature. When he calls us to rest, to practice generosity, to pursue justice, or to cultivate purity, each command points us toward abundant life.

The truly blessed person has discovered that God's commands are not obstacles to joy but pathways to it. They have learned what the world often misses: that genuine freedom is not found in the absence of all restraint, but in willing alignment with the way things were meant to be. A fish finds freedom in water, not on dry land. We find our truest freedom and deepest delight when we live according to our Creator's design.

This verse also reminds us that blessedness is not primarily about comfortable circumstances but about a right relationship with God. The person who fears the Lord and delights in his commands may face trials, opposition, or hardship. Indeed, Psalm 112 goes on to acknowledge that "evil tidings" may come. Yet they possess an unshakable foundation. Their security rests not in their ability to control their circumstances but in their connection to the unchanging God whose commands they cherish.

In our contemporary culture, which often views any form of authority with suspicion and celebrates autonomy above all else, this psalm offers a countercultural vision. It invites us to consider that submitting to God's authority is not diminishment but fulfillment. The blessed life is not found in crafting our own moral universe, but in joyfully embracing the reality of who God is and what he has revealed.

As we reflect on Psalm 112:1, we might ask ourselves: Do we approach God's Word with reverence? Have we moved beyond seeing his commands as burdensome requirements to discovering them as treasures? Are we cultivating both the healthy fear that recognizes his majesty and the deep delight that savors his wisdom?

The blessing promised here is available to all who will receive it. It begins with a heart posture that honors God as God, and it deepens as we experience the goodness of his ways. May we be numbered among those who fear the Lord and find great delight in his commands.

PRAYER

Heavenly Father, give us hearts that rightly fear you, not with paralyzing dread, but with reverent awe. Open our eyes to see the wisdom and love behind your commands. Transform our duty into delight, our obligation into joy. Help us discover that, in your boundaries, we find true freedom, and in your ways, we find abundant life. May we be counted among the blessed. In Jesus' name, Amen.

THE ETERNAL PRAISE OF GOD'S NAME

Let the name of the LORD be praised, both now and forevermore.
From the rising of the sun to the place where it sets, the name of
the LORD is to be praised (Psalm 113:2–3).

Psalm 113 opens with a summons to praise that arrests the attention of any serious reader of the Psalter. The initial verse, "Praise the LORD," serves as a clarion call, establishing the fundamental posture that frames everything that follows. Yet it is verses 2 and 3 that expand this command into a cosmic and temporal vision of unprecedented scope. "Let the name of the LORD be praised, both now and forevermore. From the rising of the sun to the place where it sets, the name of the LORD is to be praised." These words invite us to contemplate what it means to offer praise that transcends the limitations of our moment and acknowledges the majesty that spans creation itself.

The phrase "the name of the LORD" appears throughout the Psalter with particular intensity and theological significance. In Hebrew thought, the name does not merely serve as a label for identification; rather, it represents the character, presence, and power of the one named. When the psalmist calls us to praise "the name of the LORD," we are invited to celebrate not merely a title but the very essence of divine nature. This name encompasses God's holiness, justice, mercy, and redemptive power. To praise the name is to acknowledge and celebrate who God fundamentally is.

The temporal dimensions presented in these verses deserve careful attention. The phrase "both now and forevermore" anchors our praise in two essential realities. First, praise must be our present posture. We are not instructed merely to anticipate future worship or to commemorate past encounters with God. Rather, the "now" demands our immediate allegiance and vocal acknowledgment. In our contemporary moment, with all its complexities and challenges, we are called to recognize God's worthiness of praise. This present tense is radical in its implications. It suggests that regardless of our circumstances, God remains worthy of our worship.

Yet this present praise is inseparably linked with "forevermore," the eternal dimension that extends beyond our comprehension. The Hebrew word often translated as "forever" or "everlasting" conveys the sense of an indefinite, limitless future. This eternal perspective transforms our understanding of praise. We do not offer worship merely because God meets our immediate needs or because we experience his blessing in this moment. Rather, we acknowledge a reality that transcends our temporal existence, that the God we praise is eternal, unchanging, and worthy of worship regardless of the ages or centuries that may pass.

The geographical dimension in verse 3 provides yet another layer of meaning. "From the rising of the sun to the place where it sets" employs a poetic expression that encompasses the entire known world. The Hebrews understood the sun's arc across the sky as a marker of completeness and totality. This phrase suggests that from every corner of creation, from east to west, from wherever human beings exist beneath the heavens, the name of the Lord deserves to be praised. This is not a call limited to any particular nation, culture, or religious community exclusively. Rather, it envisions a universal recognition of God's worthiness that spans geographical and cultural boundaries.

There is profound significance in recognizing that this universal and eternal praise is presented not merely as a description of what happens, but as a command regarding what ought to happen. The psalmist does not simply observe that people worldwide will eventually recognize God's majesty. Instead, these verses function as an imperative, calling us to align ourselves with a reality that transcends our compliance. In other words, God's worthiness of praise is not dependent upon whether we actually offer that praise. Rather, our calling is to recognize and participate in a worship that is fundamentally true whether or not we acknowledge it.

For those of us living in the twenty-first century, these verses carry particular power. We live in an age of relativism, where truth claims are often met with skepticism. Yet the psalmist boldly asserts that there are realities not subject to our opinions or preferences, that there is indeed one God whose name is worthy of praise. This God is not confined to our sanctuaries or to moments of religious observance. Rather, the psalmist invites us to recognize that wherever the sun rises and sets, wherever human consciousness exists beneath the heavens, the name of the Lord claims allegiance.

Our response to these verses must involve both gratitude and commitment. We give thanks for a God who is eternal, unchanging, and universally worthy of worship. We commit ourselves to becoming voices of praise, not merely in our privileged moments but in the totality of our lives, joining in a chorus that spans creation and time itself.

PRAYER

Eternal God, we come before you with hearts humbled by the vastness of your eternal nature. You who existed before time itself and will endure long after all earthly things have passed away, accept the praise of our lips and the worship of our hearts. Help us recognize your worth not only in moments of abundance but also in seasons of struggle. May our lives become a living testimony to your glory, reflecting your character in all that we do and say. Grant us the grace to join in that eternal chorus of praise that rises from creation itself. Let our hearts be aligned with the truth that your name is indeed worthy of praise, both in this present moment and forevermore. Amen.

SPRINGS FROM STONE

Tremble, earth, at the presence of the LORD, at the presence of the God of Jacob, who turned the rock into a pool, the hard rock into springs of water (Psalm 114:7–8).

The psalmist's words thunder with awe. Earth itself is summoned to tremble, not in terror, but in reverent recognition of divine presence. This is not a poetic exaggeration; it is a theological declaration. The God of Jacob, the covenant-keeping God, is not a distant God but one whose presence reshapes reality. Mountains skip, seas flee, and rocks yield water. Nature itself becomes pliable under his touch.

Psalm 114 is a liturgical celebration of the Exodus, a recounting of Israel's deliverance from Egypt and their journey through the wilderness. But verses 7–8 shift the focus from historical retelling to cosmic reverence. The earth is personified as trembling before the Lord, echoing Sinai's quaking when God descended in fire and cloud. This trembling is not fear alone; it is recognition, submission, and worship.

The image of water springing from the rock derives from Exodus 17 and Numbers 20, where God provides water for his people in the desert. These were not mere miracles of survival; they were revelations of character. God does not abandon his people in barren places. He transforms barrenness into abundance. The hard rock, symbol of impossibility, becomes a source of life. In the wilderness, where no human ingenuity could suffice, God alone sustains.

This verse invites us to consider our own "hard rocks," those places in life that seem unyielding, lifeless, and resistant to change. Perhaps it is a relationship calcified by years of silence, a vocation that feels dry and fruitless, or a heart hardened by disappointment. The God of

Jacob is not intimidated by hardness. He specializes in transformation. He does not merely soften the rock; he makes it gush with springs.

There is a depth to this image that extends beyond the wilderness narrative. The apostle Paul, writing to the Corinthians, recalls the water from the rock and identifies that rock with Christ: "they drank from the spiritual rock that accompanied them, and that rock was Christ" (1 Corinthians 10:4). What the psalmist celebrated as the sovereign act of the covenant God, Paul understood as a foreshadowing of the one in whom all God's provision would find its fullest expression. The springs of water in the desert were not merely a historical mercy; they were a sign, pointing forward to the one who would stand on the last day of the feast and cry out, "Let anyone who is thirsty come to me and drink" (John 7:37). To read Psalm 114 through this lens is to discover that the God who struck the rock in the wilderness has, in Christ, become the rock himself—broken, so that living water might flow.

Notice the dual emphasis: "the rock into a pool" and "the hard rock into springs of water." The first is a miracle of provision; the second, a miracle of abundance. God does not give just enough; he gives overflow. Springs suggest continuity, renewal, and refreshment. They are not one-time events but ongoing sources. This is the nature of grace: not a drop, but a deluge.

The trembling of the earth is also a call to us. Do we tremble at the presence of the Lord? In a culture that often treats God casually, Psalm 114 reminds us that divine presence is weighty. It is not to be domesticated or diluted. When God draws near, the appropriate response is awe. Not dread, but wonder. Not panic, but praise.

Yet this trembling is not reserved for mountains and seas alone. It is the trembling of a heart that knows it stands before holiness. It is the trembling of gratitude when grace breaks through. It is the trembling of joy when the impossible becomes possible. It is the trembling of hope when springs emerge from stone.

The God of Jacob is our God. He is not only the God of deliverance but the God of presence. He does not remain in the past, confined to Exodus and Sinai. He is present now, in our deserts, in our dryness, in our hardness. And where he is present, transformation is possible.

It is worth pausing to consider how this psalm functioned in the life of Israel's worship. Psalm 114 belongs to the Egyptian Hallel (Psalms 113–118), sung at the Passover meal in celebration of the Exodus. Every year, at the table, the people of God rehearsed their deliverance. They did not simply remember it as a distant historical event; they inhabited it.

The trembling of the Jordan and the skipping of the mountains were recited as present realities, because the God who acted then was the God who was present now. This liturgical rhythm teaches us something essential: we, too, need regular rehearsal of what God has done. Memory is not nostalgia; it is the soil in which faith grows. When we gather to worship, to sing, to read the Scriptures, we are doing what Israel did: reminding ourselves and one another that the God of past deliverance is the God of present help.

Let the earth tremble. Let our hearts awaken. The God of Jacob is here.

PRAYER

Lord of wonder, you are the God who makes springs flow from stone. Teach my heart to tremble at your presence, not in fear, but in awe. Where I am dry, pour out your Spirit. Where I am hardened, soften me with grace. May your presence reshape my reality, and may I never lose the wonder of who you are. Amen.

FLOURISHING UNDER GOD'S BLESSING

May the LORD *cause you to flourish, both you and your children. May you be blessed by the* LORD, *the Maker of heaven and earth* (Psalm 115:14–15).

These final verses of Psalm 115 arrive like a benediction, a graceful closing to a hymn that has traced the contours of faith, the emptiness of idolatry, and the reality of God's sovereignty. Yet they offer far more than a ceremonial conclusion. They present a vision of what blessing actually means and how it flows through the generations, grounded not in human effort or circumstance, but in the character of the God who made all things.

To understand this blessing, we must first consider the context of Psalm 115. Throughout this psalm, the psalmist has contrasted the living God with the dead idols worshiped by the nations: gods of silver and gold that have mouths but cannot speak, eyes but cannot see, ears but cannot hear. These are the products of human hands, representations of human fantasy rather than realities of divine power. Against this backdrop of spiritual emptiness, the psalmist calls Israel to trust in the Lord, to recognize that our God is in the heavens and does whatever he pleases. It is precisely this God, the only true God, the active and all-powerful one, who now pronounces a blessing upon his people.

The word "flourish" in verse 14 carries profound significance. The Hebrew word suggests increase, abundance, and growth. But this is not the kind of frantic multiplication that consumerism promises or the status anxiety that worldly systems cultivate. This flourishing is organic, rooted, and purposeful. It suggests the growth of a well-watered, well-tended tree or a garden that produces in its proper season. The Lord does not merely wish prosperity upon his people; he causes it. He is the active agent of our increase. This is not a passive blessing but a dynamic abundance flowing from the One who sustains all creation.

What makes this promise remarkable is its inclusiveness: "both you and your children." The blessing does not end with the individual who receives it but extends through the generations. This speaks to a fundamental biblical truth: that God's covenant is never merely personal; it always has a communal and generational dimension. Abraham's blessing flowed to Isaac and Jacob. David's covenant extended beyond his own reign. When we receive God's blessing, we become conduits through which it flows to those who come after us. Our faith, our obedience, and our surrender to God's purposes create channels through which blessing can reach our children and grandchildren.

This has profound implications for how we live. It means that our choices matter not only to ourselves but also to generations yet unborn. It means that investing in our children's spiritual formation is not a burden but a privilege. We are cooperating with God's desire to extend his blessing through time. It means that when we commit ourselves to following the Lord, we make a statement that reverberates through time, affecting those we love most deeply.

The second part of the promise shifts perspective: "May you be blessed by the LORD, the Maker of heaven and earth." Here, the psalmist grounds blessing in the fundamental truth of creation. The God who blesses us is not a localized deity, not one god among many, but the creator of the cosmos itself. Every star, every creature, every atom exists because of his word. When God blesses us, it is not because we have earned it through merit or achieved it through ingenuity. It is an act of grace flowing from the One who has absolute authority and power over all that exists.

This identification of God as "the Maker of heaven and earth" also serves as a gentle but firm correction to the entire preceding section of the psalm. The idols cannot bless because they cannot do anything; they are merely things made by hands. But our God, having made all things, stands utterly apart from and above his creation. His blessing is effective precisely because it comes from the One who sustains everything by his power.

For us today, these verses offer an invitation into trust. In a world where we are constantly tempted to secure our own flourishing through ambition, accumulation, or achievement, the psalmist calls us to a different posture. He calls us to recognize that true increase comes from alignment with the God who made heaven and earth. He invites us to think beyond ourselves and our immediate circumstances to consider the legacy we are creating for those who follow. And he reassures us that the God who oversees all creation cares deeply about our individual flourishing and that of our children.

PRAYER

Almighty God, maker of heaven and earth, we thank you for the promise of your blessing upon our children and us. Free us from the anxiety that comes from trying to secure our own flourishing, and teach us to trust in your provision and care. Help us see our lives not as isolated moments but as part of a sacred story that extends across generations. May your blessing flow through us to those who come after, that they too might know the abundance of your grace. In Christ's name, we pray. Amen.

PSALM 116

THE GIFT OF BEING HEARD

I love the LORD, *for he heard my voice; he heard my cry for mercy. Because he turned his ear to me, I will call on him as long as I live* (Psalm 116:1–2).

There is something profoundly human about the need to be heard. We spend much of our lives longing for someone to truly listen, not just to our words, but to the desperation behind them, the hope buried within them, the fear that colors them. The psalmist begins this beautiful song not with theological abstraction, but with the most intimate declaration possible: "I love the LORD." And remarkably, the reason given is beautifully simple: because God listened.

The Hebrew word for "heard" used here carries a weight beyond mere auditory perception. It implies attention, understanding, and response. God did not simply register sound waves from heaven. He turned toward the psalmist with full divine attention, bending low to catch every syllable of a desperate prayer. The image of God turning his ear toward us is stunning in its tenderness. The Creator of galaxies, the One who spoke light into existence, inclines himself to hear our trembling voices.

Notice what prompted this love: a cry for mercy. This was not eloquent prayer or polished liturgy. It was raw, desperate pleading. Perhaps you know this kind of prayer, the kind that comes in hospital waiting rooms, in seasons of crushing loneliness, in moments when circumstances have stripped away all pretense and left you with nothing but need. The psalmist reminds us that these are precisely the prayers that reach God's heart. He does not require us to clean up our desperation before approaching him. He hears the cry itself.

The response to being heard transforms everything. "Because he turned his ear to me, I will call on him as long as I live." This is the anatomy of a relationship with God. We cry out, he hears, and that hearing creates such gratitude and confidence that we commit ourselves to a lifetime of calling upon him. One answered prayer becomes the foundation for decades of faith. One moment of being truly heard by God creates an unshakeable conviction that he will always listen.

This passage challenges our consumer approach to prayer, where we measure God's goodness by whether he gives us what we want. The psalmist celebrates not necessarily getting a specific answer, but being heard. Sometimes God's greatest gift is not solving our problem immediately, but assuring us that we are not alone in it. His attentive presence becomes the answer, even when circumstances have not changed. To be heard by God is to be valued, known, and loved, and sometimes that is exactly what our souls need most.

Consider what it means that God "turned his ear" to you. In our distracted age, true listening is increasingly rare. We half-listen while checking phones, formulating responses, or waiting for our turn to speak. But God offers something radically different: his complete, undivided attention. When you pray, you are not competing with a billion other voices for divine attention. The infinite God somehow gives each of his children his full focus, as though you were the only one calling his name.

This personal experience of being heard should shape our entire spiritual lives. Like the psalmist, our commitment to pray "as long as I live" flows not from obligation or fear, but from gratitude and confidence. We keep praying not because we are supposed to, but because we have tasted what it means for God to turn toward us in our need. We have experienced the relief of being fully known and still fully loved.

The beauty of Psalm 116 is that it invites us into this same experience. Whatever you face today, whether crushing sorrow or quiet desperation, whether dramatic crisis or the slow ache of ordinary struggle, God is ready to hear. He does not wait for you to find the right words or achieve the proper spiritual state. He simply asks you to cry out, to let your voice reach toward heaven with whatever honesty fills your heart.

And when you do, you may find yourself echoing the psalmist's wonderful declaration: "I love the LORD, for he heard my voice." Not for what he gave, but for how he listened. Not for removing all problems, but for being present in them. The God who hears is the God worth loving, worth calling upon, worth trusting with every day of your life.

PRAYER

Lord, thank you for hearing my voice, even when my prayers are messy and my faith is small. Thank you for turning your ear toward me, for giving me your attention when I cry out. Help me to call upon you not just in crisis, but every day of my life, confident that you always listen. In the name of Jesus, who taught us to pray. Amen.

PSALM 117

THE GLOBAL CALL TO PRAISE

Praise the LORD, *all you nations; extol him, all you peoples.*
For great is his love toward us, and the faithfulness of the LORD
endures forever. Praise the LORD *(Psalm 117:1–2).*

Psalm 117 stands out as the shortest chapter in the Bible, just two verses, yet it speaks with astonishing breadth and depth. In its brevity, it captures the essence of God's redemptive purpose: that all nations, not just Israel, would come to know, love, and worship the Lord. Its message is universal, timeless, and deeply personal. Beneath its simple call to praise lies a vast theology of inclusion, mission, and covenant faithfulness.

The psalmist begins with a command that reverberates across the ages: "Praise the LORD, all you nations; extol him, all you peoples." This is not a suggestion or a private invitation; it is a global summons. Every culture, tongue, and tribe is invited to lift their voices in worship. The psalmist envisions a world united not by political power or cultural dominance but by shared adoration of the living God. Thousands of years before Jesus gave the Great Commission, Psalm 117 was already proclaiming God's heart for all people.

This call to universal praise reminds us that God's glory was never meant to be confined to one group. His love is boundless, reaching into every heart that will receive it. The psalmist's language suggests not mere acknowledgement of God but joyful celebration, an overflowing response to his goodness. "Extol him" means to lift high, to magnify, to exalt with fervent devotion. Worship, then, is not a duty but a delight; it is the natural expression of hearts transformed by grace.

Why this call to universal praise? Verse 2 gives us the reason: "For great is his love toward us, and the faithfulness of the LORD endures forever." The Hebrew word for "love" here, *hesed*, carries the weight of covenant loyalty, mercy, and steadfast kindness. It is God's unwavering commitment to love his people despite their failures, a love that is both tender and strong. And his faithfulness means reliability, truth, and firmness. Together, these words paint a portrait of a God whose character never changes and whose promises never fail.

This psalm reminds us that divine love is not an abstract concept but a lived reality. God's *hesed* connects heaven to earth, eternity to time, divinity to humanity. His love became visible in Jesus Christ, who embodied God's faithful love and truth. Through Christ's death and resurrection, the doors of worship were thrown open to every nation, tribe, and language. In him, Psalm 117 finds its ultimate fulfillment. The nations now sing not only because they are invited but because they have been redeemed.

When we meditate on these two verses, we are called to widen our perspective. Worship is not limited to our own experiences or circumstances. It ties us to the global church, the unseen multitude of believers praising God at this very moment in every corner of the world. From rural villages to bustling cities, from whispered prayers to resounding choirs, the song of Psalm 117 continues to rise. Each believer adds a note to the eternal chorus that one day will fill heaven itself.

Yet this psalm is also deeply personal. When we reflect on God's faithfulness "toward us," it invites us to consider how he has proven himself true in our own lives. Think of the moments when his mercy sustained you, when his promises held firm despite uncertainty, when his love reached you in your weakness. Every act of God's faithfulness in your life is a reason to praise him anew. Gratitude becomes the melody that fuels our worship.

Psalm 117 teaches us that authentic praise flows from recognition. We praise God because he has loved us greatly and unconditionally. We extol him because his truth endures despite our doubts and failures. And we join the global call of worship because his story of redemption extends to all creation. True worship is never hollow repetition; it is the echo of love received and returned.

In a world divided by borders, languages, and ideologies, this psalm offers a vision of unity that transcends all earthly divisions. It reminds us that in praising God together, we discover what truly binds humanity: the faithful and enduring love of the Lord. Every time we lift our voices in praise, we participate in the fulfillment of this ancient call, a foretaste of heaven itself, where countless nations will praise the Lamb who was slain.

Let Psalm 117 shape how you pray, sing, and live today. As you go about your day, remember that your worship joins a global symphony of praise. You are part of something far larger than yourself: the eternal response to God's unfailing love.

PRAYER

"Lord God, thank you for your steadfast love and unending faithfulness. Teach my heart to praise you, not only for what you have done for me but for who you are to all people everywhere. Let my worship echo the joy of the nations and unite my voice with the chorus of your creation. May my life reflect your mercy today and always. Amen."

THE ANCHOR OF PRAISE

You are my God, and I will praise you; you are my God, and I will exalt you (Psalm 118:28).

There is a profound difference between saying "God is great" and saying "You are my God." The first is a theological statement, a declaration about the nature of God that could be spoken at arm's length, from the comfortable distance of doctrine or tradition. The second is something altogether different. It is personal. It is relational. It is the language of covenant love, the kind of language a child uses when reaching for a parent's hand in a crowd, or a traveler uses when finally returning home. In simple words, the psalmist collapses the infinite distance between heaven and earth and makes the boldest claim a human being can make: *You are mine, and I am yours.*

Psalm 118 is a song born of survival. Scholars widely believe it was composed as a liturgical hymn of thanksgiving, likely sung in procession by worshippers entering the temple gates after a season of great trial. The opening verses set the tone unmistakably: "His love endures forever," a refrain repeated like the chorus of a man who has nearly drowned and cannot stop marveling at dry ground. By the time we reach verse 28, the psalmist has walked through rejection ("The stone the builders rejected"), through near-death ("I will not die but live"), and through the narrow gate of salvation. When he finally arrives at this verse, the praise he offers is not the praise of someone who has never suffered. It is the praise of someone who has seen the pit and been pulled from it. That context is everything.

It is worth pausing here to note that this psalm was never meant to be a private confession. It was liturgy, spoken aloud, sung in community, passed from voice to voice as worshippers moved through the temple courts together. There is something quietly important in that. Praise, in the biblical imagination, is rarely a solitary act. When the psalmist declares "You are my God," he does so surrounded by others who know the same God, who have walked through their own narrow gates, who are adding their own voices to the ancient chorus. Our individual declarations of faith do not exist in isolation; they are woven into something larger than ourselves, a great ongoing conversation between God and his people across every generation. To praise is to join that conversation. To fall silent is to step out of it.

Notice, too, the deliberate repetition: *"You are my God . . . you are my God."* This is not poetic padding. In Hebrew poetry, repetition is rarely accidental. It functions like hammering, driving a nail deeper into the heartwood. The psalmist seems to know that what we declare once we may forget, but what we declare twice, and then live by, becomes the architecture of our souls. He is not merely informing God of something God does not already know. He is reminding himself. He is anchoring himself against the current of doubt, loss, and forgetfulness that so easily sweeps our devotion downstream.

This is the discipline of praise: it is not always spontaneous. Sometimes praise is a decision made before the feeling arrives, a flag planted in enemy territory. "I will praise you," the psalmist says, the future tense carrying the weight of intention, of resolve, of a will submitted to something greater than circumstance. He does not say "I praise you when life is good" or "I praise you when I understand what you are doing." He says *I will*, a declaration of ongoing commitment that does not wait for perfect conditions.

There is fuel for that resolve, and the psalmist knows where to find it: in memory. Notice how much of Psalm 118 is retrospective. Before verse 28 arrives, the poet has spent twenty-seven verses rehearsing what God has done: the deliverances, the mercies, the moments when the walls closed in and then, inexplicably, did not. This is not nostalgia. It is a spiritual practice. When we rehearse God's faithfulness in the past, we are not living backward; we are building the foundation on which present praise can stand. "I will praise you" is easier to say after you have taken the time to remember all the reasons you already should. Gratitude has a long memory, and the discipline of praise is fed by it.

And then comes that beautiful word: *exalt*. To exalt is to lift up, to elevate, to make known the greatness of something that might otherwise go unnoticed or forgotten. In a culture saturated with noise, there is something quietly countercultural about a person who lifts up the name of God, not on a stage, not for applause, but in the daily posture of their life.

You may be reading these words in a season of great joy, or in one of great weariness. You may be processing grief, navigating uncertainty, or simply moving through the quiet ordinary days that make up most of a human life. Whatever your season, the invitation of Psalm 118:28 remains the same: to plant your stake in the ground, to look upward, and to make the most personal, most defiant, most freeing declaration available to you: *You are my God.* Not a distant force. Not an abstract concept. Yours. And you, his.

That is where praise begins. That is where it never has to end.

PRAYER

Lord, in the middle of everything, the noise, the uncertainty, the ordinary and the extraordinary, I choose to say it: you are my God. You are not a stranger to me, and I am not a stranger to you. Where I have forgotten this, awaken me again. Where I have withheld my praise out of pride or pain, loosen my heart. Teach me to make exaltation a daily habit, a steady rhythm, a returning home. May the praise I offer you today not be the praise of easy days alone, but the deeper praise that rises from a soul that you have held through hard ones. You are worthy. You have always been worthy. Amen.

THE PATH OF PURITY

How can a young person stay on the path of purity? By living according to your word (Psalm 119:9).

The psalmist asks one of the most urgent questions of every generation: How can we maintain integrity in a world that constantly pulls us toward compromise? This verse does not romanticize the journey or promise that it will be easy. Instead, it acknowledges a fundamental truth: staying pure requires intentionality, and that intentionality must be anchored in something greater than our own willpower.

The question itself is profound. The psalmist does not ask if purity is possible, but how it can be achieved. This presupposes that God has made a way, that there is indeed a path we can walk. Yet the inquiry also reveals humility. The writer recognizes that without divine guidance, we are prone to wander, to lose our way in the maze of competing voices and desires that surround us daily.

Notice that the verse addresses "a young person," though its wisdom transcends age. Youth represents a season of formation, when patterns are established and character is shaped. Young people face unique pressures: identity formation, peer influence, the intoxicating rush of new freedoms, and the overwhelming weight of choices that seem to determine their entire future. But whether we are twenty or seventy, we all have areas of our lives where we are still "young," still vulnerable, still learning. We all need this wisdom.

The answer the psalmist provides is deceptively simple: "By living according to your word." Not by trying harder, not by isolating ourselves from the world, not even by sheer determination, but by aligning our lives with God's revealed truth. The Word of God becomes both a map and a compass, showing us the way and keeping us oriented when everything else seems uncertain.

Living according to God's Word means more than casual reading or occasional reference. It requires immersion. When we saturate our minds with Scripture, it begins to shape our thoughts, reframe our desires, and redirect our steps. The Word exposes the lies we have believed and replaces them with truth. It reveals what true purity looks like, not the sterile perfection of religious performance, but the wholeness and integrity that comes from being rightly aligned with our Creator.

This kind of living is active, not passive. The Hebrew concept behind "living according to" suggests careful attention, deliberate action, and constant vigilance. It is the picture of someone who studies the path ahead, who looks to the guidebook before making decisions, who returns again and again to check their bearings. We do not drift into purity; we pursue it with the Word as our guide.

But here is the beautiful paradox: while we are responsible for choosing to live by God's Word, it is ultimately the Word itself that does the transforming work. Scripture is living and active, sharper than any double-edged sword. It is not merely information to be mastered but the truth that masters us. As we consistently expose ourselves to it, the Holy Spirit uses it to cleanse, correct, and renew us from the inside out.

The path of purity is not about perfection; it is about direction. There will be stumbles and detours, moments when we lose our way. But when God's Word is our standard, we always know how to return. We have a reference point, a true north that never shifts with culture or circumstances. We can confess where we have strayed, receive forgiveness, and realign ourselves with truth.

In our current moment, when moral relativism suggests that everyone must define their own truth, this verse offers something radically different: an objective, trustworthy guide that has proven faithful across millennia. God's Word has led countless believers through temptation, persecution, doubt, and despair. It can lead us too. The invitation, then, is clear. If we want to walk in purity, in wholeness, integrity, and right relationship with God, we must commit ourselves to his Word. Not as a burden but as a gift. Not as a restrictive rulebook but as a life-giving path through dangerous terrain. The question has been asked. The answer has been given. What remains is our response.

PRAYER

Heavenly Father, thank you for your Word, which is a lamp to my feet and a light to my path. In a world of confusion and compromise, help me to anchor my life in your truth. Give me a hunger for Scripture, not out of duty but out of deep desire to know you and walk in your ways. When I stumble, remind me that your Word offers not only direction but grace to return to the path. Transform me from the inside out as I immerse myself in your truth. May my life reflect the purity that comes not from my own effort but from living in alignment with you. In Jesus' name, Amen.

FINDING GOD'S ANSWER

I call on the LORD *in my distress, and he answers me* (Psalm 120:1).

In the opening verse of Psalm 120, we encounter one of the most profound and comforting truths in all of Scripture: God hears us when we cry out to him, and he responds. This simple yet powerful declaration serves as both a testimony and an invitation, a reminder of God's faithfulness and encouragement for us to bring our own troubles before his throne.

The psalmist does not begin with platitudes or pretense. He acknowledges a fundamental reality of human existence: we experience distress. The Hebrew word translated "distress" encompasses more than temporary inconvenience or mild discomfort. It speaks of genuine anguish, pressing trouble, and circumstances that squeeze us from all sides. This word paints a picture of being caught in a tight place with no apparent way out.

How refreshing it is to find such honesty in Scripture! The Bible never minimizes our struggles or suggests that faith should exempt us from life's difficulties. Instead, it meets us in our darkest moments with truth that acknowledges our pain while pointing us toward hope. The psalmist's distress was real, pressing, and overwhelming, just like ours often is.

In our modern world, distress takes countless forms. It might be the crushing weight of financial uncertainty, the heartbreak of broken relationships, the anxiety of health concerns, or the loneliness of feeling misunderstood and isolated. Perhaps it is the burden of caring for aging parents, the stress of job insecurity, or the grief that follows loss.

Whatever form our distress takes, we can find comfort in knowing that the God who heard the ancient psalmist's cry hears ours as well. Notice the beautiful simplicity in the psalmist's response to distress: "I call on the LORD." Not "I devised a complex strategy" or "I marshaled all my resources." Simply, "I call." The Hebrew verb means to cry out, to proclaim, to summon. It is the same word used when someone calls for help in an emergency.

This calling is not about eloquent prayers or theological sophistication. It is about turning toward God in our moment of need, with the same instinctive urgency we might feel when facing physical danger. It is the cry of a child who runs to a parent when frightened, the desperate plea of someone who has reached the end of their own strength and wisdom.

Too often, we complicate prayer. We think we need to have the right words, the proper posture, or sufficient faith before we can approach God. But the psalmist's example teaches us otherwise. In distress, we simply call. We cry out from wherever we are, however we are, with whatever words we can manage. God does not require perfection from us; he requires honesty.

The most remarkable part of this verse is its confident declaration: "he answers me." Not "he might answer" or "I hope he will answer," but "he answers." This is not wishful thinking or positive psychology; it is testimony born from experience.

God's answers do not always come in the form we expect or within our preferred timeline. Sometimes his answer is a dramatic deliverance that removes us entirely from our circumstances. Other times, his answer comes as strength to endure, wisdom to navigate difficulty, or peace that transcends understanding. His answer might be a change in our situation or a change in our hearts. It could come through Scripture, through other people, through circumstances, or through the quiet whisper of his Spirit.

What matters most is not the method of his answer but the certainty of his response. When we call on the Lord in our distress, we are heard by the One who knows our needs before we speak them, who loves us with an everlasting love, and who has the power to intervene in our circumstances according to his perfect will and timing.

This verse transforms how we approach life's inevitable difficulties. Instead of being overwhelmed by distress, we can see it as an opportunity to experience God's faithfulness in new ways. Rather than trying to handle everything in our own strength, we can learn the sacred discipline of calling on the Lord.

This does not mean we become passive or irresponsible. We still take appropriate action, seek wise counsel, and use the resources available to us. But we do all of this from a foundation of prayer, recognizing that our ultimate help comes from the Lord who made heaven and earth.

As we face the challenges of today and tomorrow, may we carry with us the confidence of Psalm 120:1. In our distress, whatever form it takes, we have a God who hears, who cares, and who answers. This is not merely ancient poetry; it is present reality for all who call upon his name.

PRAYER

Heavenly Father, thank you for the promise that when we call on you in our distress, you answer us. Help us remember, in our darkest moments, that you are only a prayer away. Give us the faith to cry out to you with honest hearts, trusting in your perfect timing and wisdom. When answers seem delayed, strengthen our faith. When your response differs from our expectations, help us to trust your goodness. May we live each day with the confidence that you hear us, you love us, and you will never leave us to face our troubles alone. In Jesus' name, Amen.

PSALM 121

THE SOURCE OF OUR HELP

I lift up my eyes to the mountains—where does my help come from? My help comes from the LORD, the Maker of heaven and earth (Psalm 121:1–2).

The ancient Israelite pilgrims who sang the psalms of ascent understood something profoundly human that we often forget in our modern age of self-reliance and technological solutions: sometimes we are simply overwhelmed. The mountains that dominated the landscape of ancient Judea stood as towering reminders of human limitation. They were not mere geographical features but symbols of the great obstacles and uncertainties that every generation faces. When the psalmist declares, "I lift up my eyes to the mountains—where does my help come from?" he articulates a question that transcends ancient Israel and speaks directly to our contemporary hearts.

The opening verb in Psalm 121:1 carries weight in the Hebrew. The psalmist does not passively gaze; he actively "lifts up" his eyes. This is a deliberate, purposeful act. The mountains command his attention, but more importantly, they provoke a fundamental question about human existence. Where does help come from? The question itself is rhetorical, yet it reflects genuine spiritual wrestling. The mountains represent everything we cannot control: illness, loss, injustice, uncertainty, and the passage of time itself. They tower above us, seemingly indifferent to our individual struggles.

But the psalmist does not remain paralyzed by this contemplation. The declaration that follows is unmistakably clear: "My help comes from the LORD, the Maker of heaven and earth." Here we encounter one of Scripture's most profound statements about the nature of divine aid. The word "help" suggests not merely passive comfort but active assistance and support. This is the word used when God becomes our "helper" or "helper," someone who renders concrete aid in moments of genuine need. The parallel in Genesis 2:18, where God provides Eve, as a helper to Adam, demonstrates that this term carries the weight of real, meaningful support.

The confession moves beyond simple assertion to grounding itself in theological reality. The Lord is not merely one help among many options; He is identified as "the Maker of heaven and earth." This phrase connects the psalm to the creation narrative and affirms a doctrine of divine sovereignty that is frequently lost in our therapeutic age. The God who shaped the cosmos, who established the mountains themselves, is precisely the One to whom we lift our eyes when mountains loom before us. There is profound irony in this: the very mountains that initially provoke the question about help are themselves creatures of the God who answers that question.

This theological grounding distinguishes genuine faith from mere wishful thinking. Many ancient Near Eastern religions offered their adherents comfort through various deities, yet the psalmist makes an audacious claim: the Creator of all things has covenanted himself to his people. He is not one deity among many, not a localized god confined to a particular mountain shrine, but the Lord who "made heaven and earth." Such a God cannot be overwhelmed by our circumstances because he stands above and beyond all created reality.

The placement of this psalm within the collection of "Songs of Ascent" (Psalms 120–134) suggests these verses accompanied a literal pilgrimage to Jerusalem. The mountains, then, might represent both physical obstacles along the journey and the spiritual mountain of Zion itself, where God's temple stood. Yet the psalmist recognizes that true help does not ultimately reside in geography or religious institution but in the God whom the temple represents. This distinction proves essential for authentic faith. We may sometimes invest our hope in places, people, or programs, but the psalmist calls us back to the fundamental source: the Lord alone.

For contemporary believers, this psalm speaks with particular relevance. We live in an age of unprecedented access to information and resources, yet we are simultaneously riddled with anxiety. We scroll through an infinite array of help options: therapeutic, pharmaceutical, financial, spiritual, yet the psalmist suggests that true help requires a reorientation of our vision. We must lift our eyes beyond the immediate mountains of circumstance to recognize the God who stands behind and above all creation.

The movement from question to answer in these opening verses establishes the trajectory for the entire psalm. It is not a movement from despair to unrealistic optimism, but rather from honest questioning to grounded confidence. The psalmist does not deny that mountains exist or that help is needed. Rather, he relocates the source of help where it belongs: in the eternal God who neither slumbers nor sleeps, who guards the believer's life with constant, faithful attention.

PRAYER

O God, Creator of heaven and earth, I confess that my eyes often focus upon the mountains that rise before me: the obstacles I cannot overcome, the burdens that press upon me, the uncertainties that cloud my tomorrow. Grant me the grace to lift my gaze beyond these circumstances to behold you, the One who made all things and who alone can provide the help I truly need. Strengthen my faith to trust not in my own resources or in the systems of this world, but in your constant faithfulness and infinite power. May I walk forward today, confident in your presence and your provision. In Jesus' name I pray. Amen.

THE JOY OF GOING TO GOD'S HOUSE

I rejoiced with those who said to me, "Let us go to the house of the LORD" (Psalm 122:1).

There is something profoundly beautiful about the word "rejoiced" in this verse. David does not say he agreed, consented, or even willingly went. He rejoiced. His heart leaped at the invitation. The very mention of going to worship filled him with delight, as if someone had just announced the most wonderful news imaginable.

Think about what makes your heart leap with joy. Perhaps it is hearing from an old friend, receiving an unexpected gift, or anticipating a long-awaited reunion. For David, that unbridled joy came from the simple invitation to worship. This was not dutiful religion or obligatory attendance. This was desire, delight, and deep spiritual longing finding its fulfillment.

What strikes me most about this verse is that David rejoiced "with those who said." Worship was not a solitary endeavor for him. The invitation came from the community, and his joy was shared joy. There is something about corporate worship that multiplies our gladness. When we gather with other believers, our individual flames of devotion join together to create something warmer and brighter than any of us could produce alone. We sing louder, pray bolder, and sense God's presence more deeply when we are surrounded by others who are also seeking his face.

In our modern context, where individualism reigns and convenience often dictates our choices, this verse challenges us profoundly. We live in an age where we can stream sermons from our couches, sing worship songs in our cars, and read Scripture on our phones. All these things have value, but they cannot replace the communal experience David describes. There is an irreplaceable grace that flows when God's people physically gather, look each other in the eyes, lift their voices together, and declare their faith in unison.

But perhaps the most convicting aspect of this verse is the state of our own hearts. Can we honestly say we rejoice at the invitation to worship? Or has church become routine, predictable, even tedious? Do we look forward to Sunday morning, or do we calculate how much sleep we will sacrifice? Do we eagerly anticipate gathering with God's people, or do we scroll through our mental list of excuses?

David's joy reveals an essential aspect of his relationship with God. The house of the Lord represented God's presence, and David was a man who desperately craved that presence. Throughout the Psalms, we see his spiritual hunger: "As the deer pants for streams of water, so my soul pants for you, my God" (Psalm 42:1). When you long for someone, every opportunity to be with them is precious. David's rejoicing shows us that worship was not about checking a religious box but about encountering the living God he loved.

This verse also reminds us of our responsibility to extend the invitation ourselves. "Let us go" is a call to companionship in worship. We are meant to encourage one another, to invite the hesitant, to walk alongside those whose faith is faltering. Perhaps someone near you needs to hear those words today: "Come with me to worship." Your invitation might be the very thing that rekindles someone's spiritual passion or introduces them to the joy David knew.

The beauty of Psalm 122:1 is that it presents worship as it was meant to be: joyful, communal, and eagerly anticipated. It reminds us that our gatherings are not obligations but privileges, not burdens but blessings. When we truly grasp what is happening when God's people assemble, the presence of Christ among us, the work of the Spirit in us, the fellowship of saints with us, and the attention of the Father upon us, how can our response be anything less than joy?

As you reflect on this verse, ask yourself: What would it take for worship to become a source of rejoicing again? Perhaps it begins with remembering who awaits you, not just the congregation, but the Lord himself, eager to meet with his beloved children who have come home.

PRAYER

Heavenly Father, forgive us for the times we have treated worship as duty rather than delight. Rekindle in us the joy David knew, the eager anticipation of being in your presence with your people. Help us say "yes" with gladness when we are invited to gather in your name, and give us boldness to extend that invitation to others. May our hearts leap at the opportunity to worship you, and may we never take for granted the privilege of coming before you. In Jesus' name, Amen.

THE GAZE OF DEPENDENCE

I lift up my eyes to you, to you who sit enthroned in heaven. As the eyes of slaves look to the hand of their master, as the eyes of a female slave look to the hand of her mistress, so our eyes look to the LORD our God, till he shows us his mercy (Psalm 123:1–2).

The psalmist opens with a simple yet profound gesture: lifting the eyes heavenward. In ancient Near Eastern and biblical imagery, the eyes represent not merely the organs of sight but the entire orientation of one's being, the direction of hope, trust, and expectation. When the psalmist declares, "I lift up my eyes to you, to you who sit enthroned in heaven," the act itself becomes an expression of faith. The physical movement mirrors the spiritual reality: we redirect our focus from the anxieties and distractions of earthly existence toward the One who transcends all temporal concerns.

The Hebrew verb rendered "lift up" carries weight throughout the Old Testament. It suggests elevation not only of the eyes but of the entire person, a raising up that implies both humility and hope simultaneously. The psalmist is not gazing horizontally toward peers or superiors who might fail; rather, the upward gaze orients toward heaven itself, where God "sits enthroned." This throne language evokes the sovereignty and stability of divine rule. In a world of shifting circumstances and unreliable human authorities, the enthroned God remains constant, immovable, and absolutely secure.

Yet what follows in verse 2 introduces an image that modern sensibilities often find uncomfortable: the comparison of our relationship to God with that of slaves to their masters and mistresses. We must resist the temptation to soften this metaphor through contemporary lens grinding. The psalmist deliberately employs this imagery, and understanding why deepens our appreciation for the text's theology.

In the ancient world, a slave's survival and welfare depended entirely upon the master's or mistress's hand. The metaphor "as the eyes of slaves look to the hand of their master" captures an almost desperate watchfulness, the servant's gaze fixed upon that hand which might distribute food, inflict punishment, grant rest, or demand labor. There is no ambiguity about the dependency here. The slave has no resources of their own, no independent means, no alternative source of provision or protection. Every need must be met by the master's hand; every moment of safety depends upon the master's disposition.

The psalmist invites us to understand our relationship with God through the lens of radical dependence. In a culture that celebrates self-reliance and autonomy, this is indeed countercultural. Yet the biblical tradition consistently teaches that we are not self-sufficient. We did not create ourselves; we cannot sustain our own existence; we cannot ultimately protect ourselves from harm or death. We are dependent creatures addressing a sovereign Creator.

But here lies the crucial difference between the slavery metaphor and the relationship it describes: We are beloved dependents, not despised servants. The slave fears the master's hand because it might bring harm. Our eyes turn toward the hand of God with the confidence of children who know that hand dispenses mercy. This shift from fear to trust transforms the entire dynamic.

The conclusion of verse 2 crystallizes this hope: "so our eyes look to the LORD our God, till he shows us his mercy." The word "till" indicates both a duration and an expected culmination. We gaze upward not in endless desperation but in confident expectation of divine intervention. The mercy (*hesed*), that covenant loyalty and steadfast love so central to biblical theology, will surely come. The gaze itself becomes an act of faith, a refusal to look away from God even in the face of difficulty.

This psalm speaks to the faithful in distress. The superscription suggests a song of ascents, likely sung by pilgrims journeying toward Jerusalem. These were individuals on a journey, between destinations, vulnerable and dependent. Much like them, we find ourselves in liminal spaces: between what we have lost and what we hope to gain, between present hardship and anticipated deliverance. In such seasons, this psalm offers profound wisdom: fix your eyes upon God, acknowledge your radical dependence, and wait in confidence for the mercy that will surely come.

The practice of lifting our eyes heavenward remains as vital today as in ancient Israel. In moments when circumstances overwhelm us, when human resources fail, when we face our own insufficiency, we are invited to perform the psalmist's gesture: to lift our eyes, to acknowledge our dependence, and to wait in hopeful trust.

PRAYER

Eternal God, we lift our eyes to you this day. We acknowledge that we are but creatures, dependent upon your sustaining grace for every breath and every blessing. Teach us to gaze upon you with the trust of beloved children rather than with the fear of despised servants. When our circumstances overwhelm us and our own resources fail, grant us the courage to maintain our gaze upon your throne of mercy. We wait upon your hand and your steadfast love. Amen.

PSALM 124

THE LORD IS OUR HELP

Our help is in the name of the LORD, *the Maker of heaven and earth* (Psalm 124:8).

There is something profoundly reassuring about knowing where to turn when life overwhelms us. Psalm 124:8 offers us not merely comfort, but an anchor, a declaration of where true help is found. This single verse, which concludes David's song of deliverance, distills a truth that reverberates through every season of our lives: our help comes from the One who spoke galaxies into existence.

The psalmist does not say our help is in our own strength, our careful planning, or our accumulated wisdom. He does not point to human allies, financial security, or favorable circumstances. Instead, he directs our gaze upward to "the name of the LORD." In Hebrew culture, a name was far more than a label; it represented a person's very essence and character. The name of the Lord encompasses his faithfulness, his power, his covenant love, and his unshakeable promises. To call upon his name is to invoke all that he is.

Notice the comprehensive nature of this help. The Lord is identified as "the Maker of heaven and earth," a phrase that should stop us in our tracks. This is not a limited deity with regional jurisdiction or specialized interests. This is the sovereign Creator who fashioned the vast expanse of the cosmos and the intricate details of our planet. The same hands that set stars in their courses and established the foundations of mountains are the hands that reach down to help us. No problem we face is too complex for the One who designed the laws of physics. No relational tangle is too knotted for the One who knit us together in our mother's womb.

This truth confronts our tendency toward self-reliance. We live in an age that celebrates independence and self-sufficiency, where admitting we need help can feel like a sign of weakness. Yet the psalmist declares with confidence what we often resist acknowledging: we are creatures who desperately need our Creator. This is not a shameful admission but a liberating one. When we recognize that our help is in the Lord, we stop exhausting ourselves trying to be our own savior.

The placement of this verse is significant. Psalm 124 recounts how the Lord delivered Israel from enemies who would have swallowed them alive, swept them away like a flood, and torn them like prey. Only after rehearsing these specific acts of deliverance does the psalmist make this concluding statement. In other words, this is not merely a theological proposition; it is a testimony born from experience. The people had seen the Lord's help in action, and now they anchored their future confidence in his proven character.

We, too, can look back at our own stories and see evidence of God's help. The crisis that did not destroy us. The provision that came at just the right moment. The strength we found that was not our own. The door that opened when we had exhausted our own efforts. These are not coincidences but confirmations that our help truly is in the name of the Lord.

Yet this verse also calls us forward. When we face new challenges, when illness threatens, when relationships fracture, when purpose feels lost, when fear crowds in, we do not have to wonder where to turn. Our help has a name, and he is the Maker of heaven and earth. He does not change. His resources do not diminish. His attention does not waver. The same God who parted the Red Sea, who sustained his people in the wilderness, who sent his Son to redeem us, is available to us right now.

This verse invites us to stop striving in our own limited strength and instead to call upon the limitless One. It reminds us that dependence on God is not a fallback position for when we have failed; it is the proper posture of the human heart. We were designed to draw our strength, our wisdom, our courage, and our hope from God.

So today, whatever you are facing, let this truth settle deep into your soul: your help is in the name of the Lord. Not partially. Not as a last resort. But fully, immediately, and sufficiently. The Maker of heaven and earth bends his attention toward you. Call upon his name.

PRAYER

Lord God, Maker of heaven and earth, I confess that I often turn to lesser sources for help: to my own understanding, to human solutions, to temporary fixes. Thank you that your name is my true refuge and strength. Help me remember that, in every circumstance, you are both willing and able to help me. Teach me to call upon your name first, not last. May I rest in the assurance that the One who created all things holds my life securely in his hands. In Jesus' name, Amen.

UNMOVABLE TRUST

Those who trust in the LORD *are like Mount Zion, which cannot be shaken but endures forever* (Psalm 125:1).

Psalm 125:1 opens with one of the most evocative images in the Psalter, comparing those who trust in the Lord to Mount Zion, that immovable, eternal landmark of God's presence and protection. The psalmist offers a metaphor of geological permanence to describe spiritual stability, a promise that resonates across millennia with anyone who has felt the tremors of doubt, fear, or uncertainty.

The Hebrew word for "trust" conveys not merely intellectual assent but also genuine reliance and security. It suggests a leaning upon, a placing of weight upon something solid enough to bear it. In the ancient Near Eastern context, trust in one's god was not merely a matter of faith but an act of political and personal alignment. When the psalmist speaks of trusting in the Lord, he speaks of a comprehensive commitment, intellectual, emotional, and volitional, to the God of Israel as one's ultimate security.

Mount Zion itself was far more than a geographical feature to Israel. It was the seat of David's dynasty, the location of the Temple, the dwelling place of God among his people. When Isaiah later speaks of Zion as God's holy mountain (Isaiah 56:7), and when the Psalmist elsewhere proclaims "God is in the midst of her; she shall not be moved; God will help her when morning dawns" (Psalm 46:5), Zion becomes a theological statement about divine protection and permanence. The mountain cannot be shaken, not because of its stone composition, though that is real, but because God himself has established it as his sanctuary and throne.

The parallelism of the verse deepens its meaning. "Cannot be shaken" and "endures forever" create a temporal and physical stability that encompasses both present security and future permanence. This is no temporary refuge but an eternal anchor. The psalmist uses the language of immovability because the ancient listener would have understood that mountains symbolize stability amid chaos. When earthquakes, both literal and metaphorical, shake the earth, mountains stand firm. When political empires crumble and human plans collapse, God's purposes remain unshaken.

Yet we must ask ourselves: what does it mean practically to be "like Mount Zion" in our contemporary experience? Surely the psalmist does not suggest that believers will never face adversity, tremors, or seasons of spiritual questioning. The very existence of the Psalms of Lament, nearly one-third of the Psalter, testifies that the faithful experience genuine distress. Rather, the promise is that those whose trust is rooted in the Lord possess a foundation that cannot ultimately be destroyed, even when they themselves may feel profoundly shaken.

This distinction is crucial. The believer is not promised exemption from life's earthquakes. Rather, we are promised that our ultimate foundation, our trust in God, cannot be dislodged. We may feel the tremors of illness, loss, injustice, or doubt. Our circumstances may shift dramatically. But the bedrock of our security, if it truly rests upon the Lord, remains immovable. This is not the false promise of prosperity theology, which suggests that faith guarantees comfort and ease. Rather, it is the deeper promise that God himself is eternally reliable, unchanging in his character, and faithful to his covenant.

The structure of Psalm 125 reinforces this theme. The psalmist moves from the security of those who trust (verses 1–2) to the assurance that God will not leave the righteous to evil (verses 3–5). The psalm acknowledges that the wicked may prosper and the righteous may experience the "scepter of wickedness" resting upon their land. But God will not abandon his people. This is not naive optimism but mature faith, a recognition that faithfulness does not guarantee an easy path, but it does guarantee that we walk that path with God.

For those of us engaged in serious biblical scholarship and teaching, this promise takes on particular weight. We encounter the complexities of biblical text, the tensions between what we wish the Scripture said and what it actually says, and the difficulties of communicating faith to a skeptical age. Yet if our trust is in the Lord rather than in human approval, scholarly accolades, or perfect certainty, we remain on solid ground.

The invitation of Psalm 125:1 is to examine the foundation upon which we have built our trust. Is it shallow and circumstantial, dependent upon favorable conditions? Or is it deep and enduring, rooted in the character and covenantal faithfulness of God himself?

PRAYER

Eternal God, grant me a trust as unmovable as Mount Zion itself. When the tremors of doubt, fear, and uncertainty shake my soul, remind me that I rest upon your eternal foundation. Give me the courage to trust not in my own understanding but in your infinite wisdom and unfailing love. May my faith be not dependent upon circumstances but rooted in the character of Christ Jesus, in whom all your promises find their yes and amen. Strengthen me to stand firm in your presence forever. Amen.

PSALM 126

SOWING IN TEARS, REAPING IN JOY

Those who sow with tears will reap with songs of joy. Those who go out weeping, carrying seed to sow, will return with songs of joy, carrying sheaves with them (Psalm 126:5–6).

There is something profoundly counterintuitive about the image the psalmist paints for us: a farmer weeping as he scatters seed across the soil. We might expect tears at harvest time if the crops have failed, but tears at planting? This striking paradox contains one of Scripture's most hope-filled promises about the nature of faith and the character of God.

The historical context of Psalm 126 helps illuminate this imagery. This is a song of ascent, likely sung by Jewish pilgrims journeying to Jerusalem, celebrating the return from the Babylonian exile. The opening verses overflow with joy: "When the LORD restored the fortunes of Zion, we were like those who dreamed." Yet the latter verses acknowledge an ongoing struggle. The returned exiles faced overwhelming challenges: ruined cities, hostile neighbors, and the backbreaking work of rebuilding. They sowed their precious seed with tears, uncertain whether the land would yield enough to sustain them, wondering if their investment would bear fruit.

But the psalmist does not merely describe their current hardship. He offers a divine guarantee: those tears will give way to songs of joy. The weeping sower will return as a rejoicing reaper.

This promise speaks to a spiritual principle woven throughout Scripture and confirmed in the life of every believer who has walked through seasons of difficulty: faithful obedience in times of sorrow yields a harvest of blessing. Notice that the farmer does not stop sowing because of his tears. Despite his grief, despite his uncertainty, despite his exhaustion, he continues the work. He carries the seed and scatters it, trusting that what he cannot see beneath the soil will one day break forth into abundant life.

How often do we face our own tearful seasons of sowing? We invest in relationships that seem hopelessly broken. We serve faithfully in ministries that show little visible fruit. We parent children through rebellious years, praying prayers that seem to bounce off the ceiling. We remain obedient to God's calling even when every circumstance suggests we are wasting our time. We scatter the seed of God's Word into hearts that appear hardened beyond softening. These are the moments when faithfulness feels like foolishness, when obedience requires pushing through tears.

Yet the psalmist's promise stands: the harvest is coming. The question is never whether God will prove faithful, but whether we will continue sowing in the meantime. Will we trust him enough to invest our precious seed, our time, our resources, our hope, our very lives, into soil that looks unpromising? Will we keep scattering when our eyes are too blurred with tears to see clearly?

The transformation from tears to joy is not merely emotional; it is eschatological. It points us toward the ultimate harvest, when Christ returns and every seed sown in faith will yield its full fruit. But it also offers hope for the present. God delights in bringing beauty from ashes, joy from mourning, and harvest from what seemed like waste. He specializes in resurrections.

Consider Jesus himself, who "for the joy set before him endured the cross" (Hebrews 12:2). He is the supreme example of sorrowful sowing leading to joyful reaping. His tears in Gethsemane, his suffering on Calvary, his burial in the tomb, all were the planting of the seed that would produce a harvest of redeemed humanity, an innumerable multitude from every nation singing songs of joy around his throne.

When we sow in tears, we participate in this same pattern. We join the great company of the faithful who trusted God's promise that their labor was not in vain. We align ourselves with the character of the kingdom, where death produces life, where weakness reveals strength, and where the last become first.

So if you find yourself in a tearful season of sowing today, take heart. Your faithfulness matters. Your obedience, even through tears, is seen by the God who stores every tear in his bottle (Psalm 56:8). The harvest is coming. The songs of joy await. Continue scattering the seed. The reaping will come, as surely as God is faithful.

PRAYER

Father, when the season of sowing feels long and my tears blur the path ahead, strengthen my faith. Help me to trust your promise that this labor is not in vain. Give me the courage to continue scattering seed even when I cannot see the harvest. And when the time of reaping comes, may every song of joy give you the glory. In Jesus' name, Amen.

PSALM 127

THE FUTILITY OF HUMAN LABOR

Unless the LORD builds the house, the builders labor in vain. Unless the LORD watches over the city, the guards stand watch in vain. In vain you rise early and stay up late, toiling for food to eat—for he grants sleep to those he loves (Psalm 127:1–2).

The Psalm of Ascents collection opens with a meditation that strikes at the heart of human ambition and labor. Psalm 127 stands as a corrective to the cultural assumption that our success depends entirely upon our own effort and vigilance. The psalmist invites us to examine the fundamental relationship between divine providence and human responsibility, a tension that persists in contemporary life with undiminished force.

The opening couplet establishes a parallelism between two fundamental human endeavors: building a house and guarding a city. Both represent essential activities of civilization itself. A house represents the security and shelter of a family; a city represents the collective security and order of a community.

The Hebrew word translated "vain" appears three times in these two verses, creating an emphatic refrain. It conveys not mere disappointment but absolute futility, labor without meaningful results. Yet this is not the psalmist's final word. The "unless" that frames these statements points to a condition: all such labor becomes vain, specifically when divorced from the Lord's blessing and presence.

The superscription attributes this psalm to Solomon, a detail that enriches its theological message. Solomon, who undertook the most ambitious building projects in Israel's history, was uniquely positioned to reflect on the relationship between human enterprise and divine blessing. He erected the Temple in Jerusalem, expanded the royal palace, and fortified cities throughout the kingdom. Yet even with all of this activity, Solomon understood that the Lord's blessing was the decisive factor in any human endeavor. The attribution of this wisdom to Israel's master builder lends the psalm a note of hard-won authority. Its instruction is not the counsel of one who has never labored, but of one who labored on the grandest of scales and came to recognize that divine providence, not human ingenuity, is the foundation upon which all lasting achievement rests.

The third statement intensifies the teaching by moving from the collective (houses and cities) to the profoundly personal: your rising early and staying up late, your toiling for bread. Here is where the ancient wisdom meets modern anxiety. How many of us measure our worth by our productivity? How many have believed the lie that sufficient effort, sufficient hustle, sufficient sacrifice guarantees provision? The psalmist acknowledges the reality of labor; there is no romanticization of idleness here, yet insists that human exertion alone cannot secure what truly matters.

But notice what follows: "for he grants sleep to those he loves." The Hebrew word for "sleep" implies more than physical repose. In this psalm's context, it represents peace, the peace that comes when we entrust our security to the Lord rather than bearing it entirely on our own shoulders. Sleep becomes possible not because we have done enough, worked hard enough, or planned carefully enough, but because we have faith that the Lord watches over us. This is the spiritual rest that Jesus would later offer to his disciples: "Come to me, all you who are weary and burdened, and I will give you rest" (Matthew 11:28).

The second half of Psalm 127 extends this principle of divine gift into the most intimate sphere of human life: the family. The psalmist declares that children are a heritage from the Lord, and the fruit of the womb is his reward (Psalm 127:3). As the building of a house and the guarding of a city require the Lord's blessing, so too does the continuation of a family line rest upon divine grace rather than human initiative alone. In the ancient world, children represented not only personal joy but the security of one's legacy, the labor of one's fields, and the defense of one's household. To possess sons was to possess strength. Yet the psalmist is careful to frame even this most tangible of human blessings as a gift given by God. The logic of the psalm is unified: just as no city wall and no midnight toil can guarantee security apart from the Lord, so no human striving can manufacture what only divine grace bestows. Life in all of its dimensions, public and private, collective and personal, depends upon the sovereign generosity of God.

The teaching of Psalm 127 does not argue against work. Biblical theology has always affirmed the dignity and necessity of human labor. Rather, it argues against the idolatry of human effort, the worship of self-reliance. We are called to build, to guard, to rise, and to labor. But we are called to do so within the context of trusting divine providence. We work diligently, and then we sleep peacefully, knowing that ultimate security rests not in the strength of our hands but in the faithfulness of God.

PRAYER

Gracious Father, we confess the ways we have sought to build our security through our own effort alone. We have worked long hours, driven by anxiety rather than purpose, believing our provision depends entirely upon our strength. Forgive us for this anxiety that dishonors your sovereignty and exhausts our souls. Teach us to labor with integrity and purpose, yet to rest with genuine trust in your care. Help us to understand that our worth does not rest in our productivity but in your love. Grant us the spiritual rest that comes from knowing you watch over us, and give us the wisdom to balance our responsibilities with the peace that only you can provide. In Jesus's name, Amen.

THE PATH OF BLESSING

Blessed are all who fear the LORD, who walk in obedience to him (Psalm 128:1).

In a world obsessed with self-fulfillment and personal autonomy, the opening words of Psalm 128 strike a countercultural chord. Blessing, the psalmist declares, comes not from independence but from reverent dependence on God. This simple verse establishes a profound connection among fear of the Lord, obedient walking, and the blessed life, one that reshapes our understanding of what it means to flourish.

The concept of fearing the Lord often puzzles modern readers. We might wonder how fear relates to the loving relationship God desires with his children. But biblical fear is not the cowering terror of a slave before a tyrant. Rather, it is the awe-filled reverence of a creature before the Creator, the healthy recognition of God's holiness, power, and rightful authority over our lives. To fear the Lord is to take him seriously, to acknowledge that his ways are higher than our ways, and to approach him with the profound respect he deserves.

This fear is not paralyzing but liberating. When we truly grasp who God is, his infinite wisdom, his unchanging faithfulness, and his perfect love, we discover that surrendering to his lordship is not a burden but a relief. We were never meant to be our own gods, carrying the crushing weight of self-determination. The fear of the Lord frees us from the exhausting work of self-sovereignty and invites us into the rest of trusting someone greater than us.

Notice how the psalmist connects this fear with walking in obedience. These are not separate spiritual achievements but two dimensions of the same reality. Fear without obedience is merely sentiment; obedience without fear becomes legalism. True reverence for God naturally flows into alignment with his will. When we rightly understand who God is, following his commands becomes not a reluctant duty but a reasonable response.

The imagery of walking is particularly significant. Walking suggests movement, progression, a journey. Obedience to God is not a single decision made once and forgotten, but a daily, step-by-step following. Some steps are confident strides on clear paths; others are tentative movements through uncertain terrain. Yet each step taken in obedience, whether large or small, public or private, constitutes walking in God's ways.

This walk of obedience encompasses the whole of life. It shapes how we conduct our business, how we treat our families, how we steward our resources, how we speak about others, and how we respond to suffering. There is no area of human experience exempted from God's loving authority. To walk in obedience means allowing God's word to illuminate every corner of our existence, submitting every choice and habit to his scrutiny.

And what does this fear and obedience produce? Blessing. The Hebrew word for "blessed" conveys a sense of happiness, contentment, and flourishing. But this is not the fleeting happiness of circumstances aligning in our favor. It is the deep-rooted blessedness of a life rightly ordered under God's governance. It is the satisfaction of living in harmony with reality as God designed it, the peace that comes from knowing we are walking the path our Creator intended.

This blessing may or may not include material prosperity, physical health, or worldly success, though the following verses in Psalm 128 do speak to family and abundance. More fundamentally, it is the blessing of God's presence, the blessing of a clear conscience, the blessing of purpose and meaning, the blessing of being part of God's eternal story. It is the blessing available to all who fear the Lord, not just the prominent or powerful, but every person who chooses reverence and obedience.

As we reflect on this verse, we might ask ourselves: Do we truly fear the Lord in our daily decisions? Are we walking in obedience, or merely standing still in theological agreement? The blessed life beckons not to those who admire God from a distance but to those who daily, humbly, walk in his ways.

PRAYER

Gracious Father, cultivate in my heart a proper fear of you, not terror, but reverent awe. Give me the grace to walk daily in obedience, taking each step according to your will. May I know the deep blessing that comes not from pursuing my own path but from following yours. Where I have wandered, draw me back. Where I have been reluctant, strengthen my resolve. Lead me in the way everlasting. In Jesus' name, Amen.

RESILIENCE THROUGH OPPRESSION

*"They have greatly oppressed me from my youth," let Israel say;
"they have greatly oppressed me from my youth, but they have not
gained the victory over me"* (Psalm 129:1–2).

The opening words of Psalm 129 strike a note of defiance born from painful experience. Here stands a community, Israel personified, reflecting upon a history marked by relentless adversity. The psalm does not deny the reality of oppression; rather, it celebrates the inexplicable persistence of those oppressed. This is not the language of naive optimism or superficial encouragement. This is the testimony of those who have survived.

The Hebrew verb translated "oppressed" conveys a sense of oppression that goes beyond mere difficulty. It suggests systematic, prolonged affliction, the kind that wears upon the soul through its constancy rather than its intensity. The repetition of this verb in verse 1, combined with the phrase "from my youth," emphasizes that this oppression is not a recent development but a fundamental aspect of Israel's historical experience. The psalmist reaches back to the earliest memories of national consciousness and finds oppression already present, already woven into the fabric of existence.

Yet the most striking element of this passage lies in the conjunction "but" that introduces the triumphant second half of verse 2. Despite everything, despite the duration of the suffering, despite its intensity, despite its presence since youth, there stands an unshakeable conviction: "they have not gained the victory over me." This is not a statement about the absence of harm; it is a declaration about the absence of ultimate victory. The oppressors have wounded, but they have not destroyed. They have afflicted, but they have not conquered the essential self, the inviolable core of identity.

This paradoxical coexistence of suffering and unconquered spirit appears throughout Scripture in moments of profound faith. When Israel contemplates its history, the enslavements in Egypt and Babylon, the dispersions and persecutions, the exile and return, the community recognizes that oppression has marked every generation, yet the people survive. The oppressors come and go; their empires rise and fall, but Israel continues. This is not because Israel is stronger militarily or politically, but because something deeper sustains the people: a covenantal relationship with God that transcends the vagaries of historical circumstance.

For the contemporary reader, this psalm offers a remarkable gift. It neither denies suffering nor counsels passive acceptance of injustice. Instead, it models a mature spiritual response to systematic oppression: acknowledgment of reality combined with refusal to grant oppressors ultimate authority over one's being. This distinction proves crucial. To recognize oppression without surrendering one's dignity, to endure affliction without surrendering one's hope, to suffer without surrendering one's identity, this is the victory the psalmist celebrates.

The medieval Jewish commentator Ibn Ezra understood this psalm as Israel's response to those who sought to prevent the Jewish people from living according to their covenantal calling. The oppressors aimed not merely to inflict pain but to silence, to erase, to negate. The psalm's defiant affirmation rejects precisely this totalizing assault. The people have been oppressed, yes, but they remain: unchanged in their essential commitment to God, unbroken in their capacity to hope, unbowed in their determination to continue.

What oppression threatens your own spirit? Perhaps it comes in the form of circumstances that seem to press upon you from every side, that have haunted your years since childhood, that convince you of your smallness and powerlessness. The psalmist invites you to make a distinction: between what has happened to you and who you are, between the wounds you bear and the victory others might claim over you. The oppression is real; do not minimize it. But neither grant it dominion over your deepest self.

This defiant testimony ultimately points beyond itself toward God. The psalmist does not credit personal strength or human solidarity alone for the survival he celebrates. Verse 4 will make this more explicit, but already in these opening verses, we sense that the "I" who stands unconquered is ultimately the "I" who belongs to God. The victory that oppressors could not achieve is not because of human invincibility, but because human worth and dignity rest upon a foundation that tyrants cannot reach.

PRAYER

Merciful Father, I bring before you my own experiences of oppression, sometimes obvious, sometimes subtle, but always present. Grant me the courage to acknowledge these afflictions without surrendering my identity to them. Help me to distinguish between what has happened to me and who I am. When adversaries press upon me, help me to remember that my deepest self belongs to you and cannot be conquered by their hostility. Give me the resilience of the psalmist, the courage to say with ancient Israel, "They have not gained the victory over me." Through Jesus Christ, my Lord and deliverer. Amen.

WAITING FOR THE LORD

I wait for the LORD, *my whole being waits, and in his word I put my hope* (Psalm 130:5).

The psalmist stands in the depths of despair, crying out from what he calls "the depths" (Psalm 130:1). Yet from this dark place emerges one of Scripture's most profound declarations about hope: "I wait for the LORD, my whole being waits, and in his word I put my hope" (Psalm 130:5). This verse captures the essence of what it means to trust God when circumstances offer no earthly reason for confidence.

The Hebrew word translated as "wait" appears throughout the Psalms and wisdom literature, carrying a rich array of meanings. Unlike the passive English word "wait," which sometimes suggests mere inactivity, the Hebrew word conveys active expectation; it carries the idea of stretching forward in earnest anticipation. It is the attitude of one who has placed a wager on God's faithfulness and now stakes everything on his promised character. The psalmist is not waiting passively; he is waiting with intention, with the whole orientation of his being directed toward the Lord.

This comprehensive nature of his waiting becomes evident in the phrase "my whole being waits." The Hebrew here uses the word *nephesh*, often translated as "soul" or "life." The parallel structure of this line creates emphasis through repetition, "I wait . . . my whole being waits," suggesting that waiting is not merely an intellectual assent or a surface-level acknowledgment. Rather, it encompasses the totality of the person: emotions, will, intellect, and spirit all locked in expectant hope. The psalmist has integrated his waiting into the very fabric of his existence.

What makes this waiting possible amid despair? The second half of the verse provides the answer: "in his word I put my hope." Here we encounter a crucial theological principle that bridges the chasm between doubt and faith. The psalmist's hope does not rest on changed circumstances or the resolution of his distress. Instead, it is grounded in God's word: his promises, his revealed character, and his covenant faithfulness. In Hebrew, the term "word" encompasses both the spoken utterance and the promise; it is the declaration of God's intent and commitment.

This foundation distinguishes biblical hope from mere optimism. Optimism hopes that things will improve. Biblical hope holds that God will remain faithful to his promises, regardless of external circumstances. The psalmist has learned a difficult but essential truth: when earthly circumstances crumble, they cannot be the foundation for hope. Only the immutable Word of the Lord can bear such weight.

The theological context of Psalm 130 enriches our understanding of this verse. This psalm belongs to the Psalms of Ascent, songs pilgrims sang while traveling to Jerusalem for worship. Yet it opens with imagery of profound distress and concludes with a declaration of redemptive hope. The psalmist moves from crying out for mercy (Psalm 130:1–2) to acknowledging God's gracious forgiveness (Psalm 130:3–4), then to patient waiting (Psalm 130:5–6), and finally to inviting others to embrace the same hope (Psalm 130:7–8). This progression shows that waiting is not a station at which one remains stuck, but rather a stage in a journey toward fuller understanding of God's redemptive purposes.

In our contemporary context, we live in an age of immediacy. We expect rapid responses, quick solutions, and instant gratification. The virtue of waiting has become alien to our cultural sensibilities. Yet Psalm 130 calls us to a different rhythm, one that has sustained believers across millennia. The psalmist invites us to ask ourselves: On what foundation do I build my hope? Is it upon favorable circumstances, upon the approval of others, upon financial security, or upon the unchanging Word of God?

Consider the implications for our spiritual lives. When we wait for the Lord with our whole being, we submit our anxieties to his care. We acknowledge that our understanding is limited and our vision is shortsighted, yet we believe his purposes will ultimately prevail. This waiting is not resignation; it is active trust. It involves prayer, meditation upon his Word, obedience to his commands, and confidence that he hears our cries from the depths.

The promise embedded in this verse is revolutionary: my whole being does not need to be consumed by circumstantial anxiety because it can be wholly devoted to waiting for the One who is worthy of all trust. In his word, tested across centuries, proven in countless lives, and culminating in the person of Christ, I find my hope secure.

PRAYER

Gracious Lord, teach us to wait. In this moment of impatience and anxiety, we surrender our demand for immediate solutions. Help us to reorient our whole being toward you, stretching forward in earnest expectation of your faithfulness. When circumstances tempt us to despair, remind us of your promises. When our hope falters, anchor it afresh in your immutable Word. Give us the courage to trust you when trust is all we can offer. In Jesus' name, Amen.

THE PEACE OF HOLY CONTENTMENT

My heart is not proud, LORD, my eyes are not haughty; I do not concern myself with great matters or things too wonderful for me. But I have calmed and quieted myself, I am like a weaned child with its mother; like a weaned child I am content (Psalm 131:1–2).

There is a particular restlessness that marks our age, a persistent sense that we should be more, do more, achieve more. We scroll through curated lives on social media, measure ourselves against others' accomplishments, and exhaust ourselves in the pursuit of significance. Into this frenzy of striving, Psalm 131 speaks with startling gentleness: there is another way.

David, the psalmist-king who had every reason to be proud, begins with a confession of humility. "My heart is not proud, LORD, my eyes are not haughty." This is not false modesty or self-deprecation. David knew who he was: a shepherd boy turned king, a giant-slayer, a man after God's own heart. Yet he had learned something profound: true peace comes not from inflating ourselves but from accepting our proper place in God's order.

The second part of his confession is equally important: "I do not concern myself with great matters or things too wonderful for me." In a culture that celebrates ambition and self-promotion, these words sound almost countercultural. Is not ambition good? Should we not dream big? But David is not advocating laziness or a lack of vision. He is describing something far more sophisticated: the wisdom to know what is ours to carry and what belongs to God alone.

We exhaust ourselves trying to control outcomes beyond our reach, understand mysteries beyond our comprehension, and solve problems beyond our capacity. We lose sleep over global issues we cannot fix, family members we cannot change, and futures we cannot predict. David invites us to release these burdens, not through apathy, but through trust. Some matters are simply "too wonderful" for us, requiring a wisdom and power we do not possess. And that is okay.

The image David offers next is breathtaking in its tenderness: "But I have calmed and quieted myself, I am like a weaned child with its mother; like a weaned child I am content." Notice that David does not say he *is* calm; he says he *has calmed* himself. This suggests effort, intention, a deliberate turning away from anxiety toward peace. Peace is not something that simply happens to us; it is something we cultivate through spiritual discipline and surrender.

The metaphor of the weaned child is particularly rich. A weaned child no longer cries for milk at every discomfort. The child has learned to rest in the mother's presence without constantly demanding something from her. The child's contentment comes not from what the mother provides but from who she is. This is the essence of mature faith, learning to rest in God's presence without constantly petitioning, bargaining, or striving. We learn to be with God, not just to get things from God.

This is radically different from the relationship of a nursing infant, who seeks the mother primarily for what she can provide. The weaned child has moved beyond a transactional relationship into something deeper: trust, companionship, security in simply being held. This is what our souls long for, not to manipulate God into meeting our demands, but to rest in the assurance of his love.

In our own lives, this might mean letting go of the need to have all the answers. It might mean releasing our white-knuckled grip on circumstances we cannot control. It might mean accepting our limitations without shame, recognizing that we are creatures, not the Creator. It certainly means ceasing the exhausting performance of trying to prove our worth through achievement, productivity, or the approval of others.

David's contentment did not come from having no challenges or from understanding everything. He faced enormous pressures as king.

Rather, his peace flowed from a settled confidence in God's goodness and sovereignty. He had learned what we all must learn: that our value does not depend on our accomplishments, our understanding does not need to be comprehensive, and our peace does not require having everything figured out.

The question for us is this: Will we continue exhausting ourselves with pride, anxiety, and the burden of things too wonderful for us? Or will we choose the posture of the weaned child: content, quiet, resting in the presence of the One who holds all things? The invitation stands: to calm ourselves, to quiet the noise, to rest like a child in the arms of God.

PRAYER

Father, quiet my restless heart. Forgive me for the pride that drives me to strive and prove myself, and for the anxiety that makes me grasp at control. Teach me to release the burdens that are yours alone to carry. Help me to rest in your presence like a contented child, finding my peace not in what you give but in who you are. Let me know the freedom of accepting my limitations and the joy of trusting your limitless wisdom. In Jesus' name, Amen.

THE VOW THAT CHANGED EVERYTHING

He swore an oath to the LORD, *he made a vow to the Mighty One of Jacob: "I will not enter my house or go to my bed, I will allow no sleep to my eyes or slumber to my eyelids, till I find a place for the Lord, a dwelling for the Mighty One of Jacob"* (Psalm 132:2–3).

The most binding commitments in biblical life come not from casual promises but from vows sworn before God. Psalm 132 presents one such extraordinary vow, attributed to David in this royal psalm, a commitment so consuming that the psalmist renounces all personal comfort until a sacred task is completed. This passage invites us to examine not merely what David promised but what his vow reveals about priorities, faith, and devotion to God.

The Hebrew text employs two distinct terms for commitment: "swore an oath" and "made a vow." This linguistic doubling is not redundant but emphatic. When these terms appear together, they underscore the absolute solemnity of the promise. David does not casually mention finding a place for the Ark of the Covenant; he invokes the divine name itself as witness to his determination. The phrase "to the LORD" and "to the Mighty One of Jacob" brackets the vow in sacred language, indicating that this promise transcends personal preference; it becomes a covenant between David and God.

The Mighty One of Jacob deliberately recalls the patriarchal narratives. Jacob, the ancient ancestor, had his own encounters with God at Bethel and Peniel. By employing this archaic designation, the psalmist connects David's vow to the continuity of God's covenant people, suggesting that what David undertakes is not innovative but rather a participation in Israel's larger story of faithfulness.

The vow itself employs what scholars call "negative parallelism:" a series of negations that accumulate to create absolute resolve. David will not enter his house. He will not go to his bed. He will grant no sleep to his eyes, no slumber to his eyelids. These are not mere rhetorical flourishes; they represent the systematic renunciation of every human comfort and need.

In the ancient Near Eastern context, a man's house was more than just a place for shelter; it symbolized his identity and authority. His bed represented both rest and marital union. Sleep itself, which Hesiod called "the brother of death," stood for surrender and vulnerability. By relinquishing all of these, David commits himself to a sacred purpose with nearly ascetic dedication.

Yet we must read this carefully. This is not self-mortification for its own sake, nor is it a rejection of embodied life. Rather, it demonstrates that certain purposes transcend personal preference. David's vow exemplifies a hierarchy of values: the establishment of a dwelling place for the Lord supersedes the fundamental human needs for rest, domesticity, and comfort. This is a kingdom priority given its flesh-and-blood expression.

Notice the conditional clause: "till I find a place for the Lord." The word "until" indicates not permanent renunciation but temporary sacrifice oriented toward a specific goal. This distinction is crucial. David is not vowing permanent homelessness but a sustained effort until the objective is achieved.

Historically, this vow contextualizes David's attempts to bring the Ark of the Covenant to Jerusalem (2 Samuel 6). For years, the Ark had rested in inadequate locations, housed by Abinadab at Kiriath-Jearim. David's vow reflects his conviction that God's tangible presence in Israel demanded a permanent, worthy sanctuary, which was eventually realized in Solomon's Temple.

Yet the spiritual significance transcends historical narrative. The psalm asks us: What are we willing to sacrifice for what truly matters? Where do our genuine priorities lie? If asked to relinquish comfort for the sake of establishing God's presence in our lives or communities, would we do so?

In our contemporary context, this passage challenges our tendency to compartmentalize. We often construct strict boundaries between sacred and secular, relegating devotion to designated times and spaces. The psalmist presents a different vision: genuine commitment to God's purposes integrates all of life, from the mundane (sleep, home, rest) to the transcendent.

This does not mean we must pursue asceticism or reject God's good gifts. Rather, it calls us to examine what we truly value. Do we arrange our lives around comfort or around the kingdom? Do we compartmentalize devotion, or does it permeate our choices? David's vow invites radical reorientation, not through guilt but through renewed clarity about what ultimately matters.

PRAYER

Almighty God, God of Jacob and Father of our Lord Jesus Christ, I stand before you humbled by David's vow and convicted by my own easy compromises. Too often I have settled for comfort when you have called for courage, chosen convenience when you sought commitment. Realign my priorities this day. Let me see my home, my rest, my very life as instruments of your purposes rather than refuges from them. Grant me the grace to surrender what must be surrendered so that your presence dwells not in distant sanctuaries alone but in the transformed center of my daily existence. Make me, I pray, a dwelling place for your Spirit, and shape my choices to reflect that sacred purpose. In Christ I pray. Amen.

THE BEAUTY OF UNITY

How good and pleasant it is when God's people live together in unity (Psalm 133:1).

The opening words of Psalm 133 invite us to meditate on one of the most challenging and elusive realities in Christian experience: genuine unity among believers. Yet the psalmist does not approach this theme with hesitation or conditional language. Instead, there is a bold proclamation of affirmation, "How good and pleasant it is," that suggests unity is not merely desirable but fundamentally good, intrinsically pleasant, a reflection of divine order itself.

The Hebrew word translated "good" is *tov*, a term rich with theological significance throughout the Old Testament. It appears first in Genesis 1, where God repeatedly beholds creation and declares it *tov*, good. This is not utilitarian goodness, not merely instrumental value, but rather a declaration that something exists as it should, in proper order and harmony with divine intention. When the psalmist uses *tov* to describe unity among God's people, the implication is profound: unified believers embody something that aligns with God's creative vision and redemptive purpose.

The second evaluative term, "pleasant," adds an aesthetic dimension to this assessment. The word carries connotations of sweetness, delight, and beauty. The psalmist is not arguing that unity serves some external purpose, though it certainly does. Rather, unity itself possesses an intrinsic beauty. It is pleasant to behold, delightful to experience, like a melody that is simply good to hear. In a world fractured by division, suspicion, and competing loyalties, the psalmist testifies to the profound aesthetic and spiritual pleasure of witnessing believers dwelling together in harmony.

Yet we must pause and ask what kind of unity is being celebrated here. The context of Psalm 133 suggests we are not dealing with superficial agreement or coerced conformity. The superscription identifies this as "a song of ascents," placing it within a collection of psalms likely sung by pilgrims ascending to Jerusalem for festival celebrations. The unity referenced here emerges not from external pressure but from a common destination, a shared purpose rooted in a covenant relationship with the God of Israel. The pilgrims climbing toward Jerusalem are united not because they are identical, but because they are traveling together toward the same holy center.

This distinction matters profoundly for contemporary faith communities. The unity the psalmist celebrates is not the uniformity demanded by totalitarian systems or the surface agreement manufactured through social pressure. Rather, it is the unity of pilgrims who acknowledge a common destination, who share allegiance to the same God, and who are willing to journey together despite their differences.

The implications of this understanding transform how we approach Christian community. If unity emerges from a common destination rather than a demand for sameness, then our communities need not enforce conformity to be truly unified. A congregation may include Democrats and Republicans, contemplatives and activists, scholars and simple believers, yet remain genuinely unified when all are oriented toward Christ, when all are ascending toward that holy mountain where God dwells. This is the unity that is truly good and pleasant: the unity of diversity held together by something greater than ourselves.

The psalm testifies that this fractured condition is not the norm God intends for his people. It is a reminder that when believers do experience genuine unity amid real differences, we are touching something that reflects divine intention, something with an almost transcendent quality of goodness and beauty.

This does not mean that unity requires the absence of disagreement or the suppression of honest dialogue. Rather, it means that our disagreements occur within a framework of shared commitment, mutual respect, and common purpose. It means that even when we differ about important matters, we remain willing to journey together toward the kingdom of God. This kind of unity requires vulnerability, humility, and a willingness to prioritize our shared faith above our individual preferences.

As you reflect on this verse, consider the communities of faith to which you belong. Where do you experience that good and pleasant quality of unity? How might you contribute to building or strengthening such unity, even amid the real differences that exist within your faith community? The psalmist invites us not merely to admire unity from a distance, but to participate in creating the conditions where it can flourish.

PRAYER

O God of mercy and grace, we thank you for the gift of your people, the body of Christ scattered across this earth in countless communities and congregations. We acknowledge that we are called to live in unity, yet we confess how often we settle for less, for hollow agreement, for tolerance that masks indifference, for the absence of conflict that is not the same as genuine harmony. Teach us the difference between the unity you desire and the false uniformity our fractured world tries to impose. Help us to see in one another, even in those with whom we disagree, fellow pilgrims on the same journey toward your kingdom. Grant us the courage to be authentic in our community while remaining committed to one another. And help us to taste and see, even now, the goodness and pleasantness of genuine unity in your Spirit. Through Christ our Lord, we pray. Amen.

THE GOD WHO BLESSES

May the LORD bless you from Zion, he who is the Maker of heaven and earth (Psalm 134:3).

The Book of Psalms concludes its collection of Songs of Ascent with a benediction so rich it deserves our lingering attention: "May the LORD bless you from Zion, he who is the Maker of heaven and earth" (Psalm 134:3). In this single verse, we find a profound truth that bridges the particular and the universal, the intimate and the infinite.

This blessing comes "from Zion," that specific, sacred place where God chose to dwell among his people. Zion represents God's dwelling place, the location where heaven touched earth, where the transcendent became accessible. For the ancient Israelites, Zion was the beating heart of their worship, the place where God's presence was most tangibly felt. When the priests pronounced this blessing from Zion, they were not speaking from just any location; they were channeling God's favor from the very place he had consecrated as his own.

Yet the verse does not stop with the geographical. It immediately expands our vision to encompass all of creation: "he who is the Maker of heaven and earth." Here lies one of Scripture's most beautiful paradoxes. The God who dwells in a specific place, Zion, is simultaneously the Creator of all that exists. The One who seems localized is actually limitless. The God who meets us in the particular moments and places of our lives is the same God whose creative power spans galaxies we have yet to discover.

This dual reality transforms our understanding of divine blessing. When God blesses us, he does so with the intimate knowledge of one who has chosen to dwell near his people, and with the unlimited resources of one who spoke worlds into existence. The blessing does not flow from a distant deity who occasionally glances our way, nor from a local god whose power ends at the city limits. Instead, it comes from the Lord who is both near enough to know our names and great enough to number the stars.

Consider what this means for your life today. Whatever you are facing, whether it is a decision that keeps you awake at night, a relationship that needs healing, a dream that seems impossible, or a burden that feels unbearable, the God who blesses you is both intimately present and infinitely capable. He is not scrambling to figure out how to help you, nor is he too small to handle your situation. The hands that formed mountains and carved out oceans are the same hands extended toward you in blessing.

The verse also reminds us that genuine blessing always flows from God's presence. The priests could only pronounce this blessing because they stood in the place where God had chosen to dwell. For us, believers, God's presence is within us through the Holy Spirit. We have become mobile temples, portable Zions. Wherever we go, we carry the potential for divine blessing, both to receive it and to channel it to others.

This should fill us with confidence and humility in equal measure. Confidence, because we serve a God whose blessing is backed by all the power of creation itself. When he speaks favor over your life, no force in heaven or earth can ultimately override it. Humility, because we recognize that such a blessing is pure grace. The Maker of heaven and earth does not bless us because we have earned it, but because he has chosen to set his love upon us, just as he chose Zion.

As you go about your day, remember that you are not navigating life in hopes of a blessing from a disinterested universe. You are held in the attention of the God who made everything you see and much that you do not. His blessing upon you is intentional, personal, and powerful. From his dwelling place, now not only Zion but within the hearts of his people, he extends favor, protection, provision, and peace.

The ancient blessing still rings out: "May the LORD bless you." It is not a hesitant wish or a vague hope, but a confident prayer, one that expects God to act, turning ordinary moments into encounters with the divine.

PRAYER

Lord, you who made heaven and earth, I receive your blessing today. Thank you for being both near enough to care about the details of my life and powerful enough to move mountains on my behalf. Help me to walk in the reality of your favor, carrying your presence wherever I go, and becoming a channel of blessing to others. May your name be praised from Zion to the ends of the earth. Amen.

FINDING HOPE IN GOD

Your name, LORD, endures forever, your renown, LORD, through all generations. For the LORD will vindicate his people and have compassion on his servants (Psalm 135:13–14).

In a world obsessed with legacy, we are surrounded by monuments to human achievement. Names are carved in stone, etched on buildings, and preserved in history books. Yet how many of these names truly endure? Empires rise and fall, celebrities fade from memory, and even the most influential figures eventually slip into obscurity. Against this backdrop of human transience, Psalm 135:13–14 offers us something radically different: a name that endures forever, a reputation that spans all generations, and a God who actively vindicates and shows compassion to his people.

The psalmist's declaration that God's name endures forever is not a mere poetic flourish. In Hebrew thought, a name represented a person's essential nature and character. When we speak of God's name enduring, we are speaking of his unchanging character, his unwavering faithfulness, and his eternal presence. While human reputations can be destroyed by scandal, rewritten by critics, or simply forgotten with time, God's renown remains constant across every generation. The God who walked with Abraham is the same God who strengthens us today. His character does not shift with cultural trends or fade over the centuries.

This truth carries profound implications for how we navigate the uncertainties of life. We live in an age of constant change, where what seems solid today may crumble tomorrow. Technologies become obsolete, institutions fail, relationships fracture, and even our own bodies betray us as we age and fall ill. In such a world, the permanence of God's name becomes an anchor for the soul. When everything else proves temporary, we have a God whose nature is eternal, whose promises are unbreakable, and whose love never wavers.

But the psalmist does not stop with God's eternal nature. He moves immediately to action: "For the LORD will vindicate his people and have compassion on his servants." The God of enduring renown is not distant or detached. He is intimately involved in the lives of his people, actively working to vindicate them and extending compassion to his servants. This connection is crucial. God's eternal character is not an abstract theological concept but the foundation for his present-day involvement in our lives.

The promise of vindication speaks to our deep human need for justice and restoration. We all face moments when we are misunderstood, falsely accused, or treated unjustly. We experience seasons when our faithfulness seems unrewarded and our obedience appears futile. In these moments, the promise that God will vindicate his people becomes a lifeline. Vindication is not primarily about proving ourselves right before others; it is about God's ultimate justice prevailing, his purposes being fulfilled, and his people being restored to right standing. This vindication may not come according to our timeline, but it is guaranteed by the unchanging character of the God whose name endures forever.

Equally powerful is the promise of God's compassion. The Hebrew word used here conveys deep feeling, a visceral response of mercy and tenderness. This is not cold, calculated assistance but warm, personal care. God does not regard his servants with indifference but with genuine compassion. He sees our struggles, understands our weaknesses, and responds with mercy rather than judgment. When we fail, when we stumble, when we find ourselves overwhelmed by circumstances beyond our control, we can turn to a God who responds with compassion rather than condemnation.

These verses invite us to a posture of trust. When we face uncertainty about the future, we can rest in the knowledge that God's name endures forever. When we struggle with injustice or difficult circumstances, we can hope in his promise to vindicate his people. When we feel weak, inadequate, or overwhelmed, we can draw near to the God who has compassion on his servants. Our confidence is not based on our own strength, wisdom, or righteousness but on the unchanging character of a God whose renown spans all generations.

As you face this day, remember that you serve a God whose nature does not change with circumstances. The compassion he showed yesterday is available today. The vindication he promises will surely come. His name, which has endured through countless generations before you, will continue long after you have finished your earthly journey. Let this truth shape how you approach both your trials and your triumphs.

PRAYER

Eternal God, whose name endures forever, I anchor my hope in your unchanging character. When the world around me shifts and my circumstances threaten to overwhelm me, remind me that you remain constant. Thank you for your promise to vindicate your people and for the compassion you show to your servants. Help me to trust you more deeply today, knowing that your eternal nature is the foundation for my present hope. In Jesus' name, Amen.

THE THREEFOLD GOODNESS

Give thanks to the LORD, for he is good. His love endures forever. Give thanks to the God of gods. His love endures forever. Give thanks to the LORD of lords: His love endures forever (Psalm 136:1–3).

The opening verses of Psalm 136 present us with a rhythmic incantation that seems almost hypnotic in its repetition. Three times the psalmist commands us to give thanks—to the LORD, to the God of gods, to the LORD of lords, and three times comes the refrain: "His love endures forever." This is not accidental repetition. Rather, it is the very structure of worship itself, the beating heart of gratitude that should characterize the people of God. To understand these opening verses is to grasp something essential about the nature of thanksgiving in the biblical tradition.

The command to give thanks opens this psalm with a directness that demands our attention. To give thanks in Hebrew carries the sense not merely of gratitude but of confession and acknowledgment. To give thanks is to confess the character and the acts of God. It is to align ourselves with reality as God has established it. The very first words invite us into a posture of recognition: we are commanded to acknowledge that the Lord is good. This is not a suggestion or an invitation to consider; it is a declarative imperative. The goodness of God is not contingent upon our circumstances, our feelings, or our understanding. It simply is. In a world where evil prospers and the righteous suffer, where injustice seems to reign and compassion appears bankrupt, the psalmist insists that we acknowledge the fundamental goodness of the God who stands behind all creation.

What, then, is this goodness? The Hebrew word *tov*, "good," encompasses both moral excellence and benevolence. God is not merely good in character; He is good toward us. His goodness is not abstract but concrete, expressed in his covenant love toward His people. This goodness forms the foundation upon which all thanksgiving rests. We do not give thanks to God because life is always pleasant or circumstances are always favorable. We give thanks because God, the very source of being itself, is fundamentally good. Our thankfulness participates in a reality that transcends our momentary experience.

The second command expands our vision: "Give thanks to the God of gods." Here, the psalmist employs a form of expression common in ancient Near Eastern literature to assert the supreme sovereignty of the God of Israel. Among all the divine beings, whether we understand these as angelic powers, the gods worshipped by the surrounding nations, or simply the forces that appear powerful in our experience, there stands one who is preeminent. The *God* of gods is the God above all gods, the One who towers above every other power, authority, and dominion. In making this declaration, the psalmist invites us to a perspective that is both humbling and liberating. Whatever powers we fear, whatever authorities constrain us, whatever seems to threaten our peace, all of these exist within the sovereignty of the one true God.

Then comes the third assertion: "Give thanks to the LORD of lords." Here we move from divine hierarchy to human authority. Kings rule, emperors command, governors establish laws, yet over them all stands the Lord of lords. This confession carries profound significance for those living under oppressive regimes or unjust systems. The ultimate authority does not rest with human rulers, however powerful they may appear. Thanksgiving becomes an act of resistance, a refusal to grant ultimate allegiance to any earthly power. When we give thanks to the Lord of lords, we declare that our trust, our hope, and our obedience belong finally and ultimately to the God who rules above all human authority.

Yet what binds these three assertions together, what makes each command for thanksgiving cohere into a unified declaration, is the repeated refrain: "His love endures forever." The Hebrew *hesed* defies easy translation. It encompasses loyalty, mercy, steadfast love, and covenant faithfulness. This is not sentimental affection but a binding commitment between two parties. God's love is not a passing emotion; it is eternal, unchanging, and sure. It *endures forever.* In a world characterized by impermanence, where empires crumble, relationships fracture, and life itself inevitably ends, God's love remains constant. It is the one thing upon which we may absolutely depend.

The structure of these verses teaches us that thanksgiving is not the expression of optimism or positive thinking. Rather, it is grounded in the character of God: his goodness, his supreme sovereignty, and his eternal covenant love. When circumstances overwhelm us, when injustice seems victorious, when our resources fail and our strength ebbs, we may still give thanks, not because everything is well, but because he is good and his love endures forever.

PRAYER

Eternal God, teach us to give thanks not for our circumstances alone, but for your goodness that transcends all circumstances. Help us to acknowledge your supreme sovereignty over all powers that threaten us, and to trust in your steadfast love that endures when all else fails. May our thanksgiving become a declaration of faith, an affirmation that you alone are God, and that your mercies truly are new every morning. In the name of Jesus, we pray. Amen.

GRIEF MEETS
THE DEMAND FOR JOY

By the rivers of Babylon we sat and wept when we remembered Zion. There on the poplars we hung our harps, for there our captors asked us for songs, our tormentors demanded songs of joy; they said, "Sing us one of the songs of Zion!" (Psalm 137:1–3).

The exiles sat by Babylon's rivers, instruments silenced, hearts broken. Their captors wanted entertainment, a cruel request that revealed a profound misunderstanding of what worship truly means. "Sing us one of the songs of Zion!" they demanded, as if sacred music were merely performance, as if praise could be extracted from captive hearts like forced labor.

This moment in Psalm 137 captures something deeply human: the collision between authentic grief and the world's expectation that we perform happiness. The Israelites could not sing because their songs belonged to a specific place, a specific relationship, a specific hope, and all of it lay in ruins behind them. To sing Zion's songs in Babylon at the command of their oppressors would have been to empty those songs of meaning, to reduce worship to entertainment, to pretend their trauma did not matter.

We live in a culture that often demands we hang our harps on the willows of our own lives. "Do not be negative," we are told. "Just be grateful for what you have." Social media creates endless pressure to perform joy, to curate happiness, to demonstrate that we are thriving. Churches sometimes contribute to this burden, implicitly suggesting that sufficient faith should always produce visible gladness, that doubt or sorrow indicates spiritual deficiency.

But the Psalms make space for lament in a way our modern world often does not. Fully one-third of the Psalter consists of lament psalms, honest cries of pain directed toward God. Scripture does not ask us to pretend our grief does not exist. It invites us to bring that grief into God's presence, to sit by our own rivers and weep, to acknowledge what we have lost.

The exiles' refusal to sing was not faithlessness; it was faithfulness. They understood that worship is not performance but relationship, that God desires truth in our innermost being, not manufactured cheerfulness. They knew that to sing Zion's songs as mere entertainment would have been to betray both the songs and the God to whom those songs were addressed.

Yet notice what the exiles did: they remembered. Even in their refusal to sing, their silence testified to what mattered. They hung their harps where they could see them, visible reminders of what they had lost and what they still loved. Their grief itself became a form of devotion, a way of saying that Zion mattered too much to be reduced to a show for Babylonian amusement.

This is the paradox of faithful lament: sometimes the most profound worship happens when we refuse to pretend everything is fine. Sometimes honoring God means sitting with our sorrow instead of rushing past it toward forced positivity. The exiles' tears were as much an offering as their songs had ever been, because those tears flowed from genuine love for what God had given and what had been lost.

For us, this psalm offers permission to grieve losses large and small, dreams deferred or destroyed, relationships broken, and hopes disappointed. It reminds us that God is big enough to handle our honest pain, that we do not have to perform joy we do not feel. The Christian life includes resurrection, but resurrection always comes through the tomb, never around it.

At the same time, this is not a psalm of despair. The very act of remembering Zion kept hope alive. The exiles did not forget who they were or whose they were. Their identity was not determined by Babylon's rivers but by God's promises. They trusted that their silence was temporary, that God had not forgotten them even if they could not yet sing.

We who follow Jesus have even more reason for this kind of hope. We serve a God who entered our grief, who wept at gravesides, who cried out in abandonment from a cross. Christ did not bypass suffering but walked straight through it, transforming it from the inside. Our laments are never the final word because the tomb is empty, but the path to resurrection runs through Gethsemane and Golgotha.

So, when life demands songs you cannot sing, when the world wants you to perform joy your heart does not feel, remember the exiles by Babylon's rivers. Bring your honest grief to God. Refuse to reduce worship to performance. Trust that your tears, like theirs, are seen and held by the One who promises that those who sow in tears will reap with songs of joy, but in his time, not at the tormentors' demand.

PRAYER

Gracious God, you know our griefs before we speak them. When we cannot sing, sit with us in our silence. When the world demands joy we do not feel, give us the courage to offer honest tears instead. Help us trust that you are near to the brokenhearted, that our laments reach your ears as surely as our praise. Keep hope alive in us even when we cannot yet see its fulfillment. Through Christ, who wept with us and for us. Amen.

PSALM 138

THE GOD WHO BENDS

Though the LORD *is exalted, he looks kindly on the lowly; though lofty, he sees them from afar. Though I walk in the midst of trouble, you preserve my life. You stretch out your hand against the anger of my foes; with your right hand you save me* (Psalm 138:6–7).

David stands in the presence of overwhelming opposition, yet his voice rings with unshakeable confidence. In Psalm 138:6–7, the psalmist articulates one of Scripture's most profound paradoxes: the God who dwells in transcendent majesty simultaneously bends low to notice the afflicted. This tension between divine exaltation and divine compassion forms the beating heart of authentic faith.

The opening phrase, "Though the LORD is exalted, he looks kindly on the lowly," establishes an unexpected theological foundation. The Hebrew word for "exalted" suggests absolute elevation, supremacy beyond compare. God occupies a position of unquestionable authority and power. Yet immediately the psalmist introduces the divine paradox: this supremely exalted God "looks kindly" (literally, "knows" or "regards") the lowly, the humble, the one brought low, the insignificant.

Ancient Near Eastern literature frequently portrayed gods as capricious and indifferent to human suffering. The powerful deities concerned themselves with temples, sacrifices, and the affairs of kings. The common person remained invisible, irrelevant. Against this cultural backdrop, David announces something revolutionary: the Creator of all things intentionally focuses his attention upon those whom the world dismisses. The lowly are not invisible to God; they are the objects of his intimate knowledge and gracious regard.

The second clause extends this paradox: "Though lofty, he sees them from afar." The apparent distance, seeing "from afar," initially suggests remoteness, yet the context transforms this statement entirely. God sees from afar precisely because his vantage point encompasses all creation. His distance is not indifference but omniscience. From his exalted throne, he perceives what happens in the valleys of human experience with perfect clarity. The God who is unreachably high possesses the capacity to discern and care for the minutest details of the lowly person's struggle.

This theological affirmation provides the foundation for David's personal testimony in verse 7: "Though I walk in the midst of trouble, you preserve my life." The Hebrew word for "preserve" means to keep alive, to sustain vitality, to maintain life itself. David does not claim that God removes him from trouble; rather, God sustains him within it. The psalmist walks deliberately, actively progressing through trouble, yet in this very movement through difficulty, God preserves his essential being.

This represents a crucial distinction for believers navigating suffering. The promise is not escape from adversity but preservation through it. God does not necessarily eliminate the narrow places; he sustains life within them. Such preservation suggests both protection from destruction and provision of strength to continue. The God who exalts himself demonstrates his exaltation partly through his ability to maintain and sustain the lowly in the midst of their greatest challenges.

The final lines consummate David's testimony with concrete divine action: "You stretch out your hand against the anger of my foes; with your right hand you save me." Notice the language: God stretches out his hand, raises his right hand. These are the gestures of a God who actively intervenes. The "hand against the anger" suggests God standing between the psalmist and the destructive power of his enemies. The "right hand" in biblical imagery represents God's power and strength. This is not passive observation but aggressive defense.

The parallelism between the two lines, "you stretch out your hand against" and "with your right hand you save me" emphasizes active divine intervention. The same hand that works against the enemies simultaneously executes salvation. These are complementary divine actions: the removal of threat and the establishment of safety occur together.

For contemporary believers, Psalm 138:6–7 shatters several false comfort narratives. God's greatness does not distance him from our pain. His exaltation does not preclude his intimate involvement in our struggles. The God who sustains the cosmos extends himself protectively over the person who feels insignificant. Moreover, God's preservation of our lives encompasses not merely physical survival but the deeper sustenance of our spiritual vitality through trials.

The psalmist invites us to embrace this paradox: to trust that the transcendent God is simultaneously the personal God who knows us by name and knows the particular anguish we face. In the midst of trouble, we need not depend upon our own resources or the mercy of our foes. We serve a God exalted yet graciously engaged, distant yet intimately aware, powerful yet protective.

PRAYER

Almighty God, you alone dwell in unapproachable light, yet you incline your ear to hear the cry of the afflicted. Grant us faith to believe that your exaltation does not distance you from our sorrow. Strengthen us to trust that you see us from afar with perfect knowledge and deep compassion. In our troubled days, preserve our lives. Stretch out your hand against the fury of our enemies and save us with your mighty power. May we live as those who have experienced both your transcendence and your tender care. Amen.

THE COURAGE TO BE KNOWN

Search me, God, and know my heart; test me and know my anxious thoughts. See if there is any offensive way in me, and lead me in the way everlasting (Psalm 139:23–24).

There is something deeply counterintuitive about David's prayer in Psalm 139:23–24. Most of us spend considerable energy managing what others see, carefully curating the image we present to the world. We hide our insecurities, mask our anxieties, and desperately hope that our worst thoughts and motivations remain concealed. Yet here, David does the opposite. He invites God to search him completely, to know him fully, to test and examine every hidden corner of his inner life.

This invitation only makes sense in light of what comes before it. Psalm 139 begins with a stunning declaration: "You have searched me, LORD, and you know me." David has already acknowledged that God knows when he sits and when he rises, that God perceives his thoughts from afar, that even before a word is on his tongue, God knows it completely. There is nowhere David can flee from God's presence: not in the heights of heaven, not in the depths of the sea, not even in the darkness of night, which to God shines bright as day.

So why, after acknowledging that God already knows everything, does David ask God to search him? Because there is a profound difference between being known and choosing to be known. God's omniscience is a given, but David's invitation transforms that reality from something potentially terrifying into something deeply relational. He is not merely resigned to being seen; he is actively opening himself to divine examination. This is the move from hiding to surrender, from shame to trust.

Notice the specificity of David's request. He does not ask God to search his achievements or his public reputation. He asks God to know his heart, the center of his desires, motives, and true character. He asks God to test him and know his "anxious thoughts," those troubling inner dialogues that we often keep hidden even from ourselves. David understands that our greatest spiritual danger often lies not in our outward sins but in the subtle misalignments of our hearts, in the anxieties we nurse, in the offensive ways we do not yet recognize in ourselves.

The phrase "offensive way" is particularly telling. David is not concerned only with obvious sins but with anything that might grieve God or lead him away from God's path. He is asking God to reveal blind spots, to show him patterns of thought or behavior that he may have rationalized or overlooked. This requires remarkable humility, the willingness to be wrong about ourselves, to discover that we have been harboring attitudes or habits that do not align with God's character.

But David does not stop with examination; he moves toward transformation. "Lead me in the way everlasting," he prays. The goal of divine searching is not condemnation but direction. God's examination of our hearts is not meant to shame us but to guide us toward life, toward the ancient paths that lead to wholeness and peace. David understands that true freedom comes not from hiding who we are but from allowing God to transform us into who we were meant to be.

This prayer challenges our modern tendency toward self-protection and image management. We live in an age of carefully filtered social media profiles and personal branding, where vulnerability is often seen as weakness. Yet David models something radically different: the spiritual maturity to invite scrutiny, to desire transformation over comfort, to trust that God's knowing leads not to rejection but to redemption.

What would it mean for us to pray this prayer authentically? It would mean pausing our self-justifications long enough to ask honest questions: What anxieties am I nursing that reveal misplaced trust? What attitudes have I defended that might actually be offensive to God's heart? Where have I settled into patterns of thinking or living that seem normal to me but diverge from the way everlasting?

The invitation to be fully known by God is ultimately an invitation to freedom. When we stop hiding, we stop exhausting ourselves with pretense. When we invite God's searching light into our darkest corners, we discover that divine love is strong enough to meet us there. And when we ask God to lead us, we open ourselves to a path more beautiful than any we could construct on our own.

PRAYER

Loving God, I join David's ancient prayer and make it my own today. Search me and know my heart. Test me and reveal what I cannot see in myself. Show me the anxious thoughts I have grown comfortable with, the offensive ways I have justified, the paths I have chosen that lead away from your life. Give me the courage to face what you reveal and the grace to receive your transformation. Lead me in the way everlasting. In Christ's name, Amen.

WHEN GOD TAKES UP YOUR CASE

I know that the LORD *secures justice for the poor and upholds
the cause of the needy. Surely the righteous will praise your name,
and the upright will live in your presence* (Psalm 140: 12–13).

There is a particular kind of exhaustion that comes from fighting a battle you did not start. It is the weariness of the person who has been overlooked, underpaid, or dismissed; who has told the truth and not been believed; who has worked hard and not been rewarded; who has cried out and heard nothing but silence echo back. If you have ever stood in that place, Psalm 140:12–13 was written for you.

The psalm as a whole is a raw, urgent plea for deliverance. David is surrounded by enemies, schemers who "stir up war every day," whose tongues are as sharp as a serpent's. By the time we reach these final verses, David has spent his energy laying out the case against his adversaries. But something shifts in verse twelve. The prayer pivots from desperation to declaration. David stops describing the problem and begins describing the God who is bigger than the problem.

"I know that the LORD secures justice for the poor and upholds the cause of the needy."

Notice that David does not say *I hope* or *I believe it is possible* or *perhaps, if circumstances align.* He says *I know.* This is the language of settled conviction, not wishful thinking. It is the kind of knowing that has been forged in real experience: the memory of past deliverances, the record of a God who has shown up before and can be trusted to show up again. David had seen enough of God's faithfulness to plant a flag in it.

The word translated "secures" in this verse carries the idea of executing a verdict, of bringing a legal judgment to its proper conclusion. God is not simply sympathetic toward the poor; he is active on their behalf.

He enters the courtroom. He takes up the case. He ensures the verdict matches the truth. For anyone who has ever felt that the system was rigged against them, that the powerful were too protected and the powerless too exposed, this verse is not a platitude. It is a promise with teeth.

And who precisely is God acting for? "The poor" and "the needy." These words in the Hebrew do not refer exclusively to financial poverty. They encompass anyone in a position of vulnerability: the person without leverage, without allies, without recourse. If you have ever felt profoundly helpless, unable to defend yourself or change your circumstances by your own strength, you qualify. God's attention is drawn, not repelled, by human weakness. Where the world tends to look away from need, God leans toward it.

This should change how we wait. So much of our anxiety in seasons of injustice comes from the fear that no one is watching, that nothing is being recorded, that wrong will simply be absorbed into the silence of an indifferent universe. But the Scripture insists otherwise. God is not a distant observer. He is a present advocate. The cause of the needy is not a cause that goes unnoticed on heaven's docket.

Verse thirteen draws the circle of this confidence outward: "Surely the righteous will praise your name, and the upright will live in your presence." The word *surely* mirrors the confidence of *I know* in the previous verse. David is certain not only of God's justice but of its ultimate effect: a community of people who have witnessed God's faithfulness and respond with praise. When God acts on behalf of the vulnerable, it does not just rescue the individual; it builds the faith of the whole people. Every testimony of deliverance becomes a thread in a larger tapestry of praise.

To "live in your presence" is the crowning promise. Not merely to be rescued, but to dwell, to settle into a continuous, unbroken nearness to God himself. Justice, in the end, is not merely about correcting wrongs. It is about restoring the relationship. God rights what is broken so that his people can come home.

Whatever you are waiting for God to make right today, bring it to this verse. Let *I know* replace your *I wonder*. Let the certainty of a God who takes up cases on behalf of the powerless anchor your soul.

PRAYER

Lord, I confess that waiting is hard and trust does not always come easily. But your Word declares what your character has already proven, that you are a God who sees the unseen, who defends the defenseless, and who brings every hidden wrong into the light of your justice. Secure what only you can secure. Uphold what only you can uphold. And in the waiting, draw me deeper into your presence, where the righteous find their rest. Amen.

PSALM 141

WHEN PRAYER BECOMES
OUR OFFERING

I call to you, LORD, come quickly to me; hear me when I call to you. May my prayer be set before you like incense; may the lifting up of my hands be like the evening sacrifice (Psalm 141:1–2).

There is something profoundly human about the urgency in David's voice: "Come quickly to me." These are not the measured words of a theological treatise or the polished phrases of formal liturgy. This is the cry of someone who needs God now, not later. David does not apologize for his desperation, and neither should we.

The psalm opens with what we might call the anatomy of genuine prayer. First comes the call, direct, personal, immediate. "I call to you, LORD." Then comes the plea for divine attention: "hear me when I call." David understands something we often forget in our age of instant communication: that being heard is not automatic, even with God. Not because God is distant or distracted, but because we must position our hearts to truly seek his presence rather than simply reciting requests.

But it is in the second verse where David's prayer transforms from urgent petition into something transcendent. He asks that his prayer might be "set before you like incense" and that his raised hands might be "like the evening sacrifice." Here, David is drawing on the rich vocabulary of temple worship, where incense rose twice daily, morning and evening, filling the Holy Place with fragrant smoke that symbolized prayers ascending to heaven. The evening sacrifice was part of Israel's daily rhythm, a sacred moment when the day's activities paused for worship.

What David is requesting is remarkable: he wants his raw, desperate prayer to have the same value before God as the carefully prescribed temple rituals. He suggests that a heart genuinely lifted to God in prayer carries the same weight as the formal sacrifices offered by priests. This would have been a radical thought in ancient Israel, where the temple system was central to religious life. Yet David, himself a king familiar with both palace and battlefield, understands that God desires authenticity over mere ceremony.

The image of incense is particularly powerful. Incense does not rush or force its way upward; it rises slowly, permeating everything in its path. It lingers. It transforms the atmosphere. This is what prayer does in our lives: when we truly pray, we are not just sending urgent messages heavenward; we are allowing our very existence to become an offering that rises to God, changing us in the process.

The lifted hands speak to our posture, both physical and spiritual. In ancient times, raising one's hands was a gesture of both supplication and surrender. It is the universal human signal of "I have nothing, I need help, I give up trying to control this." When David compares this gesture to the evening sacrifice, he is acknowledging that sometimes the most sacred thing we can offer God is our emptiness, our need, our honest dependence.

For us today, these verses offer a corrective to two opposite errors in prayer. On one hand, we can become too casual, treating prayer like a spiritual vending machine where we insert our requests and expect immediate results. On the other hand, we can become so concerned with "praying correctly" that our prayers lose all authenticity and become performances rather than encounters.

David shows us a third way: prayer that is both urgent and reverent, desperate and worshipful, immediate and enduring. He does not wait to pray until he feels composed or spiritual. He comes as he is: needy, urgent, even demanding God's attention. Yet he simultaneously understands that this very act of coming to God is itself worship, as valuable as any sacrifice.

This psalm challenges us to ask: What is the quality of our prayers? Are they merely wish lists rushed through in a moment of need? Or are they offerings, fragrant, lingering, transformative, that change us even as they rise to God? Do we come to God with lifted hands, acknowledging our dependence, or with clenched fists, still trying to maintain control?

The beauty of David's prayer is that it does not require perfection. It requires presence. It does not demand eloquence. It demands honesty. The incense he speaks of is not manufactured prayer that sounds impressive; it is the genuine cry of the heart that rises naturally when we come to God as we truly are.

PRAYER

Lord, hear me when I call you. Receive my prayers, these ordinary words and desperate pleas, as precious incense rising before your throne. When I lift my hands to you, whether in worship or surrender, let them be an offering of my whole self. Teach me to pray with both urgency and reverence, knowing you welcome me as I am while transforming me into who you have called me to be. Come quickly to me, Lord. Amen.

POURING OUT OUR SOULS BEFORE GOD

I cry aloud to the LORD; I lift up my voice to the LORD for mercy. I pour out before him my complaint; before him I tell my trouble (Psalm 142: 1–2).

The Psalms capture humanity at its most honest. They do not offer sanitized expressions of faith or polished theological abstractions. Instead, they give voice to believers' raw, unfiltered experience of despair, confusion, anger, and abandonment. Psalm 142:1–2 exemplifies this unvarnished authenticity. The psalmist does not begin with praise or thanksgiving. He does not lead with confidence or assurance. Rather, he begins where so many of us actually reside: in a place of desperate need, crying out with an urgency that demands to be heard.

The Hebrew verb translated as "cry aloud" carries the sense of raising one's voice with intensity and emotion. This is not a whispered prayer or a casual petition. This is vocalization born of genuine distress. The psalmist lifts his voice deliberately, intentionally, as if volume itself might convey the severity of his circumstances. He approaches God not with formal protocol but with the comportment of someone who has exhausted all other remedies and now throws himself entirely upon divine mercy.

What strikes us immediately is the directness of the address. "I cry aloud to the LORD; I lift up my voice to the LORD for mercy." The repetition of "to the LORD" in consecutive phrases is not redundant. Rather, it emphasizes the singular focus of the psalmist's attention. In the midst of whatever affliction he faces, his gaze remains fixed upon God. He does not distribute his energy among multiple potential sources of help. He does not hedge his bets by appealing to lesser powers. His entire appeal is directed toward the one God who alone possesses the authority and compassion to intervene.

The phrase "for mercy" reveals the psalmist's understanding of his own condition. He does not approach God as one who makes demands or insists upon rights. Rather, he appeals for mercy, for *hesed*, the steadfast covenant love that characterizes God's nature. This is the language of one who recognizes his own insufficiency and throws himself upon divine compassion. He comes not as a creditor demanding payment but as a debtor pleading for grace.

The second verse deepens this vulnerability. "I pour out before him my complaint; before him I tell my trouble." The Hebrew verb translated as "pour out," originally referred to pouring or spilling liquid, an image of absolute abandonment and complete release. The psalmist does not carefully measure his words or strategically calculate what revelations might be advantageous. He pours out everything. His complaint, his frustration, his perplexity; all of it flows out before God in an unrestrained torrent.

This act of pouring out is profoundly spiritual. It acknowledges that God is not threatened by human emotion or confusion. God does not require us to suppress our legitimate grievances in favor of false piety. The divine throne room is spacious enough to accommodate complaint alongside praise, wrestling alongside worship. This is revolutionary in its implications. Many believers attempt to approach God only with carefully curated sentiments, believing that authentic faith demands the suppression of doubt, frustration, or pain. Psalm 142 teaches otherwise. The integrity of our prayer life depends upon bringing our whole selves before God, not the sanitized version that we present to others, but the true self that knows confusion and despair.

Notice that the psalmist does not merely tell God his trouble; he tells it *before* God, in his presence. This suggests a relational dimension. The psalmist is not simply downloading his emotions into a cosmic complaint box. He is engaging in dialogue, even if his part of the dialogue consists entirely of complaints. He positions himself before the one who sees, hears, and cares. The very act of bringing one's trouble into the presence of God carries implicit acknowledgment of God's sovereignty and concern.

For contemporary believers, this passage invites us to reconsider our prayer practices. Do we permit ourselves the honesty that the psalmist models? Do we bring our whole selves to prayer, or do we curate what we feel comfortable expressing? Do we understand God as one who welcomes our complaints and griefs, or do we fear that such vulnerability will somehow diminish our standing before him?

The Psalms teach us that authentic faith includes the freedom to cry aloud, to pour out, to complain before God. This freedom itself becomes an act of worship, a demonstration of trust that God is great enough to handle our questions and compassionate enough to welcome our tears.

PRAYER

Almighty God, we come before you as the psalmist came: with urgent voices and unrestrained hearts. Grant us the courage to pour out our true selves before you, without pretense or fear. Teach us that you welcome our complaints alongside our praise, and that honest prayer strengthens rather than diminishes our faith. Hear our cries, gather our troubles, and in your great mercy transform our despair into trust. In Christ's name, we pray. Amen.

FINDING DIRECTION
IN GOD'S LOVE

Let the morning bring me word of your unfailing love, for I have put my trust in you. Show me the way I should go, for to you I entrust my life (Psalm 143:8).

The psalmist's morning prayer in Psalm 143:8 captures something profoundly human: the need to begin each day anchored in something beyond ourselves. Before the demands pile up, before uncertainty clouds our vision, before we make a single decision about the path ahead, we need to hear from God. This is not just poetic sentiment; it is spiritual survival.

Notice the deliberate timing in this verse. The psalmist does not ask for God's love as an afterthought at day's end, when exhaustion has set in and choices have already been made. Instead, he seeks it at the morning's first light, recognizing that how we begin shapes everything that follows. There's wisdom in this sequence. When we ground ourselves in God's unfailing love before the day unfolds, we establish our spiritual center of gravity. The challenges still come, the uncertainties still loom, but we face them from a different foundation.

The phrase "unfailing love" deserves our attention. In Hebrew, this is *hesed*, a word so rich that no single English translation captures its full meaning. It speaks of covenant loyalty, steadfast mercy, loving-kindness that persists regardless of circumstances. This is not the fluctuating affection we often experience in human relationships, which depends on our performance or on someone else's mood. God's love is unfailing precisely because it does not rise and fall with our failures and successes. It simply is: constant, reliable, unshakeable.

Why does the psalmist need this reminder each morning? Because we forget. We wake up, and our minds immediately flood with worries, obligations, and uncertainties. We forget that we are loved with an everlasting love. We forget that our worth is not determined by our productivity or others' approval. We forget that underneath everything is the solid ground of divine faithfulness. The morning becomes crucial, then, as our opportunity to remember who we are and whose we are before the world tells us otherwise.

The verse then moves from declaration to petition: "Show me the way I should go." Here we encounter the psalmist's vulnerability. He does not know the way forward. He is not pretending to have it all figured out. In a culture that celebrates certainty and self-sufficiency, this kind of admission feels countercultural, even uncomfortable. Yet it is profoundly honest. Most of us wake up with decisions to make, crossroads to navigate, and choices whose outcomes we cannot fully predict. The psalmist models what it means to bring that uncertainty directly to God rather than masking it with false confidence.

Notice, too, that guidance follows the relationship. The request for direction comes after the affirmation of trust and love. This is not a transactional prayer: "Tell me what to do so I can get on with my day." It is relational. The psalmist wants to know the way precisely because it is God's way, because the path matters when you are walking it with someone you trust. We do not just want divine GPS coordinates; we want to walk in step with the One who loves us unfailingly.

The final phrase intensifies everything: "for to you I entrust my life." Not just this decision, not just today's concerns, but the whole of life itself. The Hebrew word for "entrust" carries the sense of lifting up, offering, and surrendering. It is the posture of someone placing something precious into the hands they completely trust. This is what morning trust looks like, not just asking for help with the day's schedule, but offering up the entirety of our existence into God's faithful care.

This kind of entrustment does not come naturally. Our instinct is to clutch, control, and manage our own lives. But the psalmist has learned something through his struggles: God is trustworthy in ways we can never be for ourselves. When we hold our lives with a white-knuckled grip, we exhaust ourselves. When we entrust our lives to God each morning, we discover a paradoxical freedom, not the freedom to do whatever we want, but the freedom to stop carrying burdens we were never meant to bear alone.

As we make this prayer our own, we join a tradition stretching back millennia of people who chose to begin their days not with anxiety or ambition, but with trust. We acknowledge that we need God's unfailing love, divine guidance, and the courage to surrender control. And in that acknowledgment, we find not weakness but the truest strength available to us.

PRAYER

Gracious God, as morning breaks, let me hear again of your unfailing love. When I am uncertain, show me the way. When I am tempted to rely on my own understanding, remind me that my life is safest in your hands. I entrust this day and all my days to you. Amen.

WHAT ARE WE THAT GOD CARES?

LORD, what are human beings that you care for them, mere mortals that you think of them? They are like a breath; their days are like a fleeting shadow (Psalm 144:3–4).

The psalmist's question cuts through the noise of human pretension with surgical precision: "LORD, what are human beings that you care for them, mere mortals that you think of them?" (Psalm 144:3–4). This is not the complaint of the despairing but the astonishment of the awakened. To ask what we are in light of God's attention is to ask perhaps the most important question a creature can pose.

David begins Psalm 144 surrounded by conflict, his hands trained for war (verse 1), yet his mind trained for theology. From this context of struggle, he does not demand God's intervention based on human merit or achievement. Instead, he positions himself within the vast chasm between human insignificance and divine regard. The Hebrew term translated as "care for" is *yada*, whose root meaning is "to know" or "to recognize." God does not merely see us from a distance; He knows us, acknowledges us, and recognizes us as persons of significance despite our creaturely limitations.

The Hebrew text employs two different words for humans, creating a rhetorical parallelism that deepens the paradox. "What are human beings?" receives its answer in the second line: "What are mortals?" The deliberate repetition suggests not diminishment but intensification. We are asked twice, in different terms, to contemplate our insignificance. The first word emphasizes our earthly origin and composition; the second, our vulnerability and mortality. Yet despite this double emphasis on human limitation, the structure of the psalm declares that God thinks of us.

Verse 4 crystallizes this paradox through vivid imagery. We are "like a breath"—the Hebrew literally means "vapor," a term the Preacher in Ecclesiastes would later use it repeatedly to describe life's transience. Our existence is not merely brief; it is as insubstantial as morning fog, as ephemeral as the breath leaving our lips on a cold day. Yet the psalmist does not stop there. We are further compared to "a fleeting shadow." A shadow has no substance whatsoever; it exists only as the absence of light. It moves with its object but possesses no independent reality. The shadow passes; the light remains.

This double metaphor, breath and shadow, presents human existence from two perspectives. Breath emphasizes what passes through us and away; shadow emphasizes what we cast during our momentary existence. Both are transitory. Both are insubstantial. Both will vanish. Yet this is precisely the context in which the psalmist marvels at God's attentiveness.

What transforms this meditation from nihilism into wonder is its theological framework. The question, "What are human beings that you care for them?" is not chiefly about our insignificance; it is about God's worth, God's nature, and God's mysterious love. The psalmist does not ask in despair but in awe. That the Eternal One, before whom all history is an instant and all space the span of a hand, should turn his thought toward fleeting creatures like us: this is the miracle that awakens faith.

This recognition carries profound spiritual implications. If we truly grasped our momentariness and God's eternality, our petty anxieties would lose their grip. The social status we chase, the material accumulation we pursue, the reputation we defend, all scatter like shadows when confronted with this reality. Yet paradoxically, recognizing our insignificance before God elevates our true significance. We matter to God not because we are impressive but because we are his. The brevity of our days becomes precious precisely because they are numbered and known by him who counts them.

The knowledge of our littleness brings the kingdom of heaven near. When we cease pretending to a grandeur we do not possess and acknowledge what we truly are, breath and shadow, we open ourselves to receive what we do not deserve: the love and attention of the God who numbers our days and cares for our souls.

As we face this day, with its unfinished tasks and uncertain outcomes, we might ask the psalmist's question not in complaint but in wonder: How remarkable that God thinks of me! How astonishing that this one day, this fleeting shadow that I shall live, matters to the Eternal! This realization, rather than crushing us with a sense of insignificance, liberates us into authentic faith.

PRAYER

Eternal God, before whom all creation is as the morning mist and all history as a passing shadow, grant me the grace to understand my own smallness. Free me from the illusion that my worth depends upon my achievements or the esteem of others. And yet, O Lord, teach me to marvel that you, in all your infinity, care for me. Let this knowledge transform my anxieties into trust, my restlessness into peace, and my fear of insignificance into wonder at your love. In the brief days you have given me, may I live not for myself but for you, whose attention makes even a shadow precious. In Christ's name, Amen.

PSALM 145

GOD'S FAITHFULNESS

The LORD is trustworthy in all he promises and faithful in all he does. The LORD upholds all who fall and lifts up all who are bowed down. The eyes of all look to you, and you give them their food at the proper time (Psalm 145:13–15).

There is something profoundly human about falling. We stumble under the weight of grief, collapse beneath disappointment, buckle under pressure we never asked to carry. We bow down, sometimes in worship, but often in exhaustion, defeat, or despair. The psalmist does not shy away from this reality. Instead, he places it directly alongside one of Scripture's most magnificent declarations: God is trustworthy in all he promises and faithful in all he does.

This juxtaposition matters. The psalmist does not present us with a distant deity whose reliability exists only in theoretical perfection. Rather, he shows us a God whose faithfulness becomes most evident precisely where human frailty is most acute. His trustworthiness is not merely an abstract attribute to be admired; it is an active force that meets us at our lowest points.

Consider the weight of that word "all." The Lord is trustworthy in *all* he promises. Not most. Not the convenient ones. Not only those that align with our expectations or timelines. Every word he has spoken carries the full force of his character behind it. When we read the promises scattered throughout Scripture, that he will never leave us, that he works all things for good, that his mercies are new every morning, we are not reading beautiful poetry meant to inspire positive thinking. We are reading binding commitments from One who has never broken faith.

And faithful in *all* he does. This challenges us. Because God's faithfulness does not always look like comfort. It does not always manifest as an immediate rescue. Sometimes his faithfulness appears to strengthen us to endure rather than remove what we endure. Sometimes it looks like closed doors that protect us from paths we desperately wanted to walk. His faithfulness is tethered to his wisdom and his love, not to our limited understanding of what we need.

The psalm then moves to something beautifully specific: "The LORD upholds all who fall and lifts up all who are bowed down." Notice the active verbs. Upholds. Lifts. This is a God who does not wait at a distance for us to pull ourselves together. He enters into our falling, our bowing down. He does not shame us for our weakness or demand we demonstrate strength before he will help. He meets us in the dust.

Think of Peter sinking beneath the waves, crying out in terror. Jesus did not wait for Peter to swim closer or for him to compose himself. Immediately, he reached out his hand. Think of the woman bent double for eighteen years, unable to straighten herself. Jesus called her forward and released her from her bondage. The pattern throughout Scripture is clear: our God is drawn to the lowly, the broken, the ones who cannot save themselves.

Then comes this stunning image: "The eyes of all look to you, and you give them their food at the proper time." Every creature, from the sparrow to the whale, from the infant to the aged, looks to God for sustenance. And he provides. Not always according to our schedules. Not always in the abundance we imagine we need. But at the proper time, in the proper measure, from his inexhaustible hand.

This speaks to more than physical hunger. We look to him for strength when ours is depleted. For hope when despair clouds our vision. For direction when we are paralyzed by confusion. For comfort when grief feels unbearable. And he feeds these hungers too, not always instantly, but faithfully, at the time his wisdom deems proper.

Living in light of God's faithfulness means learning to trust the character behind the promise even when we cannot yet see the fulfillment. It means believing he upholds even when we still feel ourselves falling. It means continuing to lift our eyes to him even when the provision has not yet arrived. It means remembering that the same God who numbers the stars and calls them each by name also numbers our tears and knows our needs before we voice them.

When you feel yourself falling today, remember you are falling into faithful hands. When you find yourself bowed down, know that the God who lifts up sees you and moves toward you even now. When hunger of any kind gnaws at your soul, turn your eyes upward in trust. Our God has never failed to keep his word, and he will not begin with you.

PRAYER

Faithful God, when my strength fails and I fall, uphold me. When the weight of this world bows me down, lift me up. Teach me to trust not only your promises but also your timing. As I look to you today, feed my deepest hungers with the bread of your presence and the certainty of your unfailing love. In Jesus' name, Amen.

THE GOD WHO LIFTS UP THE FALLEN

He upholds the cause of the oppressed and gives food to the hungry. The LORD sets prisoners free, the LORD gives sight to the blind, the LORD lifts up those who are bowed down, the LORD loves the righteous (Psalm 146: 7–8).

The psalmist concludes his hymn of praise by pivoting from the theological assertion that human princes and earthly rulers ultimately fail (v. 3–4) to the magnificent reality that our God remains eternally faithful and actively engaged in the lives of the vulnerable. Psalm 146 stands as a clarion call to trust not in temporal authorities but in the God who establishes justice for those whom society has abandoned.

The Hebrew verb translated "upholds the cause" literally means "does" or "makes." The psalmist uses this simple yet profound verb to show that justice is not merely something God announces; it is something God actively performs. The cause of the oppressed, the poor, and the marginalized is not a peripheral concern in the divine economy but a primary expression of God's character and power. This is not poetic sentiment but theological precision: the God worthy of our praise is one who acts on behalf of the downtrodden.

What follows is a stunning catalog of divine compassion expressed through concrete actions. The Lord "gives food to the hungry," a straightforward statement that material provision belongs within God's redemptive agenda. The parallelism between justice and sustenance is intentional. One cannot separate spiritual salvation from physical well-being. The God who saves also feeds.

The next three couplets employ a distinctive structural pattern, each beginning with the emphatic "The LORD," creating rhythmic weight and drawing attention to six specific divine actions. Setting prisoners free invokes both literal liberation and the spiritual freedom that comes through God's redemptive work. In the context of ancient Israel, this would have resonated with Jubilee theology and the covenant stipulation requiring the release of slaves in the seventh year. Yet it extends beyond the merely temporal; it speaks to emancipation from the chains of sin and oppression.

Giving sight to the blind moves beyond the miracle narratives of the Gospels, though Christ would certainly fulfill this pattern. Here, the psalmist uses blindness metaphorically and literally; those unable to see their way forward, those trapped in darkness, both physical and spiritual, receive illumination through God's intervention. The Hebrew verb translated "give sight" carries the sense of opening, revealing, and making plain. God removes the barriers that obscure vision.

The image of lifting up those who are bowed down, literally "straightening the bent ones," is particularly poignant. The Hebrew verb translated "lifts up" means to straighten or erect. The psalmist envisions humanity in a posture of depression and despair: bent over by grief, sorrow, and injustice, and declares that God actively restores them to an upright position. This is not merely psychological encouragement; it is the restoration of dignity and hope. Those whose weight of suffering has pressed down are raised to new heights.

Finally, the catalog concludes with a statement of relational intimacy: "The LORD loves the righteous." The righteous are those who align with God's justice and seek to live in accordance with his covenant. The Hebrew verb translated as "loves" denotes not sentimental affection but committed covenant loyalty. God's love for the righteous is active, protective, and enduring.

The cumulative effect of these six divine actions is to assure us that God is not distant or indifferent to human suffering. He is intimately involved in the restoration and liberation of the broken. More than this, these actions reveal God's fundamental character: He is the God of justice, compassion, and transformation.

As we reflect on these verses today, we must ask ourselves: Do we truly believe that our God is engaged in these liberating actions? Do we see his hand in the feeding of the hungry, the freeing of prisoners, the restoration of sight and dignity? And perhaps more searchingly: Are we participating with God in these same acts of justice and mercy? The God we praise is not a God of abstract theology but of concrete action. He calls us to join him in upholding the cause of the oppressed, in providing for the hungry, in liberating those bound by injustice, and in restoring dignity to those who have been brought low.

PRAYER

Lord, grant us eyes to see your justice at work in this world and courage to participate in your redemptive mission. Transform our hearts that we might love what you love and act as agents of your compassion toward the oppressed, the hungry, the imprisoned, and the broken. May we never place our trust in earthly powers but always in you, the eternal God who lifts up the fallen. Amen.

THE INFINITE GOD WHO SEES YOU

Great is our LORD *and mighty in power; his understanding has no limit. The* LORD *sustains the humble but casts the wicked to the ground* (Psalm 147:5–6).

In a world obsessed with measurements and limitations, the psalmist invites us to contemplate something breathtaking: a God whose understanding has no limit. This is not merely poetic exaggeration. It is a profound theological anchor for weary souls navigating the complexity of human existence.

Consider what "no limit" truly means. Our brightest minds can map galaxies and decode DNA, yet every discovery reveals ten more mysteries. The most brilliant strategist cannot account for every variable. The wisest counselor cannot fathom every human heart. But God's understanding encompasses it all: every quantum fluctuation, every human thought, every sparrow's fall, every tear shed in darkness. Nothing escapes his comprehension. Nothing surprises him. Nothing overwhelms his capacity to know and care.

This infinite understanding flows from infinite power. The psalmist does not separate God's might from his wisdom, because they work in perfect harmony. A god who was all-powerful yet lacking wisdom would be terrifying: a cosmic brute wielding force without purpose. A god who was all wisdom but lacking power would be tragic: an impotent observer of suffering, full of good intentions but unable to act. But our Lord is both mighty in power and limitless in understanding, which means his strength is always directed by perfect wisdom, and his wisdom is never frustrated by lack of ability to accomplish his will.

Yet here is where the psalm takes a deeply personal turn. This God of infinite power and understanding does not remain distant or indifferent. He actively engages with human affairs according to a clear moral vision: he sustains the humble but casts the wicked to the ground.

Notice the word "sustains." It suggests ongoing care rather than a one-time intervention. The Hebrew word carries the sense of supporting, upholding, nourishing. It is the picture of a father lifting up a stumbling child, a gardener staking a young plant against the wind, a friend who keeps showing up when everyone else has moved on. The humble, those who recognize their dependence on God, who approach him without pretense or arrogance, find in him a constant source of strength.

The contrast with the wicked is stark. While the humble are sustained, lifted, upheld, the wicked are cast down. This is not divine cruelty but divine justice. The wicked, in their pride, position themselves against God's order, against his compassion, against the flourishing of others. They build their kingdoms on exploitation and lies. And though they may prosper for a season, they are building on sand. The very power that sustains the humble ensures that evil will not have the final word.

But we must ask ourselves: which posture characterizes our lives? Humility is not weakness or self-hatred. It is the clear-eyed recognition that we are creatures, not the Creator. It is acknowledging that our wisdom has limits, our power has boundaries, and our understanding is incomplete. It is the willingness to receive rather than always needing to achieve, to admit need rather than project invincibility, to bend the knee rather than always demand the throne.

In our achievement-oriented culture, humility can feel like failure. We are taught to market ourselves, never to show weakness, to be our own saviors. But the psalmist reveals a stunning reversal: the path to being sustained is not self-sufficiency but humble dependence. The one who admits their limits encounters the God whose understanding has none.

This is the beautiful paradox at the heart of faith. When we acknowledge our smallness, we are embraced by infinite greatness. When we confess our limited understanding, we are guided by limitless wisdom. When we admit our weakness, we are upheld by mighty power. The humble do not have to carry the weight of the world on their own shoulders because they have discovered a God who carries them.

Today, as you face challenges that exceed your wisdom or strength, remember: great is our Lord and mighty in power. His understanding has no limit. And that limitless God sees you, knows you, and promises to sustain you as you walk humbly before him.

PRAYER

Almighty God, forgive us for the pride that makes us forget our need for you. We confess that our understanding is limited, our power is small, and our wisdom is incomplete. Yet you are great and mighty, infinite in understanding and perfect in all your ways. Sustain us, we pray, as we seek to walk humbly before you. Give us grace to trust your wisdom when ours fails, and strength to stand when our own power is exhausted. May we never forget that in our weakness, you are strong. In Jesus' name, Amen.

PRAISE FROM HEAVEN'S COURT

Praise the LORD. *Praise the* LORD *from the heavens; praise him in the heights above. Praise him, all his angels; praise him, all his heavenly hosts* (Psalm 148:1–2).

The Book of Psalms reaches its crescendo in the final psalms with an unrelenting imperative: "praise." Psalm 148 stands as one of the most expansive and inclusive expressions of worship in Scripture, opening with an exuberant double command that establishes both the scope and urgency of the call. From the very first words, we encounter "Hallelu Yah"—Praise Yah—a verb form that carries the weight of joyful celebration and fervent adoration in the Hebrew tradition.

The opening command resounds twice in quick succession, creating what scholars call a rhetorical intensification. This repetition is not mere poetic embellishment; rather, it functions as a wake-up call to creation itself. The psalmist stands at the threshold between the earthly and celestial realms, commanding praise to emanate from every region of the cosmos. When the writer calls for praise "from the heavens," the Hebrew word encompasses not merely the visible sky but the totality of the heavens, the vast expanse where God dwells and his throne is established.

The phrase "heights above" (literally "heights of height" in Hebrew, emphasizing supreme elevation) further expands this cosmic geography. This is not the domain accessible to ordinary human experience. The psalmist directs our attention upward, progressively higher, to those celestial regions where God reigns supreme and where his glory manifests without obstruction or shadow. In the ancient Near Eastern cosmology reflected in Scripture, these heights represented the ultimate reality, the realm where God is fully known and where his character appears most luminously.

Yet the psalmist does not stop with geographical description. He summons the inhabitants of heaven itself to join this universal chorus of praise: "Praise him, all his angels; praise him, all his heavenly hosts." The angels, those who have never known sin, never experienced rebellion against their Creator, never required redemption, are enlisted in the cosmic worship. In Hebrew, the word translated "angel" literally means "messenger," and these celestial beings are presented not as distant, passive observers but as active participants in the eternal adoration of God.

What strikes us most profoundly is that the psalmist includes these heavenly beings as models for human worship. If the angels, with their perfect understanding of God's nature and their unobstructed view of his glory, offer unceasing praise, how much more should we, who glimpse divinity only partially through faith and revelation? The juxtaposition of the celestial and earthly realms suggests that worship is not something reserved for the perfected or the privileged. Rather, it represents the fundamental response of creation, whether angelic or human, to the reality of the Creator.

The inclusive language throughout these opening verses deserves particular attention. "Praise him, all his angels; praise him, all his heavenly hosts" extends the invitation comprehensively. No angel is excluded. No member of the heavenly court is exempted from this imperative. This totality prefigures the broadening scope of the psalm, which will eventually encompass all creation, from the sun and moon to mountains and trees to rulers and peoples, both young and old. The entire universe, visible and invisible, earthly and heavenly, is summoned to worship.

For those of us who pray in the twenty-first century, separated by vast distances from those heavenly heights, Psalm 148:1–2 offers a remarkable gift: an invitation to join the cosmic choir. We are not called to create our own worship or to invent reasons for praise.

Rather, we are invited to align ourselves with what is already occurring in heaven: the unceasing adoration of the one true God who alone is worthy of worship.

When you struggle to find words of praise, remember that you stand not alone but shoulder-to-shoulder with the angelic hosts themselves. When doubt clouds your sense of God's worthiness, recollect that the heavenly beings who see God's glory directly are even now offering him unending praise. When your voice seems small and inadequate, remember that your worship joins a chorus that spans both visible and invisible creation. You are not merely an observer of worship; you are a participant in the eternal testimony of creation to the glory of the Creator.

PRAYER

Eternal God, I stand in wonder contemplating the vastness of your creation and the multitude of your worshipers. Grant me the faith to join the heavenly chorus, even as I walk upon the earth. Help me to see beyond my limited circumstances to perceive the cosmic reality that all creation, visible and invisible, bends its will toward your honor and glory. May my praises, however humble, align with the eternal adoration of the angelic hosts. I offer to you this day my voice, my heart, and my whole being, that I might truly say with all heaven: Praise the Lord. Amen.

THE CROWN OF HUMILITY

For the LORD *takes delight in his people; he crowns the humble with victory. Let his faithful people rejoice in this honor and sing for joy on their beds* (Psalm 149:4–5).

There is something profoundly counterintuitive about the kingdom of God, and Psalm 149:4–5 captures it perfectly. In a world that celebrates self-promotion, personal achievement, and the relentless pursuit of recognition, these verses offer a radically different vision: God delights in his people, and he crowns the humble with victory.

Consider the word "delight" for a moment. This is not mere tolerance or passive acceptance. The Lord does not simply put up with us or grudgingly acknowledge our existence. He takes delight in his people. This is the language of joy, of pleasure, of a parent watching their child take their first steps or of an artist stepping back to admire her masterpiece. Before we accomplish anything, before we prove ourselves worthy, God already delights in us. This truth alone should transform how we approach our relationship with him.

But notice who receives the crown: the humble. Not the self-sufficient. Not those who have clawed their way to the top through their own strength. Not the proud who demand recognition. The humble, those who have laid down their illusions of self-sufficiency and acknowledged their complete dependence on God; these are the ones he adorns with victory.

This seems backwards to us. We have been taught that victory comes to the bold, the confident, the assertive. Yet God's economy works differently. James 4:6 reminds us that "God opposes the proud but gives grace to the humble." When we humble ourselves before the Lord, we position ourselves to receive what only he can give. Humility is not weakness; it is the recognition of truth. It is acknowledging that every breath we take, every talent we possess, every opportunity we encounter comes from his hand.

The victory God promises is not always what we expect. It is not necessarily triumph over our circumstances or the elimination of our struggles. Sometimes God's victory looks like peace in the midst of chaos, strength to endure when we thought we would break, or the ability to forgive when we have been deeply wounded. His victories are often internal before they are external, transforming our hearts, renewing our minds, and reshaping our desires to align with his purposes.

The response to this incredible truth, that God delights in us and crowns the humble with victory, should be joy. Not the fleeting happiness that depends on circumstances, but deep, abiding joy that springs from knowing who we are in Christ. The psalmist tells us that God's faithful people should "rejoice in this honor and sing for joy on their beds."

There is something intimate about this image of singing for joy on our beds. This is not public worship or corporate praise, though those have their place. This is the joy that bubbles up when we are alone, when the day is done, when there is no one to impress or perform for. It is the kind of joy that makes you smile in the darkness, that causes songs to rise from your heart in the quiet moments before sleep. It is the joy of knowing you are loved, delighted in, and crowned by the King of the universe.

How different our lives would look if we truly believed this. If we stopped striving to prove our worth and instead rested in the delight God already has for us. If we approached each day not with anxiety about proving ourselves, but with the confidence that comes from being crowned by God himself. If our nights were filled not with worry and rehearsing our failures, but with songs of joy for the honor of being called his own.

The call to humility is not a call to think less of ourselves, but to think of ourselves less. It is freedom from the exhausting work of self-promotion and the liberating realization that our identity is secure in Christ. When we humble ourselves, we make room for God to work. We create space for his strength to be perfected in our weakness. We open ourselves to receive the crown that only he can give, a crown not of our own making, but of his grace.

PRAYER

Loving Father, thank you for taking delight in me, not because of what I have accomplished, but simply because I am yours. Teach me the beauty of humility. Help me to lay down my pride, my need for recognition, and my illusions of self-sufficiency. Crown me with your victory, Lord, and fill my heart with joy that overflows, even in the quiet moments, even on my bed at night. Let my life be a song of praise to you, the One who delights in his people. In Jesus' name, Amen.

PRAISE THE LORD

Let everything that has breath praise the LORD (Psalm 150:6).

The final verse of the final psalm of the Psalter stands as one of Scripture's most expansive and inclusive calls to worship. "Let everything that has breath praise the LORD" represents the culmination of one hundred and fifty psalms, each ascending toward this crescendo of universal praise. To understand this verse, we must first appreciate its context in Psalm 150, then explore the profound implications of its sweeping claim about who should worship and why.

Psalm 150 itself is a brief composition, containing only six verses, yet its architectural significance cannot be overstated. The entire psalm functions as a doxology, a declaration of praise encompassing heaven and earth, affirming that all creation, indeed, everything possessing breath, owes worship to the Lord. The psalm begins by declaring where God should be praised ("in his sanctuary," "in his mighty heaven") and proceeds through the various instruments of worship (trumpet, harp, lyre, tambourine, strings, pipe, and cymbals) before arriving at its climactic conclusion in verse six.

The Hebrew word translated here as "breath" carries profound theological weight throughout Scripture. This term appears in Genesis 2:7, where the Lord breathes into Adam "the breath of life," creating human beings as living souls. In Job 27:3, Job declares that "as long as my breath is in me, the spirit of God is in my nostrils." The use of the word in Psalm 150:6 intentionally echoes this Genesis narrative, suggesting that every creature possessing this divine breath is inherently called to participate in praise.

The scope of this call proves remarkably expansive. The psalmist does not restrict worship to a particular group, not only the righteous, not only Israel, not only humanity. Rather, the inclusive "everything that has breath" encompasses all living creatures. This reflects a theological perspective that permeates the Psalter: creation itself is engaged in constant worship of its Creator. Psalm 19:1 declares that "the heavens declare the glory of God," Psalm 98 calls upon the earth, rivers, and mountains to break forth in singing, and Psalm 148 summons angels, celestial bodies, sea creatures, animals, and all humanity to praise. Psalm 150:6 serves as the ultimate summation of this creation-wide doxology.

Yet there is particular significance in the fact that this universal call concludes the Psalter itself. The five books of Psalms move progressively from lament and complaint in the earlier psalms toward increasing praise and worship. Book One (Psalms 1–41) grapples with suffering and doubt; Book Five (Psalms 107–150) is characterized by unrelenting praise. The Psalter thus models a spiritual journey, from wrestling with God to wholehearted worship, and Psalm 150:6 represents its destination: a place where all resistance has ceased and everything that breathes joins in universal acclamation.

This verse also carries profound implications for our contemporary spiritual lives. In our modern context, where skepticism, cynicism, and despair easily take root, this psalmist's call reminds us that praise is not primarily about our emotional state or our circumstances. Rather, praise is the appropriate response of any creature possessing breath to the Creator who gave that breath. When we are discouraged, when we question God's providence, when suffering clouds our vision, still, we have breath, and therefore the fundamental calling upon our lives remains: to praise the Lord.

Moreover, the universality of this call challenges our tendency to compartmentalize worship. We often restrict praise to specific times, places, or emotional dispositions. Yet this verse suggests that praise should be as continuous and natural as breathing itself. Just as breath fills our lungs and sustains our physical life, so too should the praise of God fill and sustain our spiritual existence.

The verse also invites us to participate in something larger than ourselves. We are not solitary worshipers, isolated in our personal devotion. Rather, we join with all creation: the celestial hosts, the creatures of earth and sea, and believers throughout history and around the world, in a grand symphony of praise. This expansive vision can profoundly reshape our prayer lives, reminding us that our individual acts of worship connect us to the worshiping community of all creation.

As we conclude our meditation on this final verse of the Psalter, we recognize that it serves as both a benediction and a commission. The psalmist has led us through one hundred and fifty poems, and now sends us forth with a clear directive: everything that breathes must praise the Lord, and that includes us.

PRAYER

Eternal God, Creator of all life and Author of breath, I pause in this moment to acknowledge the gift of the breath that fills my lungs. I confess that so often I take this gracious gift for granted, moving through my days without recognizing that each breath is a renewed opportunity to worship you. Transform my heart and mind so that my entire being, my thoughts, words, and actions, become a continual offering of praise. Help me to see that worship is not confined to moments of devotion but is the fundamental calling upon my life. And grant that my praise might join with the endless chorus of creation, bringing honor and glory to your holy name. Amen.

POSTCRIPT

As you come to the end of this work, you have spent nearly five months in the company of ancient worshipers of God — men and women who knew, in the depths of their experience, the steadfast love and the unfailing faithfulness of the God of Israel. These were not merely poets composing lines of beauty; they were souls who brought the full weight of human life before the throne of God: their fears, their failures, their doubts, their grief, and their joy. I pray that in their voices you have heard your own, and that the God who heard their prayers has heard yours as well.

The book of Psalms has been a constant companion throughout my many years of ministry — in the pulpit, in the classroom, and in those quiet hours when the needs of the soul outrun the resources of the scholar. The words and prayers of the psalmists have sustained me in seasons of joy and carried me through seasons of deep trouble. They have spoken to me not as ancient relics behind glass but as living words breathed by the Spirit of God and given to every generation that would receive them. My prayer is that these meditations have opened something of that same treasury to you, and that you have been blessed in reading them as I have been in writing them.

Perhaps, now that you have walked through all one hundred and fifty psalms, it is time to begin again. That is not a counsel of mere repetition; it is an invitation to discovery. The second reading is rarely the same as the first, because the reader is not the same. Life will have changed. Circumstances will have shifted. New griefs and new mercies will have accumulated since you first opened these pages. When you return to the psalmist and hear his words again, you will find that he meets you where you are now, just as he met you where you were then. The words spoken in the distant past carry a relevance that refuses to grow old, because the God to whom they are addressed is the same: yesterday, today, and forever.

There is one more thing I must say before I close, and it is perhaps the most important of all. The prayers of the Psalms have never been intended for private possession alone. Over and over, the psalmists call their readers to tell the story, to declare what the Lord has done, to share the blessing with those who have not yet received it. "I will tell of your name to my brothers," sings one psalmist (Psalm 22:22). "Let the redeemed of the LORD say so," declares another (Psalm 107:2). "Come and hear, all you who fear God, and I will tell what he has done for my soul" (Psalm 66:16). These are not merely liturgical formulas. They are testimonies born of experience, and they carry within them a commission.

You are now such a witness. You know, from your own journey through these pages, that the same God who blessed the psalmist in his days of need is the same God who has carried you in yours. There are people in your life, perhaps closer than you realize, who are struggling with loneliness, with fear, with doubt, with grief, with the silence of God and the weight of unanswered prayer. These are people who need to encounter the God whom the psalmists encountered. These are people who need to find their own voice in Israel's prayer book.

The reason many people remain unblessed by the Psalms is not that the Psalms have nothing to say to them. It is that no one has ever placed the book in their hands and said, "Read this. It was written for you." The Psalms are the prayer book not only of ancient Israel but of the church in every age. They belong to every believer. But many believers do not yet know what they possess. You can change that, for at least one person, by sharing what you have received.

If this book has blessed you, I encourage you to pass that blessing along. Recommend it to a friend who is going through a difficult time. Give a copy to someone whose faith is fragile. Tell someone who has never prayed: "Here is a book of prayers already written for you." In doing so, you will be doing what the psalmists themselves did:

transmitting a faith that was entrusted to you so that it might reach those who come after.

And for yourself, return to these devotionals again and be blessed a second time. You are not merely the reader of these ancient songs. You are, in a profound sense, one of their intended recipients, an inheritor and a transmitter of the faith that was once entrusted to the saints of Israel and has been passed down, generation by generation, until it reached you. Read these psalms again. Pray them again. And then share them with someone who has not yet found their voice in the prayer book of the people of God.

ANNOTATED BIBLIOGRAPHY:
SELECTED WORKS ON THE PSALMS

Brueggemann, Walter. *The Message of the Psalms: A Theological Commentary*. Minneapolis: Augsburg, 1984.

This landmark work organizes the Psalter into three movements: psalms of orientation, disorientation, and new orientation, drawing on the insights of Paul Ricoeur to map the full range of Israel's life with God. Brueggemann argues that the Psalms do not simply reflect pious sentiment but engage the raw reality of human existence, from confident trust to anguished complaint. The framework is theologically rich and exegetically grounded, making this an essential reference for any serious study of the Psalms.

For lay readers in the church, Brueggemann's tripartite model is immediately recognizable in the rhythms of their own spiritual lives. His honest treatment of lament psalms is particularly liberating, permitting congregants to bring their grief, anger, and confusion into honest prayer. Pastors and small group leaders will find this volume an excellent resource for guiding congregations to a more mature and truthful engagement with Scripture and prayer.

Brueggemann, Walter. *Spirituality of the Psalms*. Minneapolis: Fortress Press, 2002.

This slender but substantive volume is an accessible distillation of Brueggemann's larger theological framework for the Psalter, retaining his orientation-disorientation-reorientation schema while presenting it in a form suitable for a broader audience. The book traces how Israel's prayers move from settled confidence to profound disruption and finally to renewed trust, a movement that mirrors the paschal pattern of death and resurrection. It is particularly valuable as an introduction to Brueggemann's approach for those who may find his larger commentary more demanding.

For lay church members, this is one of the most approachable and spiritually nurturing books on the list. Its brevity and clarity make it ideal for adult Sunday school classes, women's or men's Bible study groups, or individual devotional reading. Brueggemann's central insight, that honest speech before God is itself an act of faith, has the potential to transform how ordinary believers understand and use the Psalms in their personal prayer lives.

Brueggemann, Walter. *Praying the Psalms: Engaging Scripture and the Life of the Spirit.* 2nd ed. Eugene, OR: Cascade, 2007.

In this practical and pastoral work, Brueggemann addresses directly the question of how the ancient prayers of Israel can become genuine vehicles of contemporary Christian prayer. He focuses particularly on the psalms of lament and praise, arguing that the full range of human emotions, including rage, grief, and vengeance, belongs within the life of prayer. The second edition expands on the original with additional reflections, making it an even more complete guide to spiritually appropriating the Psalms. The work bridges Old Testament scholarship and spiritual formation with unusual effectiveness.

This book speaks directly to lay readers who have found portions of the Psalms bewildering or even disturbing. Brueggemann's frank engagement with imprecatory psalms, for instance, offers a theologically responsible way to understand texts that trouble many Christians. Church small groups, retreat leaders, and spiritual directors will find this an invaluable resource for helping believers move from reading the Psalms as ancient poetry to praying them as living words.

Kidner, Derek. *Psalms 1–72: An Introduction and Commentary.* Tyndale Old Testament Commentaries 15a. Downers Grove, IL: InterVarsity Press, 2008.

Derek Kidner's two-volume commentary on the Psalms stands as one of the finest examples of evangelical Old Testament scholarship accessible to a wide readership. Written with characteristic precision, theological sensitivity, and literary elegance, this first volume covers Psalms 1–72 with careful attention to the Hebrew text, the structure of individual psalms, and their place within the canonical Psalter. Kidner is alert to both the original historical context and the Christological dimensions of the Psalms, making his commentary equally useful for academic study and devotional reflection.

For lay readers, Kidner is a particularly rewarding guide because he never sacrifices clarity for erudition. His commentary is concise without being superficial, and his prose is a model of readable scholarship. Church members who wish to study specific psalms in depth, whether individually or as part of a Bible study group, will find Kidner's notes illuminating and spiritually enriching. Pastors preparing sermons on the Psalms will also find this an indispensable starting point.

Kidner, Derek. *Psalms 73–150: An Introduction and Commentary.* Tyndale Old Testament Commentaries 15b. Downers Grove, IL: InterVarsity Press, 2008.

The second volume of Kidner's commentary completes his magisterial treatment of the Psalter, covering the final three books of the Psalms (Psalms 73–150). This volume includes some of the most celebrated and theologically significant psalms in the collection, including Psalm 73 on the problem of theodicy, Psalm 119 on the Torah, and the great Hallel psalms (113–118), and Kidner handles each with his characteristic blend of textual precision and spiritual insight. His brief but incisive notes consistently illuminate the meaning of difficult passages without overwhelming the reader with technical apparatus.

Taken together with the first volume, this commentary equips lay readers to engage the entire Psalter with a reliable and trustworthy guide. The Tyndale series is designed for precisely this purpose: to make solid scholarship available to students, teachers, and ordinary church members, and Kidner's volumes are among the finest examples of what that series can achieve. Church libraries should regard both volumes as essential acquisitions.

Lewis, C. S. *Reflections on the Psalms*. New York: Harcourt Brace Jovanovich, 1958.

Written not as a formal commentary but as a series of personal reflections by a layman, this volume by C. S. Lewis addresses candidly the difficulties that modern readers encounter in the Psalms, including their expressions of hatred toward enemies, their apparent self-righteousness, and the seeming crudity of some passages. Lewis brings his formidable literary intelligence, theological depth, and characteristic honesty to bear on texts that have puzzled and disturbed readers for centuries. His reflections on the second meanings of the Psalms, their Christological and typological dimensions, are particularly illuminating.

This book is arguably the single most valuable entry on this list for lay church readers, precisely because Lewis writes as one of them rather than as a professional scholar. His willingness to say plainly what troubles him about certain psalms, and then to work through those difficulties with rigor and charity, models exactly the kind of honest engagement that leads to genuine spiritual growth. Bible study groups, adult education classes, and individual readers will find this book not only instructive but genuinely enjoyable.

Mays, James L. Psalms. *Interpretation: A Bible Commentary for Teaching and Preaching*. Louisville: John Knox Press, 1994.

James Mays's contribution to the Interpretation series is a mature and theologically sophisticated commentary on the Psalter, written with the explicit purpose of serving those who preach and teach from the Psalms. Mays situates individual psalms within the larger canonical context of the Psalter, paying particular attention to the role of the Torah and the kingship of Yahweh as organizing theological themes. His exegesis is careful and informed by the best of contemporary scholarship, while his canonical sensitivity ensures that the commentary remains useful for Christian proclamation.

The Interpretation series was designed from its inception with both scholars and practitioners in mind, and Mays's volume exemplifies the series at its best. Pastors preparing sermons will find his theological summaries and homiletical suggestions particularly useful. Educated lay readers who wish to move beyond introductory treatments will appreciate the depth of engagement that Mays brings to each psalm, and the volume works well for either systematic study of the Psalter or focused attention on specific texts.

Peterson, Eugene H. *Answering God: The Psalms as Tools for Prayer*. San Francisco: HarperSanFrancisco, 1989.

Eugene Peterson, pastor, scholar, and author of The Message, approaches the Psalms in this volume as the divinely given school in which Israel learned to pray, and in which Christian believers are still being taught. Drawing on his pastoral experience and his deep engagement with the Hebrew text, Peterson argues that the Psalms do not simply express human emotions to God but shape and form those emotions in ways that conform to the character of God. The book is an extended meditation on the Psalms as the grammar of prayer, indispensable for the formation of a genuinely biblical spirituality.

For lay readers, this is a deeply practical and spiritually rich guide. Peterson writes with the warm, direct voice of a pastor who has spent a lifetime praying the Psalms and leading others to do the same. His central thesis, that prayer is not self-expression but response to the living God, challenges much of the shallow therapeutic spirituality that often passes for prayer in contemporary churches. This book is ideal for personal devotional reading, for new Christians seeking to develop a prayer life, and for congregations exploring what it means to be a genuinely praying community.

Wright, N. T. *The Case for the Psalms: Why They Are Essential for the Christian Life*. New York: HarperOne, 2013.

In this characteristically accessible and theologically robust volume, N. T. Wright makes an impassioned argument for restoring the Psalms to their central place in Christian worship and personal piety. Drawing on the historical practice of the church, Wright demonstrates how the Psalms have formed the devotional backbone of Christian prayer from the earliest centuries, and how their displacement from contemporary worship has impoverished the church's spiritual life. He gives particular attention to the eschatological dimensions of the Psalter, showing how the psalms of lament, praise, and kingship point toward and are fulfilled in Jesus Christ.

Wright's accessibility and his reputation as one of the most widely read New Testament scholars of our time make this book an excellent entry point for lay readers who may be unfamiliar with the riches of the

Psalter. His argument that the Psalms form Christian character and imagination in ways that no other literature can is both compelling and practically urgent. Churches considering a renewed commitment to singing and praying the Psalms will find this book a persuasive and energizing guide.